REFORMING LONDON

The London Government Problem
1855–1900

JOHN DAVIS

CLARENDON PRESS OXFORD
1988

Oxford University Press, Walton Street, Oxford OX2 6DP

Oxford New York Toronto
Delhi Bombay Calcutta Madras Karachi
Petaling Jaya Singapore Hong Kong Tokyo
Nairobi Dar es Salaam Cape Town
Melbourne Auckland

and associated companies in
Beirut Berlin Ibadan Nicosia

Oxford is a trade mark of Oxford University Press
Published in the United States
by Oxford University Press, New York

British Library Cataloguing in Publication Data
Davis, John
Reforming London: the London government problem, 1855–1900.—(Oxford
historical monographs).
1. London (England)—Politics and government
I. Title
352.0421   JS3571
ISBN 0–19–822937–2

Library of Congress Cataloging in Publication Data
Davis, John, 1955—
Reforming London: the London government problem, 1855–1900
John Davis.
p.   cm.—(Oxford historical monographs)
Bibliography: p.   Includes index.
1. London Metropolitan Area (Eng.)—Politics and government.
2. London County Council—History—19th century.
I. Title.   II. Series.
JS3625.D33   1988   352.0421—dc19   87–22911
ISBN 0–19–822937–2

Set by Butler & Tanner Ltd,
Frome and London
Printed in Great Britain
at the University Printing House, Oxford
by David Stanford
Printer to the University

Preface

The abolition of the Greater London Council in March 1986 ended almost a century of democratic metropolitan administration in London and stirred the embers of the London government debate. The new combination of first-tier 'quango' authorities and a limited devolution to the second tier represents one response to the problem of reconciling the divergent political and material interests likely to exist within a metropolitan community. That problem was first faced in the nineteenth century; indeed many of its present elements—the need for equity between local areas, the danger of two-tier rivalry, the tensions generated by the politicization of local government—were familiar to the governors of Victorian London. This study seeks to assess the Victorians' solutions.

My chief debt is to Philip Waller, supervisor of the Oxford D.Phil. thesis upon which this book is based, who suggested the topic and provided help, encouragement, and advice throughout. Mr A. F. Thompson also served beyond the call of duty as temporary supervisor during Philip's absence in 1979. Professor F. M. L. Thompson and Mr M. G. Brock examined the doctoral thesis upon which this book is based, and I have endeavoured to incorporate here their valuable criticisms and suggestions. Nicky Allen read the entire text as amended for publication, and I am glad to acknowledge her incisive and invariably constructive criticism. Peter Mandler, Roland Quinault, Sir Norman Chester, John Rowett, and Susan Pennybacker read and commented upon all or part of the draft at various stages, and I am grateful for their helpful advice. I am also grateful to the Duke of Devonshire, Miss Anne Farrer, the Duke of Norfolk, the Earl of Onslow, Brigadier Llewellyn Palmer, the Marquess of Salisbury, the Earl of Wemyss, Birmingham University Library, the Bodleian Library, the British Library, the British Library of Political and Economic Science, the Greater London Record Office, the House of Lords Record Office, the Hereford and Worcester Record Office, the London School of Economics, the National Library of Scotland, and the Scottish Record Office for permission to quote from material in their possession.

J.D.

Contents

List of Figures

List of Maps

List of Tables

Abbreviations

Add. MS(S)	British Library Additional Manuscripts
DB	District Board
GLRO	Greater London Record Office
HHP	Hatfield House Papers (Papers of the Third Marquess of Salisbury)
LCC	London County Council
LGB	Local Government Board
LLRU	London Liberal and Radical Union
LMRL	London Municipal Reform League
LMS	London Municipal Society
MBW	Metropolitan Board of Works
MMA	Metropolitan Municipal Association
MOH	Medical Officer of Health
NUCCA	National Union of Conservative and Constitutional Associations
OP	Onslow Papers
PP	Parliamentary Papers
PRO	Public Record Office
RA	Ratepayers' Association
RC	Royal Commission
RP	Rosebery Papers
SC	Select Committee
SNRA	Stoke Newington Ratepayers' Association
WP	Wemyss Papers

I

Introduction: The Metropolitan Problem

1. 'METROPOLOGY'

The metropolitan problem is the problem of devising a system of local government suited to an urban area too large for the conventional unitary municipality. The single municipality 'is best suited for the government of a small and distinct town';[1] it assumes an essential identity of interest within its boundaries which makes acceptable the direction of municipal policy from one centre and the effective redistribution of resources between areas through a uniform city rate. The metropolis, though, is by definition an aggregation of previously separate localities—'not an assemblage of individuals so much as a collection of communities in which individuals are already assembled'.[2] These communities will have separate identities, probably sharpened by metropolitan encroachment and by the contrast with a deteriorating inner city. They are likely to have particularist governments anxious to protect local autonomy. But the physical evolution of the metropolis is bound also to create common administrative needs and to generate problems which can be most effectively tackled over the whole area. A degree of metropolitan co-operation is demanded in equity by the economic interdependence of the component areas. The wealth isolated in a highly assessed central business district will be the product of the activity of the metropolitan community; responsibility for the alleviation of inner-city problems might be the just price of suburban segregation. The essence of the metropolis has been well described as 'a tension between unity in the economic sphere and diversity in the social sphere';[3] most of the elements of the 'metropolitan problem' derive from this tension.

The metropolitan problem has been most exhaustively studied in North America, where it is most pressing. In the United States the strength of ideas of particularism and self-determination in the political

[1] V. Jones, *Metropolitan Government* (Chicago, 1942), xix.
[2] T. H. Reed, quoted ibid. 144.
[3] K. Young, ' "Metropology" Revisited: On the Political Integration of Metropolitan Areas', in K. Young (ed.), *Essays on the Study of Urban Politics* (London and Basingstoke, 1975), 135.

tradition has inhibited integration. Metropolitan growth has been met by
the multiplication of 'special districts' and other *ad hoc* authorities, so
that the number of governmental agencies has expanded at an even faster
rate than the number of metropolitan areas.[4] In the largest cities this has
given rise to a structural complexity that can hardly be conducive to
popular identification with local government.[5] In the larger Canadian
cities, however, some form of federal two-tier system has been adopted,
following the success of the Metro Toronto experiment of 1953.[6] Under
a two-tier system local bodies coexist with a metropolitan authority, and
all or most municipal powers are shared between the two levels. This
system assumes a significant demand for, or acceptance of, administrative
integration, at least within the metropolitan boundaries. The problems
of managing a city under a two-tier system therefore differ in degree from
those generated by the sometimes chaotic fragmentation of American
cities. American 'metropologists' have cast envious glances at a system
which provides institutional recognition of both unity and diversity within
the metropolis, but which refuses to take root in the USA.

The two-tier system does, though, give rise to delicate organizational
questions of its own: how much political and financial control will be
centralized within the system and how much localized; to what extent
will the subsidiary areas be subject to metropolitan direction; to what
extent should the wealthier areas support the poorer ones. The allocation
of powers within the system is at the heart of these questions. It is often
treated as a dispassionate, 'scientific' problem, on the assumption that
some powers are best handled on an 'area-wide' basis, others best tackled
locally. This is too simple. Clearly functions extending over all or most
of the metropolitan area, such as main drainage, can only be handled by
the metropolitan body, while those requiring minute execution, such as

---

[4] In 1962 the 212 Standard Metropolitan Statistical Areas contained 18,442 local governments (average 87 each); in 1967 227 SMSAs contained 20,703 agencies (91.2); in 1977 272
SMSAs contained 25,869 agencies (95.1): J. C. Bollens and H. J. Schmandt, *The Metropolis:
Its People, Politics and Economic Life* (New York, 1965), 142-3 and 4th edn. (1982), 89;
C. A. McCandless, *Urban Government and Politics* (New York, 1970), 136. The Committee
for Economic Development noted in 1970 that the increase was chiefly due to the proliferation of single-function authorities—'units spawned by the inadequacies of traditional
governments': Committee for Economic Development, *Reshaping Government in Metropolitan Areas* (New York, 1970), 42.

[5] For example, in New York, administration is shared between 3 state governments, 22
county governments, several hundred municipal governments, and over 1,500 special
districts: I. M. Barlow, *Spatial Dimensions of Urban Government* (Chichester, New York,
Brisbane, and Toronto, 1981), 21.

[6] Bollens and Schmandt, *The Metropolis* (1st edn.), 477 ff.

street lighting, are best handled locally. But these clear-cut cases are the minority, and the 'grey area' is substantial. Some functions, like education management, are susceptible to economies of scale but also require detailed personal execution. Some, like fire protection, benefit from central direction but necessarily operate from several local service-points. Even some indisputably local functions may require metropolitan supervision to ensure a uniform standard of service.

In any case, two-tier allocation is dependent upon the size of the secondary areas. In a system with several small local units, functions which might not ideally be handled centrally might still be handled better centrally than locally. Further, if all local functions are financed locally and all metropolitan functions supported by rates levied across the metropolis, it is possible that an imbalance of resources between areas might necessitate the centralization of some essentially local functions. The advantage of an effective redistribution of metropolitan wealth through the action of area-wide authorities might justify the consequent erosion of local autonomy. Such redistribution would most obviously benefit inner-city areas with high levels of social deprivation and inadequate tax-bases, but could also be sought by developing suburban areas where 'the central city provided superior services at a lower cost'.[7] Too centralized a system, however, risks the alienation of wealthy areas forced to support the bulk of metropolitan expenditure. Even on the theoretical level these questions are delicate. In the real metropolis, where they are likely to widen divisions of class and locality, they become political questions, subject to the tensions and rivalry that politics generates.

In the more prescriptive analyses,[8] the wish to avoid such contention has led to attempts to identify 'natural' first- and second-tier functions, but this only pushes the question back further, as the range of duties which can be handled locally depends upon the size and strength of the second tier. Avoiding contention here has led some to the search for natural local areas with 'high levels of local community initiative'; stressing that 'how a community perceives its identity becomes important, as well as the number of people it contains'.[9] The idea that local authority areas should reflect local community perception is unexceptionable, but

[7] J. C. Teaford, *City and Suburb* (Baltimore and London, 1979), 63. Teaford shows that American suburbanites generally favoured integration in the second half of the 19th c.

[8] See e.g. the conclusions of the 1963 Advisory Commission on Intergovernmental Relations, in Bollens and Schmandt, *The Metropolis* (1st edn.), 311–12; Barlow, *Spatial Dimensions of Urban Government*, 93–4.

[9] Committee for Economic Development, *Reshaping Government*, 46–8.

is it realistic in the modern metropolis? We can approach this question by looking at the modern world's first metropolis, and the city where the metropolitan two-tier system was first applied—nineteenth-century London.

2. THE VICTORIAN METROPOLIS

In the Herbert Commission's view the concept of the metropolis, covering 'something bigger than but including the City [of London]',[10] dated back to the late eighteenth century. The establishment of the Metropolitan Police in 1829, the passing of the Metropolis Building Act in 1844, and the creation of the Metropolitan Commission of Sewers in 1847 indicated legislative recognition of the term in the first half of the century. In 1851 the Registrar-General's extended definition of census London[11]—to be adopted for the 1855 reform—confirmed these suggestions that London's expansion had invalidated existing administrative boundaries.

This early awareness of metropolitan unity probably facilitated acceptance of a consolidated system in 1855. London expanded from a single core; allowing for the early fusion of Westminster and the City, it was not a conurbation in the sense of an accretion of previously separate cities,[12] and certainly not a 'megalopolis'.[13] The twentieth-century American metropolis generally grew through motor transportation, with its 'revolutionary effect upon local spatial relations'[14] linking disparate communities overnight, so that 'the people of the United States became metropolitan before realising their change from rural to urban'.[15] Victorian London, on the other hand, did not owe its expansion primarily to a transport revolution but to the steady spread of bricks and mortar as its population grew. Growing from a single centre, and growing organically, London possessed an underlying unity that could never convincingly be dismissed as artificial.

There was none the less no shortage of polemicists anxious to stress the diversity of London. 'What commonness of interests and management', asked the antiquarian localist Toulmin Smith in 1852, 'can

[10] RC Local Government in Greater London 1957–60, *PP 1959–60*, XVIII, Report, 35.
[11] Classified as Division I in the 1851 Census, *PP 1852–3*, LXXXV.
[12] RC Local Government in Greater London, *PP 1959–60*, XVIII, Report, 19–20.
[13] Jean Gottmann's term for the built-up North-eastern seaboard of the USA: *Megalopolis* (New York, 1961).
[14] R. D. MacKenzie, *The Metropolitan Community* (New York and London, 1933), 69.
[15] Victor Jones, quoted in Bollens and Schmandt, *The Metropolis* (1st edn.), 12.

Whitechapel have with Paddington, or Lambeth with Hackney?'[16] There was an inevitable lag between the physical and economic integration of London and the emergence of any strong sense of metropolitan identity. Most of the more exaggerated images of sprawling anonymity were propagated by non-Londoners—Cobbett's 'Great Wen', Rosebery's vision of 'a tumour, an elephantiasis, sucking into its gorged system all the life and blood and bones of the rural districts',[17] Engels's portrait of 'restless and noisy activity ... brutal indifference ... narrow-minded egotism'[18]—but the metropolis remained a foreign concept even to its natives. Despite the existence of a Metropolitan Police force, metropolitan sanitary and building legislation, and a host of statutory definitions of the metropolis, the Victorian Londoner remained long diffident about his metropolitan identity. London remained by convention not so much a city as, in the haunting phrase of the 1854 Royal Commissioners, 'a province covered with houses'.[19] The only strictly local daily newspaper for the whole of London in the nineteenth century, William Saunders's *The Circle* of 1874, survived just four months.[20] The Victorian Londoner's cast of mind remained primarily localist, only occasionally influenced by what Asquith called 'a fitful and irregular pulse of a common life'.[21]

Localism survived and flourished in the metropolis. It survived most easily in places less than fully integrated, on the fringes of the built-up area, where the effect of greater distance from the centre was compounded by the survival of links with the hinterland. The villages of Kentish London were only slowly transformed into metropolitan suburbs; Woolwich remained a market centre for West Kent, with a wage level distinct from that of the rest of London.[22] Localism survived also where the 'social severance' effect of rivers, railways, main roads, and other physical barriers contributed to spatial division. The greatest obstacle of all, the

[16] J. Toulmin Smith, *The Metropolis and its Municipal Administration* (1852), 24.

[17] Quoted by Sir Henry James at Chelsea, *The Times*, 4 Mar. 1892.

[18] F. Engels, *The Condition of the Working Class in England*, trans. W. O. Henderson and W. H. Chaloner (2nd edn., 1971), 30–1. Lucy Newlyn has described how the Londoner Charles Lamb was impelled by 'intense local attachments' to defend the metropolis from Wordsworth's anti-urbanism: 'These are thy Pleasures, O London with-the-many-sins—O City abounding in whores—for these may Keswick and her Giant Brood go hang.' (L. Newlyn, ' "In City Pent": Echo and Allusion in Wordsworth, Coleridge and Lamb, 1797–1801', *Review of English Studies*, 32 (1981), 408–28.)

[19] RC Corporation of London, *PP 1854*, xxvi, Report, xiv.

[20] W. Wellsman, 'The Local Press of London', *Newspaper Press Directory* (1898), 13.

[21] Quoted in the *Daily Chronicle*, 8 Dec. 1894.

[22] G. Crossick, *An Artisan Elite in Victorian Society: Kentish London, 1840–1880* (1978), 40; E. J. Hobsbawm, 'The Nineteenth Century London Labour Market', in Centre for Urban Studies, *London: Aspects of Change* (1964), 9.

Thames, determined the deep-seated distinction between north and south London. Where the Seine acts as a focus, the Thames has always been a barrier. Only one nineteenth-century local newspaper bridged it for any significant period.[23] The two short-lived attempts made in the west in the 1860s suggest the measurable degree of contact between Chelsea and Battersea,[24] but the east and south-east remained clearly separated, with neither bridge nor foot-tunnel across the widening river before the 1890s. Other obstacles isolated individual areas. The severance effect of docks was notorious. The Isle of Dogs became a self-contained promontory, isolated by the East and West India Docks, its residents 'strangely remote from the stir of London ... neither in it nor of it'.[25] The area's tradition of isolation survived to contribute to the Island's quixotic Unilateral Declaration of Independence in 1970.[26] In Wapping 'the shut off character of the place' made it 'really like a village' to Booth's witnesses, and the same image was used of Rotherhithe, isolated by the Surrey Docks.[27] Kellett has described the role of urban railways in marking out social areas;[28] even so slight an obstacle as the Regent's Canal could produce distinct spatial divisions.[29]

Nevertheless, the 'urban village' did not depend upon physical isolation. It should be seen as a characteristic feature of urbanization rather than a transmission from the rural past,[30] a form of social protection against the disorientation inherent in city life.[31] Village identity was most consciously cultivated in the outer suburbs, where a succession of antiquarian and devoutly nostalgic local histories commemorated the

---

[23] George Hill's *Westminster and Lambeth Gazette*, between 1881 and 1891.

[24] The *Battersea and Chelsea News* was published between Jan. 1866 and July 1869; the *Independence* (Chelsea, Fulham, Wandsworth, and Battersea) between Jan. 1862 and Mar. 1863.

[25] C. Booth (ed.), *Life and Labour of the People in London* (1902–3), 3rd ser., i. 20. Bedarida argues that docks and railways created subdivisions even within Poplar: F. Bedarida, 'Urban Growth and Social Structure in Nineteenth Century Poplar', *London Journal*, 1 (1975), 166.

[26] J. D. Eyles, *Environmental Satisfaction and London's Docklands: Problems and Policies in the Isle of Dogs* (Queen Mary College Dept. of Geography, Occasional Paper No. 5; 1976), 8.

[27] Booth MS, A 39, 20: Booth, *Life and Labour*, 3rd ser., iv. 154.

[28] J. R. Kellett, *The Impact of Railways on Victorian Cities* (London and Henley, 1969), 15–17, 303, 342, etc.

[29] In Hackney: Booth, *Life and Labour*, 1st ser., i. 29; and later in Bow: M. Young and P. Willmott, *Family and Kinship in East London* (1957), 87.

[30] D. Ward, 'Victorian Cities: How Modern?' *Journal of Historical Geography*, 1 (1975), 150.

[31] D. Harvey, *Social Justice and the City* (1973), 281.

disappearance of the bucolic past.[32] Deliberate estate policy created select enclaves in Dulwich, Hampstead, and Highgate. Dyos believed that Victorian suburbs failed to breed local loyalties, but 'nevertheless remained surprisingly peninsular';[33] in the twentieth century their insularity would generate an 'intense suburban separatism'[34] which stiffened resistance to overspill housing and other aspects of integration. Working-class localism derived from the hearsay transmission of cheap rented housing and 'the extraordinary short-term immobility of the nineteenth-century worker'.[35] The pattern (familiar from mobility studies in other Victorian cities[36]) of moves which were frequent but confined to a limited area was observable in London, giving rise to Booth's simile of fish in a river.[37] This was itself enough to reinforce attachment to particular localities, and there are some signs even in the Booth material of a growing residential stability in working-class areas.[38] By 1911, when the census first classified place of birth by locality, it was clear that working-class boroughs had the highest proportions of 'natives'.[39] Over the first half of the twentieth century kinship ties, increasing working-class domesticity, and an effectively hereditary rental tenure would combine to create an attachment to home, street, and neighbourhood in working-class areas as tenacious as that in the owner-occupied suburbs.[40]

[32] For example, F. E. Baines, *Records of the Manor, Parish and Borough of Hampstead* (1890); W. H. Blanch, *Ye Parish of Camberwell: Its History and Antiquities* (1875); J. Tanswell, *The History and Antiquities of Lambeth* (1858).

[33] H. J. Dyos, *Victorian Suburb: A Study of the Growth of Camberwell* (Leicester, 1961), 30.

[34] K. Young and J. Kramer, *Strategy and Conflict in Metropolitan Housing: Suburbia versus the GLC, 1965–1975* (1978), 12.

[35] Hobsbawm, 'London Labour Market', 8.

[36] R. Dennis and S. Daniels, '"Community" and the Social Geography of Victorian Cities', *Urban History Yearbook* (1981), 9 ff.; C. G. Pooley, 'Residential Mobility in the Victorian City', *Transactions of the Institute of British Geographers*, NS 4 (1979), 258–77.

[37] Quoted in P. J. Waller, *Town, City and Nation: England 1850–1914* (Oxford, 1983), 27.

[38] For example, Booth MS A 32 (District 10), 12; A 36 (14), 8; A 39 (8), 22. R. M. Pritchard identified a sharp fall in working-class mobility after 1900 in his study of Leicester, *Housing and the Spatial Structure of the City* (Cambridge, 1976), 108–9.

[39] The areas with the highest percentages of the population born in London were Shoreditch (85·71), Bermondsey (83·45), Bethnal Green (83·43) and Poplar (79·52): *PP 1913*, LXVIII, Table 2, 42–63.

[40] For the origins of working-class domesticity see M. J. Daunton, *House and Home in the Victorian City* (1983), ch. 11. For the sanctity of the home in Greenwich see E. W. Bakke, *The Unemployed Man* (1933), 153. For kinship networks see M. Young and P. Willmott, *Family and Kinship in East London, passim;* and for hereditary rentals, ibid. 19. For localism see ibid. 86–9; J. H. Robb, *Working-Class Anti-Semite* (1954), 57; J. Westergaard and R. Glass, 'A Profile of Lansbury', in Centre for Urban Studies, *London: Aspects of Change*, 169 ff.

All of this suggests that there was a strong case for a degree of metropolitan integration tempered by an acknowledgement that a sense of localism was emotionally potent, and was being strengthened rather than weakened by metropolitan development. This argues for a two-tier system, but it cannot determine the size or shape of the secondary areas. Here the problems inherent in any attempt to fashion administrative areas in the metropolis according to local identity become clear. No ready definition of metropolitan localism presents itself. Immediate neighbourhood perception might be very limited—especially as both middle- and working-class communities displayed increasing residential stability; modern studies suggest that even in the car age, neighbourhood perception tends to be bounded by convenient walking distance.[41] Booth's rental surveys show a variegated pattern which suggests the lack of long-distance residential mobility,[42] but the pattern is modified by the consistent outward drift of the better-off. Again, Hobsbawm stresses the immobility of the casual labourer, but also points out that the horizons of the skilled worker were wider, and argues for only three employment zones in the whole city.[43] The existence of a single wage-rate for almost the whole metropolis suggests that the potential for labour mobility was greater still. The process of social segregation associated with metropolitan growth created large tracts of socially homogeneous territory which might develop a sense of common interests. This was most evident with the polarization of the East and West Ends; by the end of the century the East End had a clear collective image as the appointed centre of 'darkest London', despite the distinctiveness of most of its components— Whitechapel, Stepney, Bethnal Green, etc. Similarly, local newspapers, which both shaped and reflected local identity, generally needed large circulation areas to pay their way. While London boasted over eighty local papers by the 1880s, this reflected more the proliferation of titles following the abolition of stamp and paper duties a generation earlier than any fine sensitivity to localism. Most of those which survived covered very large areas—the *South London Press*, the *East London Observer*, the *West London Observer*.

[41] T. Lee, 'Cities in the Mind', in D. T. Herbert and R. J. Johnston (eds.), *Social Areas in Cities: Processes, Patterns and Problems*, 2nd edn. (Chichester, New York, Brisbane, and Toronto, 1978), 267. J. D. Eyles's study of Highgate suggested that the perceived neighbourhood contracted in proportion to length of residence: *The Inhabitants' Images of Highgate Village*, (LSE Graduate Geography Dept. Discussion Paper No. 15; 1968), 16.

[42] Summaries of local rents follow the chapters in the third series; the raw material is in the Booth manuscripts, but awaits comprehensive analysis.

[43] Hobsbawm, 'London Labour Market'.

It may be that the larger and more complex a city, the less probable it is that the different types of local area will overlap. The metropolis is not likely to throw up discrete and self-contained social areas for local government purposes, and if the second tier will not define itself then subjective construction becomes necessary. The evolution of the London government problem in the late nineteenth century was the story of attempts to replace an inherited structure by other structures designed with particular social or political ends in view. It began with the creation of the world's first two-tier metropolitan system in 1855.

2

The London Government Problem

I. THE METROPOLIS MANAGEMENT ACT

The Metropolis Local Management Act of 1855 marked a triumph for parochial democracy. It consummated the reaction to the utilitarian, centralizing, anti-democratic concept of administration propagated by Edwin Chadwick in the 1840s, and provided legislative recognition of the resurgence of the London Vestry system over the previous decade. This revival was part of the broader mid-century movement for local self-determination that could be seen as a muted but lasting British response to European nationalism and the events of 1848. The localists' case was pressed with greater urgency in London than elsewhere because the capital lacked the reformed municipal institutions that saved the provinces from centralization. Thus while the overthrow of the Chadwickian regime might have marked the victory of 'dirty parties' over 'sanatarians', it was also an assertion that the spirit of 'local self-government' could not safely be neglected in any measure of administrative reform. By 1855 the Benthamite rationalism of Chadwick was an anachronism, however progressive its motives to modern eyes, and the antiquarian localism of Joshua Toulmin Smith was fashionable, however retrogressive its effects. Future local government reforms would have to acknowledge the requirements of representative democracy as well as those of administrative efficiency.

Had London been reformed at the time of its investigation by the Municipal Corporations Commissioners in 1837, it would presumably have received something close to the single metropolitan municipality that they recommended.[1] In the event its congeries of disparate authorities survived into an age more deferential towards local pluralism. The most obvious beneficiary was the ancient and unreformed City Corporation, London's only municipality, claiming an ancestry which stretched back to the ninth century, and obsessively jealous of its historical independence. It covered only one square mile out of 120 (the City proper), having long since abandoned the absorption of areas beyond its limits. At first sight

---

[1] RC Municipal Corporations, Second Report, *PP 1837*, xxv, 4–5.

the remainder of the metropolitan area appeared to be governed as if it had never been built up. The usual objects of county administration were handled by the Justices of the Peace for Middlesex, Surrey, and Kent, with only the Middlesex Justices actually sitting in London. Parochial management fell to the Vestries of nearly eighty civil parishes, varying enormously in size and character. Broad but largely inoperative drainage powers had belonged to the eight bodies of Commissioners of Sewers, of Tudor origin, until the supersession of seven of them by Chadwick's Metropolitan Commission in 1847.[2] The most obvious concession to urbanization lay in the 300 or so *ad hoc* boards or trusts empowered by around 250 local Acts to pave, light, or maintain specific areas,[3] which had regulated to a limited extent the rapid growth of early nineteenth-century London.

Many elements of the *ancien régime* had appealed as little to the self-government theorists as to Chadwick. The Justices were unelected and socially uncomfortable as urban administrators, although they would survive attempts to democratize their executive role until 1888. Some of the central Vestries had become 'close'—i.e. self-elective—authorities, and the seven Sewers Commissions outside the City had always been Crown-appointed. Few of the *ad hoc* boards were directly accountable to those they rated. Nevertheless, the wardmote system of the City, the surviving open Vestries, and the five parishes that had adopted the representative machinery of the 1831 Hobhouse Act[4] embodied a tradition of local democracy imperilled by the new centralism of Chadwick's Commission.

The public health battles had centred upon two related but distinct issues. Chadwick's Commission had been offensive because it was Crown-appointed and because it was a unitary metropolitan authority which paid no regard to parochial autonomy. It represented at once both national and metropolitan centralization. The disputes between the Commission and the Vestries, and between the centralizers and the parochial representatives within the Commission, reflected both of these issues. For most of the self-government school, the threat of governmental centralization appeared the more pressing; Toulmin Smith had been prepared to advocate extensive consolidation of the existing authorities in

[2] S. E. Finer, *The Life and Times of Sir Edwin Chadwick* (1952), 316–17.
[3] Figures from Hall's speech in Hansard, *Parliamentary Debates*, 3rd ser., CXXXVII, 705–12 (16 Mar. 1855).
[4] F. Sheppard, *Local Government in St Marylebone, 1688–1835* (1958), 301.

order to bring municipal institutions to London.[5] In practice, however, this was a battle that had been fought and won by 1855, following the overthrow of the Chadwickian General Board of Health in the previous year. The new settlement was bound to acknowledge local democracy. Of greater importance for the future of the London government problem was the question of whether the new system would be founded upon the existing parish network, upon the sort of single municipality recommended in 1837, or upon some kind of municipal federation of consolidated local authorities of the kind envisaged by Toulmin Smith.

In the event, Sir Benjamin Hall's Metropolis Local Management Act of 1855[6] rewarded the Vestries for their opposition to Chadwick. It attempted to refurbish and thus preserve the Vestry system by defining the Vestries' duties, providing a uniform franchise and election procedure (largely borrowed from the 1831 Hobhouse Act[7]), and transferring to them the powers of bodies set up under Local Acts. To meet the Chadwickian criticism of fragmentation, Hall created a new central body—the Metropolitan Board of Works—to handle functions common to the whole metropolis; but to ensure that the centre of gravity within the new system remained at the parish level, the MBW was to be an indirectly elected body chosen by the Vestries.

Of the 78 metropolitan civil parishes and 8 non-parochial areas outside the City, not one lost its separate identity under the Act.[8] The 23 parishes deemed suitable for self-government were listed in the Act's Schedule A; each would be managed by a directly elected Vestry of a size varying according to population from a minimum of 18 to a maximum of 120 members. The remaining 55 parishes, listed in Schedule B, elected Vestries in the same way, but were then grouped into 15 District Boards of Works, elected by and from their component Vestries. The District Boards exercised the same powers as the Schedule A Vestries; the Schedule B Vestries existed to do little more than choose their District Board delegates—'the same breath which calls them into being deprives them of vitality'.[9] By this curious form of local federalism, about a third of London's population was subject to an indirectly elected local administration, while the remaining two-thirds enjoyed direct elections. That

---

[5] J. Toulmin Smith, *The Metropolis and its Municipal Administration* (1852), 56–7.
[6] 18 & 19 Vict., c. 120.
[7] 1 & 2 Wm. IV., c. 60.
[8] See Appendix 1.
[9] J. Toulmin Smith, *The Metropolis Local Management Act* (1855), 78 n.

Hall could regard this anomaly as a fair price for the preservation of some quite insignificant parishes is a measure of his parochialism. The 8 non-parochial areas, consisting of small enclaves without a significant population—mainly the Inns of Court—did without representation of any sort, although contributing to the expenses of the Metropolitan Board of Works.[10] All the other bodies taxed by the MBW were represented on it, in imprecise proportion to rateable value and inhabited houses. The City Corporation elected three members, the six largest Vestries two each, and most of the remaining Vestries and District Boards one each. Thus constituted, the Metropolitan Board consisted of 45 elected members, who themselves chose a chairman from within or outside their ranks. Apart from the chairman of the MBW and the rectors and churchwardens who were ex-officio members of their Vestries, every member of every representative body under the Act was elected for three years at a time, with one-third of each body retiring annually. Each year therefore saw the election of one-third of each Vestry, each District Board, and the Metropolitan Board of Works. Finally, the Commissioners under the adoptive Acts for Baths and Libraries, and the parish Burial Boards, remained semi-autonomous, constitutionally separate from the Vestries but usually nominated by them.

The 1855 Act produced the world's first metropolitan two-tier administrative system, but the structure created displayed an awkwardness and complexity that owed much to the circumstances of its conception. The public health crisis had shown that the growth of the metropolis had created problems requiring metropolitan solutions, problems beyond the capacity of a fragmented parochial network to handle. This evidence had been so deployed by Chadwick and his followers as to pose a threat to Vestry autonomy, but Hall had responded by creating what appeared a rather residual metropolitan body precisely in order to preserve the separate identity of every major and minor parish, liberty, and inn of court within the second tier. In what was perhaps the most significant policy decision behind the 1855 Act, he rejected the 1854 Royal Commission on the Corporation of London's rather hesitant advocacy of large secondary municipalities covering the areas of the eight metropolitan parliamentary boroughs, claiming that they would be too large for local

[10] The Schedule C areas remained outside the Act for second-tier purposes. By the 1855 Act (s. 175) they were valued by an assessor appointed by the MBW, while by the 1862 Amending Act the Board was empowered to issue precepts to them (25 & 26 Vict., c. 102, s. 12).

authority areas.[11] The Metropolis Management Act made London safe for the Vestries.

This was a political rather than an administrative decision. No legislator charged with constructing an efficient second tier *de novo* would have created the London Vestry system. Parish boundaries, if they reflected anything, reflected a long-vanished pattern of settlement. A cluster of tiny parishes in the oldest quarters of London—the Strand area, the inner East End, inner Southwark and, pre-eminently, the City[12]—mirrored medieval population density, while the outer parishes, now beginning to fill up, included some of the largest in the country. The metropolitan parishes ranged in size from Lewisham, with 5,774 acres, to six of less than 10 acres each. This disparity was compounded by the fact that the movement of population in Victorian London was broadly centrifugal—from the centre to the 'inner ring' areas, and from the centre and the 'inner ring' to the new suburbs. Consequently, even by 1861 the six largest London parishes each contained a larger population than Bolton, Bradford, Dundee, Huddersfield, Hull, Leicester, Newcastle, Plymouth, and Salford, while the four smallest contained under a thousand residents apiece.[13] By 1891, when the outward movement was largely complete, Islington was more populous than all but seven British cities, Lambeth larger than Belfast, and both Camberwell and St Pancras larger than Newcastle, Nottingham, and Hull, while the six parishes of the Strand District Board could muster only 25,000 inhabitants between them and St Martin-in-the-Fields only 14,000.[14] The administrative significance of the very smallest parishes was limited by their amalgamation into District Boards, but even with this proviso the range of local authority remained large. In 1861 the most populous parish, St Pancras, contained more than ten times as many inhabitants as Hampstead, the smallest Schedule A parish, or St Olave's, the smallest District Board. By 1891 Islington was twenty-five times as populous as the St Olave's district.

Such population disparities were not in themselves barriers to efficient administration—greater divergence could be found amongst the provincial municipalities—but they presented serious problems in the metropolitan context. Metropolitan growth emphasized the differentiation of

---

[11] RC Corporation of London, *PP 1854*, xxvi, Report, xxxv; *Hansard*, 3rd ser., cxxxvii, 717 (16 Mar. 1855).

[12] The City contained over a hundred parishes within its square mile. They were not, of course, administrative authorities under the 1855 Act.

[13] 1861 Census, Population Tables, *PP 1862*, l, 223–4.

[14] 1891 Census, Preliminary Report, *PP 1890–1*, xciv, 16.

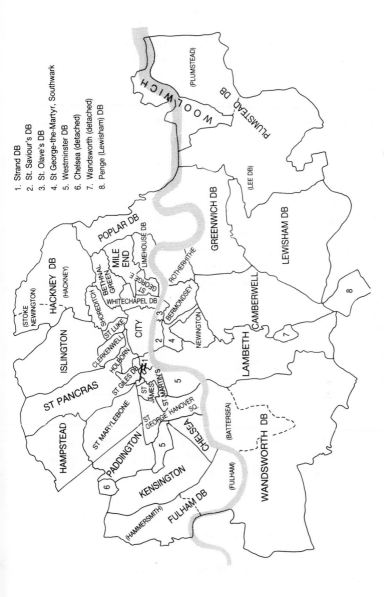

Local Areas under the Metropolis Local Management Act, 1855

1. Strand DB
2. St. Saviour's DB
3. St. Olave's DB
4. St George-the-Martyr, Southwark
5. Westminster DB
6. Chelsea (detached)
7. Wandsworth (detached)
8. Penge (Lewisham) DB

(PLUMSTEAD)

PLUMSTEAD DB

WOOLWICH

(LEE DB)

GREENWICH DB

LEWISHAM DB

POPLAR DB

LIMEHOUSE DB

MILE END

ST GEORGE I.E.

HACKNEY DB

(HACKNEY)

(STOKE NEWINGTON)

BETHNAL GREEN

SHOREDITCH

WHITECHAPEL DB

ROTHERHITHE

BERMONDSEY

NEWINGTON

CAMBERWELL

ST LUKE

ISLINGTON

CLERKENWELL

CITY

HOLBORN

ST GILES DB

ST PANCRAS

ST MARTIN'S

ST JAMES

LAMBETH

8

7

HAMPSTEAD

ST MARYLEBONE

ST GEORGE HANOVER SQ.

(BATTERSEA)

WANDSWORTH DB

PADDINGTON

CHELSEA DB

6

(FULHAM)

KENSINGTON

FULHAM DB

(HAMMERSMITH)

5

5

2

3

4

localities. In the most generalized model, a formerly heterogeneous city develops a central business area in which the cost of land precludes all but commerce, an inner ring occupied by the working classes evicted from the centre but dependent upon it, and a suburban belt comprising those able to live at a distance from their work. London displayed the additional feature of a wealthy and exclusive central *residential* area in the West End. This movement emphasizes social differentiation at a time when the metropolis is becoming economically more integrated, and thus generates much of the tension inherent in the 'metropolitan problem'. In choosing local boundaries, therefore, it is virtually impossible to avoid creating significant differences in wealth among the secondary area if the demands of localism—often accentuated by social differentiation—are to be respected. It may be desirable, none the less, to minimize these differences if the second tier is to be effective as an administrative layer. This the parish structure failed to do.

Most of the outer parishes were large enough to be socially heterogeneous. Islington, St Pancras, Hackney, Lambeth, and Camberwell all reached far enough into the centre to include sizeable working-class communities, and there were patches of poverty even in Wandsworth and Hampstead. Further in, however, the smaller central parishes saw their populations diminished and their assessments enhanced by commercialization and the arrival of the railways. The City, above all, became a place 'where wealth accumulates and men decay'.[15] The displaced population gathered, for the most part, in the 'inner ring', giving rise to Masterman's 'Ghetto'—the circle drawn from Shepherd's Bush to the docks and from Deptford to Battersea, and forming 'the enclosure into which is penned our labouring population'.[16] Where smaller parishes fell entirely within this enclosure they pocketed poverty just as the central and West End parishes pocketed wealth. The disparities thus caused lay at the heart of the metropolitan problem.

2. THE 1855 SYSTEM IN OPERATION

Few modern local government institutions can have attracted such uninhibited historical abuse as those created for London in 1855. The second

---

[15] Harcourt, quoting Goldsmith, in *Hansard*, 3rd ser., CCLXXXVII, 42 (8 Apr. 1884).

[16] C. F. G. Masterman, 'Realities at Home', in C. F. G. Masterman *et al.*, *The Heart of the Empire* (1901), 13.

tier has cornered most of the odium. A generalized contempt for the Vestries, for the pomposity and triviality of 'Bumbledom', in the Dickensian image, was as old as the Vestries themselves. It was sharpened in the 1880s by the emergence of the 'social problem' in London, and consequent suspicion of the Vestries' capacity and commitment to alleviate it. Some of Booth's witnesses suggest a public awareness of the considerable increase in Vestry activity in the 1890s, but the conventional image of self-interested neglect was assertively restored by the Progressive polemicist Henry Jephson in his *Sanitary Evolution of London* (1907). Jephson's trenchant attack upon 'vested rights in filth and dirt'[17] has conditioned most modern analysis of public health and housing questions. It was amplified in 1939 by W. A. Robson's influential *Government and Misgovernment of London*, a Fabian treatment which depicted the Vestries, like their successors the Metropolitan Boroughs, as agents of the fragmentation of London's civic consciousness and obstacles to the assumed greater efficiency of unitary management: 'There is almost unanimous agreement among those who have enquired into the subject that the minor authorities created in 1855 failed miserably to fulfil with credit or efficiency the tasks which Parliament had assigned to them.' on account of their 'apathy, indifference and jobbery'.[18] Although the semi-official historians of the London County Council, writing in the same year as Robson, suggested that 'the difference between 1855 and 1888 is in some ways more startling even than that between 1888 and the present day',[19] it is the Robsonian image of Vestrydom that has achieved historiographical currency; Brian Keith-Lucas thought it axiomatic that London's forty or so separate sanitary authorities were 'hopelessly corrupt and inefficient'.[20] Until recently the first tier has been subjected to much the same treatment as the second, intensified by the fact that the Metropolitan Board's jobbery was proven rather than assumed. To Robson the Board suffered from the 'fundamental defect ... that it completely failed to awaken any civic spirit in the minds of London's inhabitants'.[21] The more functional, less ethical, preoccupations of the present day have brought a tendency to stress the administrative achievements of both the MBW and the Vestries—'in retrospect their corruption seems petty, their delays

---

[17] H. Jephson, *The Sanitary Evolution of London* (1907), 89–90, 217, etc.
[18] W. A. Robson, *The Government and Misgovernment of London* (1939), 66–7, 69.
[19] G. Gibbon and R. W. Bell, *History of the London County Council, 1889–1939* (1939), 27.
[20] B. Keith-Lucas, 'London Government', letter in *Public Administration*, 50 (1972), 214.
[21] Robson, *Government and Misgovernment*, 65.

understandable, and their accomplishments astonishing'[22]—but revisionism has generally been hesitant.

This hesitancy may reflect a nagging awareness that the London system was indeed not a very effective one. The objection to the traditional approach should not be that it has traduced what was actually a successful system, but that it has perpetuated a polemical and unanalytical form of criticism that has changed little since the days of the Vestries. Most of the Vestries' failings are taken to be intrinsic to the authorities themselves and, particularly, to their members. Vestrymen were 'socially inferior, ill-educated, petty-minded'.[23] The Vestries were composed overwhelmingly of tradesmen, who, 'like French peasants', resented spending money on public services, and were 'not particularly interested in good government'.[24] This kind of *ad homines* approach typified much local government history until fairly recently, culminating perhaps in Professor Hennock's attempts to correlate municipal performance in Birmingham and Leeds with the social standing of councillors.[25] But the tradesman and the petty bourgeois have dominated the British local government system, for good or ill, since its inception; if London was less successful than provincial towns and cities during Britain's municipal 'golden age', it should be asked in what ways London differed from them. Obviously it was a vastly larger city than any other in Britain, with a more complex and variegated social structure. So far as local government was concerned, London's size had necessitated the adoption of a two-tier system, which generated problems foreign to the simple unitary municipality elsewhere—the balance of power and authority between the tiers, the size of the second-tier bodies, the degree of administrative and financial integration within the system. London's special circumstances raised problems more difficult than those tackled by the 1835 municipal system elsewhere. The two-tier system of 1855 was an experimental attempt to solve those problems, which happened not to be very successful.

In the provinces, municipal authority reflected a balance of social, economic, and political power which varied from one town to the next. In the most straightforward élitist model, municipal power could be simply an extension of the all-pervasive civic authority enjoyed by a

---

[22] D. J. Olsen, Introduction to D. Owen, *The Government of Victorian London* (Cambridge, Mass., and London, 1982), 16.

[23] Ibid.

[24] Owen, *The Government of Victorian London*, 38, 126.

[25] E. P. Hennock, *Fit and Proper Persons* (1973). Hennock's thesis is criticized by M. J. Daunton, *Coal Metropolis: Cardiff 1870–1914* (Leicester, 1977), 150–1.

landed family or an integrated industrial caste. In practice this simple
deference model was rare; municipal politics were too involved to allow
the direct transmission of the sort of personal power wielded over an
estate or a factory. Municipal authority is the least clearly defined aspect
of Joyce's picture of factory paternalism;[26] Garrard has outlined more
involved, less monolithic, local political structures within a fundamentally
élitist framework in three Lancashire towns.[27] Aristocratic paternalism
was always less secure in the municipal setting; the influence of the
Dartmouths in West Bromwich and the Dudleys in Dudley was a function
of power-sharing with middle-class groups, and marked a retreat from
earlier attempts to maintain 'feudal' influence.[28]

Only in small towns and single-industry towns was the deferential
model viable in its purest form. Elsewhere municipal politics reflected
battles within and between élites.[29] These would generally take political
shape, because they usually reflected social or religious divisions which
had already assumed political form. Thus Fraser has shown that political
divisions within mid-century communities could permeate their entire
local administrations down to the election of churchwardens.[30] In due
course party politics gave rise to party organization. Organization enabled
minority groups within the élite to establish an ascendancy by mobilizing
those outside it. Organization enabled Manchester's dissenting Liberals
to move from a minority position to dominance in the twenty years after
incorporation;[31] it underpinned what became Chamberlainite Liberal
municipalism in the Birmingham of the 1870s.[32] In the years after the
second Reform Act the party politicization of local government developed
a momentum of its own, as the increasingly sophisticated requirements
of registration and organization for national politics made local politics
a valuable means of oiling the wheels of the party machinery.[33] In

---

[26] For Blackburn, see P. Joyce, *Work, Society and Politics* (Hassocks, 1980), 169.

[27] J. Garrard, *Leadership and Power in Victorian Industrial Towns, 1830–80* (Manchester, 1983), 57, etc. The towns were Bolton, Rochdale, and Salford.

[28] R. Trainor, 'Peers on an Industrial Frontier: the Earls of Dartmouth and of Dudley in the Black Country, c 1810 to 1914', in D. Cannadine (ed.), *Patricians, Power and Politics in Nineteenth-century Towns* (Leicester, 1982), esp. 107–13.

[29] D. Fraser, *Urban Politics in Victorian England* (Leicester, 1976), 14.

[30] Ibid., ch. 2.

[31] See V. A. C. Gattrell, 'Incorporation and the Pursuit of Liberal Hegemony in Manchester, 1790–1839', in D. Fraser (ed.), *Municipal Reform and the Industrial City* (Leicester, 1982), esp. 22.

[32] Hennock, *Fit and Proper Persons*, 82, etc.

[33] Ibid. 131. For Conservative interest in municipal elections in the early 1870s, see the views of Gorst quoted by H. J. Hanham, *Elections and Party Management* (1959), 389.

Cardiff over the last quarter of the century, the currents of party politics determined the nature and intensity of municipal activity in a city where an identifiable economic élite existed but played no part in local gover-nemnt.[34] In London in the 1890s party politics breathed life into the municipal system of a city where no identifiable élite existed.[35] The end-product was the evolution of party municipal programmes in towns where contests were regular—a stage beyond the sort of politicization described by Fraser, which amounts to the replication of existing divisions in the arena of local politics.

In so far as these various systems empowered groups commanding either deference or a popular mandate, they retained public confidence. The London system lost public confidence because it produced neither élite leadership nor participatory politics. London, like most of the larger cities, displayed too complex a social structure to sustain a straightforward paternalistic system. If the metropolis had a natural élite it was the West End aristocracy, but the 'upper ten thousand' spent much of their lives outside the capital, and were generally taken to be extra-metropolitan in outlook—'hardly Londoners', in Arthur Hobhouse's dismissive words.[36] Their society was exclusive, and not one in which civic service was seen as a social duty. Few peers participated in local government; those that did were confined to the West End Vestries. Employer paternalism was patchily present in London.[37] Individual industrialists participated in local politics, and generally stressed their place in the local economy when they did so, but London remained 'overwhelmingly a city of small masters',[38] lacking the factory proletariat necessary to sustain industrial deference and lacking, above all, the interlinked, consolidated employer caste of the factory towns.[39] London's local authorities consequently lacked the instinctive leadership of either a social or an economic élite, and concern over the 'councillor calibre' problem became a constant undercurrent in the London government debate.

If élites were absent by default, many of those below them were absent by exclusion. In London, as in the provincial municipalities, while the franchise was conferred upon all householders, a minimum rating quali-

---

[34] Daunton, *Coal Metropolis*, 155 ff., 165 ff.

[35] See below, ch. 5.

[36] Quoted in L. T. Hobhouse and J. L. Hammond, *Lord Hobhouse: A Memoir* (1905), 162–3.

[37] P. Thompson, *Socialists, Liberals and Labour: The Struggle for London, 1885–1914* (1967), 73–4.

[38] G. Stedman Jones, *Outcast London* (Oxford, 1971), 29.

[39] Joyce, *Work, Society and Politics*, ch. 1.

fication was required to serve on the local authority. Garrard has argued that popular involvement in Rochdale local politics was increased by the adoption of a low £15 qualification.[40] In London the 1855 Bill had stipulated a £40 minimum, drawing this figure from the 1831 Hobhouse Act; in committee the qualification had been reduced to £25 in areas where fewer than one-sixth of all tenements satisfied the £40 requirement.[41] It is impossible to say whether, given London's higher rental levels, the Hobhouse provision was more restrictive than the £30 Municipal Corporations Act qualification. It is clear, however, not only that the 1855 system was, like the 1835 system, socially exclusive,[42] but also that the imposition of an overall qualification level, even with the £25 amendment, was more arbitrary in a metropolitan system than in a provincial town. Provincial municipalities were socially heterogeneous, embracing rich and poor quarters. In London, however, the combination of a fragmented second tier and increasing social segregation through metropolitan growth meant that the effect of the qualification varied enormously between areas. In wealthy St Martin's it was considered 'very low' even in the 1860s,[43] but in suburban Hampstead the Ratepayers' Association considered it 'far too high' as late as 1886,[44] and in the poorest areas it could cause a shortage of eligible candidates.[45]

All these circumstances help explain the breakdown of Vestrymen's occupations in Table 2.1. There is no indication of a dominant élite— either social or industrial—in any of the authorities chosen. While St George, Hanover Square was already in 1871 displaying the trend towards upper-middle-class involvement that would eventually characterize most

[40] Garrard, *Leadership and Power in Victorian Industrial Towns*, 13–14, etc.

[41] For the change, see the amended Bill in *PP 1854–5*, IV, Bill No. 234, clause F. The original provision had derived from 1 & 2 Wm. IV, c. 60.

[42] No breakdown of any quinquennial valuation survives before 1901, by which time both the Vestries and the qualification had been abolished. The 1901 figures (*London Statistics*, XII (1901–2), 18–59) show that despite the upward drift of valuation since 1855, some 75% of assessments still fell below the £40 mark, and 54% below £25. In Wandsworth 82.9% of householders were excluded before the 1881 valuation and 81.27% after (Wandsworth Vestry Minutes, 9 Sept. 1880 and 3 Feb. 1881). In Battersea 91% of assessments fell under £40, 71% under £25 in 1896 (LCC Local Government and Taxation Com., Presented Papers, 26 June 1896). Less than a thousand of the 12,000 houses in Bermondsey in the 1890s satisfied even the £25 qualification; F. W. Soutter, *Recollections of a Labour Pioneer* (1923), 157.

[43] SC Metropolitan Local Government and Taxation, *PP 1866*, XIII, Q. 3057 (J. Dangerfield).

[44] See Stoke Newington RA Minutes, 6 Sept. 1886 (Hackney Archives).

[45] Plumstead contained only 400 eligible householders for 96 places in 1893, even with the £25 qualification (*Local Government Journal*, 2 Dec. 1893).

TABLE 2.1. Occupations of Vestrymen

	Camberwell Vestry, 1871		Hampstead Vestry, 1871		St George, Hanover Sq. Vestry, 1871		St George in the East Vestry, 1871		St George-the-Martyr Vestry, 1857		St Pancras Vestry, 1888	
	No.	%	No.	%	No.	%	No.	%	No.	%	No.	%
Trade:												
Drink	1	1·2	4	16·7	2	1·9	2	5·7	1	2·1	11	9·2
Building	3	3·6	4	16·7	8	7·4	1	2·9	1	2·1	14	11·7
Shopkeepers	14	16·9	4	16·7	20	18·5	11	31·4	16	33·3	39	32·5
Others	10	12·0	3	12·5	20	18·5	14	40·0	18	37·5	28	23·3
Industry, Commerce	9	10·8	0		13	12·0	4	11·4	3	6·3	9	7·5
Professional	20	24·1	5	20·8	8	7·4	1	2·9	4	8·3	15	12·5
Clerks	11	13·3	1	4·2	1	0·9	0	—	0	—	2	1·7
Gentry, house proprietors, etc.	8	9·6	2	8·3	30	27·8	0	—	0	—	0	—
Unidentified	7	8·4	1	4·2	6	5·6	2	5·7	5	10·4	2	1·7
TOTAL	83		24		108		35		48		120	

Sources: 1871 figures compiled from Post Office Directories and 1871 Census street returns. St George-the-Martyr (1857) from the list of occupations given in A. M. Wilkinson, 'The Work of the Medical Officers in Three Parishes, 1856–1900', D.Phil. thesis (Oxford, 1980), 84–5. St Pancras (1888) from the letter 'What are Vestries Made of?' by 'Nemo' in *Holborn Guardian*, 20 Oct. 1888.

of the West End Vestries,[46] one would not gather from the composition of its authority that it was the most aristocratic parish in London. The 'shopocratic' tone of Vestrydom is clear. It may or may not have impaired performance, but the example of St George's-in-the-East shows that where a parish lacked a resident middle class, and the qualification ruled out the predominant working-class householders, the 'shopocracy' virtually monopolized the Vestry and provided a seriously unrepresentative local authority. St George's had still to attain the degree of social uniformity that would impress Booth, but it was already a sufficiently homogeneous working-class community to ensure that very few householders satisfied even the £25 qualification, and that eligibility usually depended upon assessment being enhanced by trade or a licence.

The politicization of the Vestries could have provided leadership and, by increasing public involvement, could have offset the constitutional defects of representation. This failed to happen because the nature of London politics worked against involvement in local government. In the 1850s and early 1860s the pattern of London parliamentary politics had been one of Conservative weakness and Liberal dominance by default.[47] As a result borough Liberal Associations rather than the borough itself became the focus of dispute, and Whig/Radical divisions became more important than Liberal/Tory ones. Where parliamentary contests occurred they were most likely to be between Liberal factions, and the support of the party association would generally determine the result.[48]

From the mid-1860s this pattern changed. In 1865 and particularly in 1868, when the Conservatives contested every London borough for the first time since the 1832 Reform Act, the Tory challenge was more potent. With the return of party contests it became more necessary to nurse the constituency than the association, and effective registration became essential. The massive boroughs created in 1832 took some nursing once London's growth had swelled their populations to half a million—in the cases of Finsbury and Marylebone—by the 1880s. The London boroughs acquired the reputation of being beyond the reach of caucus methods.[49]

---

[46] By the end of the century St George, Hanover Square, would parade 'a small army of generals, colonels, admirals, honorables and persons with double-barreled names', Booth MS B 255, 75 (interview with Mr Nesbit, Vestry clerk).

[47] M. B. Baer, 'The Politics of London, 1852–1868: Parties, Voters and Representation', Ph.D. thesis (Univ. of Iowa, 1976), 166 ff.

[48] Of the twelve sitting MPs defeated between 1852 and 1867, ten were opposed by their borough associations: ibid. 189.

[49] 'I have always a doubt or a dread of the London constituencies. There is greater power among them, but it is not coherent, and it is difficult to excite among them any common

Certainly borough elections were expensive to fight. A growing premium was placed upon the wealthy candidate, and the balance between candidate and association tilted in favour of the former. W. H. Smith topped the poll at Westminster in 1868 after paying nearly four times the combined election expenses of his opponents.[50] Between 1869 and 1880 he contributed £7,935 to the Westminster Conservative Association, 59 per cent of its entire subscription income in that period.[51]

The London boroughs did not, therefore, see a direct transition 'from the caucus-type cadre party to the branch-type mass party'.[52] The fifteen years or so between the introduction of household suffrage and the development of Birmingham-model constituency organizations provided an interlude during which the metropolitan boroughs became among the last refuges of the Independent Member, flaunting his Burkean autonomy at every opportunity. Thus W. M. Torrens, *bête noire* of the revived Finsbury Liberal Association in the 1880s, prided himself that 'if I had done nothing but vote with Gladstone I never should have held the half million community against his candidates for twenty years'.[53] Fawcett, in Hackney, who fought economical campaigns with subscription funds, 'never condescended to conceal his hostility to some of the favourite nostrums of the party to which he belonged' and refused to be introduced to the Commons by the Liberal whips.[54] In Marylebone Thomas Chambers, who 'never would permit himself to be called a "Radical"', a name he much disliked', who strongly objected to the lowering of the franchise, and who would die a Liberal Unionist, decided that 'canvassing was out of the question with such a huge electorate'. With 'hardly any Liberal organization, properly so called', he held the seat on the strength of 'about two political meetings in a year' in the late 1860s.[55] Smith believed that

feeling and action.' John Bright to Thorold Rogers, 4 Feb. 1879: Thorold Rogers Papers, Correspondence Box 3.

[50] Election expenses from the Return in *PP 1868–9*, L, 23.

[51] From Westminster Conservative Association, Cash Book 1869–86 and Index to Donors 1866–86, in Westminster Archives 487/3 and 487/4.

[52] Baer, 'The Politics of London', 209, n. 86, referring to the Westminster Conservatives. By virtually ignoring the question of party funding, Baer exaggerates the extent of local party control.

[53] W. M. Torrens to the tenth Earl of Wemyss, 30 Mar. 1892, WP, National Library of Scotland, RH 4/40/12. The *Echo* (5 July 1884) described Torrens as 'one of those vastly "independent" Members who find it necessary to emphasise their freedom from control by habitually supporting and voting with the party they were sent to Parliament to oppose'.

[54] L. Stephen, *Life of Sir Henry Fawcett* (1886), 385; S. Gwynn and G. M. Tuckwell, *The Life of the Right Hon. Sir Charles W. Dilke* (1917) i. 173.

[55] Lady Southwark, *Social and Political Reminiscences* (1913), 52, 55.

the Member for Westminster 'may retain his seat pretty nearly for life', and proved himself right.[56]

Organizational decay was not inevitable, but the accelerating cost of metropolitan elections did have important effects upon organization. Where most of the organizational expenses were borne by the candidate or sitting Member, there was a clear danger of the association becoming a vehicle for the man. While a figure like Smith could subsidize his association but remain genuinely sensitive to its views, such magnanimity could not be guaranteed; when the Chelsea Liberal Association was reformed along caucus lines in 1878, one of its first actions was to set up a registration fund to relieve the candidates.[57] Even where this was not the case, the sheer magnitude of a metropolitan campaign meant that organizations tended to be geared to producing a massive effort in anticipation of a general election—fund-raising and canvassing for Morgan Howard's 1874 campaign in Lambeth began in May 1873[58]—and exhibited little activity at other times.

What London lacked was the kind of regular, standing, constituency party organization which, in many provincial towns in the late 1860s and 1870s, came to use local elections as a means of oiling its machinery.[59] The Vestries were not seen as a means of cultivating a political base or as an outlet for aspirant politicians; Vestrydom produced no Chamberlain. This absence of party involvement was important in an emergent metropolis. Party organization, and in particular the development of party municipal programmes, could have served as an integrative force, providing a dimension to local politics beyond that of the needs of the parish. Underlying the development of the London government debate over the second half of the century was the transformation of a metropolitan system dominated by issues of local particularism into one accommodating both local interests and questions of political principle. The weakness of London's party political organization down to the 1880s retarded this transformation. Without party organization, Vestry politics was dominated until the mid-1880s—and in some areas later—by parochial ratepayers' associations.

Ratepayers' associations were generally concerned with overtly

---

[56] Viscount Chilston, *W. H. Smith* (London and Toronto, 1965), 49.

[57] Report of first annual meeting in *Chelsea News and Kensington Post*, 10 May 1879.

[58] Sir Edward Clarke, *The Story of My Life* (1918), 103–4. Torrens spoke of canvassing lasting 'eight or nine months' in Finsbury in 1865; W. M. Torrens, *Twenty Years of Parliamentary Life* (1893), 15, 18.

[59] Hennock, *Fit and Proper Persons*, 133; Daunton, *Coal Metropolis*, 168.

parochial issues—the repair of streets, the condition of the drains, the
lighting of thoroughfares. They were not, of course, apolitical; like the
Vestries they reflected social, religious, and cultural divisions within the
community which could take political form. Nevertheless, they generally
adopted the public stance that the interests of the parish were indivisible,
and consequently that local government was above party politics. The
rules of the Plumstead Ratepayers' Association stated aggressively that
'This Association is strictly non-political; should any member introduce
any such question at any of its meetings, the Chairman is authorised to
suppress it at once, and no appeal can be made against such decision'.[60]
This taboo survived until the widespread intervention of party organizations in the 1880s. In the absence of élite leadership, and given the
obscurity of most Vestrymen, Vestry politics came to appear to consist
of battles between cliques, which inhibited wider popular involvement.

This was exacerbated by the anxiety of most ratepayers' associations
to limit the number of contested Vestry elections. In part this was
financial. Many associations ran on a shoe-string and were reluctant to face
the cost of annual contests; in Bethnal Green the so-called Ratepayers'
Permanent Association charged its candidates for the board of guardians
10s. 6d. per head to defray the cost of their campaigns.[61] Nevertheless,
associations were not invariably penniless. The Kensington RA had an
income of over £100 p.a. in the 1890s,[62] that in St George, Hanover
Square, £45 p.a. in the 1880s,[63] and the Stoke Newington RA—in a
smaller parish—received over £20 annually in subscriptions for most of
its life.[64] The resistance of these bodies to contests usually reflected their
success in infiltrating the Vestry. When an association commanded an
authority, contests were clearly undesirable, and unnecessary until a
challenge came from a rival association. This usually happened when an
association had become so completely identified with the Vestry that it
was as much tainted by rising local taxation as the 'old gang' that it had
originally supplanted. Secession was the most frequent cause of death for
ratepayers' associations,[65] which tended to 'live a butterfly existence and

---

[60] Rules of the Plumstead RA (est. 1887), Rule 12 (Greenwich Archives).
[61] Bethnal Green Ratepayers' Permanent Association, East Ward, Minutes, 23 Nov. 1894
(Tower Hamlets Archives).
[62] Kensington RA, *19th Annual Report* (1890), 15.
[63] Annual meeting reported *Westminster Times*, 25 Feb. 1888.
[64] SNRA Minutes, 1884–94 (Hackney Archives).
[65] For an example in Paddington see *Marylebone Mercury* 26 July 1879.

soon die'.[66] It could be resisted by accommodation with the rival body, which could occasionally lead to its successful absorption. In Islington in 1887, for example, the Upper Holloway RA amalgamated with the secessionist North Islington RA to create an association allegedly three-quarters composed of Vestrymen. In due course, though, the view that 'the object of a ratepayers' association was to keep vestrymen in check' led to the formation of a North Islington Ratepayers' Protection Association, in which sitting Vestrymen were denied voting rights.[67]

The two most extensive surviving sets of ratepayers' association minutes—in Stoke Newington and De Beauvoir Town—provide examples of the life-cycle characteristic of these bodies. In each case a successful assault was mounted upon an unsuspecting 'old gang' in the association's first year. In Stoke Newington the association met in the following year with a counter-attack by 'the Vestry Party, supported by the Church & working for days beforehand & spending a lot of money', and was defeated at a poll. In subsequent years the chairman was authorized to contact 'the other side with a view of avoiding a contest' and sparing 'the expense and perhaps bad feeling that might be engendered'. For four years the Vestry elections were uncontested, until in 1890 two rival candidates were run by a dissident member of the association.[68] In De Beauvoir Town a rival organization emerged within eighteen months of the original association's birth, and despite a resolution to 'take no notice of the new organization as it would soon die a natural death', an accommodation was sought to prevent a contest in the 1881 Hackney Vestry elections. Although these approaches failed, contests appear to have been avoided between 1884 and the association's demise in 1890.[69]

Thus, even where ratepayers' associations did provide some degree of electoral organization, their energies were often overtly devoted to restricting the extent of public involvement. The 1855 system helped them. By what Sidney Webb considered 'the most hugger-mugger electoral machinery that even the early Victorian era ever produced',[70] ratepayers assembled first to choose their representatives by show of hands, subject to a poll on the demand of five electors. A ratepayer contemplating turning out for the show of hands would therefore have faced a wasted

[66] Letter from C. Fox on 'Ratepayers and their Associations' in *Islington Gazette*, 18 May 1887.
[67] For these events see ibid., 13 May 1887.
[68] SNRA Minutes, 27 Jan. 1885, 1 June 1885, 17 May 1886, 11 June 1888, 9 June 1890.
[69] De Beauvoir Town and Dalston RA Minutes, 8 Feb. 1881, 12 Apr. 1881, 28 Mar. 1890 (Hackney Archives).
[70] S. Webb, 'London's District Councils', *Methodist Times*, 29 Nov. 1894.

journey if the election was uncontested, or if it was contested and a poll was demanded. In 1885 three-quarters of all Vestry elections were either uncontested or polled.[71] Even at a poll, turnout was limited by the short notice—twenty-four hours—stipulated by the 1855 Act, and by the consequently restricted publicity. Ratepayers' associations seldom made any attempt at widespread canvassing, and concentrated their efforts upon the poll itself, where, in the absence of official ballot papers, they would assail the electors with their own private lists.[72] In Paddington this practice was said to have given rise to scenes 'resembling the betting rings of a racecourse' outside the poll, encouraging double voting and allowing 'false imitation papers [to be] forced into the hands of unsuspecting voters who by using them have voted contrary to the manner they wished'.[73] The results of Vestry polls often indicate a pattern of ticket voting; at Limehouse in 1885, for example, where the representative of the ratepayers' association emerged from the count 'with a wild hurrah' announcing that 'the Association candidates were "right in it and the rest nowhere" ', the twenty-three men elected polled between 246 and 304 votes, with nobody else securing above 72.[74] In Paddington in the same year the five successful candidates in one ward polled between 201 and 182 votes, the five defeated candidates between 66 and 51.[75]

Two systematic surveys of Vestry election results—one 'vertical', from a single parish throughout the life of its Vestry, the other 'horizontal', covering all the parishes in a single year—show the very low level of public participation in Vestry elections down to the mid-1880s.[76] In Camberwell the highest vote recorded by a Vestryman in any of the first ten elections was 67, and on three occasions men topped the lists with single-figure votes. Only one of 60 ward elections in these years was polled, and 25 were uncontested. By 1880 there had still been only 19 polled elections and 47 uncontested out of 150. The parliamentary return of Vestry results in 1885 suggests that the apathy from which Camberwell was starting to emerge in the mid-1880s was still generally prevalent. Of

[71] 'Return of the Result of the Latest Vestry Elections . . .', *PP 1886*, LVII, 329–62.
[72] The 1855 Act did not prohibit this; see Dunham's report to Newington Vestry, *South London Press*, 20 May 1893.
[73] Report by churchwarden (G. D. Thomas) on Vestry elections, Paddington Vestry Minutes, 20 May 1884.
[74] *East End News*, 2 June 1885.
[75] *Metropolitan*, 16 May 1885.
[76] Summary of Vestry elections, 1855–99, Camberwell Vestry *Annual Report*, (1899–1900), 291–2; 'Return of the Result of the latest Vestry Elections', *PP 1886*, LVII, 331–60.

the 200 electoral areas—wards or single-ward parishes—only 90 were even contested, and only 40 polled. In 32 cases candidates topped the poll with fewer than 50 votes. These were derisory figures even by the conventionally unimpressive standards of local government elections.

The breakdown of Schedule A and B parish results reveals further problems.[77] Whereas 61 of 110 Schedule A wards were contested, with 29 polled, only 29 out of 90 Schedule B areas were contested, and 11 polled. With elections, as with much else, the District Board system amplified the shortcomings of the Vestries. Several Schedule B parishes were far too small to sustain an independent political vitality. Holy Trinity, Minories, in the Whitechapel District, considered itself 'too small to elect a vestry' in 1885. Another Whitechapel parish, St Katherine-by-the-Tower, contained only eleven rated householders in 1891. Elections being rather a luxury in these circumstances, 'all the ratepayers are deemed vestrymen', although the Act stipulated a minimum of eighteen. The smaller Schedule B parishes were in any case often condemned to form permanent minorities on their District Boards. In Whitechapel, where St Mary's parish provided 27 of the 58 District Board members, eight parishes shared the other 31 seats. In the Holborn District, three out of the four component parishes shared only 16 of the 49 seats. In the period before the development of party municipal programmes in London, municipal identities were primarily local; the actual duties of a Schedule B Vestry were nugatory,[78] and if its representatives were constitutionally incapable of protecting the interests of the parish on the District Board, the chances of arousing popular interest in their election were slight. For most of the system's life, Schedule B elections were significant only in some of the larger parishes which formed the majority of their District Board—Hackney, Wandsworth, Lewisham. Generally, turnout was pitiful. As Table 2.2 shows, the members of the St Olave's District Board for 1882–3—a body with an annual budget of around £20,000—were returned by a total of 67 votes in nine elections.

About a third of London's population lived in Schedule B parishes; by the 1890s the LCC Progressive B. F. C. Costelloe was convinced that

---

[77] For this paragraph see *PP 1886*, LVII, 331–60.

[78] Consisting chiefly of electing the District Board members and formally voting rates to meet the precepts imposed upon them. Members of the Schedule B Vestry of St Nicholas, Deptford, met 'once in two months or as often as is required' (Report on the Union of St Paul and St Nicholas, Deptford, LCC Local Government and Taxation Com., Presented Papers, 10 Dec. 1897, p. 21).

TABLE 2.2.   Attendance at Vestry Elections, St Olave's District, 1880–1882

	1880	1881	1882
St Olave	8	6	15
St Thomas	2	5	4
St John, Horselydown	8	9	10

Sources: St Olave's Vestry Minutes, 5 May 1880, 4 May 1881, 3 May 1882; St Thomas, Southwark, Vestry Minutes, 5 May 1880, 12 May 1881, 3 May 1882; St John, Horselydown Vestry Minutes, 5 May 1880, 11 May 1881, 3 May 1882.

'one of the first essentials in any reform of London areas is that as far as possible the District Board system should be done away with'.[79]

The paralysing effects of indirect elections were also shown in the Metropolitan Board of Works. Vestries were aware in choosing their MBW representative they were nominating to a body entitled to tax them heavily, but with that proviso, the choice of MBW member resembled the election of committee men or of delegates on co-optive authorities. It was rare for the selection of an MBW representative to be contested, rarer for a sitting member to be opposed for re-election and rarer still for one to be defeated; by 1878 only thirteen out of the 132 Board members elected since 1856 had been unseated by their Vestries.[80] A striking example of the different effects of direct and indirect election was provided in 1888 in Lambeth, where F. H. Fowler, revealed by the Royal Commission on the MBW to have benefited from extensive peculation during his years as a Board member, was heavily defeated in the Vestry election but still came within three votes of being re-elected by the Vestry to the Board.[81]

Vestries tended to choose as their representatives the men with the longest municipal experience, often, even down to the 1880s, returning men schooled in the pre-1855 Vestries. John Reddish of Islington was *first* elected to Spring Gardens at the age of seventy-nine in 1878.[82] W. H. Dickinson's memory in the 1890s was of Wandsworth being represented by two near octogenarians.[83] This tendency, coupled with the practical

[79] RC Proper Conditions under which the Amalgamation of the City and County of London can be Effected, *PP 1894*, XVII, Q. 13962.

[80] According to Earl Beauchamp in Hansard, 3rd ser., CCXXXVIII, 1027–8 (11 Mar. 1878).

[81] *Metropolitan*, 23 June 1888.

[82] *Islington Gazette*, 21 Oct. 1878. The *Gazette* complained that 'the position is not an ornamental one, to be bestowed like churchwardens' vellum or a testimonial tankard on one whose only claim can be for past services, not present fitness'.

[83] RC Amalgamation, *PP 1894*, XVII, Q. 13664.

security of MBW tenure, turned the Board into a municipal gerontocracy. In 1885 at least sixteen of its forty-six members were over sixty-five, and five over seventy; thirteen would be dead by the end of the decade. The average age of the forty-four members whose dates of birth can be traced was over sixty-one, against an average of forty-six for the directly elected members of the first London County Council in 1889.[84] The difference between the 'town improvement' municipalism of the MBW and the social municipalism of the LCC was generational as well as ideological. One effect was to make the Board slow to reflect changes in the second tier. The emergence of Radical minorities in some Vestries in the 1880s had no echo on the Board, and the fact that Radical reformers in the 1880s sought to attack the London system from without, through legislative change, rather than alter it from within may reflect this failing.

London government remained ostensibly apolitical for virtually all the MBW's life, and as long as neither Board nor Vestries adopted overtly party political stances, MBW politics broke down primarily along local or parochial lines. The ambassadorial attitude identified by Sir Edwin Herbert as characterizing members of federal, indirectly elected bodies[85] was evident on the MBW. A readiness on the part of many Vestries to believe that their 'ambassador' was not responsible for the actions of the Board as a whole shielded MBW members from parochial resentment of rising first-tier precepts and of the corruption scandal of the late 1880s. Local particularism could have hampered the Board as an executive body. It did not do so—and in fact the Board was arguably a more effective authority than its successor—because with only forty-six members and no party political divisions the MBW was small enough to be managed by an 'inner cabinet' of five or six senior members, who fixed agendas and influenced discussion.[86] One of them, John Runtz of Hackney, was criticized at his District Board in 1885 for seeming 'to regard his position as a freehold', for poor attendance at the DB and for voting against 'the

---

[84] MBW members from F. Boase, *Modern English Biography* (1892–1921); where applicable, Census street returns, and obituaries in the *Metropolitan*. LCC members from *Pall Mall Gazette Extra on the London County Council* (1889), and *Dod's Handbook to the London County Council* (1889).

[85] RC Local Government in Greater London, 1957–60, Minutes of Evidence, vol i. Q. 262.

[86] See the evidence of G. Edwards, MBW, to the RC Metropolitan Board of Works, Interim report, *PP 1888*, LVI, Q. 11102–3. Edwards's evidence was supported by J. Jones, MBW (Q. 12467), who, however, claimed that Edwards belonged to the 'ring'. J. Runtz, MBW, whom both Edwards and Jones believed to belong to the cabinet, denied its existence (Q. 12568). See also Owen, *The Government of Victorian London*, 191.

decisions of Hackney' at Spring Gardens.[87] Generally the Board came to develop a corporate will and identity of its own over the years, which would show itself most clearly in the 'dangerous unanimity'[88] with which it at first resisted public investigation of the surplus lands scandal in the 1880s. Corruption may not be an inevitable concomitant of indirect election, and the Board's most recent historian has robustly defended its role in the most famous of the early scandals,[89] but it remains the case that the MBW attracted an inordinate number of allegations in its thirty-three years, that even within five years of its creation the chairman thought it necessary to dispel the taint of jobbery,[90] and that its introversion under pressure encouraged public suspicion. The low public image of the MBW became increasingly important as the system developed. Hall's determination to make the Vestries what would now be called the primary authorities within the system, and to underline their primacy by electing the first tier from the second, was justifiable at a time when second-tier issues—paving, lighting, and local sanitation—formed the greater part of municipal activity. By the 1870s, however, many provincial cities had graduated to a more ambitious 'town improvement' municipalism of public utility purchase and comprehensive civic improvement. Their unitary municipal structure allowed this to be accomplished in most cases without undue friction, despite the inherent limitations of the rating system, because borough boundaries embraced both high and low assessments and (in the case of the utilities) provided adequate catchment areas for municipal provision. The limited areas and resources of many London Vestries prevented their adoption of town improvement municipalism and contributed to the progressive enervation of the second tier. At the height of the debate over parochial incorporation in 1897 one Lambeth Vestryman argued that 'Birmingham and Glasgow had developed their municipal life while London had become hopeless' because

the citizens of the two former cities were not called to serve upon their municipal corporations solely to supervise the cleansing of streets and sewers, but to take a hand in the management of such important subjects as the police, the trams, the water and the electric lighting.[91]

---

[87] *Eastern Argus and Borough of Hackney Times*, 28 Mar. 1885.
[88] M. H. Judge, *The Working of the Metropolitan Board of Works* (1888), 7.
[89] Owen, *The Government of Victorian London*, 85–6.
[90] SC Metropolis Local Taxation, *PP 1861*, VIII, Q. 2410 (Sir John Thwaites).
[91] W. Wightman, quoted in the *South London Press*, 13 Nov. 1897.

The MBW was the only plausible agency of town improvement municipalism in London, and it was indeed responsible for most of the capital's
early municipal monuments—the main drainage system, several major
street improvements, and the Thames Embankment. The coincidence of
its attempts to purchase London's gas and water supply in 1875–8 and
the comprehensive street improvements programme of 1877 suggests a
sensitivity on the Board's part to the favourable climate for municipal
enterprise in the years after Chamberlain's Birmingham mayoralty. But
the MBW's constitution, and growing public doubt about its honesty,
meant that it lived most of its life under a cloud of suspicion. In the
1870s, when the Borough Funds and Local Loans Acts worked to lib-
eralize provincial loans and encourage municipal activity, the MBW had
to endure the tightening of Treasury control over its own borrowing and
the parliamentary defeat of its gas and water schemes.

   The Board's modern defenders generally argue that, uninspiring, irresponsible, and corrupt as it was, the Board was at least effective; similarly,
the current of revisionism has created a readiness to see the Vestries as
competent if unexciting local bodies. In fact the London system as a
whole did not function well, however proficient individual authorities
were within it. Most of its failings derived from the fragmentation of the
second tier. Fragmentation meant that local areas were more likely to
encapsulate pockets of poverty or wealth within the metropolis, which
created a substantial disparity of resources between second-tier bodies
from the start. At the time of the first uniform valuation, in 1871, the
richest London parish, St James, Piccadilly, had a rateable value per head
nearly seven times that of the poorest, Bethnal Green.[92] The process of
metropolitan growth, by which rising land values turned the central area
over to commerce and depopulated it, sending more refugees into the
poorest quarters, exacerbated this problem. By 1901 the richest of the
former Vestry and District Board areas, now St Martin's, had a rateable
value per head thirteen times that of the poorest, now Mile End.

   This was a very wide divergence of resources between authorities
expected to fulfil the same statutory duties. It meant that a substantially
higher rate in the pound was required to raise a given sum in a poor
parish than in a rich one, so that the London rating system was, in effect,
inversely graduated between areas. Table 2.3 shows the consequences of
this inequality for the levels of poundage rates in the earliest years for

---

[92] From the comparative table of rateable value per head in *London Statistics*, XIII (1902–
3), 350–1.

TABLE 2.3. Rateable Value per Head and Rates Raised, 1878–1882

Parish/District	R.v./hd. (£) 1881	Av. Rate in £ 1878, 1880, 1882		
		s.	d.	rank
St James	22·27 (1)	3	$8\frac{3}{4}$	(36)
St Martin's	21·86 (2)	3	5	(38)
St George, Hanover Sq.	18·75 (3)	3	$6\frac{3}{4}$	(37)
St Olave's DB	17·12 (4)	4	$5\frac{1}{2}$	(27)
Strand DB	13·39 (5)	3	9	(35=)
Paddington	11·10 (6)	3	$9\frac{1}{2}$	(33)
St Saviour's DB	10·63 (7)	4	$3\frac{1}{4}$	(30)
Kensington	10·10 (8)	3	$10\frac{1}{4}$	(32)
Westminster DB	10·00 (9)	3	9	(35=)
Hampstead	9·18 (10)	4	8	(25)
Marylebone	8·93 (11)	4	$4\frac{3}{4}$	(29)
Holborn DB	8·13 (12)	5	$5\frac{1}{4}$	(12)
St Giles DB	7·90 (13)	5	$4\frac{3}{4}$	(14=)
Lewisham DB	7·12 (14)	4	$11\frac{3}{4}$	(23)
St Pancras	6.31 (15)	4	$7\frac{1}{4}$	(26)
St Luke's	5·94 (16)	5	10	(5=)
Wandsworth DB	5·62 (17)	5	1	(19)
Limehouse DB	5·44 (18)	5	10	(5=)
Rotherhithe	5·36 (19)	4	10	(24)
Chelsea	5·28 (20)	5	0	(22)
Whitechapel DB	5·25 (21)	5	$6\frac{1}{2}$	(11)
Plumstead DB	5·16 (22)	5	$10\frac{1}{4}$	(3)
Islington	5·11 (23)	3	$11\frac{3}{4}$	(31)
Lambeth	5·06 (24)	5	$0\frac{3}{4}$	(20)
Hackney DB	5·05 (25)	4	$5\frac{1}{4}$	(28)
Fulham DB	4·75 (26)	5	9	(7=)
Clerkenwell	4·73 (27)	5	$4\frac{3}{4}$	(14=)
Greenwich DB	4·70 (28)	5	7	(10)
Shoreditch	4·55 (29)	5	$0\frac{1}{4}$	(21)
Bermondsey	4·35 (30)	5	$3\frac{3}{4}$	(15)
Camberwell	4·31 (31)	5	2	(18)
Poplar	4·28 (32)	5	$8\frac{3}{4}$	(8)
St George-in-the-East	4·22 (33)	6	0	(2)
St George-the-Martyr	4·04 (34)	5	9	(7=)
Newington	3·69 (35)	5	$3\frac{1}{4}$	(17)
Woolwich	3·19 (36)	5	$7\frac{3}{4}$	(9)
Mile End Old Town	3·18 (37)	5	3	(16)
Bethnal Green	2·82 (38)	6	3	(1)

which complete figures have survived. The disparity of Vestry rates is in fact partly disguised in this table, as the total rate figures include the poor rate, supported by a partial equalization scheme, and the first-tier levies, met by a uniform rate across London. Table 2.4 isolates the rate for Vestry services alone in the five wealthiest and five poorest areas in 1880.

TABLE 2.4.   Vestry/District Board Rates, 1880

5 Wealthiest Areas	s.	d.	5 Poorest Areas	s.	d.
1. St James, Piccadilly	0	$9\frac{1}{2}$	Bethnal Green	2	$2\frac{1}{2}$
2. St Martin-in-the-Fields	0	$10\frac{1}{2}$	Mile End Old Town	1	$10\frac{1}{2}$
3. St George, Hanover Square	0	$9\frac{1}{2}$	Woolwich	1	$8\frac{1}{2}$
4. St Olave's DB	0	$10\frac{1}{2}$	Newington	1	$11\frac{1}{2}$
5. Strand DB	0	11	St George-the-Martyr	2	$1\frac{1}{2}$

Source: MBW 'Unnumbered Report' 0153. Figs. given for DB rates are averages of component parish rates weighted according to 1881 population.

Even these figures conceal the extent of rating disparities by looking only at the Schedule A Vestries and the District Boards. In fact rates would vary even within District Board areas, between the component Schedule B parishes. There was no obligation to spread expenditure across the district, despite the extreme fragmentation of some districts.[93] Nine parishes, all in Schedule B, paid higher Vestry rates than Bethnal Green in 1880, including the Whitechapel parish of Tower Without, whose 233 inhabitants were rated at 3s. 3d. in the pound. Highly assessed parishes in poor districts did not necessarily support their neighbours. St John, Wapping, in the very poor Limehouse District, paid Vestry rates of 1s. $2\frac{1}{2}d$. against 2s. or more in the other Limehouse parishes; All Saints, Poplar, paid 1s. 4d. against 2s. $0\frac{1}{2}d$. and 2s. $5\frac{1}{2}d$. in the other Poplar District parishes.[94]

The material effect of fragmentation was that the occupier of a 10s.

[93] The 1855 Act was silent on the matter, but the decision in *Overseers of St. Botolph, Aldgate* v. *Whitechapel District Board* (1861) (29 LJ (NS) MC, 228) entitled District Boards to charge their parishes according to expenditure incurred within each. A committee of Greenwich Vestry in 1891, angered by the Greenwich DB's failure to equalize rating, found that Hackney and Plumstead Districts remained unequalized and that Limehouse had only changed in 1888 (Greenwich Vestry Minutes, 20 July and 17 Aug. 1891). Greenwich remained unequalized in 1897; see Report on Union of St Paul & St Nicholas, Deptford, LCC Local Government and Taxation Com., Presented Papers, 10 Dec. 1897, p. 17.

[94] MBW 'Unnumbered Report' 0153. For the special circumstances of Tower Without see *London*, 19 Oct. 1893.

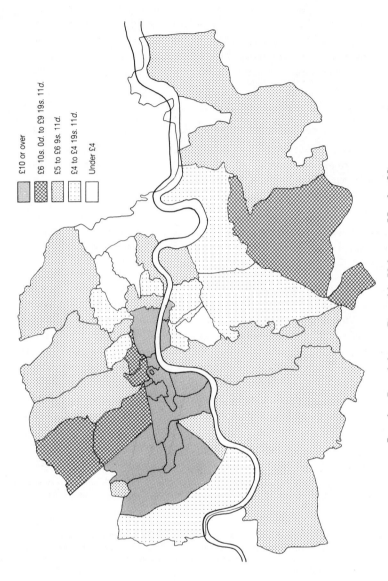

£10 or over

£6 10s. 0d. to £9 19s. 11d.

£5 to £6 9s. 11d.

£4 to £4 19s. 11d.

Under £4

London Local Areas: Rateable Value per Head, 1881

weekly tenement, with a rateable value of perhaps £15 per annum, in Bethnal Green, would pay annually £1. 1s.—over two weeks' rent—more in rates than would a similarly assessed occupier in St James, for the same basic services. In provincial municipalities expenses were generally covered by a uniform town or city rate across the whole borough, providing some degree of effective redistribution between areas. Even in London, the redistributive principle had been admitted for poor rates with the creation of the Metropolitan Common Poor Fund in 1867, taxing rich unions in aid of poor ones, but Vestry rates remained entirely unequalized until 1894, only six years before the Vestries' demise.

This localization of Vestry rates was an inefficient way of funding services intended, presumably, to be executed to a similar standard across London. Fig. 2.1 shows that the inequality in poundage rates, considerable though it was, mitigated rather than corrected the disparity of resources. There remained a fairly strong correlation between rateable value per head and expenditure upon the basic Vestry services of paving, lighting, and sewerage. St James spent over six times as much as Bethnal Green from a rate one-third as heavy.

The significance of this discrepancy was enhanced by the fact that sanitary problems, forming the bulk of the Vestries' concerns, were also localized to a considerable extent, with the poorest parishes facing the greatest difficulties. Sanitary powers constituted a dubious prize for the localists to have wrested from Chadwick. They were mostly trivial and unappealing, and more conspicuous in the breach than in the observance.[95] The Vestries' poor sanitary reputation, which would be turned against them at a critical time in 1883–4, derived chiefly from the fact that weak authorities faced overwhelming difficulties. This is not to deny the in-built parsimony of the second tier; even that was in a sense structural. The members of the Bethnal Green Vestry regarded schemes under the 1868 Artisans and Labourers' Dwellings Act 'from a financial rather than a sanitary point of view' because they were 'large ratepayers themselves'.[96] This was the effect of the Vestry qualification, and of the resultant dominance of the 'shopocracy' in working-class areas. W. H. Dickinson estimated in 1897 that rateable value represented 12 per cent of a shopkeeper's net income, 14 per cent of a builder's or factory owner's

---

[95] The St Luke's Medical Officer, interviewed by Jesse Argyle for the Booth survey in 1898, complained of the 'difficulty in squeezing the Vestry up to the mark in sanitary matters: the work is not showy enough for them—they want to see more for their money'. Booth MS B 235, 167 (G. E. Yarrow).

[96] Stedman Jones, *Outcast London*, 190.

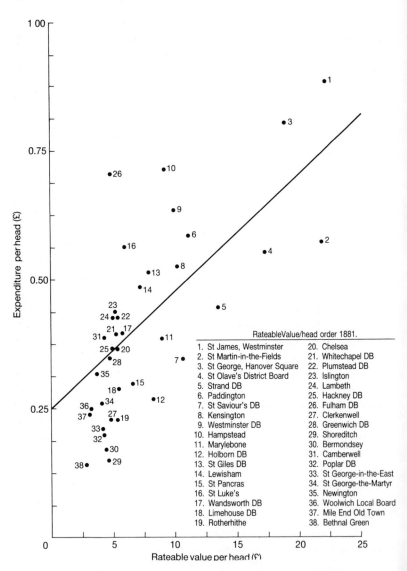

FIG. 2.1   Vestry and District Board Expenditure on Streets, Lighting, and Local Drainage, 1880/1
Source: Local Taxation Returns (Metropolis) 1880–1, *PP 1882*. LVII.

and 26 per cent of a publican's, against 9 per cent for an average householder.[97] The problem was aggravated by the fact that a Vestryman satisfying even the £25 qualification was unable to benefit from compounding agreements, subject to a £20 ceiling in London. This left him paying in full a poundage rate swollen, in working-class areas, by extension discounts to others. One consequence of the very high Vestry qualification was that the second tier was manned by those with the greatest material interest in retrenchment. In working-class areas this was particularly the case.

Overall Vestry expenditure increased as the range of Vestry duties expanded, but down to the late 1880s the increase was only broadly in step with that in rateable value, and did not preclude several 'operational' economies. As late as 1885 there were only 103 sanitary inspectors for the whole of London, the four sparsest areas providing one for every 116,000 people.[98] Twenty Vestries and District Boards paid their Medical Officers £200 or less in 1888–9, presumably making do with part-time service. The entire establishment of Bermondsey Vestry in that year numbered only eleven, including an 'office lad' and messenger. Six other bodies employed even fewer, St Olave's District Board making do with four men.[99] Of the Vestries employing their own road sweepers in the early 1890s, fifteen paid below Charles Booth's poverty line of 21s. per week. Hammersmith and St Giles allowed no holidays and no sick pay.[1] It is true that analysis of the provincial authorities in this age of municipal awakening would still reveal considerable disparity in expenditure, with even some of the largest municipalities content with low levels of service,[2] but many of the failings of the London system reflected directly its

[97] Memorandum in LCC Local Government and Taxation Com., Presented Papers, 26 May 1897.

[98] Jephson, *The Sanitary Evolution of London*, 308–9.

[99] 'Return of Salaries, Fees, etc.' *PP 1890–1*, LXIX, 29–82.

[1] Return of Vestry wages in *London Statistics*, II (1891–2), 523–34.

[2] Comparison of Vestry performance with that of the provincial municipalities is rendered difficult both by the fact that the Vestries were confined to second-tier duties and by the different bases on which the metropolitan and non-metropolitan sections of the parliamentary Local Taxation Returns were compiled. A comparison of highways expenditure—one category in which the returns appear to be comparable—for the five years 1875/6 to 1879/80 shows that the average annual expenditure (£/hd.) of the five largest provincial municipalities in England was exactly equal to that of the London Vestries (0.27), but that expenditure in the five richest Vestries and District Boards (0.45) was substantially above the average, while that in the five poorest areas (0.18) was appreciably below it (based on 1881 r.v. and population figures). Nevertheless, even the poorest Vestries compare well with some large cities outside the top five, e.g. Hull (0.13) and Nottingham (0.08), and with Birmingham (0.16).

structure and its uneven distribution of the capital's wealth. By the 1890s 'the East End is badly lighted and poorly cared for in sanitation, street maintenance, and other matters, chiefly because the burden of rate is already so severely felt that even the smallest increase is a terror'.[3]

The problem was not merely that the lifetime of the Vestries saw the quickening of the process of metropolitan growth which had increased the resource imbalance, but also that the same period saw a general expansion of local taxation in London and elsewhere as local authorities became the thin end of the Welfare State wedge. The total rate burden in London rose from below £3 million in the 1860s to over £11 million by the turn of the century. The second tier was unable to accommodate this expansion, and the shock was necessarily absorbed by the various first-tier bodies. The first tier's share of this growing burden rose from under 30 per cent in the early 1870s to almost 50 per cent in the late 1890s, by which time the three equalization levies accounted for a further 22–3 per cent. Less than a third of London's rating was localized by the turn of the century.[4]

The rapid change in the ratio of first- to second-tier rates in the last quarter of the century is the principal structural factor behind the events covered by this study. Its immediate effect was to enhance the importance of the Metropolitan Board. The victorious localists in 1855 had seen the MBW as the small price to be paid for banishing Chadwick's Metropolitan Sewers Commission. Its task was to settle the main drainage question and other metropolitan problems which threatened parochial autonomy. Toulmin Smith saw it as 'a standing conference of Committees on special points'.[5] It is unlikely that Hall was ever quite so dismissive of the MBW. The 1855 Act itself not only constituted the Board as the main drainage authority, but also made it the main road authority, empowered it to contribute to Vestry improvement schemes, to approve local sewerage plans, and to sanction Vestry loans.[6] By the new London Building Act of the same session it was given control of the building inspectorate.[7] From its inception, then, it possessed powers of a metropolitan nature—

[3] B. F. C. Costelloe, 'Memorandum on the Effect of the Equalisation Bill, LCC Local Government and Taxation Com., Presented Papers, 12 July 1893.

[4] See Appendix 3.

[5] Toulmin Smith, *Metropolis Local Management Act*, 38. One modern writer rather loosely compares the MBW to the modern 'special authority'; F. Nicholson, 'The Politics of English Metropolitan Reform: The Background to the Establishment of the London County Council, 1876–89', Ph.D. thesis (Toronto, 1972), 58.

[6] 18 & 19 Vict., c. 120, ss. 69, 138, 144, 183.

[7] 18 & 19 Vict., c. 122, s. 32.

powers covering more than one area, powers to supervise the second tier, embryonic 'resource allocation' powers in the provision for contributions to local schemes, and powers of inspection requiring uniform execution across London. It is unlikely, however, that Hall ever anticipated that an indirectly elected authority of only forty-six members would be raising over a million pounds in rates by the end of its life.

Much of the Board's expansion reflected the fact that metropolitan growth required metropolitan oversight.[8] Work on the main drainage network was begun in 1858 after new rating and borrowing powers had been granted. The closely related work of embanking the Thames was authorized by Acts of 1862 and 1863. The duty implicit in the 1855 Act of improving London's arterial road network was first approached in March 1859 when the Board's Works and General Purposes Committee reported upon a reference to draw up a general plan for metropolitan street improvements. Two years earlier the Board had secured authorization by private Act for its first new street. Fourteen such Acts had been passed by the time of the Board's fall, creating such important thoroughfares as Charing Cross Road, Commercial Road, Northumberland Avenue, and Shaftesbury Avenue. In 1865 the Board assumed control of the newly consolidated Metropolitan Fire Brigade. In 1870 and 1871 it became the local authority—outside the City—under the Tramway Act and the Metropolis Water Act.

The Board's inspection role was increased in 1865 when the need for concerted action in the face of a threatened cattle plague led to its being given power to regulate slaughterhouses and dairies.[9] Similar inspection powers were subsequently acquired for the storage of petroleum and explosives, the sale of gas, and infant life protection. These inspection powers are not intrinsically expensive and required detailed local execution. They could have been handled by the second tier—as the Adulteration Acts indeed were from 1860—but for the growing belief that uniformity of execution was impossible with forty secondary authorities. The centralization of slaughterhouse and dairy regulation was a significant invasion of the public health stronghold of the second tier by an authority without a medical officer or a sanitary establishment. The

[8] For this paragraph see D. M. Corlett, 'The Metropolitan Board of Works, 1855—1889', Ph.D. thesis (Univ. of Illinois, 1943); Owen, *The Government of Victorian London*; D. S. Elliott, 'The Metropolitan Board of Works, 1855–89', M.Phil. thesis (Univ. of Nottingham, 1971); J. F. B. Firth and E. R. Simpson, *London Government under the Local Government Act* (1888), Appendix I.
[9] Corlett, 'The Metropolitan Board of Works', 177.

same step was taken in the housing field in 1875, when the MBW became local authority outside the City for large-scale clearance schemes under the Cross Act,[10] although earlier housing legislation had empowered the Vestries. The anomalies caused by this two-tier division, by which 'places which are notoriously bad remain so because each authority maintains that the other authority ought to deal with them', would arouse comment in the 1880s.[11]

They were inevitable, though, without better funding of the second tier. Clearance schemes involved the frustrating process of buying out slum landlords, often at inflated prices and with a premium for compulsory purchase. Like sanitary operations, they were most necessary where they could be least afforded. Housing was an extreme example of a pattern visible in other fields. The MBW became London's parks authority by virtue of its actions first by private legislation and then under the Metropolitan Open Spaces Acts of 1877 and 1881.[12] The provision of parks was not necessarily a metropolitan function, but it too involved a heavy capital outlay likely to be beyond the local bodies. One of the Board's earliest steps in this direction—the acquisition of Hampstead Heath in 1856—followed a petition by three local Vestries.[13]

Such requests were common throughout the Board's life. Sometimes, as with Hampstead Heath and Southwark Park, they prompted particular MBW projects. During the 1870s and 1880s, however, the Vestries came increasingly to rely first on the Board's powers to contribute to local capital projects, at a rate which became standardized at 50 per cent,[14] and secondly on the opportunity to take advantage of the cheap borrowing powers available to the MBW after the metropolitan financial reconstruction of 1869–71.[15] Although the comparison with the modern 'stra-

[10] 38 & 39 Vict., c. 36, s. 2.

[11] RC the Housing of the Working Classes. *PP 1884–5*, xxx, Report, pp. 34–5. The Strand Medical Officer took pride in his 'astute management' in so drawing up the Clare Market rehousing scheme as to get it classified as a metropolitan improvement: 'Had it been smaller it might have been regarded as a local improvement and the District Board been called upon to pay one half; whilst had it been too large the L.C.C. might have been afraid to undertake it at all.' Booth MS B 245, 127 (Dr Allen).

[12] Firth and Simpson, *London under the Local Government Act*, 347–8.

[13] Corlett, 'The Metropolitan Board of Works', 115.

[14] Ibid. 86.

[15] Between 1855 and 1869 the MBW borrowed over £8 million, either privately, at $4\frac{1}{2}\%$ or more, or through the Bank of England or the National Debt Commissioners at better rates but on very short terms. The Embankment was initially financed by a $16\frac{1}{4}$ year loan. In 1867 the MBW investigated the funding of Haussmann's Parisian improvements, and in 1869 Ayrton introduced on its behalf a Bill empowering the Board to create a 60 year stock at $3\frac{1}{2}\%$. This was estimated to have saved London ratepayers £2 million by 1888 (RC

tegic' resource allocation role of the metropolitan authority is tempting, the Board was anxious not to appear to use its power in an arbitrary, or even a discretionary, way to offset differences in local resources. The Board saw its duty as being to encourage those second-tier operations bringing metropolitan benefits; when the propriety of subsidizing an improvement mooted by the City Corporation, which had a massive rateable value and private estates to call upon, was questioned, Sir John Thwaites, first MBW chairman, laid down the principle that 'the main consideration was whether the improvement in question was of a pressing character and demanded by public convenience and was not a matter of locality'.[16] Without positive discrimination the poorer areas were likely to be as diffident of capital projects as of other enterprises, and it is possible that the MBW's widely alleged West End bias partly reflected the greater propensity of wealthy parishes to apply for metropolitan help. Nevertheless, there can be little doubt that the £1 million or so made available to the Vestries in aid of local improvements,[17] and the unquantifiable saving in interest charges brought about by the relending of MBW stock, allowed the second tier as a whole to embark upon capital projects which it would not have contemplated unaided.

The Vestry attitude to the Metropolitan Board was therefore necessarily ambivalent. They were grateful for first-tier support for their own projects, and aware that it could make otherwise forbidding enterprises acceptable to their ratepaying electorate.[18] They were also aware, however, that the Metropolitan Board, like the School Board, raised its revenue by precepting the Vestries, and that first-tier precepts constituted a growing burden upon Vestry rates. The fear was that the undiscriminating ratepayer would blame his Vestry for all the rates that it levied,[19] despite attempts to indicate on rate demands the extent of

Metropolitan Board of Works, *PP 1888*, LVI, Q. 11317 (G. B. Richardson)). By its 1871 Loans Act (34 & 35 Vict., c. 47, s. 10) the Board was empowered to relend to the secondary authorities. For this, see the return of MBW borrowing in *PP 1867–8*, LVIII and MBW Report 236 II, 'Translation of a Letter from the Prefect of the Seine...'.

[16] Quoted in Corlett, 'The Metropolitan Board of Works', 86.

[17] The return (MBW 2410) of Board expenditure on metropolitan and local improvements gives a total of £1,073,718 contributed by the Board to local bodies by 1888. The total excludes contributions for parks and housing schemes.

[18] In 1886 the SNRA resolved to oppose any scheme for the acquisition of Clissold Park which would throw the cost on the local rates. Fourteen months later it unanimously applauded the acquisition of 'so splendid a recreation ground as Clissold Park at the small cost to this parish of £10,000'. (SNRA Minutes, 6 Sept. 1886, 7 Nov. 1887.)

[19] 'It is questionable whether the vestry as vestry had a right to complain of the expenditure of outside bodies ... Yet as the odium attached to the vestry who had the making and collection of the rates it was necessary the Ratepayers should know who

second-tier responsibility.[20] The incidence of electoral blame for local taxation is impossible to determine, but the Layfield Committee's researches in the mid-1970s suggested that the burden of guilt is most likely to be ascribed to the rating authority (usually the second-tier) rather than the precepting authority.[21] In 1863–4 the MBW had accounted for about 24 per cent of the rates raised by the Vestries. By 1888–9 the Board and the London School Board, created in 1870, absorbed about 54 per cent of Vestry rates. Most of this increase was, of course, due to the School Board, which prompted incessant parochial criticism of its assumed extravagance, but the MBW's levies had themselves grown by a factor of 3.7 over the period, and the overall effect was to create a broad suspicion of first-tier action.[22] In any case, the School Board was subject to direct election every three years; the Metropolitan Board was not, and its lack of accountability came to appear more serious as its levies grew.

This had several consequences. In the first place, the Vestries became increasingly conscious of their success, or lack of it, in gaining their share of the metropolitan cake. Before the eventual party politicization of London government in the late 1880s metropolitan local politics reflected the clash of parochial interests far more than the clash of municipal principles. Since the MBW levies were met by a uniform charge across London, while very few MBW functions benefited the whole metropolis equally, there was unlimited scope for parochial complaint. Thus Marylebone grumbled at paying $\frac{1}{13}$ of the fire brigade's charges while bearing only $\frac{1}{50}$ of the risk,[23] Hackney resented paying $\frac{1}{35}$ of the MBW rate but receiving only $\frac{1}{97}$ of its expenditure,[24] the parishes without a river front objected to flood prevention becoming a metropolitan charge in 1878–9,[25] Woolwich complained that the MBW had spent only £7,000 in the

expended the rates', T. Huggett, Kensington Vestryman and Member of the London School Board, quoted in North Kensington RA *Annual Report* (1894), 21.

[20] In what appear to be the only surviving Vestry rate demands for this period, those from Islington, 1881–2 (MS Harcourt, Dep. 107/24–35), those parts of the total rate over which the Vestry had no control were ostentatiously asterisked.

[21] Committee of Inquiry on Local Government Finance, *PP 1975–6*, XXI, Report, pp. 54–5; Appendix 10 (microfiche), 'Report on a Survey of Public Attitudes to Local Government Finance', fiche 16. Only 9% of those questioned were aware that more than one tier of authority was involved in making the rate. Of the 71% who identified one or the other tier exclusively, 56% believed that responsibility lay with the lower-tier authority, against 15% for the upper tier.

[22] See Appendix 3.

[23] Owen, *The Government of Victorian London*, 129.

[24] De Beauvoir Town and Dalston RA Minutes, 5 Aug. 1886.

[25] Owen, *The Government of Victorian London*, 67; Corlett, 'The Metropolitan Board of Works', 77.

parish in thirty years,[26] and the Board encountered 'the greatest difficulty in the world to get the representatives of outlying districts to vote for internal [i.e. central] improvements'.[27] Such attitudes hardly assisted the process of metropolitan integration; the MBW remained subject to recurrent parochial sniping for most of its life. Until its final years it struck a delicate balance—whether deliberately or not is unclear—by directing much of its largesse towards the chief contributors. This was tactful because in the wealthiest areas high assessments meant that pound-age rates were low, so that a uniform metropolitan levy formed a larger proportion of total rates than elsewhere. The MBW's penchant for street improvements meant that much of its expenditure was directed to the City and the West End, where they were most necessary. The waning of the intense hostility shown by the City Corporation to the MBW in the mid-1860s was largely due to the drop in the MBW precept after the 1869 Loans Act, but was helped by the fact that between 1868 and 1880 MBW contributions to the City amounted to 49 per cent of its precept.[28] The alienation of the West End in the late 1880s would leave the Board almost defenceless.

The second effect was to engender among the Vestries a deeply rooted protectiveness towards their statutory functions. Continued local exercise of second-tier powers was seen as essential in order to apply some sort of brake to the apparently inexorable increase in local taxation. This attitude should not be taken—as it was taken by some Conservatives in the 1890s—to imply an anxiety to decentralize first-tier functions. For the two-thirds of London's secondary authorities whose rateable value per head lay below the metropolitan average, wholesale devolution would have been overwhelming even had it been administratively feasible. They remained grateful that the wealth of the City and West End could be requisitioned in aid of such mundane first-tier tasks as slaughterhouse inspection. Nevertheless, the second tier was unanimous in its resistance to further encroachment: the rumour of an increase in MBW powers in 1866 brought a wave of second-tier protest, Whitechapel District Board admonishing Sir George Grey in language reminiscent of the battles with Chadwick.[29]

[26] C. Butler, 'Some Aspects of the Work of Local Boards of Health, with Special Reference to Woolwich Local Board of Health between 1848 and 1875', diss. (South Bank Polytechnic, n.d.), 59.

[27] William Newton, MBW, quoted in Owen, *The Government of Victorian London*, 146.

[28] From MBW 1000, Return of precepts upon and contributions to the City, 1856–1880.

[29] 'To be deprived of a right which is based upon principles so universally admitted and so essentially English, would be to abolish a system which all Englishmen regard as freedom,

The third consequence was the development of a far tighter parliamentary and departmental control over the Metropolitan Board's activities than was applied to other municipalities. The principle of central intervention in the MBW's financial affairs dated from as early as 1858, when the Treasury guaranteed the first main drainage loan in order to mitigate the severe interest rates that the Board faced.[30] It became more restrictive in 1869 when the Treasury was authorized to oversee borrowing under the MBW Loans Act, and parliamentary sanction was made mandatory for loans beyond a ceiling of £10 million.[31] The Act was passed when metropolitan reform appeared imminent, but by the time the ceiling was approached, in the mid-1870s, the position had changed. The early 1870s saw increasing concern over the growth in local rates, with Goschen's report of 1870,[32] with the warnings of the 1871 Sanitary Commission about the expansion of local debt,[33] and with the prominence of local taxation as an issue in the 1874 election. The question of MBW accountability became more urgent, but the option of constitutional change was precluded by Disraeli's determination not to wade into the mire of London government reform. The alternative was an expedient tightening of existing controls. This was effected in 1875–6 by the new Financial Secretary to the Treasury, W. H. Smith (who, as a Westminster Member, understood the resentment of central parishes at growing metropolitan levies), and the Treasury official handling MBW business, the later Permanent Secretary R. E. Welby. Welby was by conviction an 'exponent of rigid economy in the public service'.[34] He believed that metropolitan debt was 'assuming imperial proportions'[35] and that the Treasury had, however inappropriately, acquired a controlling power denied to London ratepayers.

The MBW Loans Act of 1875, apparently Smith's work,[36] extended the Board's borrowing powers for its regular services for a year only, inaugurating the regime of annual money Bills, unique to London, which survived to hamper the Greater London Council nearly a century after

and without which Englishmen would cease to be free.' 'Memorial from Whitechapel DB to Sir George Grey', 2 Mar. 1866, PRO HO 45/7741.

[30] Corlett, 'The Metropolitan Board of Works', 32.

[31] 32 & 33 Vict., c. 102, ss. 3, 4, 38.

[32] *PP 1870*, LV.

[33] Second report of the Royal Sanitary Commission, *PP 1871*, xxxv, 68.

[34] Francis Hirst in *Dictionary of National Biography* (Compact edn., Oxford, 1975) ii. 2956.

[35] Welby to W. H. Smith, n.d. but probably Mar. 1876, in PRO T1/7525A/3711.

[36] For the attribution see ibid. The Act was 38 & 39 Vict., c. 65.

the MBW's abolition. The first three Bills were so tightly drawn as to necessitate substantial supplementary votes in their successors. The Board's fond hope that this arrangement 'was not intended by the Lords of the Treasury to apply to any undertaking for which special statutory powers would be required',[37] that is to the larger projects authorized by Private Act, was scotched in 1876 by a new Standing Order, indirectly fathered by Welby, preventing the Board from including borrowing powers in such Acts.[38] Any Bill empowering the MBW to raise money was to be introduced as a Public Bill and to go to Private Bill Committee only after second reading. This enforced hybridity meant that the MBW, unlike any other local authority, was either obliged to introduce Public Bills through private members or to hive off the financial provisions of any improvement scheme for inclusion in the year's Money Bill. In practice the second course proved more reliable. Paradoxically, it may have helped some schemes to pass;[39] it certainly did not impede the new street proposals of 1877 or the Blackwall Tunnel. Similarly the Money Bill procedure loosened after the early years. The real scrutiny was departmental rather than parliamentary; the Bill's terms were fixed by correspondence with the Treasury, and it was then presented by a junior minister as a *fait accompli*, with the implicit threat that any parliamentary haggling would paralyse the London government system. Nevertheless, the new regime was in principle an obstacle to local autonomy, and offered hostages to Parliament in the event of contentious proposals emanating from the Board.

This was most pointedly demonstrated over the question of public utility purchase in the 1870s. No other enterprise so completely symbolizes the flowering of provincial civic consciousness in the 1860s and 1870s as the provision of municipal gas and water. No other services so conspicuously eluded London in the nineteenth century. Both gas and water were examples of public services provided by private companies which, having evolved from a period of price-cutting competition, enjoyed district monopolies which enabled them to exploit an inelastic demand. The MBW became interested in the gas question in the 1870s after nearly two decades of public agitation, prompted by the 'districting' of the north

---

[37] Sir James McGarel Hogg to Treasury, 1 Mar. 1876, PRO T1/7525A/3711.

[38] Standing Order 194 of 1876, *PP 1876*, LX, 145. See also PRO T1/7525A.

[39] A. A. Baumann, 'The London Clauses of the Local Government Bill', *National Review*, 11 (1888), 551–2, suggested that the Private Bills were helped by removal of their financial provisions and the relevant clauses in the Money Bill by the fact that the schemes had already been approved.

London gas companies in 1857, appeared to have demonstrated the ineffectiveness of parliamentary regulation.[40] In harness with the City Corporation, the MBW introduced three Bills in the 1875 session, one for purchase of the companies' plant, one for power to provide an alternative supply, and one for dividend regulation.[41] Both purchase—entailing compensation for loss of prospective monopoly profits—and the alternative supply were extremely expensive, and there was growing parliamentary reluctance to entrust such vast powers to the Metropolitan Board. In the event, both the purchase and supply Bills were dropped, and the threat of government action over regulation forced the companies into adopting a voluntary sliding scale by which dividend increases matched price reductions. The scheme brought significant benefits for the consumer, and moderated the effects of the gas monopolies until the advent of electric lighting ended them.

Water, however, was a more persistent problem. 'Districting' had occurred a lot earlier than in the gas industry—north of the Thames in 1817 and south in 1839.[42] The companies' position had been weakened by the public health crisis, and the Metropolis Water Act of 1852 had, for all its conspicuous shortcomings, facilitated regulation by preventing water from being drawn below Teddington Lock.[43] The need to seek parliamentary sanction for new works upstream made it possible to impose the model provisions of the 1847 Waterworks Clauses Act upon the companies, and stipulate maximum charges for the water supplied. The drawback was that the maximum rate was invariably expressed as a percentage of the valuation of the property served. That this was 'one of the most absurd "blind bargains" into which an uninformed Parliament was ever led'[44] was concealed by the primitive nature of assessment before 1869, but the Metropolis Valuation Act of that year both tightened up

[40] St Marylebone, St James, and other Vestries had combined in 1857 to press for legislation to regulate the gas monopoly (St James Vestry Minutes, 12 Nov. 1857, 2 June 1858, etc.). A Bill drafted by James Beal, St James Vestryman and later municipal reformer, was introduced in 1859 and passed as the Metropolis Gas Act (23 & 24 Vict., c. 125). In committee, however, it had been so mangled by the gas interest that, to Beal, 'we did not know the Bill again'. (SC Metropolis Gas Bill, *PP 1867*, XII, Q. 919.) By 1867 it had proved 'eminently favourable to the Companies, while the interests of the consumer have been very inadequately protected'. (Ibid., Report, ix–x.) The best analysis of the gas problem is provided by J. F. B. Firth, *Municipal London* (1876), ch. 8.

[41] For this see Corlett, 'The Metropolitan Board of Works', 165–8, Owen, *The Government of Victorian London*, 140–5.

[42] Finer, *Sir Edwin Chadwick*, 391.

[43] 15 & 16 Vict., c. 84, s. 1.

[44] B. F. C. Costelloe, 'London v. the Water Companies', *Contemporary Review*, 67 (1895), 802–3.

the practice of assessment and provided for comprehensive quinquennial valuations from 1871.[45] The rising value of London property was reflected in the assessments and consequently in water rates; the companies secured a quinquennial tribute in return for no necessary increase in supply. The average London water company dividend rose from 6·84 per cent to 8·80 per cent over the decade 1871–81. The dividend of the New River Company, which served the City, where assessments rose fastest, climbed from 7·27 per cent to 11·51 per cent, and their net profits increased by 84 per cent in the same decade.[46]

The second quinquennial valuation may have prompted the MBW to seek power to purchase the water supply in February 1876.[47] It eventually presented two Bills—again for purchase and for separate supply—in the 1878 session, only to find that Parliament was still more hesitant about entrusting the Board with powers of extensive expenditure than it had been three years earlier. As Dilke told the Commons, 'their constitution is such that they must be perfectly aware ... that they will not be permitted by the House to carry any of those large Bills'.[48] Water purchase would have been contentious in London even with a metropolitan authority beyond reproach, but the point was valid. It probably influenced Disraeli's government to embark upon its unrewarding project of 1880 for purchase by an *ad hoc* authority—a water trust in which the MBW's representation was unflatteringly small.[49] The rebuff over water supply, one of the elementary municipal powers, exercised by over four hundred authorities by 1880, was a serious setback for the Board. Cross's 1880 scheme provided another example of a government department having to assume powers which should have fallen to the local authority. Purchase at £30 million was probably a better bad bargain than London secured when the Metropolitan Water Board was eventually established in 1902, but no government department could expect to win public support for such expenditure without more adequate consultation with ratepayers. No such consultation was possible without a better representative machinery. The logic pointed to municipal reform, and was to lead that

---

[45] 32 & 33 Vict., c. 67.
[46] G. P. Bevan, *The London Water Supply: Its Past, Present and Future* (1884), ch. 3; *London Statistics*, VI (1895–6), 1–100, for a summary of water company dividends 1855–94.
[47] Corlett, 'The Metropolitan Board of Works', 154.
[48] Hansard, 3rd ser., CCXXXIX, 725 (5 Apr. 1878).
[49] *PP 1880*, V, Bill 97. The MBW would provide only 1 ex-officio and 1 nominated member out of 22. For the water episode see P. Smith, *Disraelian Conservatism and Social Reform* (1967), 294–9.

way in the early 1880s. For the moment, however, the water problem had elicited a resounding vote of no confidence in the Metropolitan Board of Works.

The Herbert Commission took the marks of a satisfactory local governmental system to be 'administrative efficiency and the health of representative government'.[50] The 1855 London system was visibly inadequate in both these respects. It did not mirror any existing pattern of urban leadership, and it operated at such a low and fitful level of political activity that the extent of popular participation was negligible. The Vestries retained the parochialism of mid-century local politics while losing its redeeming vitality. Indirect election made the first tier a reflection of the second—'a Vestry vestrified to the nth power'[51]—and ensured that a body which should have assumed public prominence in the era of town improvement municipalism remained shadowy. The second tier was too fragmented to attain uniform administrative efficiency, and although the MBW showed itself to be proficient, its lack of accountability led to its being progressively confined by central government and, in part, to London's being denied some of the essentials of municipal development elsewhere.

   The municipal inadequacy of London should not, however, be ascribed merely to the collective deficiencies of those who manned its institutions. Its complex social structure, and the political vacuum which existed for most of the period, would have made its local management a difficult art in any event. Its size necessitated a more sophisticated system than existed elsewhere, and posed problems which were not fully appreciated in 1855. Some aspects of Hall's Act were palpably inappropriate and made matters worse—the Vestry qualification and the indirect election of the first tier and much of the second. Other problems were more obviously 'metropolitan'—the two-tier balance, the extent of financial integration. They had only been dimly visible in 1855, and were brought into prominence by the experience of metropolitan growth. It is an indication of their obliqueness that the reform of London government was taken by most contemporaries to imply not the settlement of these metropolitan issues but the overhaul of the City Corporation.

[50] RC Local Government in Greater London, *PP 1959–60*, XVIII, Report, 59.
[51] *The Examiner*, 17 June 1875, quoted in Firth, *Municipal London*, 281 n.

3. THE PROBLEM OF THE CITY

'Logic has its limits', declared the Herbert Commission, 'and the position of the City lies outside them'.[52] In the nineteenth century the City's position was so resolutely anomalous as to defy attempts to rationalize the London problem. On one level the Corporation of London was simply a very wealthy central-area authority with an obvious material interest in resisting metropolitan integration, but it was always more than that. The most important corporation to escape the reform of 1835, it remained an obstacle because of its wealth and its ability to invoke a tradition of independence that still exercised a spurious attraction.

An ostensibly democratic constitution had made the City Corporation harder to stigmatize than most ancient municipalities when it was invest-igated in the 1830s.[53] At its base were the twenty-six City wards, in which rated householders assembled each December to elect the members of the Court of Common Council. This body was the Corporation's main policy maker by this time, and the City Commission of Sewers, which exercised most local government functions in the City and levied most of the municipal rates, was effectively a committee of Common Council. Above Common Council was the Court of Aldermen. Although their Court had been eclipsed politically by the rise of Common Council, the aldermen were still the grandees of the Corporation. They were elected for life, one by each ward, and served as Justices of the Peace within the City, which was a judicial county in itself. Immense wealth was a practical prerequisite for the position; the City MPs were usually, and the Lord Mayor always, chosen from the aldermanic ranks.

The allocation of the duties of local government was no less complex within the City than outside it. The aldermen, as JPs, performed most of the county functions handled by magistrates elsewhere. The MBW exercised significant jurisdiction in the City in respect of main drainage, the fire brigade, and the Building Acts, but many other MBW powers, including those under the Cross Act, the Tramways Act, and the Acts for gas and water regulation, were exercised by Common Council or the Commissioners of Sewers within the City area.[54] The powers exercised by the Vestries and District Boards elsewhere in London also fell to the

---

[52] RC Local Government in Greater London, *PP 1959–60*, XVIII, Report, 237.

[53] The most recent scholarly work on the Corporation is I. G. Doolittle, *The City of London and its Livery Companies* (1982).

[54] For a summary of these powers see RC Amalgamation of City and County of London, *PP 1894*, XVII, Report, 18.

Commissioners of Sewers. The Corporation itself had rating powers only in respect of the City Police, an independent force which had resisted amalgamation with the Metropolitan Police in 1829 and 1839, and stood as one of the most treasured symbols of City autonomy. Otherwise the Corporation possessed a variegated collection of powers and rights by charter or statute. In addition to such honorific privileges as the right to nominate the sheriff of Middlesex, it was empowered to levy a duty of 13*d*. upon every ton of coal sold within twenty miles of the General Post Office (9*d*. per ton of which it was bound to hand over to the Metropolitan Board by Acts of 1861 and 1862),[55] and to levy $\frac{3}{16}$ of a penny upon every hundredweight of grain brought into the Port of London.[56] It was sanitary authority for the Port and nominated representatives on the Thames Conservancy Board—a right denied to the MBW. The Corporation also possessed a monopoly of new market rights within seven miles of the Guildhall. Finally it acted as trustee for a number of legacies and funds, of which the most important were the revenues of the Gresham Estates, devoted to education under a trust of 1579, and those of the Bridge House Estates, to be applied to the building and freeing from toll of bridges across the Thames.[57]

Symptomatic of the Corporation's unreformed status was the involvement of the traditional craft or trading associations, the City Livery Companies or Guilds, in its constitutional processes.[58] By the 1880s there were twelve great and sixty lesser companies, each notionally linked to a craft or trade. With the freedom of most companies transmitted by inheritance and purchase as well as apprenticeship, their trading functions had become eroded and in many cases extinguished over the centuries, although the Fishmongers, the Goldsmiths and some other Companies remained active in trade regulation. Otherwise the Companies exercised their charitable and educational duties under various bequests, and, in theory, provided alms and pensions for their members. Their trust and corporate income totalled about £800,000 per annum by 1880, three quarters of which came from landed property in London, mostly in

[55] The London Coal and Wine Duties Continuance Act, 1861 (24 & 25 Vict., c. 42, s. 5) created a 'Thames Embankment and Metropolis Improvement Fund', which was appropriated by the MBW under the Thames Embankment Act, 1862 (25 & 26 Vict., c. 93, s. 45).

[56] 35 & 36 Vict., c. c.

[57] For trust accounts see G. L. Gomme's summary of Corporation finance in RC Amalgamation, *PP 1894*, XVIII, Appendix XI, 417–518.

[58] For this paragraph, see the report of RC City of London Livery Companies, *PP 1884*, XXXIX, Pt. I; and Doolittle, *The City of London*, ch. 6.

the City, the provinces, and Londonderry. Some £100,000 of this was spent each year upon 'entertainments', mostly banquets for the Companies' ruling courts, conspicuous consumption which prompted the apparently unjustified belief of reformers that the Companies abused trust income.

The liverymen were attached to the constitution of the Corporation by virtue of their membership of the City's third Court, the Court of Common Hall. Common Hall assembled annually in September to elect the City sheriffs and forward two names to the Court of Aldermen as a short list for the mayoralty. In practice the Lord Mayor was generally the senior alderman who had not already served. He held office for one year, but although he continued to perform judicial duties and had a court of his own, his role was largely honorific. The assumption, common among those unfamiliar with the London government labyrinth, that the Lord Mayor was the capital's chief executive made his position a standing provocation to the Corporation's many enemies.

This somewhat baroque constitution differed in many respects from the reformed municipal model—in the size of Common Council, in the direct election of the aldermen and their existence as a separate Court, and in the involvement of the Guilds. The most obvious argument for the assimilation of the City to the 1835 system was that of conformity, but it was not clear that the Corporation's constitution impaired its municipal efficiency. In the 1840s the peculiarities of the Corporation's constitution had commended it to the antiquarian defenders of local self-government who, like Toulmin Smith, saw the 1835 Act as a Whiggish sham, inhibitive of true municipal spontaneity. During the third quarter of the century, however, the City's position in the reform debate changed dramatically.

Prompting this change was the steady commercialization of the City area over the second half of the century. The replacement of much of the City's housing stock by offices, warehouses, and railway stations brought both rapid depopulation and an enormous rise in the City's assessment, movements reflected, as Table 2.5 shows, in the inflation of the City's rateable value per head. By 1901 the City's rateable value per head was more than twenty times that of the County of London as a whole (£8.77) and almost four times that of the richest of the former Schedule A parishes (St Martin's at £48.53).

The first casualty of this development was the City's vaunted local democracy. The ratepaying democracy of the earlier nineteenth century

TABLE 2.5. Population, Rateable Value, and Rateable Value per Head in the City, 1861–1901

	Population	Rateable Value (£)	R.V./Head (£)
1861	111,784	[1,319,188]	[11·80]
1871	74,688	2,500,714	33·48
1881	50,618	3,500,968	69·16
1891	37,678	4,087,746	108·49
1901	26,293	4,756,404	180·90

Sources: Censuses and Local Taxation Returns for census years, excepting the 1861 r.v. figure, which is the aggregate consolidated rate valuation of the City for January 1862, from *PP 1864*, L, 65.

had made an impression upon the Whig Commissioners of 1837 and provided the backbone of City opposition to Chadwick. Toulmin Smith saw the wardmote system as 'local self-government in its reality'.[59] But with twenty-six wards within a square mile it required intense popular participation to keep the system alive, and a population decline of the order indicated precluded this. By the 1870s the ward system was moribund. Of the 416 Common Council elections between 1866 and 1881 only 59 (14 per cent) were contested; seven wards did not see a single contest in that time.[60]

The previously dominant City Radicalism was hardest hit by this depopulation. With poorer property taken first by the process of commercialization and improvement, Radicalism lost its constituency. Meanwhile the more drawn-out movement of the free-trade Liberals of the 1860s into Conservatism or, later, Liberal Unionism depleted Liberalism's higher ranks in the City. The Conservatives' capture of three of the four City seats in 1874 therefore resulted from a double weakness in City Liberalism, structural flaws which converted the City into a permanent Conservative stronghold. The City Liberal Association stagnated over the last quarter of the century, and was said to have been kept alive largely by inadvertent subscriptions from Conservatives and Liberal Unionists, paid by uncancelled bankers' orders 'long after they had ceased to be Liberals'.[61] On becoming CLA secretary in 1904 F. W. Galton found the Association a refuge for

[59] Toulmin Smith, *Metropolis Municipal Administration*, 42.
[60] Return in *PP 1882*, LII, 361–9.
[61] F. W. Galton, MS Autobiography, ch. 8, 16.

old-fashioned Free Traders—the bankers, shipowners, etc., whose business interests were—or they thought they were—bound up with free trade and free competition. As for all the schemes of social reform and greater equality in the distribution of wealth which I considered the essence of Liberalism, they had either never heard of or were violently hostile to them.[62]

Conservative conquest of the City was therefore accompanied by the alienation of what survived of City Liberalism from the party's mainstream.

The commercialization of the City also served to swell the Corporation's own coffers. A large part of the Corporation's income came from its freehold property, most of which was in the City itself. Between 1850 and 1890 income from general rents—from property in the City, around Broad Street, Aldgate, and the Minories, together with other holdings such as the Conduit Mead estate in Westminster[63]—more than trebled, as Table 2.6 indicates.

TABLE 2.6. Corporation Income from General Rents, 1850–1890

	Rental Income (£)	Decennial % Increase	% Increase since 1850
1850	50,477	—	—
1860	59,452	17·78	17·78
1870	76,228	28·22	51·02
1880	111,141	45·80	120·18
1890	156,816	41·10	210·67

Source: The analysis of City rents, 1850–93, in *London Statistics*, V (1894–5), 354–5.

In addition the Corporation's market rights yielded around £115,000 per annum during the 1870s,[64] and its share of the coal dues—applicable only to public improvements under the Act of 1862—about £100,000 per annum. Profits from the investment of the trust funds provided a further £12,000 or so per annum and the fruits of the Corporation's own investments around £4,000 per annum during the 1880s.[65]

[62] Ibid. 17–18.
[63] RC Municipal Corporations, Second Report, *PP 1837*, XXV, 200. For Conduit Mead see I. G. Doolittle, 'The City's West End Estate: A "Remarkable Omission"', *London Journal*, 7 (1981), 15–27.
[64] Firth, *Municipal London*, 190.
[65] Gomme memorandum in *PP 1894*, XVIII, 437–8.

This massive revenue supported an extensive programme of municipal activity over the second half of the century. The bulk of it was concentrated in the years 1850 to 1870, when a programme of public improvements was launched to help the City accommodate its growing commerce. Between 1850 and 1870 the Corporation built Queen Victoria Street and lengthened Cannon Street, rebuilt Blackfriars Bridge and freed Southwark Bridge from toll, restored Billingsgate Market and rebuilt Smithfield, and sank a total of £2½ million in the massive Fleet Valley scheme, including the building of Farringdon Street and Holborn Viaduct. The rest of the century saw the purchase of Epping Forest for the public, the building of Tower Bridge out of the Bridge House funds, the opening of Islington and Deptford markets, the widening of Ludgate Hill, the provision of Corporation artisans' dwellings, the construction of a new Guildhall Library and the Guildhall School of Music, and much else. The Corporation dispelled its parsimonious image of the 1840s at the expense of encumbering the City lands for the rest of the century.[66] It is seldom listed in the catalogue of heroic Victorian municipalities, but, while doing little to dispel its bloated and decadent public image, it became one of the most active local authorities in Britain.

This could not, however, prevent its steady estrangement from the local self-government movement. Each side shifted its stance. With the passing of Toulmin Smith the tone of the reform movement changed, becoming progressive rather than antiquarian, utilitarian rather than romantic. These changes helped increase respect for the 1835 Act and lower the stock of the City. The Corporation's municipal work was outweighed in reformers' eyes by the irresponsible opulence of what Mill called 'that union of modern jobbing and antiquated foppery'.[67] The City's wealth, its feasting, and its taste for ceremony provided an offensive contrast to the businesslike asceticism of the rate-dependent municipalities which reformers took as their models.[68] Both the market monopoly and the coal duties offended the free-trading principles of most reformers. More important still was the growing awareness that the City's future could not be considered in isolation from that of the rest of London. During the Chadwick years the Corporation and the parishes had united

---

[66] In 1893 the City estates were still security for £240,400 of outstanding debt, and contingent security for a further £4,708,200. See *London Statistics*, v, (1894–5), 360–3.

[67] J. S. Mill, *Representative Government* (Everyman edn., 1968), 351.

[68] £12,826 was spent upon entertaining the Tsar in 1874, £26,802 upon a reception for the Prince of Wales in 1876. See the Corporation's Special (Finance) Com. Minute Papers, 24 Feb. 1888.

in defence of the self-government tradition against governmental centralization, but after 1855 the common threat was no longer present.
During the 1860s and 1870s the shortcomings of the Hall system became
evident at the same time as some provincial municipalities became *exempla*
of energetic civic activity. The conclusion was reached that London was
weak because it was not municipalized, that it was not municipalized
because of City resistance and that the City was therefore to blame.

This was a half truth which disguised the enormous difficulty of
metropolitan local government that would have applied even had the City
not existed. It nevertheless gained plausibility from the Corporation's
consistent opposition to any reform proposals which threatened its own
interests. As the wealthiest part of London, the City was materially
threatened by the trend towards metropolitan integration over the second
half of the century. Occupying only $\frac{1}{120}$ of the metropolitan area, it
accounted for about $\frac{1}{8}$ of London's rateable value. The MBW's power,
under the 1855 Act, to precept the City for the same rate as other
authorities represented 'a very large handful of feathers ... plucked from
the civic bird',[69] and the expansion of MBW expenditure over the years
imposed a heavy burden upon the City. The very sharp increase in
the Board's rate in the 1860s fuelled intense rancour between the two
authorities, and prompted a number of disingenuous demonstrations by
City officials and Common Councilmen that the Board was exceeding its
powers.[70] A semi-official polemic under the name of the City Chamberlain, Benjamin Scott, in 1867 advanced the case for increased City
representation on the Board.[71]

From the Corporation's point of view municipal reform was likely to
make matter worse. It would entail at worst the creation of a massive
unitary authority which would absorb the existing Corporation and strip
the City of the administrative and financial autonomy that it retained.
Even at best it would entail the construction of a new two-tier system
into which a reformed Corporation, reduced to the status of a second-
tier authority, could be integrated, probably losing its estates and many
of its powers to a new and more potent central body. The City's interest
lay in promoting as decentralized a metropolitan system as was feasible,

---

[69] *The Times*, 14 Aug. 1855, quoted in Corlett, 'The Metropolitan Board of Works', 23.
[70] See e.g. the evidence of the City Remembrancer to the SC Metropolitan Local
Government and Taxation, *PP 1867*, XII, QQ. 568 ff.
[71] B. Scott, *A Statistical Vindication of the City of London* (1867), 131–47. The book was
apparently written by the City Radical James Acland; see H. J. Hanham, *Elections and Party
Management* (1959), 238.

to protect its autonomy and reduce the demands of the rest of London upon its wealth. This it did in a succession of proposals for a federation of separate municipalities, of sufficient size to allow extensive devolution to the second tier, under a central body strictly confined to tasks that were undisputably metropolitan. The ten metropolitan parliamentary boroughs[72] were the most frequent candidates for municipal areas, even after their abolition in 1885. 'Tenification' became the most enduring distraction of the whole reform debate. As an argument for large secondary bodies and for placing the centre of gravity within the two-tier system with the local rather than the metropolitan authority, it was plausible, and was indeed effectively the policy followed in the reform of 1965. As an argument for almost total decentralization, for the creation of ten or a dozen contiguous authorities virtually independent of one another simply in order to protect the City's favoured position, it was absurd. City spokesmen showed little awareness of the distinction. The Corporation, after all, was already virtually a separate municipality, exercising full local and county powers and many of the powers of the MBW. It did so, however, on the strength of a massive rateable value and lucrative estates, both advantages denied to other London areas. It was partly because the rest of London was not as wealthy as the City that the trend towards metropolitan integration, symbolized by the growing importance of the first tier, had gathered momentum. But it was a trend which, by stressing the weaknesses of the existing system, increased the pressure for municipal reform and thus the threat to the City's position. The Corporation was bound to resist it, and if the City's attitude towards its enemies from the 1860s to the turn of the century appears obstructive, its obstinacy is comprehensible.

4. THE ANCESTRY OF REFORM

In 1855 Hall had promised Corporation reform at an early date,[73] and four Bills in the next five years attempted to assimilate the Corporation to the standard municipal model.[74] None reached the statute book, however, and apart from an unsuccessful attempt to amalgamate the City and Metropolitan police forces in 1863, no government legislation threatened the Corporation until 1884. One reason for this was that by

---

[72] Eight before the creation of Chelsea and Hackney in 1867.
[73] *Hansard*, 3rd ser., CXXXVII, 718 (16 Mar. 1855).
[74] *PP 1856*, V, Bill 77; *PP 1857–8*, III, Bills 8 and 86; *PP 1859*, (Sess. 2), I, Bill 46.

the early 1860s the shortcomings of the 1855 system were becoming apparent. Corporation reform accordingly became integrated with metropolitan reform; the question was no longer simply one of fitting a remodelled Corporation into the 1855 system. Legislation consequently became more daunting. Successive governments ducked the challenge, which was taken up by individual reformers.

Pressure for reform in the Commons in the early 1860s came from some of the metropolitan Radicals, in particular from A. S. Ayrton, Member for Tower Hamlets, and John Locke, Member for Southwark. Both believed the failings of the London system to stem from the absence of a plausible metropolitan municipality. Locke's solution was the blanket application of the 1835 system to London, reforming and expanding the Corporation to form a single metropolitan municipality, absorbing all existing authorities.[75] Ayrton's position was more complex, emerging only through his statements in Parliament and the views that he expressed as chairman of two Commons Select Committees on Metropolis Local Taxation and Local Government in 1861 and 1866–7. More willing from the start than most reformers to see the MBW as a 'really useful and practical municipality',[76] he became convinced by the City's opposition to the police amalgamation proposal of 1863 that the Corporation was an irredeemable obstacle to reform, and subsequently 'devoted himself to aggrandising the Met. Board until it should be strong enough to swamp the City'.[77] In office as a junior member of Gladstone's first ministry he would introduce the important MBW Loans Act of 1869, and probably influenced the direction taken by that ministry's embryonic reform scheme. His own views on reform were outlined most clearly in the report of his second Select Committee in 1867, which recommended strengthening the MBW by turning it into a Municipal Council, with the parochial nominees supplemented by members chosen by the home county justices, by the government, and directly by the ratepayers. Unlike Locke he retained the second tier, with minor adjustment of local areas, but the Corporation lost its special status, and the emphasis remained decidedly metropolitan rather than parochial.[78]

Outside Parliament the main impetus for reform came from a group of Radicals on the St James, Piccadilly Vestry, who used the issue as a

---

[75] See e.g. *Hansard* 3rd ser. CLXV, 749 (26 Feb. 1862), CLVI, 288 (30 Jan. 1860).
[76] Ibid., CLVI, 286 (30 Jan. 1860).
[77] J. F. B. Firth to Sir William Harcourt, 4 Jan. 1882, MS Harcourt, Dep. 108/9.
[78] SC Metropolitan Local Government and Taxation, *PP 1867*, XII, Report, v–vii. The Metropolitan Board approved the scheme in 1869 (MBW Minutes, 11 June 1869).

weapon in their factional battles within the Westminster Liberal Association.[79] They were led by James Beal, auctioneer and estate agent in Regent Street, and 'wirepuller of the Westminster Radicals'.[80] He had appeared before the first Ayrton Committee in 1861 to advocate the consolidation of Westminster's ten Schedule A and B Vestries into a single Westminster municipality, extending the argument to advocate a federation of similar municipalities in the parliamentary boroughs, with an indirectly elected Metropolitan Council as a first-tier body.[81] This proposal for large secondary bodies and an indirectly elected central authority was essentially the scheme sketched out by the Commissioners of 1854. It had then and has since been associated with the City Corporation, for whom it appeared to offer the best guarantee of autonomy. Beal was never an apologist for the City, but he professed to take the Corporation as his model for the proposed secondary municipalities,[82] and after working with it over the gas question[83] was aware of the power which the Corporation's support could lend any reform movement. Beal's Metropolitan Municipal Association, formed in 1865, spent most of its formative years angling for an alliance with the City, and its spokesmen were not above taking that alliance for granted in order to soothe ministerial nerves when the reform question was broached.[84]

The division that would characterize the metropolitan debate for the remainder of the century, between predominantly centralized and predominantly decentralized systems, was already emergent, but had still to be focused. The question had yet to become party politicized; the debate was being fought between two groups of metropolitan Radicals and a still largely Liberal City. London Conservatism remained too weak to participate. Further, the ambiguity of Beal's position prevented any distinct polarization from taking place. He could not share Ayrton's veneration of the MBW. Although in 1861 he had allowed the Board faint praise,[85] the scandals of the 1860s turned him to a position of

---

[79] Baer, 'The politics of London', 157–62 and 206 for Westminster politics.

[80] F. Harrison to J. Morley, Aug. 1876, in F. W. Hirst, *The Early Life and Letters of John Morley* (1927), 15.

[81] SC Metropolis Local Taxation, *PP 1861*, VIII, QQ. 1180–1243.

[82] 'What the City is within its area, I should like each Parliamentary borough to be within its area.' SC Metropolis Local Government and Taxation, *PP 1866*, XIII, Q. 1894 (Beal).

[83] He had drafted the City of London Gas Act of 1868 (31 & 32 Vict., c. cxxv), which had been actively supported by the Corporation.

[84] 'I have reason to believe, and I greatly rejoice in the belief, that the City would not stand in the way of this proposal.' C. Buxton, *Self-Government in London ... A Letter to the Right Hon. H. A. Bruce M.P.* (1869), 14.

[85] SC Metropolis Local Taxation, *PP 1861*, VIII, Q. 1318.

unequivocal hostility, and he did not toy with indirect election in any of
his subsequent schemes. He was not, however, as eager a decentralizer
as the 'tenification' advocates in the Corporation. His work on the gas
question had convinced him of the need for a strong metropolitan authority to handle public utilities, and although his proposals bore sufficient
resemblance to those of the Corporation to encourage him to seek City
support, they were not close enough to enable him to win it.

The fate of the successive Bills sponsored by the Metropolitan Municipal Association between 1867 and 1870 removed this ambiguity. In 1867
and 1868 the reform standard was carried by John Stuart Mill, the Radical
half of the Liberal 'ticket' for Westminster in 1865.[86] Mill had seen
London government as an issue 'in which I shall have to take an active
part' on his election.[87] His chief concern was with what is now called the
'councillor calibre' question; he believed the social tone of 'shopocratic'
Vestrydom to inhibit the politically educative role that he had prescribed
for local institutions. He was therefore less concerned than most other
London reformers with the shape of the London system, and persuaded
himself without much difficulty that Beal's proposals offered the best
solution.[88] In 1867 he introduced two Private Member's Bills, emanating
from a committee appointed by the Social Science Association in the
previous year and drafted by Beal.[89] Together the Bills proposed nine
new metropolitan municipalities based upon the parliamentary boroughs,
with the tenth, the City Corporation, remaining in existence but losing
many if its powers and all of its estates to a new central metropolitan
body. The central body would be directly elected, and would handle gas,
water, police, fire, county, and other first-tier functions. The local bodies
would not be any more powerful than the Vestries; the hope was that
their size would increase second-tier efficiency and that, ornamented by
a mayor apiece and 'aldermen as thick as blackberries',[90] they would draw
better men into municipal service.

The Corporation already had a mayor and aldermen and did not wish

[86] In the days of the two-member boroughs, it was common for Liberal divisions to be
resolved by sharing the ticket. For Westminster see Baer, 'The Politics of London',
159–60; and for Mill's campaign see J. E. Smith, 'The Parliamentary Representation of
Westminster from the Thirteenth Century to the Present Day', typescript (Westminster
Archives 1923), ii. 514.

[87] Mill to T. Hare, 11 Jan. 1866, in F. E. Mineka and D. Lindley (eds.), *The Later Letters
of J. S. Mill* (Toronto, 1972), 1138–40.

[88] Mill to Beal, 8 Feb. 1869, ibid., 1555–7.

[89] *PP 1867*, IV, Bills 166 and 303.

[90] SC Metropolis Local Government and Taxation, *PP 1866*, XIII, Q. 3469 (R. Freeman,
MBW).

to be confined to the role of a Vestry or to lose its estates. *Locus standi*
given by this last provision allowed the Corporation to attack the Bill
setting up the central body, and to secure its withdrawal by the Examiners
when it was reintroduced in 1868. If the Corporation could not accept
Mill's first tier, the Ayrton group could not accept his second. Their
own proposals envisaged a fundamentally centralized system,[91] and
they suspected that Mill's separate municipalities reflected Beal's apparent deference towards the City. They provided the most effective
parliamentary opposition to the Mill proposals and, by showing the
reform movement to be divided over method, weakened the force of
the Bills.

The 1868 general election swept Mill out of Parliament—victim, he
believed, of 'the dislike of the Vestries to my Metropolitan Bill'[92]—and
returned a Gladstonian ministry which included Ayrton as Financial
Secretary to the Treasury. This and the City's coldness led Beal to alter
the emphasis of the MMA Bills, which were reintroduced by Charles
Buxton in 1869 and 1870, in the direction of centralization. By 1870 the
secondary municipalities had lost their aldermen, and their mayors had
become mere 'wardens'.[93] In November 1870 Beal embraced the single
municipality doctrine without qualification, blaming his former heresy
upon 'a creed steadfastly adhered to at the Home Office, that London
was too large for one Council'.[94]

Ayrton's 'radical objection to the Mill–Buxton compromise'[95] prevented the government from acting directly upon Beal's Bills. Instead it
promised a Select Committee and canvassed the existing authorities for
suggestions.[96] One result was to harden the Corporation's attitude to
reform. By attacking Beal's first-tier proposals and even refusing to accept
his second-tier scheme,[97] it had already cast doubt on its willingness to
accept any change. Asked to produce specific proposals, Common Council's Local Government Committee responded only with an endorsement
of the principle of municipalizing the parliamentary boroughs. In 'a sort
of collective expression of the idea that reticence is the better part of

---

[91] 'The local administration should be kept in due subordination to the central authority
so as to prevent the great inconvenience experienced in times past from the want of
harmonious action.' Ayrton in *Hansard*, 3rd ser., CLXXXVII, 887 (21 May 1867).
[92] Mill to G. Grote, 1 Dec. 1868, in Mineka and Lindley, *Letters of J. S. Mill*, 1501–2.
[93] *PP 1870*, III, Bill 65, s. 5.
[94] *Observations by J. Beal . . . 7th November 1870* in PRO HO 45/9518/22782.
[95] H. A. Bruce to Gladstone, 5 Jan. 1870. Add. MS 44086 fo. 66.
[96] *Hansard*, 3rd ser. CCI, 878 (18 May 1870).
[97] Common Council Minutes, 19, 26 Mar. 1868.

wisdom',[98] the Committee declined to make any proposals for the central
body or for Corporation reform until the government had given a lead.[99]

The Select Committee was never, in fact, appointed, probably because
the government was already moving towards legislation. Early in 1870
H. A. Bruce, the Home Secretary, had drawn up a memorandum on the
subject after consulting Ayrton and Goschen.[1] His private secretary,
A. O. Rutson, apparently acted as a medium for communication with
Beal.[2] For six weeks in September and October 1870 Godfrey Lushington
at the Home Office was 'up to the eyes in a Corporation of London Bill'
and Bruce gave the subject priority among Bills to which he was not
already pledged.[3] At the first Cabinet in November, however, Bruce's
initiative was suppressed, apparently by the Prime Minister,[4] and
although the subject was considered again in 1872,[5] no further progress
was made during Gladstone's first ministry. In his 1874 election address
Gladstone described the failure to deal with London as 'a reproach to
our Parliament'.[6]

Conservative gains in 1874 included two of the City seats, and Disraeli
became 'quite decided never to embark on a scheme for the Government
of London without the concurrence of the City Corporation'.[7] In a
negative way this was a step towards the party politicization of the London
reform question. John Bright's confidence that nothing could be expected
from a Conservative ministry[8] would be proved wrong in 1888 and
1899 but was plausible; so far as it concerned Corporation rather than
metropolitan reform it was accurate. In consequence, although the
London reform movement remained ostensibly independent of party
until the late 1880s, it, like the temperance and nonconformist pressure
groups, expected progress only from a Liberal ministry. The immediate
effect of Disraeli's resolution was to block the last of the MMA Bills,
introduced by the Association's president Lord Elcho in 1875.[9] This Bill

[98] *City Press*, 21 May 1870.

[99] Common Council Minutes, 12 May 1870.

[1] See Gladstone to Bruce, 1 Jan. 1870, Bruce Papers D/D Br. 149. (I am grateful to Mark
Curthoys for this reference.) Bruce to Gladstone, 5 Jan. 1870, BL Add. MS 44086 fo. 66.

[2] Beal to Lord Edmond Fitzmaurice, 1 Oct. 1873, PRO HO 45/9518/22782.

[3] Knatchbull-Hugesson Journal, 6 Feb. 1871, Brabourne MS U951/F27/3. (I am grateful
to Mark Curthoys for this reference.)

[4] Ibid.; see also H. C. G. Matthew (ed.), *The Gladstone Diaries*, vii (Oxford, 1982), 390
(2 Nov. 1870).

[5] Ibid., viii. 253 (3 Dec. 1872).

[6] MMA Report, Aug. 1874, in PRO HO 45/9518/22782.

[7] P. Smith, *Disraelian Conservatism and Social Reform*, 198, n. 4.

[8] J. Bright to Beal, 11 Nov. 1875, Beal Papers, F/BL/9/26.

[9] *PP 1875*, IV, Bill 61.

envisaged a simple centralized unitary municipality, with the existing secondary areas forming electoral wards. It contained a number of concessions to the City, but despite Beal's assurance to R. A. Cross that 'no difficulty need be anticipated from the Corporation'[10] and Elcho's curious assumption that permission to confiscate the City lands 'would of course be given',[11] the Bill was dismissed with derision by Common Council. The Cabinet was also unanimous in rejecting it '(1) as politically dangerous (2) because between different parts of London there is no community of interests and but little local intercourse',[12] and the Bill was left to fail.

Five years later Beal recounted rather bitterly that 'he had tried in every way to coax the City to head the movement, but the City would not listen'.[13] The Elcho Bill had certainly offered scant temptation to the City, but even the concessions that were included had weakened the Bill without winning Corporation support. Thereafter the reform movement became more unequivocally hostile to the City. Associated with this change was the decline of Beal's MMA, which apparently produced its last report in 1875, and a less tangible alteration in the character of the reform movement, which became more partisan and more radical. Its focus shifted from Westminster to Chelsea, and Beal was supplanted as its dominant spokesman by Joseph Firth.

Joseph Firth Bottomley Firth was a Yorkshireman, born in 1842, who had gravitated to the Middle Temple in the early 1870s. He was thirteen years younger than Beal and twenty-six years younger than Ayrton, and his attitude was shaped more by the provincial municipalism of the 1860s—his father-in-law had been mayor of Leeds—than by the constitutional and representative municipal theories prevalent in London in the 1840s and 1850s. This determined the somewhat blunt functionalism of his municipal doctrine, expressed with an incisive logic probably instilled by his legal training. Whereas Toulmin Smith had believed that 'not allowed to learn self-government, men naturally take to beating their wives',[14] and Mill considered local government 'a school of political capacity and general intelligence',[15] Firth declined to recognize the

[10] Beal to R. A. Cross, 3 Oct. 1874, PRO HO 45/9518/22782.

[11] Elcho to Beal, 7 Jan. 1875, WP, RH 4/40/10.

[12] Derby Diary, 12 Nov. 1874. (I am grateful to Mark Curthoys for this reference.)

[13] J. Lloyd, *London Municipal Government: History of a Great Reform, 1880–1888* (1910), 3.

[14] *Morning Advertiser*, 7 Dec. 1853, in the collection of cuttings relating to J. Toulmin Smith in the Bodleian Library, Oxford, 33.

[15] Mill, *Representative Government*, 351.

municipality as character-builder. He held that 'municipal government exists for the united benefit of aggregations of people, not for the cultivation of their tastes or their acquaintanceship. It exists because there are many requirements born of proximity which may be best met by united action.'[16] By this utilitarian criterion, Firth considered the Municipal Corporations Act to have 'proved more completely advantageous to the people affected by it' than any other measure of the century,[17] and a spell of inglorious service as a Kensington Vestryman between 1874 and 1877[18] helped convince him of the evil consequences of London's omission from the Act. He attacked the Corporation, the Vestries, the MBW and the public utility companies without discrimination, in polemics intended to pave the way for comprehensive reform.

Firth's *maximum opus* was the 763-page *Municipal London*, published in 1876. Two-thirds of the work was devoted to abuse of the existing system, while the remainder—an extensive tract in its own right—projected an ideal London under a Supreme Council.[19] This Council would comprise 240 members drawn from the whole of London, including the City. It would be elected triennially by householders and lodgers in forty geometrically defined electoral areas, bearing no necessary relation to existing parochial divisions. There would be no secondary bodies. Firth cited the existing precedents of the London School Board, to which he was elected in 1876, and, more guardedly, the MBW in its Building Act work to prove that a central body could be capable of detailed local operations.[20] A passage in *Municipal London* spells out the justification for dispensing with local bodies in Firth's usual dialectical manner, and with a clarity which makes paraphrase redundant.

It would no doubt be perfectly possible to construct Local Councils which should govern areas analogous to the present Vestry Districts, and to make such Councils responsible to a Central Body. But having constituted them, the question of the appointment of duties would arise, and if no functions were conceded to a District Council, and no administrative work given to it, except such as could be better performed by a local than a Central Body, it would probably be found that its functions would be extremely limited.[21]

[16] Firth, *Municipal London*, 600.
[17] J. F. B. Firth, *London Government and How to Reform It* (1881), 9.
[18] He attended only thirteen Vestry meetings in those years. See Kensington Vestry Minutes, 1874–7.
[19] Firth, *Municipal London*, chs. 16–23.
[20] Firth, *London Government*, 107.
[21] Firth, *Municipal London*, 614.

The committees of the Supreme Council would cover functions rather than areas, and the only concession to localism lay in the unworkable provision that each electoral area should be represented on each committee. Firth raised the single municipality to the level of strident principle, giving it an infusion of dogma that it seemed scarcely able to bear, and setting a doctrinaire tone that would afflict the reform movement for the next decade.

5. THE POSITION IN 1880

Firth's work marks the culmination of a drift towards metropolitan centralization on the part of the reform movement. Toulmin Smith had venerated the parish and the wardmote. Hall had based his system upon the parish, but provided for a constitutionally weak central body. Beal had moved from a separate municipalities system emphasizing the second tier to one emphasizing the first tier, and then to a single municipality scheme. Firth arrived at the single municipality deductively and promoted it unequivocally.

In the meantime the City Corporation had emerged as the most vocal advocate of decentralization because that had come to appear the only way to protect its advantageous position. Corporation representatives before the second Ayrton Committee had advocated a degree of devolution that was quite unworkable. J. T. Bedford, a City Deputy, contemplated 'one set of police on one side of Oxford Street, and another set of police on the other side'.[22] J. F. Bontems, of the Common Council's Local Government Committee, called for water, gas, street improvements, education, justice, and police powers to be entrusted to local municipalities.[23] The Corporation possessed or sought each of these powers in the 1860s, but to expect any scheme devised *de novo* to allocate them separately to ten contiguous authorities, and to expect any Home Secretary to dismember the Metropolitan Police, was profoundly unrealistic. The City's effective admission in 1870 that it was not prepared to consider any scheme entailing either Corporation reform or a significant first-tier authority meant in practice that it was not prepared to contemplate reform at all. The Corporation became committed to an obstructionist position in the reform debate, and maintained this stance until 1885. When pressed, its spokesmen simply reiterated their commitment

[22] SC Metropolitan Local Government and Taxation, *PP 1867*, XII, Q. 2131.
[23] Ibid., QQ. 1868–79, 1922.

to separate municipalities proposals which the Corporation's actions had rendered inapplicable.

Implicit in both single and separate municipalities schemes was the view that the parochial second tier would have to be replaced. Neither side had reached this conclusion through any assessment of the importance of parochial identity to the average Londoner. The reformer adopted the single municipality out of a desire to imitate the provincial municipal model, out of the belief that the division of London was a device to protect the City, and out of a functionalist association of size with efficiency. The Corporation adopted the devolved system with large secondary bodies in order to prevent the emergence of a first-tier authority which threatened its resources and independence. Both proposals were inimical to parochialism. The Vestry system certainly offered easy targets, but to jump from reform of the Vestries to the abolition of any localized second tier entailed either questionable assumptions about the limits of local identity in London or an arbitrary abandonment of any attempt to construct local administrative areas according to such identity. The single municipalists faced the obvious objection, thrown at them *ad nauseam* by their opponents, that no community of interest existed between the four corners of the Metropolis, but the Corporation and its supporters were vulnerable to the same charge. Even their local municipalities would throw together parishes with completely separate identities, varying greatly in wealth and social class. They were no more likely to sustain a spontaneous political life at the municipal than at the parliamentary level. The polarization of the reform issue into a battle between unification and 'tenification' had, however, suppressed such considerations by 1880. For the moment the question of local government reform depended more upon the internal dynamics of London politics than upon any appraisal of local identity.

3

The London Government Bill of 1884

I. THE BIRTH OF THE CAUCUS

The Second Reform Act had increased the electorate in the existing London boroughs by almost 30 per cent,[1] but in London, as in all the larger cities where multiple occupation made a tenurial franchise hard to define, the expansion continued throughout the 1870s and into the 1880s. The clarification of the position of indirect ratepayers by the 1869 Poor Rate Assessment and Collection Act,[2] the broader definition of a 'dwelling house' in the 1878 Parliamentary and Municipal Registration Act,[3] and the interpretation of that Act with respect to lodgers in *Bradley* v. *Baylis* of 1881[4] were necessary before the democratic implications of the new franchise worked themselves out in London. By 1883, though, the London electorate was 39 per cent larger even than in 1868.[5]

By increasing the cost of both registration work and elections, the expanding electorate had strengthened the hand of the wealthy Member in the 1870s, but in due course the concomitant accession of strength to the local party associations prompted their organizational revival. The main obstacle remained the unwieldy size of the pre-1885 boroughs and their artificiality as representative units. Organizational integration within the parliamentary boroughs proved at first as contentious as administrative integration within the metropolis; the surviving minutes of one branch of the Chelsea Conservative Union show that even in a small borough the force of separatism remained strong in component areas.[6]

[1] Comparison of 1865 and 1868 electorates in the eight pre-1867 boroughs from F. W. S. Craig, *British Parliamentary Election Results, 1832–1885* (London and Basingstoke, 1977), 3–21.
[2] By which compounding arrangements were standardized and overseers obliged to list indirect ratepayers in the ratebooks: 32 & 33 Vict., c. 41.
[3] 'Any part of a house where that part is separately occupied as a dwelling', without reference to separate rating: 41 & 42 Vict., c. 26, s. 5.
[4] By which the lodgers could be enrolled as inhabitant householders, thus evading the £10 qualification, if the landlord was non-resident: *Law Reports*, 8 QBD, 195–246.
[5] Craig, *Election Results*; and return in *PP 1884*, LXII, 213–20.
[6] Minutes of the Hammersmith Branch of the Chelsea Conservative and Constitutional Union, 1869–73 (Hammersmith Archives), 20 July, 1869 (opposition to contributing to Borough Union Com. for registration); 12 Dec. 1869 (opposition to Union reorganization);

Disorganization enhanced the independence of the sitting Member, so that 'not only was it impossible for a gentleman whose financial position was beneath that of a merchant prince to contest the constituency, but on all hands there were constant grounds for complaint at the loss of "touch" between the electors and the elected'.[7] As a result, when caucus organization was imposed in the late 1870s and early 1880s, it presented a challenge to the position of the representative.

This was more true of the Liberals because they provided most of London's sitting MPs. Liberal constituency-party life in London had been 'almost non-existent', in Firth's words,[8] down to the late 1870s, except in Chelsea where a political committee drawn from the borough's four Radical clubs formed London's first Liberal caucus.[9] The inaugural conference of the National Liberal Federation in 1877 and its propagation of the Birmingham model of local party organization led to the formation of caucus structures in most of the London boroughs, as 'the old cry of "register, register" was superseded by that of "organise, organise" '.[10] Southwark was the first metropolitan Liberal Association to adopt the Birmingham system, in October 1877, followed by Chelsea, Marylebone, and Hackney in 1878.[11] By 1884 some sort of federal organization on Birmingham lines—a general council of several hundred and a smaller executive committee, both elected by the component local organizations—existed in every Liberal Association outside the City.

The relevance of these steps towards party democracy for the London reform question lay in the number of sitting Liberal Members connected with the Corporation of London. Sir Thomas Chambers, the City Recorder, held one of the Marylebone seats for twenty years down to 1885. In Finsbury Andrew Lusk, a City alderman, sat for the same term. Two more aldermen sat for Lambeth until redistribution: J. C. Lawrence from 1865 and William McArthur from 1868. As the rivalry within borough Liberal Associations between Radicals, 'Whigs', and sitting Members crystallized around particular issues, London government reform was forced into prominence. It was at this stage essentially an activists' issue, significant to the rank and file, but of no necessary interest

---

4 July 1870 (secession of W. London Conservative Assoc.); 2 Nov. 1873 (no responsibility for election expenses incurred by central com).

[7] Editorial on Redistribution, *South London Press*, 20 June 1885.

[8] Quoted in H. J. Hanham, *Elections and Party Management* (1959), 139.

[9] 'Working Men's Clubs, V', *Echo*, 20 Feb. 1884.

[10] W. Ward to Finsbury Liberal Association, *Islington Gazette*, 3 June 1884.

[11] *The Times*, 23 Oct. 1877, 26 Feb. 1878; *Marylebone Mercury*, 26 Jan., 13 July 1878; *Hackney and Kingsland Gazette*, 28 June 1878.

to the wider electorate, as the response to the 1884 Bill was to demonstrate. Within the party, though, it was a good predictor of an individual's place in the ideological spectrum, becoming a Radical totem until the eventual triumph over the Whigs in 1885–6.

The new model caucuses were frequently accused of intruding upon the independence of the representative,[12] but in practice they usually respected the position of sitting Members willing to acknowledge the new organization. Thus while Torrens in Finsbury and McArthur in Lambeth caused party friction by their provocative assertions of independence, Locke in Southwark and even Chambers in Marylebone were readopted despite Radical misgivings.[13] The emphasis in the reorganizations of the late 1870s lay on the attainment of party unity, erasing the memory of 'the time when the Radicals, the extreme Radicals, the Anti-Vaccinators, the Tichbornites, the Local Option candidates and other sections each had an association and each a candidate in embryo'.[14] Given the size and social diversity of the parliamentary boroughs, this entailed respect for 'Whig' opinion, and advantage was often taken of the fact that the London boroughs were two-Member seats to produce balanced Whig/Radical tickets. For that reason, the belief prevailed in 'advanced' Radical circles that 'a Liberal Caucus is a mutual admiration society'.[15] The Marylebone Radical Reform Association was formed barely a year after the creation of the borough's United Liberal Association and Radical federations on the Chelsea model were formed in Hackney and Finsbury.[16] It would take the Corrupt Practices Act, redistribution, the alienation of the Liberal right over Home Rule, and the constituency party reorganization of 1886 to complete the Radicalization of local Liberal parties. In the early 1880s London Radicals had to find other outlets, in particular the political clubs and the single-issue pressure groups which flourished in that decade. One of these was the London Municipal Reform League.

---

[12] For example, W. Fraser Rae, 'Political Clubs and Party Organization', *Nineteenth Century*, 3 (1878), 926–7, for Southwark and Greenwich.

[13] For Torrens see e.g. *Islington Gazette*, 11 Apr., 2 May 1884; for McArthur, *South London Press*, 4 Aug. 1883, *South London Chronicle*, 25 Oct. 1884; for Locke, *South London Press*, 3 Nov. 1887; for Chambers, *Marylebone Mercury*, 2 Nov. 1878.

[14] Letter from H. Dann, Lambeth LA, *South London Press*, 1 Sept. 1883.

[15] *Radical*, 18 Dec. 1880.

[16] *Marylebone Mercury*, 13 Sept. 1879; *Eastern Argus and Borough of Hackney Times*, 19 July 1884; *Islington Gazette*, 8 May 1884.

2. THE LONDON MUNICIPAL REFORM LEAGUE

The League was founded by John Lloyd, an irascible Breconshire Liberal who was sufficiently offended by—of all London's municipal short-comings—the inaccessibility of Lincoln's Inn Fields to the general public, to advertise in *The Times* the formation of a municipal reform association.[17] After interrogation by Beal, Lloyd was sent on to Firth, who showed approval but no commitment. Undeterred, Lloyd and William Phillips, coal factor and Radical adventurer from Eltham, who had previously belonged to Beal's MMA, circularized the thirty friends of municipal reform whose names occurred to them. At the consequent meeting an executive committee was formed, and Firth now promised to join when the association had a hundred members. In March 1881 he presided at a provisional committee meeting to fix future policy, and by January 1882 he is listed as president in the League's first annual report, with Phillips as treasurer and Lloyd as secretary.

The League soon demonstrated that it was more substantial than most of the largely ephemeral ginger groups endemic in this period. It listed a membership of 200 in its first report, and of more than 1000 by 1884, when its annual income was £1250.[18] It was appreciably more broadly based than Beal's Metropolitan Municipal Association. It appealed both to the conventional Liberal reformism of men like Arthur Hobhouse, Arnold and Samuel Morley, Arthur Arnold, and Sir John Lubbock, and to the various elements of the emergent London Radicalism. Several Liberal Associations and Radical or Working Men's Clubs were affiliated to the League during the 1880s,[19] and the individual membership lists indicate the enlistment of members of the radical minorities on several Vestries. Nevertheless, while appreciably more 'democratic' than its predecessor, the League still displayed the centralized direction typical of most Victorian single-issue pressure groups. Although branches were founded in the parliamentary boroughs, the League's motive force during the 1880s derived almost entirely from the ruling triumvirate of Lloyd,

---

[17] For this paragraph see J. Lloyd, *London Municipal Government: History of a Great Reform, 1880–1888* (1910), chs. 2 and 3.

[18] London Municipal Reform League, *First Annual Report* (1882), 3–4 and *Fourth Annual Report* (1885), 2–16, 28–9.

[19] In 1884 affiliated associations included all four Chelsea Clubs, both the major Tower Hamlets Clubs, the Borough of Hackney Club (the largest in England: *Echo*, 12 Feb. 1884), and the Patriotic Club in Clerkenwell, as well as Liberal Clubs and Associations in Brockley, Woolwich, Whitechapel, Battersea, Paddington, and Westminster: LMRL, *Fourth Annual Report*, 30.

Phillips, and above all Firth. Whether because of organizational inadequacy or the disinclination of the hierarchy, little attempt was made to mobilize or involve what was a substantial nominal membership. The League's constitution stipulated a subscription of one shilling p.a., avowedly based upon that for the Anti-Corn Law League,[20] but the lists of donations in the annual reports indicate that there was no practical subscription mechanism. Even in 1884, the year in which the London Bill came before Parliament, only 285 of the League's 1030-strong General Council contributed anything to its funds.[21] Whereas the League's first report set a £1. 1s. 0d. affiliation fee for sympathetic associations,[22] the fee disappeared in the second and subsequent reports, and the seven published annual reports show only four individual donations from the twenty-nine affiliated societies. The League depended not upon small donors—donations under 10s. provided only 1·5 per cent of income in 1884—but upon large individual gifts: the £300 contributed by Samuel Morley between 1883 and his death in 1886, £285 from Bertram Currie, and £110 from Sydney Buxton between 1881 and 1887. Its 'income distribution' is correspondingly top-heavy; only 38 per cent of all donations in 1884 were for amounts under 10s., against 84 per cent for its successor, the more decentralized and participatory London Reform Union, in 1892–3.[23]

The corollary was a highly centralized direction of policy. Firth ran his League much as Cobden had run his, with an exclusive commitment to a single aim and a brusque treatment of dissidents. The League adopted from the outset a commitment to the full-blooded single-municipality doctrine that Firth had popularized, and the first public meeting in April 1881 demonstrated the rather totalitarian enforcement of that policy which would become familiar over the next few years. Phillips's single-municipality motion was carried by acclamation with only the conventional sprinkling of opponents, but an acrimonious correspondence followed in the *Citizen* between Lloyd and one of the dissentients, W. S. Storr, in which allegations that the meeting had been packed were raised and denied.[24] The single municipality was not a new policy and was not

---

[20] LMRL, *First Annual Report*, 23; *The Times*, 17 Mar. 1881.

[21] LMRL, *Fourth Annual Report*, 26–7.

[22] LMRL, *First Annual Report*, 22.

[23] These calculations from LMRL, 1st–7th Annual Reports (1882–8), and London Reform Union, *First Annual Report* (1894).

[24] Lloyd, *London Municipal Government*, 9. See also the League's prospectus of Oct. 1881 in the George Howell Collection.

exclusively Firthite—it had been the option favoured by the reform movement since 1870—but it was a policy unpalatable to most of the numerous Vestrymen in the League's ranks, who might have made their views known in a less hierarchical organization. As it was, the suppression of localism proposed by the 1884 Bill prompted criticism from within the League that weakened the reform cause at an important time.

More seriously, the League's career demonstrated the shortcomings of the single-issue pressure group for a cause with less emotive appeal than cheap bread, national education, or temperance. The League's hard core comprised municipal reform stalwarts who had no doubt of the compelling appeal of single-municipality theory, but its broader appeal to the emergent London Radicalism relied upon municipal reform being taken as a means to wider political ends. The League was not primarily a vehicle for broader causes, and although its publicists strained to mobilize growing public concern over metropolitan social problems, it was charged with opportunism when—as with housing in 1883–4—it sought to tie such issues to the municipal reform question. Its claims to head a mass movement for municipal reform alone laid it open to ridicule. Threats to mobilize the metropolitan *sansculottes*, to enlist 'a hundred thousand working men'[25] and launch 'such a movement that Mr. Gladstone would be unable to break his word'[26] were implausible. The view of the League as a band of faddists persistently invoking a mass support they could never hope to deploy probably led national politicians to underestimate the reform movement,[27] and gave rise to a cranky image that persisted throughout the 1880s. The League's efforts to manufacture artificial expressions of public support at the time of the 1884 Bill failed to do it serious harm only because its opponents practised the same deception more blatantly. Only with absorption into the broader programme of Progressivism in the 1890s would municipal reform become a plausible popular issue. In the early 1880s it gained ground not through the League's work but because of Firth's contact with a receptive government.

---

[25] Phillips in 1881, quoted in Lloyd, *London Municipal Government*, 21.

[26] Aeneas Smith at the Leeds conference, *Pall Mall Gazette*, 18 Oct. 1883.

[27] 'Is the pressure now being put on the government to carry the London Bill genuine or is it only Beal and Firth with a few supporters, multiplying themselves by means of public meetings in various places, with the same speeches, and mostly the same audience?' Derby to Harcourt, 21 Mar. 1883, MS Harcourt, Dep. 107/63.

3. LONDON AND THE CABINET

Firth had celebrated his election to Parliament in 1880 by introducing a Bill to create a single municipality[28] and moving successfully for a Royal Commission on the City Guilds and for a Select Committee on London's Water Supply. The Bill went the way of all previous Private Members' Bills on the subject, and the Royal Commission would spin out its deliberations until 1884, but the water problem required urgent attention as the 1881 quinquennial valuation approached. The Committee was influentially manned[29] and chaired by the new Home Secretary, Sir William Harcourt. Its report buried the Cross purchase terms and, while accepting the need for a separate water authority, made pointed reference to the want of adequate municipal institutions which could have obviated the creation of another special authority in London.[30]

The emphasis upon the connection between water supply and municipal reform reflected Firth's work upon the Committee, of which he was the member best informed on public utility questions, and his consequent influence upon Harcourt. By the end of 1881 the Home Secretary had read Firth's Cobden Club essay, a digestible version of *Municipal London*,[31] and convinced himself that the creation of a water authority 'would have involved precisely the same questions and been exposed to just the same difficulties as those which surround the creation of a Municipal Government of London ... In short, it would be almost as easy to settle the one question as the other.'[32] On 13 December he presented to the Cabinet proposals that would form the basis of the Bill of 1884.

His memorandum suggested the creation of a new Corporation of London, nominally an extension of the old one to cover the whole metropolis, with a Common Council of 240 members, directly elected on the ordinary municipal franchise. The new Corporation would exercise not only municipal but also county powers, London being constituted a county in itself.[33] The Corporation would therefore assume the authority

---

[28] *PP 1880*, v, Bill 228.

[29] It was chaired by Harcourt and included Chamberlain, Cross, Sir James McGarel Hogg, Chairman of the MBW, G. P. Goldney, City Remembrancer, two of the City members, Hubbard and Lawrence, and the two reformers Firth and Rogers.

[30] SC London Water Supply, *PP 1880*, x, Report, iii.

[31] J. F. B. Firth, *London Government and How to Reform It* (1881).

[32] Memorandum on a Plan for the Municipal Government of London, 13 Dec. 1881, MS Harcourt, Dep. 110/25, 1.

[33] A provision common to the Buxton, Elcho, and Firth Bills.

of the Metropolitan Board, the Vestries and District Boards, and of the JPs in respect of their metropolitan territory.[34]

This single-municipality proposal was transparently Firthite in origin, and Harcourt subsequently acknowledged that 'it is in a great degree by the arguments and facts which he has placed before me that I have come to the conclusion at which I have arrived'.[35] Firth had none the less been 'induced to modify his original views' to some extent,[36] symbolically with the nominal perpetuation of the City Corporation, and practically with the reintroduction of second-tier authorities. Harcourt proposed to create District Councils of between twelve and fifty members, to be elected at the same time as the Common Council. They would not, however, be entrusted with autonomous executive power or the right to raise their own funds, but were intended to act as 'a sort of "Visiting Committee" for their Municipal District and ... a good training college for the Corporation'. Each Council would be charged to 'discuss the needs of its own district, look after the Inspectors and officials of the Corporation within the district and report to the Corporation ... the requirements of the locality'.[37] The District Councils would not, therefore, greatly dilute Firth's single-municipality principle, and Harcourt made it clear that they had been devised not for administrative reasons but in order to satisfy legitimate local aspirations.

In time it would become clear that an emasculated second tier satisfied no local aspirations, but the reaction of Gladstone, whose experience of the subject during his first ministry had made him 'a staunch Unitarian',[38] was that the District Councils seemed to 'convey a slight savour of dualism'. The Prime Minister specified seven points of difference with Harcourt, of which the most serious concerned police control, but none the less professed to agree 'in everything that has the aspect of a principle'.[39] London municipal reform became government policy for the first time since 1870.

In the 1882 session London reform jostled for time with the twice deferred Corrupt Practices Bill and a projected county government measure. In the event Irish matters thwarted all three proposals, although

---

[34] Harcourt memorandum, MS Harcourt, Dep. 110/25.
[35] 'Further Memorandum on a Plan for the Government of London', 2 Jan. 1882, ibid., Dep. 110/34, 14–15.
[36] Harcourt to Gladstone, 15 Dec. 1881, Gladstone Papers, Add. MSS 44196, fo. 253.
[37] Harcourt Memorandum, MS Harcourt, Dep. 110/25, 12.
[38] Gladstone to Harcourt, 30 Mar. 1883, MS Harcourt, Dep. 9/15.
[39] Gladstone to Harcourt, 19 Dec. 1881, copy in Add. MS 44196, fo. 263.

the embryonic state of the London measure in 1882[40] probably made it the least plausible of the three candidates. In 1883 London secured an unexpected priority, as the Cabinet radicals balked at the introduction of a county measure before the reform of the county franchise.[41] The Bill, reared by an *ad hoc* committee of Harcourt, Dilke, Firth, and Beal,[42] was now in a more finished state. Harcourt was anxious to be seen to have 'done a good job and accomplished my share of the programme'.[43] Dilke had been elevated to the Cabinet as President of the Local Government Board in December 1882 and immediately promised the Home Secretary to 'slave and devil for you re. govt. of London'.[44] As the mouthpiece of Chelsea Radicalism and the only London Member in the Cabinet, he was the Bill's most consistent Cabinet supporter, and alone contemplated resigning when the 1883 proposals were dropped.[45] Gladstone sensed the importance of London reform as one of the 'great Liberal measures' from which 'the Liberal party as a whole draws its vital health'[46]—one made all the more necessary by the inertia of the previous three years.

In the event the Bill failed to be passed, or even introduced, in 1883, because of the failure of Gladstone and Harcourt to resolve their differences over police control.[47] As a result London reform collided with franchise extension in 1884, which limited the parliamentary time available for the London Government Bill and changed radically the attitude of the Liberal party towards it. A National Liberal Federation Conference at Leeds in October 1883 made clear the party's unwillingness to suffer any distraction from the progress of the Franchise Bill.[48]

The government cast around for means of softening the blow to the London Bill. Firth's idea of a Grand Committee of metropolitan Members to receive the Bill after second reading had apparently been accepted by Gladstone in November 1883, but was dropped in December when Firth rather belatedly discovered that fifteen of the twenty-two London

---

[40] Drafts are in the Harcourt Papers, MS Harcourt, Dep. 109. The earliest were disguised as the 'Manchester Extension Bill' for greater secrecy.

[41] See J. P. D. Dunbabin, 'The Politics of the Establishment of County Councils', *Historical Journal*, 6/2 (1963), 231–3.

[42] Dilke Journal, Add. MS 43937, fo. 5; S. Gwynn and G. M. Tuckwell, *The Life of the Rt. Hon. Sir Charles W. Dilke* (1917), i. 420–1.

[43] Harcourt to Lewis Harcourt, 1 Feb. 1883, MS Harcourt, Dep. 649/57.

[44] Dilke to Harcourt, 10 Dec. 1882, copy in Add. MS 43890, fo. 182.

[45] Dilke Journal, Add. MS 43937, fo. 152.

[46] Gladstone to Harcourt, 18 May 1883, MS Harcourt, Dep. 9/44.

[47] For more detail see J. H. Davis, 'The Problem of London Local Government Reform, 1880–1900', D.Phil. thesis (Oxford, 1983), 101–4.

[48] See *Pall Mall Gazette*, 18 Oct. 1883.

Members were hostile—'a nice working majority to go to a Grand Committee with', as Harcourt put it.[49] Firth's optimistic suggestion to Harcourt in January 1884 that London and the franchise proceed *'pari passu'* was unrealistic.[50] The London Government Bill was placed firmly behind Franchise in the 1884 session. It waited for its introduction until 8 April, the day after the second reading of the Franchise Bill, and for its own second reading a further three months, until Franchise had cleared the Commons. With second reading as late as 3 July, no major opposed measure could stand much chance of success.

4. THE 1884 BILL

On 8 April 1884 the Bill was finally launched,[51] backed by a powerful speech from Harcourt. It differed little in form from the measure first outlined by Harcourt in December 1881—a Common Council of 240 members, a Lord Mayor but no aldermen, and District Councils in the existing Vestry and District Board areas exercising delegated powers. Virtually all reference to the police question was avoided,[52] so that the City force passed to the new municipality under the clause transferring to it the powers of the existing Corporation,[53] and the Metropolitan Police remained under the Home Office. All powers and duties of the Metropolitan Board, the Corporation, and the Vestries and District Boards were to vest in the new municipality. Poor Law and education powers were not transferred, but the new Corporation was obliged to submit schemes as soon as possible for the purchase or regulation of gas and water supply.[54] Elections to the new central and local bodies were to be triennial, with the qualifications for both voting and membership to be the same as those in the Municipal Corporations Act. Only two significant changes of detail were made in the Bill.

The first was the inclusion of a number of quite futile *douceurs* for the MBW and the Corporation. Echoing Firth's belief that the Board 'cannot struggle much against a proposition to place them all *ex-officio* on the

---

[49] Firth to Gladstone, 13 April. 1883, Add. MS 44480, fo. 157; Dilke to Harcourt, 30 Nov. 1883, copy in Add. MS 43890, fo. 262; Harcourt to Lewis Harcourt, 14 Dec. 1883, MS Harcourt, Dep. 649/113.

[50] Firth to Harcourt, 21 Jan. 1884, MS Harcourt, Dep. 108/91.

[51] London Government Bill, *PP 1884*, v, Bill 171.

[52] The only provision was that restoring the Exchequer contribution to the City Police, ibid., s. 39(4).

[53] Ibid., s. 20(1).

[54] Ibid., s. 48(1)(*b*).

new Council',[55] the Bill proposed the incorporation of the MBW's forty-six members *en bloc* in the first, transitional, Council. They would be joined by forty-four nominees of the existing Corporation, so that three-eighths of London's first reformed council would be indirectly elected.[56] More serious was the provision that in the second and subsequent councils the City area would elect no less than thirty members of the Common Council.[57] While all the other areas were allocated members in proportion to a compound of rateable value and population, the City, with roughly one-eighth of London's rateable value but a small and shrinking population, had its representation determined by assessment alone.[58]

Neither the City nor the MBW was much impressed. If Harcourt really had believed that 'the retention *eo nomine* of the Corporation will much mollify the City',[59] he cannot have paid much attention to the Corporation's response to reform since the 1860s. The Bill would deprive the City proper of exclusive control over its estates and rob the vast majority of Common Councilmen and aldermen of their positions. This did not much mollify the City, and neither did the possibility of more local charges coming onto the central rate. The MBW could not even look to retention *eo nomine*, and the offer of a three-year term on the first council meant little to men whose tenure had previously appeared open-ended. The Board now dropped its support for even the cautious Ayrton proposals and opposed reform outright, convening a Vestry conference to condemn the Bill.[60]

The second modification to the original proposals involved the localization of some of the rate burden. Harcourt had originally seen the introduction of a single equalized city rate as 'the basis of the whole plan',[61] and the principle of a uniform rate had been qualified only in respect of local debts already contracted, existing statutory liabilities, and the adoption of the Public Libraries Act by individual localities.[62] Firth's advisers on the local financial provisions, T. E. Gibb, St Pancras Vestry Clerk and municipal reformer, and W. Kerr, a St Pancras Guardian, had

---

[55] Firth to Gladstone, 13 Apr. 1883, Add. MS 44480, fo. 157.

[56] London Government Bill, *PP 1884*, v, Bill 171, s. 52(2).

[57] Ibid., First Schedule.

[58] In his 1881 Memorandum (MS Harcourt, Dep. 110/25, 7) Harcourt had considered it 'monstrously unjust' that the City should be given '1/8oth of the representation whilst it paid 1/8th of the rate'.

[59] Harcourt to Gladstone, 15 Dec. 1881, Add. MS 44196, fo. 253.

[60] *Metropolitan*, 3 May 1884.

[61] Harcourt Memorandum, MS Harcourt, Dep. 110/25, 7.

[62] See 'Manchester Extension Bill, 1883', MS Harcourt, Dep. 109/1, ss. 45, 58, 71.

recommended that local bodies contribute half the cost of extraordinary capital projects in their area—essentially the existing practice—and Chamberlain had made the same suggestion for the provision of public parks.[63] Revisions made for the 1884 session, however, went much further. In the third 1884 draft the Common Council was given the discretionary right to declare any expenses incurred in a locality to be a local charge rather than a charge on the general city rate.[64] The Bill as introduced went further still, effectively providing that local expenses should be defrayed by local charges unless the Common Council declared otherwise.[65]

This progressive devolution of the rate burden sat uncomfortably with the constitutional emasculation of the local bodies. The district council appeared likely to become 'a mere jobbing committee'[66] of the central body, with no financial powers and, indeed, no spontaneous function at all except the annual presentation of an area budget which the Common Council could accept or reduce at will. Its duties would be specified in the binding district orders handed down by the Common Council. It would be expected to supervise the work of council officials within its district, but lacked the power to appoint or dismiss them.[67] Ratepayers seeking improvements in their own area would have to petition the Common Council for a district order to bind their local representatives— a clumsily indirect approach to self-government.[68] Whether such a high degree of centralization was to be justified on grounds of efficiency or of the essential unity of the metropolis, it was hardly consonant with the perpetuation of the existing inefficient and fragmented local taxation system. With around forty secondary bodies, any given district would elect only a small fraction of a Common Council empowered to inflict local charges upon it. The Bill threatened taxation without representation— 'centralisation with local liability', in the words of the Mile End Vestry Clerk.[69]

The reason for the move away from the uniform rate remains unclear. Possibly Harcourt or his officials had responded to public anxiety at the

[63] MS Harcourt, Dep. 108/35; Chamberlain to Harcourt, 16 Jan. 1882 (enclosure), MS Harcourt, Dep. 59/40.
[64] MS Harcourt, Dep. 109/8.
[65] London Government Bill, *PP 1884*, v, Bill 171, ss. 21(2) and 22(1).
[66] Chamberlain's criticisms of the Harcourt plan, cited in Harcourt's 'Further Memorandum', MS Harcourt, Dep. 110/34, 5.
[67] London Government Bill, *PP 1884*, v, Bill 171, ss. 7(3), 22(1).
[68] As was argued by the *Metropolitan*, 26 Apr. 1884.
[69] Milner Jutsum, quoted in the *East London Observer*, 26 Apr. 1884.

inexorable growth of first-tier rates. Over the previous five years the levies of the MBW had increased by 50 per cent, those of the School Board by 49 per cent, and those of the Metropolitan Asylums Board, handling a smallpox epidemic, by 73 per cent.[70] Nevertheless, by leaving the incidence of charge to the discretion of the Common Council, the Bill frightened virtually everybody. The fear of J. T. Bedford, Deputy for the ward of Farringdon Without, that 'as all will come out of one common fund, away goes every incentive to economy', was echoed in areas which appeared to have a greater material incentive than the City to seek metropolitan integration—in Islington and even in Shoreditch.[71] On the other hand, Plumstead District Board noted that 'local expenses are still to be defrayed by rates raised locally, so that where such rates are heavy they will remain so', and the *Hackney Express* complained that, while reducing local representatives to the impotence of School Board managers, the Bill ignored 'the very best provision of the Education Act'—the uniform rate.[72]

Fears of localized rates were probably more valid than fears of centralized rates. The Bill allocated representatives on the Common Council in proportions which would reflect rateable value more sensitively than was the case on the MBW, except in the City, which was magnanimously awarded an eighth of the entire council. Apart from virtually ensuring Conservative domination of the new authority, this allocation was likely to give control of the council to those wealthy areas with the greatest interest in devolving the rate burden. Harcourt's Bill would probably have left the metropolitan financial system still more inequitable than it stood under the 1855 Act.

5. REACTIONS TO THE BILL

The Bill proposed to abolish the MBW and the Vestries and to change the City Corporation beyond recognition; opposition from all these quarters was clearly inevitable. The City's Common Council rejected the Bill

---

[70] Comparison of levies for 1883/4 with those for 1878/9. See Appendix 3.

[71] Bedford quoted in the *Metropolitan*, 5 Jan. 1884; Islington Vestry Minutes, 2 May 1884; for Shoreditch Vestry see *[Borough of] Hackney Express and Shoreditch Observer*, 3 May 1884.

[72] Plumstead DB Minutes, 14 May 1884; *Hackney Express and Shoreditch Observer*, 17 May 1884.

comprehensively in April,[73] as did the Metropolitan Board in early May;[74] both bodies resolved to court the second tier, after years of neglect, and the MBW convened a Vestry conference at Spring Gardens within a week.[75] Vestry reaction was similarly hostile, only one of the thirty-eight sanitary authorities approving the Bill, but the degrees of opposition provided some variation from the unequivocal condemnation expressed by the first-tier bodies. Certainly many authorities limited themselves to an unqualified rejection of the Bill as 'subversive of the principles of Local Self-Government'[76] which had 'for centuries distinguished Englishmen from other nations'[77] and provided 'the great guarantee of efficiency and economy in local administration'.[78] Nevertheless, various provisos suggested that Harcourt might have been better advised to appease the second tier than the first. Signs of support for the single municipality for *first-tier* purposes[79] provided a reminder that the Vestries had little sympathy for the MBW and less for the Corporation, which had revived its advocacy of 'tenification' as reform loomed.[80] The Bill also met an appreciably less hostile reception in the suburban areas which had been thinly populated in 1855—and had consequently been consigned to Schedule B and given sparse representation on the MBW—but had since 'filled up', and resented their constitutional impotence. Lewisham District Board, which had 'as it were, two-fifths of one member' of the MBW,[81] was the only authority to support the Bill.[82] Wandsworth DB,

---

[73] Common Council Minutes, 18 Apr. 1884.

[74] MBW Minutes, 2 May 1884.

[75] For its proceedings see the *Metropolitan*, 10 May 1884.

[76] Fulham DB Minutes, 7 May 1884.

[77] Whitechapel DB Minutes, 21 Apr. 1884.

[78] Poplar DB Minutes, 29 Apr. 1884.

[79] The amalgamation of the MBW and the City to form a single first-tier body was endorsed in Bermondsey (Vestry Minutes, 5 May 1884), Greenwich (DB Minutes, 23 Apr. 1884), Paddington (Vestry Minutes, 13 May 1884), St Pancras (Vestry Minutes, 14 May 1884), St James (see *Westminster and Lambeth Gazette*, 17 May 1884), Westminster (ibid., 31 May 1884), and Woolwich (see *Kentish Mercury*, 16 May 1884), and inferentially in Hampstead (Vestry Minutes, 1 May 1884). It had earlier been approved in Shoreditch (Vestry Minutes, 21 Feb., 4 Apr. 1882).

[80] In Westminster the mover of the resolution against the Bill asserted that 'the existence of the Corporation was a fraud upon London' (*Westminster and Lambeth Gazette*, 31 May 1884). In Holborn the DB passed the motion of William Malthouse, Common Councilman, against the Bill only after removal of a reference to the need for separate municipalities in the parliamentary boroughs (Holborn DB Minutes, 28 Apr. 1884).

[81] D. K. Forbes (Lewisham DB) quoted in the *Kentish Mercury*, 2 May 1884. The other three-fifths belonged to Plumstead.

[82] Lewisham DB Minutes, 30 April 1884. The Board 'trusts the main duties of the District Councils will be stated in the Bill itself'.

which joined Lewisham in calling for increased MBW representation in
1884,[83] would have supported the Bill with provision for 'independent
local control of matters of a local character',[84] and similar motions secured
respectable minorities in Greenwich and Hackney.[85]

Nevertheless, the destruction of local independence made the Bill as a
whole quite unpalatable to the second tier. The retention of existing local
boundaries for the district councils only emphasized their impotence.
The disparity of size between first- and second-tier areas was so great
that even the largest districts could expect only a minimal representation
on the central body, and reiteration of this point characterized the Vestry
response.[86] Centuries of practice had established the parish as the perceived unit of local administration—a perception reinforced by the 1855
Act. The Bill proposed to erase parochial autonomy, giving recognized
areas only a small share of a central body 'which, considering the vast
extent of the Metropolis, could possess no adequate knowledge of local
requirements'.[87] Much of the Vestry reaction could doubtless be ascribed
to the same job-protective instincts that motivated the first tier, but
the Vestries were responding not only to their threatened abolition as
institutions, but also to the attack in principle upon the second tier.

After the first promise of legislation in 1882, Shoreditch Vestry had
resolved, while admitting the need for first-tier reform, that 'no system
of municipal Government will be satisfactory which does not provide for
the administration of purely local affairs by duly elected local councils'.[88]
The Shoreditch resolution typified the second-tier attitude to reform.
The fear that the Bill 'will authorize strangers to raise and apply funds
from local taxpayers for local purposes'[89] was universal. The Vestries had
always had an ambiguous attitude towards first-tier expenditure. An
awareness that it made possible an expansion of municipal activity that
would have overwhelmed the second tier alone was tempered by the fear
that it fuelled an explosion of local taxation that the Vestries could not

[83] Lewisham DB Minutes, 12 Mar., 16 July 1884.
[84] The Minutes have not survived. See the *Metropolitan*, 26 Apr., 3 May 1884.
[85] Greenwich DB Minutes, 23 Apr. 1884; Hackney DB Minutes, 9 May 1884. In
Greenwich it was said that 'the [District] Board was snubbed on every side, and why?
Because they were not properly elected?' (*Kentish Mercury*, 25 Apr. 1884).
[86] See, e.g. Marylebone Vestry Minutes, 1 May 1884; Poplar DB Minutes, 13 May 1884;
Lambeth Vestry Minutes, 1 May 1884; and the discussions in Lewisham (*Kentish Mercury*,
2 May 1884); Bermondsey (*Southwark Recorder*, 14 June 1884); and St George, Hanover
Square (*Westminster and Chelsea News*, 26 Apr. 1884).
[87] Shoreditch Vestry Minutes, 29 Apr. 1884.
[88] Ibid., 21 Feb., 4 Apr. 1882.
[89] Whitechapel DB Minutes, 21 Apr. 1884.

control but for which they might still be blamed by the undiscerning ratepayer. In twenty years the burden of London local taxation had increased by 124 per cent, and the share of the first tier had risen from 29 per cent to 43 per cent.[90] During the past five years first-tier levies had increased by 41 per cent against an increase of 4 per cent in those of the second tier.[91] 'So heavy are the payments to Boards over which they [Marylebone Vestry] have no control, that the strictest economy has to be exercised over the almost insufficient balance left for the necessary and ordinary expenditure of the parish'.[92] The possible loss of what remained of direct parochial control over expenditure was a potent threat, which heightened Vestry anxiety to protect existing local powers. This did not imply any eagerness to dismember the first tier in the manner prescribed by the Corporation; if anything, the Vestries were more conscious of the need for a substantial first-tier body than they had been in the 1850s, when the range of municipal activity had been so much smaller. Most Vestries sought a fine two-tier balance by which the metropolitan bodies would shoulder enough of the rate burden to prevent the second tier from being overwhelmed, while the local bodies would exercise sufficiently extensive powers to retain some direct control over municipal expenditure.

Failure to appreciate the nuances of Vestry attitudes would bedevil Conservative attempts at devolution in the 1890s. In 1884 it led the Liberals to produce a Bill so offensively centralizing as to weaken them tactically. The reformers found themselves not only fighting the obvious battle against the 'sinister interests' of the City and the MBW but also mounting an attack against the principle of second-tier autonomy which many of them found unpalatable. In the months after the Bill's publication, Hobhouse, Sydney Buxton, Corrie Grant, Samuel Morley, and even Dilke suggested amending the Bill in the direction of greater local independence.[93] Their recantation came too late to help the sizeable contingent of Liberal Vestrymen forced to choose between disowning the Bill's second-tier provisions and claiming, fraudulently, that they would really enhance local powers. Firth and Harcourt had chosen to ignore

---

[90] Comparison of years 1883/4 and 1863/4. See Appendix 3.

[91] Comparison of years 1883/4 and 1878/9, ibid.

[92] Marylebone Vestry Minutes, 1 May 1884, printed report of Parliamentary Com. on London Government Bill, 6.

[93] For Hobhouse's motions in St George, Hanover Square, see Vestry Minutes, 24 Apr., 1 May 1884, and *Westminster and Chelsea News*, 26 Apr., 3 May 1884. For Buxton, Grant, and Morley, all Leaguers, see *Metropolitan*, 3, 31 May, 21 June 1884. For Dilke at Kensington, ibid., 31 May 1884.

Vestry opinion for the same reason that they ignored the Corporation—
'when you are cleaning out a pond you don't consult the opinion of the
frogs';[94] in fact the government tried to promote the Bill by discrediting
the Vestries.[95] Yet London's three thousand or so Vestrymen formed an
almost exclusive pool of local administrative experience in a metropolis
notoriously apathetic towards local government.

Their alienation and general public apathy[96] increased the difficulty of
mobilizing credible public support. The Bill was best received in the
London borough Liberal Associations. Misgivings were expressed even
there about the local provisions,[97] and Firth was roughly received by the
Bow Liberal Club in May for the over-representation of the City at the
expense of the East End,[98] but most London Liberals saw the Bill as an
assault upon the privileged position of the Corporation, and welcomed it
as such. The London Liberal Associations were, though, as committed
to franchise reform as their provincial counterparts, and though they
supported Harcourt's Bill for its own sake, had no greater desire to see
it impede reform. A meeting of representatives of London borough
associations shortly after the Leeds conference had apparently confirmed
the national party's verdict,[99] and as a constitutional battle over franchise
became probable, interest in the London Bill diminished.

The Conservatives, emerging from a generation of impotence in
London, had still to formulate a municipal reform policy, being moved
only by a specific sympathy for the Corporation and a vaguer affinity for
localism. Salisbury, with three Lord Mayors in his lineage, translated
these premises into support for the Corporation's traditional separate
municipalities policy, and advanced this philosophy at Plymouth in June.[1]
In the Commons, though, where Northcote offered no lead, C. T. Ritchie,
Member for Tower Hamlets, 'was not prepared to say that it ['tenification'] was absolutely the best way of doing what was desired'.[2] The

---

[94] Firth, at Bow Liberal Club, *Metropolitan*, 24 May 1884.

[95] See below, pp. 89–92.

[96] Dilke admitted that 'one unfortunate fact for the London Bill is that no one in the
House cares about it except Dilke, Firth and the Prime Minister, no one outside except the
Liberal electors of Chelsea': Dilke to J. Loader, Add. MS 43886, fo. 158, quoted in Gwynn
and Tuckwell, *Dilke*, ii. 10–11. Hamilton discerned 'no real sign of enthusiasm' for the Bill
in July: D. W. R. Bahlman (ed.), *The Diary of Sir Edward Walter Hamilton, 1880–1885*
(Oxford, 1972), ii. 648.

[97] For example by Richard Strong of the Lambeth LA, *South London Press*, 3 May 1884.

[98] *Metropolitan*, 24 May 1884.

[99] According to a *South London Chronicle* editorial, 28 June 1884.

[1] *Metropolitan*, 7 June 1884.

[2] *Hansard*, 3rd ser., CCLXXXIX, 1955 (3 July 1884).

question of how far Conservative support for the City should be translated into support for its specific reform prescriptions would later become critical, but in 1884 the many targets offered by the Harcourt Bill exempted the opposition from constructive thought upon the subject.

The views of the ratepayers' associations, still dominant in Vestry politics, remain as arcane as most of their processes, and analysis is further inhibited by the intrusion of the spurious associations sponsored by the City and 'springing up about London like mushrooms'[3] during 1884. These probably account for most of the fifty-five hostile 'ratepayers' meetings' listed by the *Metropolitan* in June,[4] and it is more significant that neither of the two associations whose minutes for 1884 survive appears even to have discussed the Bill.[5] Certainly the Bill's supporters failed to project reform as a ratepayers' issue. The potential of the single municipality for rate equalization, already impaired by the retreat into ambiguity over local charges, was not stressed, and the debate was instead pervaded by the belief, surviving from the Chadwick era and reinforced by rising School Board and MBW precepts, that metropolitan bodies were intrinsically extravagant. Consequently public dissatisfaction with the existing first tier hindered rather than helped the reformers.

Overall the Bill can hardly be said to have generated much more spontaneous public support than the bodies that it threatened, and the reformers' success at what Hobhouse had described as 'that difficult art ... the art of turning a minority into a majority'[6] came increasingly to depend upon their more direct attempts to create a favourable climate of opinion. Ever since its formation the London Municipal Reform League had been anxious to promote ostentatious manifestations of support, and its efforts reached a peak in 1883 and 1884. It was, however, always in competition with the Corporation, acting through Common Council's Special Committee on London Government, formed in 1882 in response to the government's first reform pledge.[7] Disparity of resources made it a battle that the League was bound to lose. The full extent of its disposable income is unclear, as its accounted donation income of some £1,000 p.a. in 1883 and 1884 was probably supplemented by additional contributions from Firth and others. It was none the less unlikely to have even

<hr />

[3] J. H. Lile, Lambeth Vestry, quoted in the *South London Press*, 3 May 1884.
[4] *Metropolitan*, 14 June 1884.
[5] The minutes of the Stoke Newington and the De Beauvoir Town and Dalston Associations are in the Hackney Archives.
[6] Quoted in Lloyd, *London Municipal Government*, 13.
[7] Common Council Minutes, 16 Feb. 1882.

approached the resources of the Special Committee, which could disburse funds from the City cash without effective scrutiny by either Common Council or the Corporation's auditors.[8] It spent £19,500 on opposing the League between 1882 and 1885, including over £14,000 in 1884 alone,[9] money which gave it a marked advantage in almost every aspect of the campaign.

The Special Committee operated through the sponsorship of bogus societies—chiefly the London Workmen's League and the Metropolitan Ratepayers' Protection Association—while the League sought to harness the enthusiasm of Liberal Associations and the Radical Clubs.[10] Both sides paid for professional partisans to attend or disrupt the 350 or so public meetings 'got up' on the issue during 1884, with the result that many degenerated to a level of violence that 'could scarcely have been consistent with public safety'.[11] Competitive demonstrations of this sort, entailing heavy expenditure on packing and policing meetings, proved among the least cost-effective forms of self-advertisement,[12] and the drain upon resources weakened the League earlier than the Special Committee. Only two sizeable reform meetings were held in the four weeks before the second reading on 3 July, although Firth had earlier naïvely urged upon Gladstone an adequate pause between first and second readings for the convincing expression of metropolitan opinion.[13] The inequality of resources was more tellingly demonstrated with propaganda. The Special Committee sponsored some fifty polemical pamphlets and circulated 4,000 copies of its report on the Bill to Vestrymen. It notified the *Morning Post* of anti-reform meetings and engaged two freelance reporters of its

---

[8] For Corporation audit procedure see RC Corporation of London, *PP 1854*, XXIII, QQ. 4675 (Scott), 433 (Acland). Also SC Corporation of London (Charges of Malversation), *PP 1887*, X, QQ. 904, 913 (Scott).

[9] SC Malversation, *PP 1887*, X, Report, iv–v. Much of the information on the manœuvres of the League and the Special Committee comes from this Committee, instigated by Bradlaugh on Firth's behalf, following the leaking of incriminating material to the Chelsea Liberal Association.

[10] For more detail on this campaign see Davis, 'London Local Government Reform', 119 ff., and SC Malversation, *PP 1887*, X, *passim*.

[11] SC Malversation, *PP 1887*, X, Report, xi.

[12] The MRPA spent £77 policing one of its meetings at Westminster and £93 disrupting one of the League's at Kensington. The Leaguer Samuel Brighty of Clerkenwell took 'contingents of men from the "Crown Tavern", Clerkenwell Close, to vote for resolutions and eject dissentients, their price being 3s each': ibid., Report, xi; QQ. 2809–54 (Johnson); Q. 3613 (Hamilton). The League recruited a force of 'Municipal Police' from the Chelsea ironmaster Aeneas Smith—'smiths, iron-hammerers and foundrymen' euphemistically described by Firth as 'honest but powerful men', Lloyd, *London Municipal Government*, 44–5; SC Malversation, *PP 1887*, X, Q. 1634 (Firth).

[13] Firth to Gladstone, 18 Jan. 1884, copy in MS Harcourt, Dep. 108/88.

own.[14] The League's *Municipal Reform Gazette* ran to only two issues. The Special Committee also embarked upon the expensive exercise of petitioning the Privy Council for the incorporation of the parliamentary boroughs, and secured the presentation of a 15,000-signature petition from Greenwich.[15] The League frankly acknowledged its inability to bear the expense of comprehensive petitioning, adding pathetically that 'certain leading streets' taken as samples demonstrated overwhelming support for the Bill.[16]

The campaign demonstrated how easily a pressure group with genuine but limited support could be defeated by an interest with virtually no spontaneous following but practically unlimited resources. It showed the limitations of the methods of agitation favoured by London Radicals in the 1880s—the single-issue, ostensibly unpartisan pressure group and the 'monster' demonstration—in matters which did not generate significant public enthusiasm. The public campaign had been a distraction, at times squalid, at times farcical, but with no bearing upon the Bill's parliamentary progress. It had damaged the reformers' credibility more than it had enhanced the Bill's prospects. Municipal reform would become plausible as a popular issue only when built into broader political platforms—Liberal/Progressive social politics and Conservative retrenchment and anti-Radicalism.

One aspect of the 1885 campaign deserves further emphasis, in view of its effect upon the subsequent debate. This was the vilification of the second tier, and of Clerkenwell Vestry in particular, over slum housing. Vestries, like local authorities elsewhere, tended to attract small property owners keenly interested in the level of local taxation. That they might also be keenly interested in sparing themselves the cost of sanitary improvement, and anxious to use their position to discourage inspectors from investigating their property, was always a danger, but there is little to suggest that such action necessarily evolved into the wholesale obstruction of sanitary operations in their area. Self-interested interference by slum-owning Vestrymen was unlikely to have been the most potent reason for the sluggishness of sanitary work down to the 1880s; the expense and legal problems in implementing the Torrens Act,[17] the difficulties posed by unsympathetic magistrates,[18] and the general bias

---

[14] Special Com. Minutes, 22, 25 Apr., 2 May 1884, Minute Papers, Oct. 1884; SC Malversation Q. 2282 ff. (Johnson).

[15] PRO PC1/690/9.

[16] *Municipal Reform Gazette*, 25 June 1884.

[17] See Llewellyn-Davies's letter in *The Times*, 16 Nov. 1883.

[18] See e.g. Booth MS, B 381, 13 (G. P. Bate).

towards economy were more significant obstacles. It nevertheless remained true that 'the Medical Officer in any parish is about the most unpopular officer. If he does his duty he makes enemies of all the small property owners whilst he displeases the many whose first idea is to keep down the rates'.[19] The image of the earnest MOH fighting a recalcitrant Vestry was kept alive by such *causes célèbres* as those of William Rendle in St George-the-Martyr and a succession of Medical Officers in St Pancras.[20]

The explosion of concern over urban housing conditions sparked by Andrew Mearns's pamphlet *The Bitter Cry of Outcast London* in October 1883 brought renewed scrutiny of the Vestries' sanitary record. Those moved by the pamphlet included the Queen at Balmoral, who asked the Prime Minister what was being done to improve the dwellings of her poorer subjects. Gladstone faced a very full session, and was in any case inclined to believe that the limits of legislative originality in this field had already been reached. Taking the obvious escape, he assured the Queen that 'improvements in local government which he trusts are now at hand will lead to a sensible progress in this great subject'.[21] The first draft of the London Bill for the 1884 session was amended to give the Common Council a default power to enact tasks neglected by the District Councils, and in the third 1884 draft this power was explicitly related to questions of public health and housing.[22]

The polemical battle waged by Mearns and his predecessors had not been directed specifically at the local authorities, but the Vestries did possess almost all the relevant sanitary powers, as well as local slum clearance powers under the Torrens Act of 1868, and they were inferentially open to criticism on the housing question. This was fortunate for the reformers, who had been attempting to discredit the Vestries since February 1883, when Firth had engaged the Radical journalist Carey Taylor at £5 per week to gather local scandal.[23] His report, forwarded to the Home Office in March, had been random and rather anecdotal.

---

[19] Booth MS, B 214, 177 (W. J. Wetenhall).

[20] The St Pancras MOH in 1898 claimed that his two predecessors had been 'worried out of' their posts: ibid., B 214, 19 (J. F. Sykes). For details see Sheppard's ch. in D. Owen, *The Government of Victorian London* (Cambridge, Mass., and London, 1982), 299–302; and for Rendle ibid., 306–12.

[21] Victoria to Gladstone and Gladstone to Victoria, 4 Nov. 1883, copies in Add. MS 43875, fos. 146–8.

[22] MS Harcourt, Dep. 109/6 and 109/8.

[23] Firth to Harcourt, 6 Feb. 1883, MS Harcourt, Dep. 108/39. The contract and assorted papers are ibid., Dep. 108/43 and 108/61–6. Taylor's report is Dep. 108/67–83.

Harcourt appears to have made no use of it, perhaps heeding Sir Henry Jenkyns's warning that 'it is not desirable for you, as Secretary of State, to be mixed up with this mode of getting information'.[24]

By early October, however, responsibility for the generation of scandal *had* passed to ministerial level, as Dilke was reported to be scrutinizing the London Vestries.[25] *The Bitter Cry* focused his attention. On 9 November a meeting was held between Harcourt, Dilke, and Chamberlain at the Home Office at which, to quote the Dilke Journal, 'Harcourt agreed to let me do what I pleased in his name or my own as to fighting the vestries about the dwellings of the poor.'[26] On the same day Dilke wrote to Lyulph Stanley and others seeking details of London's fever dens, and in particular of 'cases as to which the Medical Officers have reported to the Vestry in the past and nothing has been done yet'.[27] A few days later he started a tour of London's black spots, which proved almost fruitless. Shoreditch, 'the worst district fifteen years ago', had now improved to the extent that 'it would be impossible to declare Shoreditch Vestry in default'. Limehouse District Board was less active but not openly culpable. Bermondsey Vestry could be attacked 'if I don't find much worse places', but could point to 'a great and steady reduction in the death rate'. St George-the-Martyr was 'not so bad as I expected'. On 19 November Dilke failed, after what must have been a cursory investigation, to 'find any really bad spots in Lambeth'.[28] He was rescued by 'a very strong and detailed anonymous letter', relating to the condition of houses on the Northampton estate in Clerkenwell, sent to Lord William Compton, son of the Marquis of Northampton.[29] Compton's investigations, which he communicated to Dilke, indicated the neglect of poorer property on the estate by the intermediate lessees, including Decimus Ball, a prominent Clerkenwell Vestryman.[30] The possibility of charging the Vestries not merely with neglecting the slums, but with exploiting them, occurred to Dilke, who forwarded the material to Harcourt, adding that 'we shall have no legal case but a splendid House of Commons case against Clerkenwell'.[31]

[24] Jenkyns to Harcourt, 16 Mar. 1883, MS Harcourt, Dep. 108/56.
[25] *Metropolitan*, 6 Oct. 1883.
[26] Dilke Journal, Add MS 43937, fo. 179.
[27] Dilke to Stanley, 9 Nov. 1883, Add. MS 43912, fo. 174.
[28] For these visits see Dilke to Harcourt, 12, 14, 15, 19 Nov. 1883, Add. MS 43890, fos. 250, 252, 254, 256.
[29] Dilke Journal, Add. MS 43937, fo. 205.
[30] W. M. C[ompton] to Dilke, 24 Nov. 1883, Add. MS 43912, fo. 181.
[31] Dilke to Harcourt, 24 Nov. 1883, Add. MS 43890, fo. 260.

In pushing the Clerkenwell housing question Dilke was, as he probably realized, wading into the mire of Finsbury Liberal politics. The reconstruction of the Finsbury Liberal Association in the early 1880s had not reconciled Liberalism and Radicalism. Finsbury had a strong and independent Radical tradition, recently invoked in the Bradlaugh case, which eventually gave rise to the Finsbury Clubs Radical Association, formed in May 1884 to federate the borough's nine Radical Clubs.[32] Membership was limited to those accepting a programme based upon that of the Chelsea clubs, a test imposed 'in order not to be swamped by Whigs',[33] and the Association was intended to 'act in healthy rivalry' with the reformed Finsbury Liberal Association. Healthy rivalry manifested itself in the interruption of Liberal Association meetings,[34] and in a series of battles on Clerkenwell Vestry. There the Radicals were led by J. F. Kelly, a Municipal Reform Leaguer, and included the two men who would testify against the Vestry to Dilke's Royal Commission on the Housing of the Working Classes in March 1884, Thomas Jennings and Samuel Brighty, both also Leaguers.[35] Their attacks were directed not so much at the FLA 'establishment' embodied by the churchwarden William Robson, author of the most articulate defence of the Vestry,[36] but at the 'Old Radical' right, and in particular John Ross, the 'dictator of Clerkenwell', and his colleague Decimus Ball. Ross and Ball both 'farmed' slum property on the Northampton estate,[37] and the emergence of the housing agitation had made them vulnerable on that front. It was almost certainly Kelly who supplied Dilke with the information behind his 'splendid House of Commons case' against Vestry house-farmers.[38]

In December 1883 the Local Government Board issued two circulars to London local authorities reminding them, first, of their responsibilities under existing housing legislation and, secondly, of their permissive powers under section 35 of the 1866 Sanitary Act to inspect and regulate houses let in lodgings or occupied by more than one family. Attached to

[32] *Islington Gazette*, 11 Apr., 8 May 1884.

[33] F. A. Ford at the Patriotic Club, ibid., 8 May 1884.

[34] See e.g. *Holborn Guardian*, 5 July 1884.

[35] LMRL, *Fourth Annual Report*, 7–8. For Brighty's earlier Reform League activities see R. Harrison, *Before the Socialists* (London and Toronto, 1965), ch. 4.

[36] W. Robson, *Sir Charles Dilke and the Clerkenwell Vestry* (1884).

[37] RC Housing of the Working Classes, *PP 1884–5*, xxx, QQ. 623–6 (Compton).

[38] Cf. Dilke to Harcourt, 4 July 1884, Add. MS 43890, fo. 292: 'As for this City agitation, I sent a good deal of similar information to Firth yesterday ... any quantity of it can be got from Kelly of Clerkenwell for nothing.' Kelly told his Vestry that 'he did not know who gave Sir Charles Dilke information, but in the interests of the public, he would not scruple to have shown such a state of affairs': *Islington Gazette*, 10 Mar. 1884.

the second circular was a set of model regulations for tenement houses to guide those Vestries, nineteen in number, that had yet to produce bye-laws of their own. These regulations were of such provocative complexity that it is difficult to resist the conclusion that they were designed to annoy the Vestries rather than to reduce overcrowding.[39] Whether or not this was their design, it was certainly their effect. St Saviour's considered them 'impracticable', Shoreditch claimed to have adopted three sets already since 1866 and found them all unworkable, and Bethnal Green complained that 'an army of inspectors would be wanted'.[40] The Vestry Clerk of Clerkenwell was not alone, therefore, in considering the regulations 'of too inquisitorial a character'.[41]

The realization that the housing question could be used to promote municipal reform led the Lord Mayor to convene a conference of housing philanthropists and Conservative politicians, including Salisbury and C. T. Ritchie, which gave birth to the Mansion House Council on the Dwellings of the Poor.[42] Salisbury himself, as a large London landlord, was moved by more than opposition to municipal reform. The housing furore spurred him to an uncharacteristically enthusiastic response to a social issue, with an article in the *National Review* in November calling for a Royal Commission on the question.[43] The government had not pressed the subject to see it buried in a Royal Commission, but had no real answer to Salisbury's motion, which was accepted at the beginning of the 1884 session.[44] It had the advantage that under Dilke's chairmanship it provided another forum for the attack upon the Vestries.

On 21 February 1884 Clerkenwell Vestry referred back to its Sanitary Committee a set of tenement house regulations framed along the lines of

---

[39] Both letters and a digest of the regulations are given in *The Times*, 2 Jan. 1884. The regulations stipulated, among other things, that each adult enjoy 300 cubic feet of air and each child under ten 150 cubic feet, that lodgers sweep all courts and communal areas and keep WCs in order, that they sweep the floors of their rooms daily and wash them weekly, and that every window be opened for at least two hours each day—weather permitting. The provisions were to be enforced by Vestries with a sanitary staff consisting usually of one Medical Officer and two or three inspectors. In Clerkenwell they would have been applicable to 4,700 houses, according to a Home Office inspector: see 'Report by D. Cubitt Nichols, Esq., on the Sanitary Condition of the Parish of Clerkenwell', *PP 1886*, LVI.

[40] See the replies to the circular sent out by Clerkenwell Vestry: Clerkenwell Vestry Minutes, 13 Mar. 1884.

[41] RC Housing of the Working Classes, *PP 1884–5*, XXX, Q. 17533 (Paget).

[42] *The Times*, 12 Dec. 1883. For the origins of the MHC see also *London*, 25 June 1896.

[43] Lord Salisbury, 'Artisans' and Labourers' Dwellings', *National Review* (1883), 301–16.

[44] *Hansard*, 3rd ser., CCLXXXV, 1–2 (26 Feb. 1884).

the LGB circular.[45] Within a month Dilke had called Thomas Jennings and Samuel Brighty, present and former chairmen of the Sanitary Committee, to testify against the Vestry before the Royal Commission. The Vestry was given only twenty-four hours' notice of their appearance,[46] and had to press for five months to secure a hearing for the Vestry clerk in its defence. Neither Jennings nor Brighty proved very forthcoming on oath; neither mentioned any other occasion of Vestry obstruction of the Sanitary Committee, and Jennings acknowledged that 'most of our recommendations have been adopted'.[47] He did, however, accept, on Dilke's prompting, that thirteen Vestrymen, from a complement of seventy, were interested in slum property.[48] In the Commons Dilke glossed this to mean that 'Chairman after Chairman of that Committee had reported in favour of sanitary reforms in that parish, which had been year after year vetoed by the Vestry, the majority of the members of which were interested in the property it was proposed to deal with'.[49] George Russell, his Parliamentary Secretary, alleged that the house-farmers had secured majorities on the Vestry's Works, Assessment and Finance Committees, although apparently not on the Sanitary Committee.[50]

The allegations against Clerkenwell did not greatly assist the London Government Bill but, amplified by the Royal Commission report in 1885, they did serve to vilify the image of the London Vestries so effectively as to convince both contemporaries and historians.[51] The argument that an otherwise adequate body of sanitary laws was blocked by recalcitrant local authorities should never have been entirely convincing, but it was allowed to prevail because both sides wished to accept it—Conservatives in order to preclude more interventionist sanitary legislation and Liberals in order to promote the reform of the existing authorities. Its most important effect was to be felt in the 1890s, when a reformist LCC, habitually convinced of Vestry malevolence, would encounter a self-defensive second tier anxious to resist first-tier encroachment. The consequent two-tier suspicion goes some way to explain the eventual shape of London reform.

[45] Clerkenwell Vestry Minutes, 21 Feb. 1884. For the regulations see ibid., 21 Jan. 1884.
[46] Robson, *Sir Charles Dilke*, 6.
[47] RC Housing of the Working Classes, *PP 1884–5*, XXX, Q. 2040 (Jennings).
[48] Ibid., QQ. 2949–70 (Jennings).
[49] *Hansard*, 3rd ser., CCXC, 70 (4 July 1884).
[50] Ibid. 534 (8 July 1884).
[51] Owen, *The Government of Victorian London*, 222; Wohl, *The Eternal Slum*, (1977), 126 ff., for rehearsals of the Clerkenwell allegations.

6. THE FATE OF THE BILL

If Harcourt was really 'never so happy as when he was fighting a hopeless battle against overwhelming odds', he must have thoroughly enjoyed his fight for the London Bill in 1884.[52] Strict subordination to the Franchise Bill ensured that its chances were always negligible. The second reading as late as 3 July was 'very much like Obstruction'.[53] It had been rumoured early in June that Harcourt had promised his back-benchers not to take the Bill beyond a second reading vote, and early in July he was pressed to drop it immediately.[54] In the event the government settled for a division on an adjournment motion on 8 July. This was won, but on the same night the Cairns amendment to the Reform Bill in the Lords led to the announcement of an autumn session devoted to franchise alone, and Gladstone took the opportunity for a wholesale sacrifice of lost causes. On 10 July the London Government Bill was dropped.[55]

The remainder of the ministry's life offered little more for the reformers. The report of the City Guilds Commission was published too late to affect discussion of the Bill; in any case, such inflated estimates had been made of the pickings to be had from the Livery Companies that the Commission's conclusions were inevitably an anti-climax.[56] There was still scope for the statutory reorganization of the Companies, and the Commissioners recommended useful reforms, but these had little bearing upon the municipal issue. Firth had wildly predicted an income of around £1 million per annum to be realized for the new municipality by an attack upon the Livery Companies,[57] but his motion to disendow and disestablish the Companies was defeated on the Commission by ten votes to two.[58] Even the report that was produced threatened to create tension within the Cabinet, Lord Selborne, a member of the Mercer's Company, being strongly opposed to legislation.[59] Dilke produced a short Bill to prevent the Companies from alienating their property in anticipation of more comprehensive legislation, but it fell a victim of the breakup of the

[52] A. L. Armstrong, in *Dictionary of National Biography* (Compact edn., Oxford, 1975) ii. 2680.

[53] C. T. Ritchie in the Commons, *Hansard*, 3rd ser., CCLXXXIX, 1944 (3 July 1884).

[54] *Metropolitan*, 7 June 1884; *The Times*, 5 July 1884.

[55] *Hansard*, 3rd ser., CCXC, 575 (8 July 1884), 666 (10 July 1884).

[56] RC City of London Livery Companies, *PP 1884*, XXXIX, 1–4.

[57] *The Times*, 6 Dec. 1883.

[58] RC Livery Companies, *PP 1884*, XXXIX, Dissent Report, 70.

[59] Dilke to Gladstone, 13 Dec. 1884, Add. MS 44149, fo. 296.

government in 1885.[60] No serious consideration appears to have been given to the reintroduction of the London Bill in 1885.

The 1884 Bill would have become law, for all its weaknesses, had it been given an unimpeded passage through Parliament. It was opposed by almost every London local authority and aroused virtually no interest among the metropolitan population, but in Britain local government reform is statute-based, and does not require the consent of endangered authorities or any evidence of popular enthusiasm. Although the City's near-illegal opposition to the Bill attracted considerable attention and left the impression of successful obstruction by a vested interest, the City could not have offered effective resistance to the parliamentary passage of a measure with committed government backing. Second-tier opposition to the Bill's suppression of parochial autonomy carried more authority, and it is possible that local powers would have been enhanced at the committee stage had the Bill got that far, but it would have remained in essence a centralizing measure. The only obstacles to its passage lay in the parliamentary timetable.

They were, though, substantial obstacles. A feature of each of the Gladstone ministries was the ministerial sponsorship of a plethora of Bills designed to satisfy sectional Liberal lobbies. The practice of 'starting bills which were certain to run into difficulties and then not allowing enough time for the resolution of these difficulties' became a routine means of keeping the 'fissiparous elements' of the party occupied, if not contented.[61] In 1883 the London Bill had benefited from the competition for priority among the various reform options, and the dissipation of its tactical promotion was fatal. In 1884 it suffered heavily from having to compete with the franchise.

In this light, reform appears dependent upon the casual ebb and flow of political opportunity and upon the Liberal leadership's assessment of the advantages to be gained by propitiating one section of the party or by deferring progress on other measures. The London system was certainly much in need of repair, but there is little to suggest that its inadequacies were the reason for the government's interest in reform. Harcourt's deference to the Firthite single municipality showed how little departmental consideration had been given to the mechanics of the London problem. The reformers themselves were scarcely more

---

[60] *PP 1884–5*, III, Bill 210.

[61] H. C. G. Matthew (ed.), Introduction to *The Gladstone Diaries*, vii (Oxford, 1982), lxvi–lxvii.

sophisticated. Their main concern lay in bringing the City to heel along with the lesser sinister interests of the MBW and the Vestries. This had determined a centralizing solution almost regardless of the objections to centralization felt by many who were not apologists for the existing bodies. Little attempt was made to exploit the real grievances that the system had generated: London reform was never convincingly presented as a ratepayers' or public utility consumers' issue, and while the housing crisis *was* dragged into the arena, the way in which it was linked to municipal reform appeared more opportunistic than was necessary. No effort was made to play off East End interests against those of the West, or the second tier against the first. Little was done to cultivate Vestry Radicalism, and the London Municipal Reform League stood aside deliberately from Vestry elections. Instead the reformers' obsessive pursuit of a centralized system put *them* on the defensive; the disadvantages of the single municipality were scrutinized *ad nauseam*, while the manifest failings of the existing structure received relatively little attention.

The consequence of this neglect was the promotion of a scheme which had very little support among Vestrymen, ratepayers, and other 'consumers' of local government services. With London government essentially a pawn in the game of élite politics in 1884, their objections need not have prevented the Bill from becoming law, but a system commanding so little enthusiasm from those to be governed by it and those likely to operate it was unlikely to survive long unamended. The 1884 agitation had brought little progress towards the solution of the structural problems of metropolitan government, except in the negative sense that the single municipality had emerged as a model to be avoided. Politically, however, London government had been forced on to the reform agenda; Firth and his League could claim at least that success.

4

The Fall of the Metropolitan Board, 1885–1889

1. RECONSIDERATION OF REFORM

By the time of the Gladstone ministry's fall in June 1885 London government reform had attained the status of 'unfinished business', and whatever the weaknesses of the 1884 Bill the view had been implanted that legislation could not be much longer deferred. It was reinforced by the effects of the 1885 redistribution, which did belated parliamentary justice to the metropolis by raising the number of MPs outside the City from eighteen to fifty-seven and reducing the City's quota from four to two. London issues would no longer be neglected on account of the capital's parliamentary weakness.

The prospect of reform galvanized both the Corporation and the second tier into action. On the day after the Harcourt Bill was dropped the City's Special Committee asked Common Council for power to consider the general question of London government and—a measure of the pressing need for a plausible Corporation alternative—to confer with other local authorities.[1] At the end of March 1885 a colloquium of Special Committee members and senior Corporation officers was held, at which the policy of incorporating the old parliamentary boroughs was hesitantly endorsed, despite the imminence of redistribution.[2] In July, after the change of government, the Committee resolved to test the intentions of the new Home Secretary, R. A. Cross. A deputation was sent on 31 July and received in a secrecy which defied parliamentary questions.[3] The Committee appears to have mooted a separate municipalities scheme based upon either the old parliamentary boroughs or the water company areas—the latter suggesting that the central body would be deprived even of

---

[1] Corporation Special Committee Minutes, 11 July 1884.
[2] Special Committee Minute Papers, March 1885. G. N. Johnson considered 'the time for separate Municipalities gone', and the Chamberlain, Benjamin Scott, believed the policy 'broken up by the Seats Bill', but Alderman De Keyser insisted that 'a number of municipalities ... is the certain future of London'.
[3] *Hansard*, 3rd ser., CCC, 1732 (11 Aug. 1885).

water supply.[4] Cross was predictably non-committal, indicating that the government had not had time to examine the question, and that any measure would have to wait for a future session—a somewhat empty promise in view of the government's minority position. He did, however, draw attention to the two most significant weaknesses of the scheme, asking the Committee what it intended to do with the Metropolitan Board and indicating that it 'would not do to have any municipality consisting entirely of poor houses'. He also appears to have suggested that, if the proposals were worked into a complete scheme, the government would give it careful consideration.[5]

The Special Committee took this hint seriously enough to mould their ideas into the most complete reform scheme to emerge from the Corporation throughout this period. Their report, presented to Common Council on 5 November 1885, was received in camera but extensively leaked to *The Times*.[6] It retained the old parliamentary boroughs as municipalities, endowing each with a mayor, aldermen, burgesses, and a commission of the peace. Grasping the nettle avoided by the Local Government and Taxation Committee in 1870, it envisaged a central body constituted in a rather awkward manner—directly elected by the ratepayers, but from a field confined to members of the secondary bodies. This amounted to an ingenious way of abandoning the indirect election which had made the MBW unpopular without allowing the unfettered direct election which could encourage the first tier to dominate the second; members would owe their primary allegiance to the local bodies. Ultimately, however, the restriction of the first tier would depend upon the extent of its powers, and here the Committee remained ambiguous. It spoke of the surrender of some central government powers over parks, public works, and buildings to the new metropolitan authority, but did not specify whether the Corporation would itself surrender any powers, or whether any first-tier functions would be devolved. This reticence frightened some City fundamentalists into projecting the creation of a 'new Frankenstein' of a central body, devouring the City lands and the Coal dues;[7] *The Times*' informant believed that it would retain most MBW functions and acquire the police.[8] In fact there was little chance

---

[4] Special Committee Minute Papers, July 1885, esp. MS Notes marked 'Mr Johnson'. See also Special Committee Minutes, 31 July 1885.
[5] See *The Times*, 6 Nov. 1885 (report of Common Council meeting), also *Metropolitan*, 16 Jan. 1886.
[6] Common Council Minutes, 1885, report No. 55; *The Times*, 6 Nov. 1885.
[7] *City Press*, 14 Nov. 1885; see also Special Committee Minutes, 16 Nov. 1885.
[8] *The Times*, 6 Nov. 1885.

that a Committee which had wasted so much Corporation income manufacturing a separate-municipalities movement in 1884 would now seek to endow any central body so lavishly. The Committee's minutes show that the only functions intended for the central body were those of main drainage, water, and light; in the report the central body was pointedly given the power 'to hand over to the respective boroughs any of such property and duties as the boroughs might conveniently hold and perform'.[9] The most interesting feature of the proposals was the provision intended to encourage this, by which the Corporation would be empowered to make an annual contribution from the City cash to each of the new boroughs.[10] Like Onslow's acceptance of rate equalization fourteen years later,[11] it indicated a realization that devolution, to be plausible, would have to be subsidized by those who sought it.

The Committee's proposals left much unclear—the financial relationship between the tiers, the fate of the two police forces and the fire brigade, the internal reform of the Corporation. Nevertheless, the scheme was sufficiently comprehensive to encourage the Corporation to communicate it to the second-tier authorities. Its reception indicated how remote the City had become from Vestry opinion. The main ground for second-tier complaint was that 'tenification' would entail the obliteration of parochial identity. If the Corporation had anticipated that the spirit of localism would allow devolution to be pursued at the expense of Vestry independence, it had been mistaken. In Marylebone 'the [Parliamentary] Committee were unable to concur in the idea of ten municipalities that would be very little better than one. The proposed arrangement was an attempt to coalise incongruous atoms. Under it St Pancras, Paddington and Marylebone, which had recently been divorced, were to be reunited for parochial purposes'.[12] The view expressed in Marylebone that 'the very fact that the scheme returned to the divisions of the old [parliamentary] boroughs condemned it'[13] was echoed in the resolution carried by thirty-one votes to three in St George's, Hanover Square.[14] That devolution should fail to carry even those West End parishes that carried so much of the burden of an integrated metropolitan system was a measure

---

[9] Special Committee Minutes, 24 Sept. 1885, Report, 3.

[10] Ibid., 2.

[11] See below, pp. 240–1.

[12] Edmund Boulnois, quoted in the *Marylebone Independent*, 9 Jan. 1886.

[13] Admiral Oliver, quoted ibid.

[14] *Metropolitan*, 16 Jan. 1886. For the terms of the resolution see St George's, Hanover Square, Vestry, *Annual Report*, (1885–6), 40.

of the lack of appeal of 'tenification' and the resilience of parochial identity.

The promulgation of the Corporation proposals led some secondary authorities to construct schemes of their own. Westminster District Board chose the softest option by calling for a Royal Commission, summoning a Vestry conference to endorse the demand for 'a searching investigation by an unbiassed authority'.[15] Islington Vestry adopted a scheme proposing a district council for Islington and each of the twenty-seven *new* parliamentary boroughs outside the City, with a central body to inherit the powers of the Corporation, the City Commissioners of Sewers, and the Metropolitan Board.[16] In December 1885 St Pancras Vestry, like Islington an authority governing an area and population larger than most provincial municipalities, voted unanimously against the Corporation's proposals[17] and in favour of its own scheme for a central municipality and independent local authorities, apparently in the new parliamentary boroughs. It too convened a Vestry conference, which met in January and February 1886.[18] The City proposals were dismissed as 'unworthy of the present day' by the author of the St Pancras scheme, the future LCC Moderate T. B. Westacott.[19] A motion tabled by G. N. Johnson, delegate of the City Commission of Sewers and a member of the Special Committee, calling for the central body to be 'confined to the management of such matters of public service as cannot be performed by the District Authorities ... such as main drainage and the supply of water and light', was defeated at the second session. Instead the conference adopted a modified version of the St Pancras scheme, calling for a central body to replace the Corporation, the MBW, and the Metropolitan Asylums Board, and to supply water and light, and for consolidated district authorities exercising *all* second-tier functions within areas to be determined.[20]

In the mid-1880s, then, there was still broad second-tier agreement on

[15] For the proceedings see the papers on the Conference on London Government, Westminster DB, 1885, Westminster Archives, E3391.
[16] *Metropolitan*, 14 Nov. 1885. See also the summary of the scheme in Special Committee Minute Papers, Jan. 1886.
[17] *Metropolitan*, 26 Dec. 1885.
[18] For its proceedings see T. E. Gibb, *The Municipal Government of the Metropolis* (1886). Young's repeated assertion (K. Young, 'The Politics of London Government, 1880–1899', *Public Administration*, 51 (1973), and K. Young and P. Garside, *Metropolitan London: Politics and Urban Change, 1837–1981* (1982), 55) that the St Pancras conference supported the City scheme and 'sent a deputation ... to press for its incorporation in legislation' is inexplicable.
[19] *Metropolitan*, 30 Jan. 1886.
[20] Gibb, *Municipal Government*.

the shape of reform. There was an almost unanimous aversion to 'a huge municipality for the whole of London as suggested by the late Home Secretary'.[21] But this stemmed from an anxiety to preserve parochial independence rather than from any sympathy for the Corporation. Consequently there was little opposition to the concept of a substantial first-tier body as long as it limited itself to recognizably metropolitan objects, and certainly no inclination to embark upon a programme of wholesale devolution that, to become feasible, would require second-tier amalgamations. In the wake of the attack of 1884 there was certainly an anxiety to see second-tier functions preserved and even expanded, but the tendency was to look for 'horizontal' transfers from other local bodies,[22] which would not affect the balance of first- and second-tier taxation, rather than devolution from the central body.

In the meantime the London Municipal Reform League had begun its own reappraisal of policy which carried it away from the single municipality. In June 1885 the League's Executive Council had approved resolutions calling for largely independent local bodies in addition to the central municipality,[23] and a Committee had been appointed to produce a new scheme. It reported in December, advocating a central body, directly elected, to handle main and local drainage, bridges, street improvements, fire brigade, licensing, water, and gas, and district councils in the Vestry areas to handle assessment, sanitation, the Adulteration Acts, weights and measures, and street maintenance. Both tiers would have powers over parks, libraries, baths, and markets.[24] Lloyd noted that 'some few of our members' opposed the departure from the single municipality principle; when the sub-committee reported, 'some difference of opinion prevailed as to whether the Report should be adopted or not'.[25] The meeting of 22 December resolved to accept it without binding the League to its proposals, and the position was only partially clarified by the adoption, at special sessions in January and February 1886, of Hobhouse's motion accepting the two-tier system in principle, without resort to details.[26] Nevertheless, even this compromise represented a

[21] T. B. Westacott to J. E. Smith (Westminster DB Clerk), 15 Oct. 1885, with Westminster DB Papers on the Conference on London Government, Westminster Archives.

[22] For example of the powers of the semi-autonomous commissioners for baths and libraries, burial boards and, occasionally, poor-law guardians.

[23] J. Lloyd, *London Municipal Government History of a Great Reform, 1880–1888* (1910), 62.

[24] Ironically, the only surviving copy of the report appears to be that in Special Committee Minute Papers, May 1886. It is summarized in *Metropolitan*, 9 Jan. 1886.

[25] Lloyd, *London Municipal Government*, 62.

[26] *Metropolitan*, 30 Jan., 13 Feb. 1886.

defeat for Firth. At the League's annual meeting in February, 'not a very jubilant function',[27] he indicated his intention to resign the presidency.

2. THE GENESIS OF THE LOCAL GOVERNMENT ACT

Whatever the shape of reform, the chances of legislation depended, as always, upon the parliamentary situation. Ominously, the approach of the 1885 election induced both parties to subordinate London to county reform. Some Conservatives saw local government measures as a means of detaching moderate Liberals from the wreckage of the Gladstone ministry. Churchill's advocacy of a 'purely popular' reform of county government, involving 'a large and liberal measure of executive and local legislative power' in order to secure the 'positive co-operation of the Whigs' disturbed Salisbury, who preferred to advance a London separate-municipalities measure to avoid committing the party to the details of a county Bill.[28] Churchill tactfully dismissed this as 'an error in tactics of the largest kind',[29] and his view appears to have prevailed as, despite defeat in the election, the Queen's Speech promised county councils for Great Britain and Ireland[30]—making no mention of London—and Balfour at the Local Government Board had produced at least two draft County Bills by the time the ministry fell at the end of January.[31]

The Liberals juggled with the unfinished business with which they had left office. In October Gladstone had believed that 'the Irish question might delay Local Government, and that London Govt. might be taken first',[32] raising the possibility that metropolitan reform could be shuffled into primacy as in 1883, but the fate of the Harcourt Bill had raised doubts about the commitment of provincial Liberals to London reform, and extension of the county franchise had removed radical anxiety about a county government measure. Chamberlain anticipated that county government would be 'the first business undertaken by any Lib. Govt'.[33] The emergence of Home Rule in December only pushed London further

[27] Ibid., 27 Feb. 1886. For his unrepentant adhesion to the single municipality in 1888 see J. F. B. Firth, *The Reform of London Government and of the City Guilds* (1888), 31–2.
[28] For this exchange see W. S. Churchill, *Lord Randolph Churchill*, 2nd edn. (1907), 431–41.
[29] On the grounds that 'no one in the country, or in London either, gives a damn about a London municipality, nor would many municipalities attract them': ibid., 441.
[30] *Hansard*, 3rd ser., CCCII, 35 (21 Jan. 1886).
[31] One at Hatfield, 8 Jan. 1886 (HHP, B29), the other, of 23 Jan., in the PRO, HLG/29/18.
[32] See Chamberlain to Harcourt, 9 Oct. 1885, Joseph Chamberlain Papers, JC 5/38/151.
[33] Ibid.

down the agenda, and although the LMRL believed Gladstone's 1886 ministry to be 'crowded with our friends',[34] the new Home Secretary, H. C. E. Childers, fended off both parliamentary questions and a proposed deputation from the St Pancras conference.[35]

At the time of the Conservatives' return to office in July 1886, therefore, the county and London reform proposals were seen as rival projects, handled by different departments—the Local Government Board and the Home Office respectively—and competing for parliamentary time. In the event partial metropolitan reform came in 1888 on the back of the county measure. The political inspiration for this fusion must have come from the new President of the Local Government Board. C. T. Ritchie was a metropolitan Member, representing St George-in-the-East since redistribution, and had led the Commons opposition to the Bill of 1884. Considered 'a little wild, but ... manageable' by Smith,[36] Ritchie radicalized the early Balfour proposals in several respects in his drafts of November 1886.[37] The creation of a new London county was one of these changes and, significantly, the only one to pass into law.

This was probably because the independent administrative arguments for grafting London first-tier reform on to a county government measure were very strong. Under the Balfour proposals the county councils of Middlesex, Surrey and Kent would each have included a significant metropolitan contingent, in Middlesex almost certainly a majority. The MBW already possessed some county powers, so that metropolitan members of the Home County councils would have been unable to act or vote upon questions relating to those powers, and equity would have demanded a two-tier county rate to avoid double-charging London ratepayers. It is true that these were to be the expedients adopted to protect the City's autonomy in 1888, but they hardly commended themselves for application on a larger scale. The issue was further complicated by the question of rate relief. The overhaul of the existing piecemeal system of Exchequer aid to rural ratepayers was an essential component of county government reform, and one of the chief motives prompting a Conservative ministry to take up the problem. By virtually

[34] LMRL, *Fifth Annual Report* (1886), 24.
[35] *Hansard*, 3rd ser., CCCII, 711 (19 Feb. 1886); Gibb, *Municipal Government*, 17.
[36] W. H. Smith to Salisbury, 25 Nov. 1886, HHP.
[37] By dropping Balfour's aldermen, introducing District Councils with poor-law powers, creating a new London county and metropolitan district councils and, at first, proposing district council status for the City. ('Heads of a Bill', 12 and 15 Nov. 1886, PRO HLG/29/18.) Forwarding the proposals Ritchie warned Salisbury that 'you will consider them rather radical': Ritchie to Salisbury, 16 Nov. 1886, HHP.

any method of apportionment of Exchequer grants the Home Counties would benefit enormously from the inclusion of their metropolitan portions, and the ratepayers of extra-metropolitan Middlesex, Surrey, and Kent would receive a substantial and unjustified windfall. The alternative, however, would have been to confine the Home Counties' grants to their extra-metropolitan portions and entrust the metropolitan grants to the MBW. By 1888, when the Board's financial affairs were under the scrutiny of a Royal Commission, this would have been politically impossible,[38] and even in November 1886 it would have been difficult for a party which had not felt the confidence in the Board necessary to entrust it even with water supply in 1880.

The measure that became the Local Government (England and Wales) Act of 1888[39] therefore created a single London county authority based, like the other county councils, upon the principles of the 1882 Municipal Corporations Act,[40] replacing the MBW and the Justices in their administrative capacity. It proposed no new secondary bodies in London, leaving the Vestries and District Boards virtually unaffected.[41] The City was to be placed in a position relative to the county similar to that of a Quarter Sessions borough elsewhere; it was not to be given the complete autonomy of a county borough. The most conspicuous feature of the Bill's London clauses was, of course, the new directly elected first-tier authority consolidating municipal and county powers. Judged by its statutory capacity, the London County Council, lacking police, public utility and all second-tier powers, was hardly the municipal juggernaut that it was constantly alleged to be, and was weaker, in fact, than all the county boroughs. Nevertheless, it covered a larger population and rateable value than any other local authority in the country, and possessed more extensive power than any of its metropolitan predecessors.

When this power fell into Radical hands, the irony of its having been conferred by a Conservative government, headed by a man deeply suspicious of the potential of a metropolitan authority, became apparent. In the 1890s Conservative leaders claimed that they had always intended to balance the LCC by strong district councils, perhaps separate municipalities, and one recent authority has refined this claim into the unlikely

[38] As Firth pointed out in the Commons, *Hansard*, 3rd ser., CCCXXIV, 1746–7 (19 Apr. 1888).

[39] 51 & 52 Vict., c. 41. The London clauses are ss. 40–5.

[40] Although triennially elected.

[41] They were empowered to seek metropolitan support for main road maintenance and for payment of half the salary of their Medical Officers. J. F. B. Firth and E. R. Simpson, *London Government under the Local Government Act, 1888* (1888), 2.

hypothesis that the government was forced by 'the demands of cabinet unity' after Goschen's admission in January 1887 to drop plans for 'relatively powerful district councils' in London.[42] In fact no district council proposals for London appear in any of the surviving drafts. The only mention of them is in Ritchie's two 'Heads of a Bill' of November 1886, and they were probably dropped with poor-law powers and provincial district councils in the same month[43]—before Goschen's inclusion. Why they were not reinstated with the provincial district councils is unclear. Possibly they were seen to present greater problems than the provincial councils because, unlike them, they entailed the reorganization and amalgamation of existing statutory authorities.[44] There may also have been the consideration that second-tier reform in London would emphasize the anomalous privileges of the City, although the government was clearly bound to stand by the Corporation whatever the consequent discomfort. Whatever the explanation, the fact remains that Ritchie's suggested second-tier bodies would have possessed only Vestry powers,[45] as indeed would those that he proposed in 1891. They could not have been intended to effect a fundamental decentralization of the London system by their mere existence. Similarly their removal from the Bill did not mean that there was to be no second tier, only that the Vestries survived for, in the event, another eleven years.

There can be no doubt that the two-tier balance effected in 1888 was of Ritchie's own devising; indeed his attempts to reinforce it in 1890–1 would offend the Vestries. The only misgivings expressed within the Cabinet appear to have come from Salisbury, who had advocated separate municipalities publicly in 1884 and privately in his correspondence with Churchill in 1885. Ritchie met them in December 1886 with the courageously misleading claims that the MBW already possessed virtually all county powers, and that his own district council proposals reflected those

---

[42] K. Young, *Local Politics and the Rise of Party* (Leicester, 1975), 37. It seems most unlikely that with a new political coalition in the making, the fate of the Union in the balance, and the chance of high office at stake, Goschen would have stalled over the structure of London's second tier. Young's claim rests entirely upon one letter from Salisbury written eight years after the event.

[43] See Salisbury to Victoria, 26 Nov. 1886, HHP.

[44] The provincial district councils would have covered existing urban and rural sanitary district areas; see Local Government (England and Wales) Bill, *PP 1888*, IV, Bill 182, s. 41. Ritchie's original 'Heads' of 12 Nov. 1886 envisaged London district councils occupying the ten School Board divisions; some rationalization would certainly have been necessary.

[45] 'Heads of a Bill', PRO HLG/29/18.

of the Corporation's Special Committee in November 1885.[46] Salisbury's response is unclear, but as late as December 1887 the Cabinet was considering the administrative and judicial implications of creating a single London county authority, and contemplating 'the half measure' of giving some county powers to the LCC and leaving others with the Home County councils.[47] If it was this uncomfortable expedient that Goschen objected to, he was unlikely to have been alone; clearly the Cabinet as a whole rejected it, as the LCC remained part of the London clauses, comparatively unfettered.[48]

In fact to assume that the Conservatives in 1888 were anxious for party reasons to inhibit the scope of the first-tier body is to anticipate a reaction that would only occur when Radicalism had captured the Council, and was not to be universal even then. Dr Young's claim that the 1888 Act was forced by the government upon metropolitan Conservatives, 'who saw it, at best, as a stop-gap measure', is at variance with the evidence.[49] 'Tenification', in the sense of the amalgamation of secondary areas to allow full-blooded devolution, was never more than a minority cause among Conservatives in this period, and certainly not in 1888. It offended

[46] Ritchie to Salisbury, 17 Dec. 1886, HHP. The county powers already exercised by the MBW were trivial—Infant Life Protection Act, cattle plague, petroleum and explosive regulation powers (see the memorandum of 8 Dec. 1887 in PRO HLG/29/20). Those to be transferred included reformatory and industrial schools, asylums (as Ritchie acknowledged), and music and theatre licensing. All except asylums were potentially controversial. Although Ritchie claimed that 'so far as the central body is concerned the body recommended by the Committee is the same as proposed in the Bill', this was quite untrue. The Special Committee envisaged a body considerably weaker than the MBW; Ritchie was proposing one still stronger. Whether or not Ritchie convinced Salisbury, he appears to have convinced Young, who argues that the Special Committee's plan 'barely differed from Ritchie's'. K. G. Young, 'The London Municipal Society, 1894–1963', Ph.D. thesis (London University, 1973), 31.

[47] Memorandum of 8 Dec. 1887, PRO HLG/29/20.

[48] It still lacked police powers, transfer of which had never been considered, and power to promote Bills (although it did inherit the MBW's private Bill powers), and remained bound by the various financial strictures applying to the MBW.

[49] Young claims that the Bill 'failed to placate Conservative feeling: a far more congenial private members' bill to establish thirteen powerful boroughs and a weak metropolitan council had been introduced in 1887 and 1888 by backbench Conservatives, but had been withdrawn under government pressure with the advent of the Ritchie bill.' K. Young, 'The Conservative Strategy for London, 1855–1975', *London Journal*, 1 (1975), 59. The Bills are in *PP 1887*, iv, Bill 82, and *PP 1888*, v, Bill 14. The 'thirteen powerful boroughs' would have possessed only Vestry and commissioners' powers and so, without poor-law functions, would have been weaker than Ritchie's original proposed district councils. The 'weak metropolitan council' would have inherited all MBW powers, along with power to frame schemes for gas and water purchase and for the amalgamation of the two police forces. There is no evidence that anybody considered the 1888 Act to be 'a stop-gap measure', and Young provides none.

the parochial instincts of most London Conservatives, instincts already aroused by the 1884 Bill. In October 1887 R. G. Webster, Conservative Member for East St Pancras and a St George, Hanover Square, Vestryman, had considered the creation of ten or twelve municipalities—'mere shams'—to be 'a great mistake'.[50] Similarly C. A. Whitmore, Dilke's conqueror at Chelsea, won applause from his constituency association by asserting that 'a great deal of the apathy of Londoners in the past had been due to the artificiality of the areas' and calling, in any district council's measure, for 'natural areas' which were 'coherent and had a vigorous local life'.[51]

London Conservatives did not accept that they had any reason to fear a popularly elected central body. The party had won forty-five out of the fifty-nine London seats in the 1886 general election. There seemed every reason to anticipate a similar majority on the municipal body, which was elected from the same areas and on what was likely to be a more conservative franchise;[52] certainly it was unlikely that anybody could have anticipated Radical control of the Council for its first eighteen years. There is no evidence of the 'profound suspicion' of the new body that Young claims was shown by metropolitan Conservatives.[53] G. C. T. Bartley, Member for North Islington and later one of the most acerbic critics of the Council, predicted in the second reading debate that 'the establishment of a County Council for London would do an enormous amount of good'.[54] A. A. Baumann, Member for Peckham and another later critic, also welcomed the Council and urged Conservatives to campaign for a party majority upon it.[55]

There was, therefore, no significant measure of spontaneous support for 'tenification' in Conservative ranks. Its only justification could have been the defence of the City, and Ritchie's Bill effected this in other ways. The Bill as introduced treated the City as a borough within a county, as indeed it now was. In the provinces the Bill recognized two types of boroughs within counties—the Quarter Sessions boroughs of over 10,000 inhabitants, which would retain such county powers as they already possessed while admitting county council jurisdiction in respect of other county functions, and the sixty-one County Boroughs, including

---

[50] *Metropolitan*, 29 Oct 1887.

[51] *West London Press and Chelsea News*, 24 Mar. 1888.

[52] Including rated women and peers, but excluding lodgers.

[53] Young, 'The Conservative Strategy for London', 59.

[54] *Hansard*, 3rd ser., cccxxv, 67 (20 Apr. 1888).

[55] A. A. Baumann, 'The London Clauses of the Local Government Bill', *National Review*, 11 (1888), 552.

all the reformed municipalities of more than 50,000 inhabitants (and four of less), which became autonomous authorities with both county and municipal powers. The City had been one of only eleven County Boroughs planned in the Balfour drafts of January 1886, and it had contained over 50,000 people in 1881, but despite the expansion of the County Borough schedule it was treated as a Quarter Sessions Borough in the final Bill.

The City's failure to achieve County Borough status was an indication that the government would not have one separate municipality in the metropolis, let alone ten. Its success in gaining Quarter Sessions Borough status, however, marked the recognition that it was more than just a London local area. The result was that the City remained a judicial county in itself, but was included in the 'administrative county of London' created by the Bill. The MBW's powers within the City passed to its successor, and the Corporation's Court of Aldermen even yielded—by a provision which would have been furiously resisted had it come from a Liberal government—some county powers to the LCC.[56] The Corporation's Special Committee, characteristically seeking the best of all worlds, deputed the City Remembrancer to press Ritchie for both County Borough status and increased representation on the LCC.[57] He came away believing that 'the City of London is to remain a county distinct from the administrative county of London',[58] but no change was made. The 1888 Act effectively ratified the position that had developed since 1855, by which the Corporation paid for substantial constitutional autonomy and the avoidance of internal reform by accepting a relatively large degree of financial and administrative integration.[59] It was not a bad bargain, and Churchill's prediction that the City would not resist a measure which did it no real harm[60] proved more accurate than Firth's claim that 'the turtle was well on its back'.[61] By gaining a distinct statutory position the Corporation secured a less anomalous status than it had occupied since 1835. Although Ritchie, who had once contemplated making the City a mere district council,[62] continued to threaten darkly

---

[56] Over music and dancing licences. Other powers were transferred to Common Council: Firth and Simpson, *London under the Local Government Act*, 1–2.

[57] Special Committee Minutes, 10 Apr., 18 June 1888.

[58] Ibid., 17 July 1888.

[59] Although, with the accession of new county powers to the central body, the City was specifically exempted from contributing to the cost of those services to which it did not already contribute. See the summary of the final draft in PRO HLG/29/20, 1345–72, and 51 & 52 Vict., c. 41, s. 41(3).

[60] *Hansard*, 3rd ser., CCCXXVIII, 1271 (13 July 1888).

[61] Quoted by Lawson, ibid., 1031 (11 July 1888).

[62] 'Heads of a Bill', 12 Nov. 1886, PRO HLG 29/18.

that the government 'hoped on a future occasion to bring in a Bill dealing with the local areas in London', and that 'one of the local areas in London, of course, would be the City',[63] 1888 saw the first step in the separation of the 'Corporation problem' from the 'metropolitan problem', a separation which was bound to reduce the City's vulnerability.

3. THE DEATH OF THE METROPOLITAN BOARD

The progress of the Bill's London clauses through Parliament was helped by the revelations concerning the MBW's last and greatest scandal which emerged during the spring and summer of 1888. The findings of the Royal Commission on the Metropolitan Board of Works, indicating extensive dealing in the Board's surplus lands by two of its officers, use by two architect Board members of their position to secure commissions as a condition of the sale of these lands, and other less significant peculation, have recently been fully described,[64] and need not be repeated in detail here. Mrs Clifton is undoubtedly right to stress that the scandal was not the direct cause of the Board's replacement;[65] county reform, and the inclusion of London in a county measure, had been decided upon well before the scandal could have gathered sufficient momentum to influence legislation, although there can equally be little doubt that had reform not already been mooted, the Royal Commission's revelations would have made it necessary. Nevertheless, the surplus-lands scandal had many implications for the 'metropolitan problem', and these should be examined.

In the first place it reflected the constitutional weakness of Hall's first-tier body. There would seem to be no reason to question W. A. Robson's contention that indirect election encouraged corruption and allowed it to flourish.[66] Corruption is not unknown in directly elected bodies, least of all in local government, but it prospered on the MBW in an almost casual manner, suggesting that some members saw a share of the municipal pork-barrel as one of the perquisites of their position. The revelations of 1888 indicated, in addition to the primary peculation of two senior officers, a

---

[63] *Hansard*, 3rd ser., CCCXXVIII, 1172 (12 July 1888).

[64] D. Owen, *The Government of Victorian London* (Cambridge, Mass. and London), esp. ch. 8. The Royal Commission's Interim Report is in *PP 1888*, LVI.

[65] G. Clifton, 'Corruption in Local Government and the Metropolitan Board of Works in the 1880s'. I am most grateful to Mrs Clifton for allowing me to read this paper, which will eventually form part of her thesis on the administration of the MBW.

[66] W. A. Robson, *The Government and Misgovernment of London* (1939), 331.

striking number of indiscretions, of various degrees of importance, on the part of elected members. The two architects, F. H. Fowler and J. E. Saunders, extorted commissions to build on former MBW sites.[67] George Phillips of Holborn sub-purchased in 1883 an MBW site in the Clerkenwell Road from F. Statham Hobson, one of the Board's favoured clients, and might have been pressed harder by the Commissioners on his claim that Hobson had been 'only too glad to get rid of it'.[68] The Commissioners had to accept the repeated testimony of Alfred Ewin of Bethnal Green that he had no interest in an MBW plot purchased by his son, but the land was in fact resold to Ewin within a week.[69] Robert Jones of Mile End pressed the owner of the new Pavilion Theatre, built on MBW land, for a private box.[70] Allegations that George Brown, MBW member for Fulham, owned insanitary property in Marylebone and had used Board labour to repair it, were never satisfactorily dismissed.[71] T. M. Fairclough of St George-in-the-East admitted voting on a matter in which he had a financial interest.[72] The son of John Runtz of Hackney handled MBW auctions.[73] The chairman of the Board since 1870, Sir James McGarel Hogg, was a director of the bank which handled its balances.[74] Many of these operations could, in themselves, be dismissed, but their accumulation, the casual manner in which they appear to have been undertaken, and the complacent tone of the Board's internal enquiry, reinforced the comment of the *Financial News* that 'public men who can look upon such things in such a light can hardly be seeing them for the first time'.[75]

The implications were that indirect election limited accountability, and that governmental supervision was no substitute for ratepayer control. These were the conclusions reached generally by metropolitan ratepayers in the 1880s with respect to London's still relatively irresponsible first tier. Of the five metropolitan first-tier authorities—the Justices, the MBW, the Metropolitan Police, the Asylums Board, and the School Board—only the School Board was directly elected. By 1885, however,

[67] R.C. Metropolitan Board of Works, *PP 1888*, LVI, Interim Report, 22–4.
[68] MBW Minutes, 7 Oct. 1887; RC MBW, QQ. 5682–91.
[69] Ibid., QQ. 12613–21; Middlesex Deeds Register, 1884, vol. xxvii, Nos. 584 and 926.
[70] MBW Sub-Committee on Officers, minutes, 16 Feb. 1887, MBW minutes, 15 July 1887.
[71] For the original allegations see *The Times*, 22 Aug., 3, 7, 14–16, and 24 Sept. 1885.
[72] RC MBW, *PP 1888*, LVI, Q. 1273.
[73] Ibid., QQ. 2675–81 (E. A. Runtz).
[74] Ibid., QQ. 11367–78 (Beal).
[75] *Financial News*, 23 July 1887.

their aggregate rates had risen by almost 150 per cent in ten years.[76] Criticism of first-tier authorities was therefore general during the mid- and late 1880s. The Asylums Board came under heavy pressure after a massive increase in its rate to combat a smallpox epidemic in the early 1880s. Criticism of the School Board was perennial, as its rate scarcely ceased to rise,[77] but was particularly intense in the mid-1880s.[78] The management of the Metropolitan Police came under fire during the unhappy Warren regime, with revived calls for popular control. The attack upon the Metropolitan Board from 1885 to 1888 should be seen against this background. Even during the debates of 1884 it had usually been seen as a more 'responsible' authority than the School Board,[79] but in its last years it became the main engine of first-tier expansion as the street improvements programme of the late 1870s got under way. In the five years 1883/4 to 1888/9 its precept increased by 50 per cent, and its poundage rate regained for the first time the levels reached before the 1869 Loans Act.[80] This is not to suggest that ostensible criticism of corruption was really criticism of rising rates, but that the growing demands of the first tier enhanced public concern with its performance and accountability, making the Metropolitan Board's dismissive treatment of its critics increasingly inappropriate.

The acceleration of MBW rates helped undermine its natural support. During the late 1880s the ratepaying metropolitan Conservative joined the London Radical in his suspicion of the irresponsibility of indirectly elected bodies. Thus at a time when Conservatives elsewhere were insisting upon a substantial proportion of aldermen as a check to 'democracy' on the county councils, those in London showed themselves very suspicious of any survival of indirect election. C. A. Whitmore's conviction that 'it was absolutely essential that any body which succeeded [the

---

[76] Comparison of first-tier rate totals 1874/5 and 1884/5, excluding the Corporation. From Appendix 3.

[77] The aggregate levy fell in only three individual years between 1873 and 1900. See Appendix 3.

[78] The Westminster conference memorial of 1885 urged consideration of 'the question of centralisation, with special reference to the economy of the administration of the Metropolitan Asylums Board and the School Board for London'. Westminster DB Papers on the Conference on London Government, Westminster Archives. Kensington Vestry convened a Vestry conference in 1890 to protest at LSB expenditure: *Annual Report* (1890–1), 62–5.

[79] See e.g. Boulnois's comments at the Marylebone Vestry Conference, in *Marylebone Mercury*, 16 Feb. 1884.

[80] See Appendix 3 and Fig. 4.1.

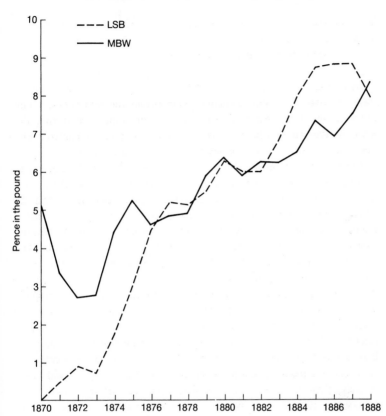

F IG . 4.1   Metropolitan Board of Works and London School Board Rate in the Pound, 1870–88.

Sources: MBW rate from the Board's final Annual Report, in *PP 1889*, LXVI, 85. School Board 1870–9 from the table in *PP 1878–9*, LVII, 183; 1880–5 from *Metropolitan*, 14 Mar. 1885; 1886–8 from the return in *London Statistics*, I (1890–1), 247–59.

MBW] should be popularly elected'[81] was widely shared. Ritchie would have been unlikely to have accepted Sydney Buxton's amendment reducing the proportion of aldermen to councillors for the LCC alone from one-third to one-sixth[82] without evidence of the extensive support of

[81] *West London Press and Chelsea News*, 24 Mar. 1888. See also Lethbridge in *Hansard*, 3rd ser., CCCXXIV, 1264 (13 Apr. 1888).
[82] *Hansard*, 3rd ser., CCCXXVIII, 1044 (11 July 1888). The eventual composition of the Council was 118 elected members (4 from the City, 2 from each of the other 57 parliamentary constituencies), and 19 aldermen.

metropolitan Conservatives. The reason for London Conservatives' lack of interest in 'tenification' in 1888 was that they believed direct election to be an adequate safeguard. Only when the rates continued to rise under the LCC did such constitutional escapism begin to appeal.

Associated with the alienation of Conservatism was the alienation of the West End. The danger had always been present. The high assessments of the central and West End parishes meant both that they contributed a significant proportion of first-tier expenses and that their own local poundage rates were low, emphasizing the first-tier levies as a proportion of the whole. For most of its life the Board had limited criticism by devoting much of its expenditure to the City and the West End. This was probably less a conscious policy than a reflection of the fact that the Board's town-improvement municipalism led it naturally to concentrate upon the central area, where improvements were most vital. By the mid-1880s, however, the rise in first-tier rates was beginning to make the West End parishes more conscious of their lack of control over the metropolitan bodies than of the benefits that those bodies provided. Fig. 4.2 shows the steady erosion of parochial control over the rates levied in Paddington. The 1886 quinquennial valuation tightened the screw, prompting a protest meeting in St Martin's to voice 'this "bitter cry" of the London ratepayers'.[83] The 1886 quinquennial also led Kensington to become the first authority to try to use parochial control over assessments as a substitute for parochial control over the first tier.[84] In his annual report for 1886/7 the St James Vestry Clerk complained that 'the efforts of the Vestry to reduce the rates by an economical administration in local affairs are ... to a large extent neutralised by the growing expenditure of Central Authorities', pointing out that £85,000 of the £147,000 raised in rates in the parish was claimed by the first tier.[85] It is significant that the attacks on the Board over the surplus-land scandal should have emanated from the West End Vestries—Paddington and St James—and from the *Financial News*, owned and edited by the Marylebone Conservative Harry Marks. In 1884 the threat that reform would entail the extinction of parochial autonomy had made it appear menacing to larger ratepayers; in 1888, with no threat to the second tier and with first-tier rates apparently

---

[83] *Westminster Times* (Supplement), 17 Oct. 1885.

    [84] By systematic under-assessment. The attempt was eventually foiled by the protests of other parishes, which had a right of appeal under the 1869 Valuation Act. For this episode see Kensington Vestry, *Annual Report* (1885–6), 28–39, and *West London Observer*, 24 Apr. 1886.

    [85] St James Vestry, *Annual Report* (1886–7), 38.

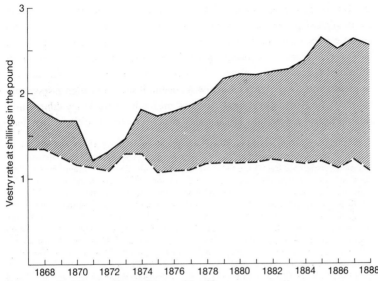

FIG. 4.2   Paddington Vestry Rates, 1867–88

Note: The continuous line marks total rates raised by the Vestry, the broken line the rates raised for Vestry purposes. The shaded area therefore represents the precepted demands of the Metropolitan Board of Works and the London School Board.

Source: Compiled from the table of rates in Paddington Vestry, *Annual Report* (1888–9), 60–3.

impervious to any control, reform became identified with retrenchment. Shortly after the Bill's introduction, C. Howard Vincent, who would become a member of the first LCC, expressed the hope to his Vestry, St George, Hanover Square, that 'whatever the new form of London Government might be, one of its first aims would be to ensure economy'.[86]

After thirty-three years the 1855 system had buckled at its weakest point. The incapacity of the system's second tier had ensured an expansion of first-tier activity which an indirectly elected body was unfit to sustain. By the late 1880s this was so clear that the Board had very few defenders outside its own ranks; its 'dangerous unanimity'[87] was symptomatic of its isolation. The London clauses of the 1888 Bill were received with 'perfect and profound apathy'[88] because no metropolitan interest wished to retain

[86] *West London Press and Chelsea News*, 7 Apr. 1888.
[87] M. H. Judge, *The Working of the Metropolitan Board of Works* (1888), 7.
[88] Baumann, 'The London Clauses of the Local Government Bill', 539.

the Board. Reformers objected to its constitution, suburban ratepayers to its alleged preference for the West End,[89] and West End ratepayers and Vestries to its part in the growth of first-tier precepts. This was, however, an artificial accord between those who sought a more economical metropolitan body and those who sought a more active one, between those anxious to reduce the burden upon the West End and those anxious to divert first-tier spending to the east and the south. It would dissolve during the 1890s as the LCC came to determine its priorities.

---

[89] 'The Metropolitan Board of Works was a warning to those who would adopt centralisation in municipal government. The West End was continually being improved and beautified; its bridges freed from tolls and new ones built all at an enormous expense; but the East End of the town is grudged the smallest outlay.': W. Davis at the AGM of the De Beauvoir Town and Dalston Ratepayers' Association, Minutes, 10 June 1886. In the first LCC election several candidates, chiefly in the south and east, stressed their intention to win more for their area from the new Council than had been secured from the MBW. See the 1889 addresses of W. M. Acworth (Dulwich), R. S. Gutteridge (Dulwich), G. Lidgett (Greenwich), R. Roberts (South Islington), C. T. Beresford Hope and H. Smallman (Brixton), H. Myer (Kennington), H. Bell (North Lambeth), H. Quelch (Walworth), J. Ambrose and A. Leon (Limehouse), W. P. Bullivant (Poplar), R. S. Sly and F. J. W. Dellow (St George's E.), J. D. Kemp (Stepney), H. W. Henderson (Whitechapel), all in the Bristol University collection of LCC election addresses.

5

The LCC and the London Government Question

I. THE LIBERAL REVIVAL AND PROGRESSIVISM

The creation of the London County Council injected party politics into London government and the London government debate. The birth of the Council followed the overhaul of the constituency Liberal Associations necessitated by the 1885 redistribution, and it gave the new Liberal organization its first metropolitan outlet. Success in 1889 would set the tone of London municipal politics for the next eighteen years.

By the early 1880s each of the old borough Liberal Associations had been or was being reconstructed along caucus lines. This was the first stage in the downfall of the Independent Member, but the size and the expense of fighting old boroughs still hindered the democratization of party organization. The 1883 Corrupt Practices Act was important to London. In April 1884 the President of the Finsbury Liberal Association remembered the time when a smaller electorate had cost £10,000 to canvass and rejoiced that 'now such an expenditure would *ipso facto* vitiate the election'.[1] In Finsbury and elsewhere Liberal Associations stressed that 'personal help is regarded ... as of greater value than mere subscription'.[2] Nevertheless, the logistical difficulties and the expense occasioned by the size of the old boroughs remained severe, and the 1885 redistribution, creating nearly sixty single-member constituencies in place of the ten two-member boroughs outside the City, was as important to the emergence of the Liberal caucus as the Corrupt Practices Act.

The next twenty years would show that redistribution had made London safe for Conservatism in Parliament by separating the suburbs from the inner-city areas that they had been joined to in the old boroughs, but the corollary of this was that the Liberal caucuses were no longer obliged to dissipate their strength over some of the infertile ground covered by the old boroughs. Liberal activists tended to assume that London lay at the party's feet—as it had done for a generation—given adequate organization, and in 1885 they paid more attention to the effects

[1] H. Spicer, quoted in the *Islington Gazette*, 30 Apr. 1884.
[2] Finsbury Liberal Association Annual Report, quoted ibid., 3 June 1884.

of redistribution on their own intra-party battles than upon the party balance. 'The newly created constituencies', claimed the Radical *South London Press* 'are glorying in the fact that they have freed themselves— let us hope for ever—from the West End clubs, with their Tadpoles and Tapers, and from mere money-bags, whose principal if not only claim was the weight of their gold'.[3]

James Stuart, already a sitting member, accepted the Liberal nomination for Hoxton in 1885 with an affirmation that it could be won for half the £500 allowed by the 1883 Act, and should be, since 'for people to allow themselves to drift into unnecessary and uncertain expense would be to jeopardise the freedom of their choice, and to place themselves at the mercy of the rich'.[4] The inference drawn in North Camberwell that 'nowadays a member was bound to do what his constituency required, and if he did not he would soon get the cold shoulder'[5] was exaggerated; in most cases the candidate continued to bear the cost of registration,[6] and all MPs had to be able to support themselves in Parliament. Nevertheless, the reduction in the cost of London elections expanded the field of available candidates and increased the associations' range of choice. It was generally true that 'the day is gone by when members are to pick their seats, as in the time of Old Sarum'.[7] No more City aldermen would represent Liberal seats.

The 1885 election nevertheless demonstrated the depth of 'Whig'/ Radical divisions within the London parties, as Radical groups in some constituencies challenged the selection of right-wing Liberals[8] and some of the sitting Members refused to acknowledge their rejection by the re-established Liberal Associations.[9] Seven independent Liberals eventually ran, four of them probably causing the loss of the seats for the party. This was the most striking feature of an unexpectedly weak Liberal performance in London in 1885, which brought the party only twenty-three of the fifty-nine seats. Inadequate local organization was blamed for the separate candidatures and for an alleged failure to bring out 80,000 registered Liberal electors. In the early months of 1886 the Central

---

[3] *South London Press*, 11 July 1885.
[4] *Borough of Hackney Express*, 21 Mar. 1885.
[5] Mr Prangle, quoted in the *South London Press*, 27 Feb. 1886.
[6] For example in Battersea, ibid., 30 Jan. 1886.
[7] *South London Press*, 27 June 1885, letter from J. D. Gilbert, W. Newington LRA.
[8] For Woolwich and Hampstead see the *Democrat*, 25 July 1885.
[9] Lawrence in Lambeth North and McArthur in Newington West ran as Independent Liberals, as did Ayrton, a past Member, in Mile End.

Liberal Association appointed an Organization Commission for the Metropolis to tackle these problems.[10]

The Commission sought to create a more effective grass-roots organization through the formation in each constituency of a Liberal Association 'so thoroughly representative in its character and formation that no candidate can hope for success who is not launched under its authority'.[11] Chaired by W. S. Caine and including Firth, R. K. Causton, G. W. E. Russell, and J. R. Seager,[12] it had a clear Radical bias, which made the endorsement of caucus supremacy likely. The need to embrace all shades of Liberalism to avoid future splits reinforced the Commission's anxiety to make the new organizations as broad-based as possible. Caine believed that once the expense of forming a new association had been met, it could support itself on 'local energy and zeal'.[13] He toured London in the spring of 1886 'entrusted with a comfortable amount of party funds'[14] to defray initial costs. He took as his model the local organization in Barrow, which returned him to Parliament in a by-election in April 1886, when 'the canvas was completed in two days because there was a Liberal Association 800 strong. Every member was willing to take his share of the labour'.[15] He invoked this evidence of the power of the activist in London, urging the new associations to dispense with money subscriptions altogether and to use volunteers for registration work.[16]

In many constituencies the Organizing Commission did little more than sanction caucus organizations that already existed; its most valuable work lay in fusing rival associations where the party was split.[17] Nevertheless, central government endorsement of the caucus was important, given the recent intra-party battles. By mid-1886 London Liberal organization was unequivocally established along Birmingham caucus lines. In less than ten years it had been transformed from a personal, hierarchical party structure, dependent chiefly upon the financial support of sitting MPs, to a broad-based structure reliant upon the grass-roots activist. The bankruptcy early in 1886 of W. M. Torrens, owing £6,630 which he

---

[10] For this paragraph see *The Times*, 18 Feb. 1886.
[11] Ibid., 4 Feb. 1886.
[12] For full membership see ibid., 18 Feb. 1886.
[13] Ibid.
[14] Address to W. Newington Liberals, *South London Press*, 20 Mar. 1886.
[15] Address to Mile End Liberals, *East London Observer*, 8 May 1886.
[16] See e.g. address to Norwood Liberals, *South London Press*, 13 Mar. 1886; to E. Marylebone Liberals, *Marylebone Independent*, 24 Apr. 1886.
[17] For example in Walworth (*South London Press*, 27 Mar. 1886), in W. Newington (ibid., 20 Mar. 1886), and in E. Finsbury (*Islington Gazette*, 18 Feb. 1886).

claimed to be 'not debts in the usual sense of the word', but money lent to support 'his very difficult and expensive position as Member for Finsbury', epitomized the decline of the 'Independent Member'.[18]

This evolution has been treated at some length because it was a precondition for party political involvement in local government in London. Only with redistribution and the reform of the constituency associations did the political intervention, frequent in many provincial municipalities since the late 1860s, become general in London as party organization became geared less towards the return of individuals to Parliament and more towards the local promotion of the party. The Liberals have been emphasized because they were to make the running in London local politics in the late 1880s and 1890s. The Vestry elections of May 1887 saw sporadic political involvement, mostly on the Liberal side.[19] Nevertheless, before the politicization of the LCC clarified party municipal platforms, intervention in Vestry elections was curiously hesitant. The West Newington Liberals could even complain that 'in London we have not the facilities of proving our strength that our provincial friends have, as, owing to the want of proper Municipal Government, we are unable to test our position year by year, as the Liberals in Birmingham and other large towns do'.[20] It took the formation of the LCC, a body with more power and more attendant publicity than the Vestries, and one elected by the parliamentary constituencies, to bring about widespread party involvement in municipal politics.

Within days of the 1888 Act's Royal Assent the London Liberal and Radical Union—formed in January 1887 as the apex of the constituency-party reorganization—convened a conference of its own General Committee and officers of the local Liberal Associations. It resolved to seek the return to the Council of men pledged to 'a Progressive Policy in all matters', defined in a draft programme produced by the Union's Executive Committee.[21] Similarly, in December 1888 a conference of representatives of Conservative Associations approved a motion, to 'find and support suitable Conservative and Unionist candidates',[22] although the

---

[18] *Islington Gazette*, 20 May 1886; *Holborn Guardian*, 27 Feb. 1886.

[19] For example in Islington (*Islington Gazette*, 16 Feb. 1887), Camberwell and Rotherhithe (*South London Press*, 21 May 1887), Fulham and Hammersmith (*West London Observer*, 28 May 1887), and Marylebone (*Marylebone Mercury*, 28 May 1887).

[20] W. Newington Liberal and Radical Association, *Second Annual Report* (1887–8) (Southwark Archives).

[21] London Liberal and Radical Union, *Second Annual Report* (1888–9), 2.

[22] See the 1889 election address of H. L. Mills (S. Paddington), in the Bristol University collection.

Conservatives remained more diffident than their opponents about overt involvement, and failed to define Conservative municipal policy as distinctively as the Liberals had done. A campaign dominated by the social policy issues central to the Liberal platform led to the election of seventy-one Liberals who took the Progressive party whip on the first Council, against forty-seven Conservatives, who styled themselves Moderates.[23]

London's 'New Liberalism' was not, therefore, handed down by salon theorists or intellectual journalists, but pushed up from the constituency parties. Too much can be made of the Progressives' ideological range 'from staid Liberal Unionist to Fabian permeator'[24] and the party's coalition appearance. The Progressive centre of gravity lay with the new Liberal and Radical Associations, which had selected the candidates and managed their campaigns. Policy was shaped in the manner most acceptable to the London Liberal activist, with an emphasis upon the Radical elements of a traditional creed. Thus social reform and the assault upon privilege and monopoly were stressed, but the older values of nonconformist 'puritanism' and temperance were also well entrenched, and were less prominent only because of their smaller municipal bearing. Most of the men who ran the Progressive party during its ascendancy were London constituency-party Radicals like John Williams Benn, B. F. C. Costelloe, W. H. Dickinson, and Thomas Mackinnon Wood, or men in sympathy with their outlook, like James Stuart and Charles Harrison. It is true that in 1889 deference to age and experience elevated to important Council positions some figures entirely untypical of London Radicalism: Rosebery, the future Liberal Imperialist, as Chairman, Sir John Lubbock, a Liberal Unionist, as Vice-Chairman, R. W. W. Lingen, who 'declined ... to give any pledges whatever as to questions that may come before the Council',[25] as chairman of the Finance Committee, and Sir Thomas Farrer, who considered London Liberalism 'faddist, schismatic, jealous, unorganized',[26] as chairman of the Local Government Committee; but this 'junta' was dethroned by defeats over the loans and attempts to form an executive in 1891–2, and never regained its authority. It is also true that from 1892 the Council acquired a 'labour bench' of working men, who took the Progressive whip and joined John Burns, the only Socialist elected in 1889. Some of them, notably Will Crooks and Will Steadman,

---

[23] The totals given at the time by the *Pall Mall Gazette* 'Extra' (1889).
[24] K. Young, *Local Politics and the Rise of Party* (Leicester, 1975), 39.
[25] *Pall Mall Gazette* 'Extra' (1889), 99.
[26] Farrer to Rosebery, ? Dec. 1891, RP, MS 10089, fo. 156. Rosebery and Lubbock were both nominees of the untypical City Liberal Association, Farrer and Lingen both aldermen.

were assiduous and effective on the Council and in committee but, whether by exclusion or through voluntary independence, they did not reach positions of authority within the Progressive party, which remained the arbiter of policy. In the period covered by the two surviving party minute books, for 1890 to 1900,[27] no labour representative appears on the party committee. Even the voice of club Radicalism, loud in the mid-1880s, was muted on the Council. Its mouthpieces, James Tims, 'the Carnot of London Radicalism'[28] and F. A. Ford, organizer of the Finsbury Radical Federation in 1884, were ineffectual.

The Progressives would control the first six Councils, until their defeat in 1907. The coincidence of a new local authority and a rejuvenated party controlling it brought a burst of municipal enthusiasm unmatched at any other point during the life of the Victorian system. Because the emergence of local Liberalism has so far been charted chiefly in terms of organization, it should not be inferred that Progressive policy was developed residually, in the heat of the party battle on the Council, as was largely true of the Moderates in the 1890s. The Progressives of 1889 came armed with a relatively cohesive and distinctively municipal policy. The creation of more democratic local Liberal organizations had coincided with the emergence of social politics in London in the 1880s. The advanced tone of London Liberalism and the prominence given to social issues in the London Liberal programme became conspicuous in the 1880s and 1890s. In a sense this was a metropolitan phenomenon—a consequence of the social segregation brought about by metropolitan growth—and one attempt at quantification has argued for a markedly higher level of class-based voting in London than elsewhere in this period.[29] Certainly the social movements of the 1880s were centred in London, with Henry George's land campaign, the Bitter Cry controversy, the unemployment riots of 1886–7, concern over sweated labour in the East End, and the match-girls, gas and dock strikes of 1888–9. The classic study of the reaction to these problems has concentrated upon the response of an apprehensive middle class,[30] but it should be stressed that social questions permeated metropolitan Liberal and Radical politics in the 1880s—that there was a populist aspect to social concern. The attempts to link municipal and social reform in 1883–4 had shown both to be elements of

---

[27] Both in the Greater London Record Office.

[28] *Pall Mall Gazette* 'Extra' (1889), 104.

[29] K. D. Wald, 'The Rise of Class-based Voting in London', *Comparative Politics*, 9 (1977), 219–29.

[30] G. Stedman Jones, *Outcast London* (Oxford, 1971).

the emergent London Radicalism. They had failed then because they had appeared an opportunistic confusion of means and ends, but in 1889 municipal reform of a sort had been enacted, and the case for devoting the new authority to social reform was at its strongest.

Virtually every element of the 'social question' had a municipal aspect. One of the chief demands of London's land campaigners was for the absorption of the 'unearned increment' of rent by local taxation. The housing crisis had been ascribed to the inadequacy of existing authorities, and some Progressives campaigned in 1889 in the belief that the new Council was empowered to enforce Vestry action against overcrowding and insanitation; more positively, the 1875 Cross Act had given local authorities the power to build their own municipal dwellings on cleared sites.[31] Responsibility for contra-cyclical action to relieve unemployment had been palmed off on the local authorities by the Chamberlain circular of 1886, although in London it remained chiefly a second-tier concern.[32] The problems of sweating and labour unrest could be met by local authorities acting as model employers—establishing wage scales for contractors and carrying out as much work as possible by direct labour— and accepting unionization. Thus, although many of the Progressives who stood for the Council in 1889 possessed only an imprecise knowledge of its statutory powers, they were aware that their programme had a distinct municipal bearing. By the mid-1890s Canon Barnett believed that 'the social unrest of the last ten years, which took form in bitter cries, royal commissions, and social schemes, seems now to be settling down to a steady demand for better local administration'.[33] Local government had become heir to the diffuse social movement of the previous decade.

There was, however, more to Progressivism than municipal philanthropy. The Progressives were intensely conscious of belonging to London's first directly metropolitan municipal authority. They believed that London's previous municipal Balkanization had left the metropolitan community prey to the various sinister interests feeding upon it— ground landlords, public utility monopolists, and the City Corporation. Hobhouse's casting of the Council, on the land question, as 'the voice of London as against one class of Londoners' characterized the Progressives'

---

[31] 38 & 39 Vict., c. 36, s. 9.
[32] J. Harris, *Unemployment and Politics* (Oxford, 1972), 75–6.
[33] Quoted in *London*, 24 Jan. 1895.

communitarian preoccupation with the assault upon vested interests.[34] The land question exemplified the way in which the obsession with entrenched privilege encouraged the evolution of a previously 'minimalist' Radicalism into assertive, interventionist Progressivism. Sidney Webb believed that 'a course of lessons in the "law of rent" will usually convert a mere Radical into something very like a Socialist'; his own notorious call in 1892 for 'unearned increment' to be rated at 20s. in the pound had been anticipated in 1887 by the 'mere Radical' and later LCC Progressive William Saunders.[35] It reinforced the conviction born of the public-utility battles that municipal intervention was necessary to defeat structural monopoly. John Williams Benn

was never a Socialist, except in the sense in which that very elastic term applies to everyone who lives in a social community. He was a Radical, who stood for equality of opportunity and for the freedom of the individual. But the public ownership of public monopolies was an indestructible part of his creed, and he held that the major task of the Council was to deliver London from the stranglehold of private corporations upon the public service.[36]

The Progressive Council pressed repeatedly for water control and exploited as best it could the twenty-one-year purchase option under the 1870 Tramways Act. The assault upon the City Corporation and the livery companies needed less theoretical justification; again the argument was that they had cornered revenues intended for the whole London community. The attack upon vested interests was an essential concomitant of the Progressives' social municipalism because it was expected to provide the revenue for social measures without reliance upon the regressive rating system. Alfred Davies, elected for North Hackney in 1889, promised in his address that the taxation of land values would fund 'imperative social reforms . . . without a farthing of increase in the rates'; Burns believed that the interception of public-utility profits could pay off the London debt; James Branch and Charles Harrison anticipated $£\frac{1}{2}$ million p.a. from the absorption of existing charitable endowments.[37]

Progressive attitudes to the London government question should be judged in the light of their overall policy. Support for the reform cause

[34] Lord Hobhouse, 'The London County Council and its Assailants', *Contemporary Review*, 61 (1892), 335.

[35] S. Webb, *Socialism in England* (1890), 87–8; RC Labour, *PP 1893–4*, XXXIX (1), QQ. 3887–90 (Webb); SC Town Holdings, *PP 1887*, XIII, Q. 11645 (Saunders).

[36] A. G. Gardiner, *John Benn and the Progressive Movement* (1925), 124.

[37] 1889 election addresses of A. Davies (N. Hackney), J. Branch and C. Harrison (Bethnal Green SW), Bristol University collection; J. Burns, 'Let London Live', *Nineteenth Century*, 31 (1892), 675.

had been widespread in the Liberal caucuses of the 1880s, and was
accordingly reflected on the Council. Progressives' hostility to the City
and their belief in the essential civic unity of London—to say nothing of
the explicit threat to the Council—made them deeply antipathetic towards
devolutionary 'tenification'. Their consequent commitment to metropolitan integration was reinforced by their social policy. So far as the
Council's own prerogative was concerned, there was a shift away from
the town-improvement municipalism which had directed the bulk of
MBW spending towards the West End, in favour of increased expenditure
on housing, parks, and other amenities in London's 'congested districts';[38]
the attitude of Aeneas Smith, who 'would not vote money for the Strand
improvement in its complete form, because he contended that if they
could spend money in London they owed a debt to the poor people in
the slums rather than in the Strand'[39] was typical. Beyond this, the
Progressives showed an increasing awareness of the redistributive power
of general first-tier expenditure. 'With regard to taxation', stressed Jane
Cobden, elected and unseated in 1889, 'I hold that the whole Metropolis
ought to be regarded as one community, having common burdens and
common responsibilities'.[40] For the Liberal Unionist Progressive Wallace
Bruce, campaigning under the threat of the Council's abolition in 1898,
the difference between London and the provincial municipalities was that
the latter 'are complete in themselves: each contains rich, poor, and
middle classes, and the rate raised is the same over the whole town, and
is spent for the common good'.[41] In London the rating system was
regressive between areas, inhibiting social expenditure where it was most
needed. First-tier social spending could deploy the resources of the City
and the West End in aid of the East and the inner South.

   The commitment to metropolitan integration was therefore an important element of social policy, but it did not preclude the existence of
second-tier bodies. More Progressives inclined to the support of parochial
democracy characteristic of Liberals in the 1890s than to the older
utilitarian single-municipality doctrines of Firth. They wanted the Vestries replaced by 'democratic district councils' open to women and
working men, and would secure this aim in 1894. This was, however, a
representative rather than an administrative goal. The question of how

[38] Costelloe's analogy, SC Town Holdings, *PP 1890*, XVIII, Q. 4529.
[39] Quoted in the *Metropolitan*, 5 Oct. 1889.
[40] 1889 election address of J. Cobden (Bow and Bromley), Bristol University collection.
Cobden was unseated on grounds of female ineligibility.
[41] 1898 election address of W. Bruce (Bow and Bromley), ibid.

to protect second-tier autonomy within an integrated system dominated by an interventionist County Council was a delicate one, which few Progressives faced squarely. Matters were further complicated by a rather uncritical acceptance by many Progressives of the Vestries' squalid public image in the wake of the housing crisis. This was strongest in 1889, and diminished during the 1890s as a result of two-tier contact and the growing strength of Progressivism in the second tier, but the sense of suspicion never entirely vanished. It accounted in large measure for the self-defensive stance taken by the Vestries during the 1890s.

Progressive views on the question of second-tier reform were therefore complex—certainly more complex than could be inferred from the brusque categorization of the party as 'centralists and rationalists almost to a man', inspired by the 'centralist authoritarianism' of the French Revolution.[42] Dr Young's argument is based largely on the assumption that since nearly all of the Progressives were associated with the London Municipal Reform League, they must all have been Firthite centralizers.[43] This rests in turn upon John Lloyd's claim in 1910 that sixty-six of the seventy-three Progressives elected in 1889 had been associated with the League.[44] It is not always wise to rely upon Lloyd; the League itself was more modest at the time, claiming only thirty-four of the whole Council in January 1889.[45] Even if his figure is accepted, its significance should not be exaggerated. It is true that the single-municipality men who led the League in the 1880s—Firth, Phillips, and Lloyd—were all elected in 1889, along with Beal, Aeneas Smith, T. E. Gibb, and Firth's Kensington protege J. F. Torr, but they were not to be the Progressive policy makers on the Council. Firth's early death in August 1889 was crucial. As the first salaried Deputy Chairman, he occupied one of the most influential positions on the Council, and his knowledge of municipal law commanded the respect of the novice Councillors. Age told against most of his former colleagues.[46] Beal, who was in any case at odds with Firth,[47] proved 'only

---

[42] K. Young and P. Garside, *Metropolitan London: Politics and Urban Change, 1837–1981* (1982), 59; K. Young, ' "Metropology" Revisited: On the Political Integration of Metropolitan Areas', in K. Young (ed.), *Essays on the Study of Urban Politics* (London and Basingstoke, 1975), 145.

[43] Young, *Local Politics*, 39–40.

[44] J. Lloyd, *London Municipal Government: History of a Great Reform, 1880–1888* (1910), 69–72.

[45] *Metropolitan*, 2 Feb. 1889.

[46] 'Hobhouse, Farrer, Beal, Lloyd and Phillips were a band of reformers who had already well nigh outrun the allotted span of active human life.' W. H. Dickinson, Introduction to W. Phillips, *Sixty Years of Citizen Work and Play* (1910), xi.

[47] *The Times*, 1 Apr. 1889.

a very useful, but not a very eminent, member',[48] and died in 1891. Phillips and Lloyd were lightweights. The men who shaped Progressive policy in the 1890s—Charles Harrison, Costelloe, Webb, McKinnon Wood, Hutton, Benn, Collins, Dickinson—had either not belonged to the League or not been prominent in it in its Firthite days.

For the other Leaguers, membership of the organization did not necessarily signify acceptance of the single-municipality principle. It usually signified a specific belief that the City Corporation should be reformed and a more general wish to correct what was manifestly an inadequate system. The centralizing district council provisions of the Harcourt Bill had disturbed many League members, and since 1886 the LMRL had been committed to a two-tier system with independent local bodies. The second-tier question was not especially prominent in the 1889 election and there is little indication that it greatly concerned most candidates. Men did not seek election to the first tier in order to suppress the second; many of the elected councillors had in fact cut their municipal teeth on local bodies.[49] Nevertheless, the candidates who *did* refer to the future of the second tier often assumed—without statutory foundation— that the Council had been created to keep the local bodies in order; Branch and Harrison envisaged reformed district councils as 'subordinate fractions' of the LCC, and other Councillors used similar language.[50]

Such attitudes were consonant with the public view in the late 1880s of the Vestries as incompetent, obstructive, and malevolent. By the mid-1890s the Vestries' rapid rejuvenation had gone some way towards improving their standing with the informed public, and Progressive attitudes changed accordingly.[51] Two considerations assisted their change of heart. First, with the omission of the City from the county reform of 1888, the anticipated District Councils Bill offered the prospect of an

[48] Obituary in *The Times*, 15 June 1891.

[49] At least 53 members of the first Council (35 Progressives and 18 Moderates) had served or were serving on Vestries or Guardian Boards at the time of their election. A further 3 (2 Progressives and 1 Moderate) had been Common Councilmen of the City. Information from the *Pall Mall Gazette* 'Extra' on the LCC (1889); *Dod's Handbook to the London County Council* (1889); the Bristol University collection of election addresses.

[50] J. Branch and C. Harrison, election address, (Bethnal Green SW), 1889, Bristol University collection. See also the portraits of N. W. Hubbard, T. E. Gibb, G. J. Cooper, J. Marsland, and J. G. Rhodes in *Dod's Handbook* (1889).

[51] For Webb's change of heart between 1888 and 1891 see A. M. McBriar, *Fabian Socialism and English Politics, 1884–1918* (Cambridge, 1962), 193–4. By 1895 Charles Harrison, whose views in 1889 are quoted above, was willing to leave the local authorities 'their autonomy and their present local powers': 'A Statement of a Progressive Policy for the London County Council', typescript (7 Jan. 1895), Benn Papers vi.

assault upon Corporation. The London Liberals had pressed Ritchie to
promise an early Bill in 1888,[52] and in the absence of subsequent legislation the call for 'democratic' district councils entered the Progressive
litany. Secondly, Progressive success on the Council was followed—and
had in some areas been anticipated—by Progressive victories in Vestry
elections, which did more than anything else to raise the status of the
second tier in Liberal eyes. The two measures which went furthest to
emancipate the local bodies before the 1899 Act—the Equalization of
Rates Act and the London clauses of the Parish Councils Act of 1894—
were both promoted by the London Liberal Members, including several
Progressive Councillors.

It was, however, one thing to advocate independent district councils
and another to reconcile their independence with the Progressives' belief
in greater metropolitan integration. Two Liberal reports on the second-
tier question which appeared in 1891 attempted this reconciliation. In
February a committee of the London Municipal Reform League advocated the creation of district councils for the existing Vestry and District
Board areas, with the 'horizontal transfer' of commissioners' and other
second-tier powers (although not those of the guardians), but no transfers
from the LCC. The Council would have extensive default powers, would
arbitrate between district councils, and could adjust their areas. County
Councillors would become ex-officio members of their local district councils, restoring the two-tier link severed in 1888 without returning to
indirect election.[53] In the autumn a committee of the London Liberal
and Radical Union produced another report, although not without some
friction between traditional single-municipalists and more pluralistic
Progressives.[54] It advocated district councils in areas coinciding with
parliamentary boroughs or divisions, 'regard being had for local sentiment'. They would inherit all Vestry powers and all other municipal
powers not reserved for the LCC. The Council would have default powers
over housing and Factory Act administration and could veto the dismissal
of medical and sanitary officers. Most interestingly, the committee
approached the equalization issue in an adventurous way, providing for
grants to the second tier corresponding to 'the necessary minimum cost
of municipal administration'—a proposal probably deriving from Sidney
Webb—and allowing further grants by the Council to defray capital

---

[52] *Hansard*, 3rd ser., CCCXXVIII, 1040 (11 July 1888) and 1172 (12 July 1888).
[53] For this scheme and its reception see *Metropolitan*, 28 Feb., 9 May 1891.
[54] See M. Barker, *Gladstone and Radicalism* (Hassocks, 1975), 140.

expenditure on sewerage, paving, and lighting subject to inspection by LCC officers.[55]

The essential features of both schemes were the retention of small secondary bodies, the augmentation of their powers by the consolidation of existing local duties rather than by first-tier transfers, and the extension of LCC surveillance. It was a plausible programme, but one which had not been fully developed or reconciled with other Progressive policies. The retention of small local areas reflected a heightened Liberal sensitivity to the value of the parish council as an instrument of local self-expression, but this was a representative rather than an administrative consideration, treating the new councils as organs of local democracy rather than as components of an integrated two-tier system. A fragmented second tier meant continuing rating disparities. Most Progressives saw the solution to that problem in rate equalization, but this would have to be reconciled with local financial autonomy. More to the point, equalization was likely to prove no more than a palliative. Some Progressives toyed with the idea of throwing the cost of supposedly 'common' second-tier functions, such as street lighting, on to the county rate, while leaving them for local execution,[56] but this necessitated some LCC scrutiny to prevent parishes from paving their streets with gold at the Council's expense. Dickinson thought it 'extremely valuable' for the LCC to have tighter control over second-tier finances.[57]

Reluctance to countenance first-tier transfers was defensible, as the nearly fruitless attempts at devolution later in the decade would prove, but it did reflect an ungracious administrative possessiveness on the Council's part, which would only harden as the argument developed. It was fortified by the continuing suspicion of Vestry honesty and com- petence which lay behind the recommendation of extensive default powers. Provision for the metropolitan body to act in default of a negligent local authority provides a guarantee of some uniformity of standards without impairing local diversity, and is logical in a two-tier system.

[55] The Report is given in full in *South London Press*, 5 Sept. 1891. For Webb's views see S. Webb, *The London Programme* (1891), 30.

[56] For example Dickinson (RC Amalgamation, *PP 1894*, XVIII, Q. 13624) and Costelloe ('The Equalisation of London Rates, I', *London*, 9 Feb. 1893). Costelloe concluded crypt- ically that 'how this can be largely done, even without any invasion of the present autonomy of the local bodies, cannot be stated here'. The increase of second-tier rates during the 1890s generated a limited degree of Vestry support for such proposals. See the criticism of the Equalization Bill by G. W. Preston, Vestry Clerk of St Luke's, in *Local Government Journal*, 31 Mar. 1894, and also the resolutions passed by Rotherhithe Vestry (Minutes, 18 Mar. 1899), on the introduction of the London Government Bill.

[57] RC Amalgamation, *PP 1894*, XVII, Q. 13616.

Nevertheless, in this context it had grown out of the received opinion that London's municipal problems derived from Vestry mismanagement. This had been generated during the housing crisis of 1883–4 and reinforced in Progressive minds by energetic vilification of the Vestries in the new and aggressively Radical London evening newspaper, the *Star*, from January 1888.[58] Criticism of the Vestries had become 'as fashionable as "slumming" was a few years ago'.[59] Several candidates for the Council in 1889 had promised rigorous enforcement of the sanitary law, in apparent ignorance of the limited extent of the Council's powers in that direction,[60] and the pursuit of default powers represented an attempt to provide the LCC with a sanitary role that was always likely to appear a slur upon the existing sanitary authorities.

This did little for two-tier harmony. The LCC Progressives failed to appreciate that recent developments had sharpened the Vestries' anxiety to protect their independence. The 1880s had seen the continued—and accelerating—encroachment of first-tier rates upon their taxable resources, the threat virtually to extinguish local autonomy in the 1884 Bill, and the severance of the Vestries' direct link with the central body in 1888. The Vestries knew that they had been granted only a stay of execution in 1888 and that, after years of unfavourable publicity, the name Vestry 'stinks in the nostrils of London'.[61] The fear that the anticipated District Councils Bill would severely curb local independence appeared well founded. The knowledge that the new Council included Firth, Beal, and other single-municipality men, coupled with the discovery that even those Progressives committed to district councils envisaged greater centralization of local finance, and cast the Council as the 'supervisory authority' over all the local authorities of London',[62] heightened this fear. It ensured that early discussions with the new Council took place in an atmosphere of some suspicion.

---

[58] 'War on Corruption' in the *Star*, 23 Jan. 1888 (Mile End), 30 Jan. 1888 (Shoreditch), 7 Feb. 1888 (Hammersmith and Fulham), 17 Feb. 1888 (Hackney), 2 Mar. 1888 (St George, Hanover Square). See also 'Corrupt Camberwell', ibid., 27 Apr. 1888, and many other attacks on 'Bumbledom' in early issues.

[59] Letter from J. Braye, ibid., 8 Feb. 1888.

[60] See e.g., the addresses of H. B. Chapman (Camberwell N.), R. Lyon (Camberwell, Peckham), T. L. Corbett (a Moderate, Clapham), T. W. Maule (Finsbury, Holborn), C. C. Cramp (a Moderate, Hammersmith), D. H. Macfarlane (Islington W.), and many others (Bristol University collection). Wren and Torr (NE Bethnal Green), and W. B. Doubleday (Lambeth, Norwood), appear to have believed that the Council was empowered to control the local authorities in sanitary matters.

[61] T. B. Westacott, of St Pancras, before RC Amalgamation, *PP 1894*, XVII, Q. 13172.

[62] Dickinson, before RC Amalgamation, *PP 1894*, XVII, Q. 8699.

2. EARLY TWO-TIER SKIRMISHES

The haphazard evolution of the London government system since 1855 had made overhaul highly desirable by the early 1890s, even if it entailed only a detailed readjustment to remove the kind of anomaly by which the LCC regulated cow-houses while the Vestries regulated pigsties.[63] Ritchie's remarks in the Commons in 1888 had suggested that second-tier reform was imminent, and the creation of the LCC had itself stimulated public discussion of the Vestries' future.

The LCC took up the question of second-tier reform *in extenso* in June 1889. The Local Government and Taxation Committee nominated a sub-committee under Sir Thomas Farrer to consider 'the completion of the scheme of London Government', including the questions of areas, the constitution of the local authorities, their functions, and their relationship to the central body.[64] The sub-committee's work revolved around draft proposals sketched out by the Moderate Councillor for Woolwich, Colonel Edwin Hughes, after an interview with Ritchie.[65] Hughes's proposals for local areas were considered first. Working on the principle that local government areas should correspond as closely as possible to existing Poor Law units and the post-Redistribution parliamentary boroughs, he had scheduled eight local areas as above dispute. After some debate the sub-committee fashioned a further fifteen areas to give what it considered an absolute minimum of twenty-three district councils.[66] The area proposals amounted to as strong a second tier as could be devised within truly localist guidelines; the range of rateable value per head ran only from £4.15 (Shoreditch) to £17.99 (Westminster) if the unavoidable exception of the City is ignored. The drawback was that the reduction of the number of secondary authorities from forty to twenty-three entailed the suppression of some quite distinctive local areas, including Holborn, Whitechapel, Bethnal Green, Rotherhithe, Bermondsey, and, fatally, Chelsea. Hughes's proposals for the allocation of powers were conservative. He proposed no transfer of functions from the LCC to the District Councils, and the sub-committee concurred that such transfers 'would not be to the public advantage'.[67] Instead it mooted

---

[63] Farrer's example in LCC Local Government and Taxation Com., Sub-Committee on Completion of London Government, Minutes: 'Memorandum by Sir T. H. Farrer', 6 Feb. 1890.

[64] LCC Local Government and Taxation Com., Minutes, 26 June 1889.

[65] Sub-Committee on Completion of London Government, Minutes, 25 July 1889.

[66] Ibid., 3 Oct. 1889.

[67] Ibid., 17, 31 Oct. 1889.

various horizontal transfers, giving the LCC some first-tier powers not already within its grasp[68] and the District Councils the second-tier functions performed by other bodies—overseers, burial boards, baths and library commissioners, and, more controversially, the guardians of the poor. Finally, the central–local relationship was handled with a nonchalance suggesting that its contentiousness was not entirely appreciated. The LCC was to be empowered to act in default of the local bodies in all matters, to arbitrate in disputes between District Councils, to approve all District Council by-laws, and to alter District Council areas.[69]

These supervisory provisions would undoubtedly have engendered controversy had the scheme ever been fully aired, but their specialized nature would have confined the argument to the experts. As it was, the scheme was sunk by a public uproar over the proposed amalgamations. Curiously, details of the Hughes scheme were circulated to Councillors before receiving the approval of the full committee, with the predictable result that details were leaked to one of the threatened Vestries. Chelsea considered itself 'a parish whose elective institutions are more ancient than Parliament itself',[70] let alone the LCC; the threat of enforced amalgamation with Kensington prompted what Dilke believed to be 'the only occasion on which the Vestry of Chelsea had ever been known to be unanimous on any subject on which difference of opinion could appear'.[71] The cause was promoted by Dilke, a Chelsea Vestryman himself and perhaps anxious to atone for his association with the 1884 Bill, in an eloquent piece in the *Speaker*, in April 1890.[72] He stressed that the 1884 Bill had respected local boundaries, whatever violence it had threatened to second-tier powers, and advanced the rather Burkean argument that if local areas were frequently changed 'all those traditions of community of life which are an essential element of good local government became lost'. He invoked Hobhouse's view that the existing parishes contained 'a multitude of old associations and sentiments which are entitled to great respect'. Such deference to parochial identity would become familiar during the 1890s. It would eventually do most damage to Conservative proposals for 'tenification', but for the moment it embarrassed the LCC.

In June 1890 Chelsea Vestry organized a public meeting under Dilke's

[68] For example the control of the Metropolitan Common Poor Fund, duties of the Thames Conservancy Board, and powers of the London Assessment Sessions.
[69] Sub-Committee on Completion, Minutes, 31 Oct. 1889.
[70] Chelsea Vestry, *Annual Report* (1889–90), 3.
[71] *West London Press*, 14 June 1890.
[72] *Speaker*, 26 Apr. 1890.

chairmanship.[73] It is a measure of the sensitivity of the question of areas that 'in response to the appeal to parochial patriotism the people of Chelsea attended in numbers that filled the Council Chamber to suffocation', and overflowed outside. The proposal received ritual burial from the meeting, and Costelloe, in the extremely embarrassing position of being chairman of the Local Government and Taxation Committee (although not on the sub-committee) as well as prospective Liberal parliamentary candidate for Chelsea, underwent something of a show trial, after which he 'had no hesitation whatever in condemning the scheme out and out'.[74] The Vestry went on to summon a Vestry conference later in June which asserted the principle that existing local boundaries should be respected as far as possible, and sent a deputation to Salisbury in August.[75] It is likely that the Chelsea protests secured the parish's autonomy in Ritchie's draft District Councils Bill of December 1890, and ensured its survival as a separate authority under the Act of 1899. They probably therefore preserved Chelsea's independence until 1965.

The Council was perhaps fortunate that it had not ratified the scheme before it leaked. In fact the proposals had not even come before the full Local Government and Taxation Committee when the parochial uproar erupted; under the circumstances 'the general sense of the Committee was that it was really of no practical utility to proceed with any scheme of the kind', and it was shelved.[76] In the wake of the Chelsea furore the emphasis of the advocates of second-tier reform within the Council shifted from areas to powers. Farrer advised Costelloe to 'avoid burning questions such as "districting" London, and take up practical questions where centralisation of some sort is obviously desirable'.[77] In directing attention to those fields in which the two-tier system had evolved in the most piecemeal and irrational manner, his recommendation paralleled the policy already being followed by the Local Government Board.

Ritchie's contribution to the flurry of social legislation produced in the last years of the 1886 ministry was the overhaul and consolidation of the corpus of housing legislation by the Housing of the Working Classes Act

[73] See the *West London Press*, 14 June 1890, for the fullest report.
[74] He admitted in 1894 that he had been 'amazed at the fury of the local feeling evoked', a measure of Progressive insouciance on the subject, RC Amalgamation, *PP 1894*, XVII, Q. 13953.
[75] See Chelsea Vestry, *Annual Report* (1890–1), 217–27, for the proceedings and resolutions of the conference.
[76] RC Amalgamation, *PP 1894*, XVII, Q. 13951 (Costelloe).
[77] Farrer to Costelloe, 14 July 1890, in LCC Local Government and Taxation Com., Presented Papers, 16 July 1890.

of 1890, and the extension of the 1875 Public Health Act to London by the Public Health (London) Act of 1891. Both measures called attention to the two-tier balance. With the housing Bill, Ritchie had the advantage that the lines of demarcation had already been drawn at the margin between the two measures. He provided greater executive flexibility by blurring this margin. The LCC was empowered to draw up Torrens Act schemes itself, to contribute to Vestry schemes, and to act in default of a secondary authority.[78] Ritchie admitted freely in the House that the default power was provided at the request of the LCC.[79] There is no evidence that this power, which had existed in the 1879 Torrens Act,[80] provoked extensive Vestry resentment, though it would have been impolitic anyway to defend the principle of second-tier negligence in so emotive a matter.

With the Public Health Bill, however, the position was different. The omission of London from the 1875 Act had saved the designers of that measure from the problem of two-tier allocation, but it left public health provision in London resting upon twenty-nine *ad hoc* statutes.[81] The consequent want of system increased the need to regularize matters, but it also made the drawing of rational lines of division more difficult. The growing conviction that the Council should have a supervisory sanitary role had been reflected in the provisions of the 1888 Act empowering the Council, unlike its predecessor, to appoint a medical officer and to pay half the salaries of Vestry MOHs.[82] This did not, however, provide any guide to the further definition of its tasks. After consulting W. H. James, Chairman of the Council's Public Health Committee,[83] a Moderate but formerly a prominent London Municipal Reform Leaguer, Ritchie introduced a Bill which underlined the Council's supervisory role. A default power similar to that in the Housing Act was introduced, for the first time in a sanitary Bill, and the LCC was also to be empowered to ask the Local Government Board to force a local body to appoint extra sanitary inspectors. The Council was to be given extensive by-law powers over sanitary matters, with an obligation upon the local authority to enforce such by-laws as the Council devised.[84]

---

[78] 53 & 54 Vict., c. 70, ss. 46(7), 45(2).

[79] *Hansard*, 3rd ser., CCCXLV, 1824–5 (24 June 1890).

[80] 42 & 43 Vict., c. 64, s. 12.

[81] Ritchie in *Hansard*, 3rd ser., CCCLII, 33 (7 Apr. 1891).

[82] 51 & 52 Vict., c. 41, s. 24(c).

[83] *The Times*, 9 Apr. 1891: 'As far as the London County Council is concerned, the credit is chiefly due to Captain James'.

[84] *PP 1890–1*, VIII, Bill 231, ss. 9, 20, 36, 37.

The Bill gave a handle to the growing ranks of Conservative back-bench opponents of the Progressive-controlled Council. For London Conservatives like G. C. T. Bartley, whom Ritchie described, with commendable restraint, as 'a good type of a pig-headed, obstinate, unreasonable and most conceited politician',[85] the Bill was seen as 'empowering the London County Council (that dreadful body) to ride roughshod over the Local Sanitary Authority, creating armies of inspectors under the London County Council, setting free the common informer to aid the London County Council etc., etc.'[86] In the Commons the knot of Conservative London MPs who had regularly sniped at the Council's Money and General Powers Bills since 1889, with some success, 'proved themselves more Vestry than the Vestries'.[87] In the Standing Committee on Law, to which the innovatory portions of the Bill were sent, Ritchie was 'only saved from his friends by the interposition of the Liberal Members of the Committee'.[88] The opposition was all the more embarrassing because it did reflect genuine Vestry unease, and when a conference convened by St George, Hanover Square, dispatched a deputation to protest at the by-law provisions, Ritchie met the Conservative London members to hammer out a compromise.[89] The result was the elaboration of a wholly artificial distinction between county and local sanitary by-laws, by which the LCC was left to regulate the times for removal of offensive matter through London and the filling up of cess-pools, while the Vestries prevented nuisances and controlled the keeping of animals. The Council made by-laws on water closets in connection with buildings, but the Vestries regulated their water supply.[90] This was the cow-house/pigsty anomaly writ large. So ended one attempt to regularize the two-tier system.

The controversy over the Public Health Act demonstrated to the government, as that over the amalgamation of Chelsea had demonstrated to the LCC, the sensitivity of the local bodies over questions of second-tier independence. It may have contributed to Ritchie's failure to pursue the district councils scheme with which he had been toying since early 1890. The Cabinet's decision not to deal with rural district councils in that year had not been taken to preclude second-tier reform in London,

[85] Ritchie to Salisbury, 2 June 1891, HHP.

[86] G. C. T. Bartley to Salisbury, 1 June 1891, Ritchie correspondence, HHP.

[87] Ritchie to Salisbury, 2 June 1891.

[88] E. H. Pickersgill in *Hansard*, 3rd ser., CCCLIV, 1618 (26 June 1891). For the proceedings of the Standing Com. see its report in *PP 1891*, XIII.

[89] *The Times*, 19 June 1891.

[90] 54 & 55 Vict., c. 76, ss. 16, 39.

which Ritchie had once believed 'can be done without much difficulty or friction'.[91] A Bill was drafted in 1890, and a promise of action was included in the 1891 Queen's Speech.[92] The draft Bill's similarity to the LCC scheme might imply common ancestry. Although Chelsea particularism was necessarily respected, the number of authorities—twenty-two outside the City, which was, of course, unaffected—was the same as in Hughes's scheme, and the principle of no transfer of power from the LCC to the districts was observed. The proposal was avowedly unspectacular; Ritchie had doubted whether it 'would have all the beneficient results which some people imagine, but it would satisfy public opinion and might possibly improve the administration of the sanitary laws'.[93] Had the Bill ever been published, it would have proved an embarrassment to those Unionist statesmen later in the 1890s who saw second-tier reform as an opportunity to impair by extensive decentralization the Radicalism of the Progressive LCC. The Public Health Act controversy demonstrated the extent to which second-tier reform was a political question when the LCC aroused such controversy.

In the meantime the Council had become entangled in the quarrel over assessment practice. The assessments battle concerned not merely the division of functions, but the very foundations of local taxation. Assessment was effectively a second-tier power, but one upon which all first-tier activity depended. Assessment policy was decided by the twenty-nine local assessment committees, appointed by the poor-law union or, where a parish was independent for poor-law purposes, by the Vestry. A minimal degree of uniformity was imposed by the Metropolis Valuation Act of 1869,[94] which stipulated that the gross assessment should reflect the 'reasonable' rent for a building, and established maximum deductions, from gross to rateable, to cover repairs and insurance. On the face of it, these guidelines might have offset the potentially anarchic fragmentation of the assessment system, but they were not sufficiently comprehensive. In the first place they offered no guide to the specialized assessment of industrial and commercial premises, a task which required professional valuation and tended to be approached in an *ad hoc* manner by amateur committees.[95] Secondly, there was no provision for the reliable assessment

---

[91] Ritchie to Salisbury, 26 Jan. 1890, HHP.
[92] For the Bill see PRO HLG 29/63.
[93] Ritchie to Salisbury, 26 Jan. 1890, HHP.
[94] 32 & 33 Vict., c. 67.
[95] For a valuable survey of assessment practice see the summary compiled by the Lewisham Union Assessment Com. in LCC Local Government and Taxation Com., Presented Papers, 8 May 1889.

of premises extending over more than one assessment area. Railways, in particular, were 'only partially assessed at the present time, because they are split up like a bundle of sticks'.[96] The administrative arguments for greater central direction were therefore considerable. They were compounded by the growing abuse, or perhaps growing awareness of the abuse, of assessment procedure during the 1880s. The cause was the increase in first-tier precepts as a proportion of local taxation. When the bulk of rate revenue had been applied to local purposes there was little incentive to tamper with valuations; if assessments were artificially depressed the poundage rate would need to be higher to raise a given sum. With the growth of the MBW and School Board levies in the 1880s, however, under-assessment offered a means of deflecting the impact of a growing burden which was subject to no direct parochial control. Under-assessment would make the first-tier poundage rates higher than they would otherwise have been, but the increase would have been spread across the whole of London, and much of the odium was likely to be borne by the first-tier bodies. Any parish or union stood to benefit from this anti-social practice, but the incentive was greatest in the City and the West End parishes, where the proportion of the rate in the pound accounted for by first-tier demands was greatest.[97] Kensington had been forced to raise its aggregate assessment in the 1886 quinquennial valuation by the threat of legal action from some of its neighbours;[98] in the battles over the 1891 quinquennial the standard of localism was raised by Marylebone, St George's, Hanover Square, and the City.

The LCC had shown a desire to tackle assessment from the early months of its existence. As well as the obvious wish to keep down the rate in the pound, which was accentuated by frequent public comparisons of the LCC's rate and those of its predecessors, the Progressives had their own reasons for attending to the problem. First the question meshed with the land taxation issue; by expressing deductions as a percentage of the gross valuation, the 1869 Act provided a hidden subsidy to the occupiers of valuable central land.[99] Secondly, the Progressives' desire to correct the disabilities of the poorer parts of London had led them to favour rate

[96] RC Local Taxation, *PP 1899*, XXXVI, Q. 13048 (W. F. Dewey).

[97] 'With the common charges staring one in the face, there is an undue temptation to a locality not to assess to the hilt, but rather to under-assess': W. C. Leete, Kensington Vestry Clerk, before RC Local Taxation, *PP 1899*, XXXVI, Q. 13395.

[98] See e.g. *Metropolitan*, 19 Dec. 1885.

[99] E. J. Harper, the Council's Valuer, estimated that £1.75 million would be added to London's rateable value if deductions were based on structural rather than gross value. RC Local Taxation, *PP 1899*, XXXVI, QQ. 12110–2.

equalization, which could have been rendered ineffective by inconsistent assessment. A sub-committee of the Local Government and Taxation Committee on the Equalization of Assessments and Rates had sat between July 1889 and June 1891,[1] preparing the ground for the LCC's scrutiny of the 1891 quinquennial.

Its investigations indicated casual but extensive under-assessment, so widespread, in fact, that the Council's Valuer put the cost of appealing in every case where the Council had *locus standi* at £25,000.[2] Faced by this bill, the sub-committee resolved to confine their attention to six parishes or unions;[3] the threat was enough to force four of them to treat, leaving the active opposition to St George's Union and Marylebone. The Council embarked upon appeals against the aggregate valuation totals in both these areas, alleging under-assessment by £82,000 in Marylebone and by no less than £200,000 in St George's.[4]

These cases provided a menacing backcloth to the Council's more amicable attempts to bring about assessment uniformity. In May 1890 it had convened a conference of assessment authorities, tactfully managed by Farrer and Hughes, at which genuine difficulties about the state of the law were resolved and a degree of standardization of procedure was agreed upon,[5] but while such voluntarism was sufficient to bring into line those authorities not seeking to use assessment as a means of tax evasion, its limitations were made evident by the intransigence of the two West End authorities which chose to resist. The tortuous progress of the Marylebone and St George's appeal need not be given in detail here; the main legal difficulty which impaired the Council's case related to the validity of challenging aggregate totals on the grounds of systematic under-assessment rather than those of arithmetical error or omission from the lists. The main practical difficulty lay simply in the unsuitability of Quarter Sessions as a forum for the enforcement of valuation procedure. Sir Peter Edlin, chairman of the London Quarter Sessions—a Disraelian appointment felt by many Progressives to lack the judicial impartiality that would have enabled him to take their side—protested stridently

---

[1] Merged with the Assessment and Valuation Sub-Committee in November 1890.

[2] LCC Local Government and Taxation Com., Sub-Com. on Equalization of Assessments and Rates, Minutes, 12 Mar. 1890.

[3] Assessment and Valuation Sub-Com., Minutes, 12 Dec. 1890.

[4] Marylebone figures in Young's memorandum in LCC Local Government and Taxation Com., Presented Papers, 8 Jan. 1891; St George's in 'Case for the Appellants . . .', ibid., 6 Feb. 1891.

[5] For proceedings see LCC Local Government and Taxation Com. Presented Papers, 11 June, 4 July 1890.

against the swamping of his court's business by individual assessment cases.[6] By March 1893 only 125 out of 586 appeals in St George's had been settled.[7] In December of that year the Council accepted a long-standing offer from the Marylebone solicitors to drop their case without costs.[8] The St George's case stumbled into the House of Lords (where the Lord Chancellor was a St George's ratepayer),[9] to be settled in the assessment committee's favour in August 1894.[10] The two appeals, together with action taken against six City parishes, had cost the Council almost £11,000 over four years.[11]

The whole exercise demonstrated to the Council the need for a more coercive and centralized assessment machinery. In July 1892 the Local Government and Taxation Committee resolved to communicate with the government with a view to introducing a Bill to establish a special assessments court.[12] A draft Bill was apparently produced by the Council's unofficial draftsman, H. L. Cripps, only to be heavily criticized by Mac-Kinnon Wood, of the Local Government Committee, because of the extent of local representation on the proposed central assessment committee, and because the burden of appeal remained with the central authority.[13] In December a sub-committee under Costelloe recommended that the Council seek by-law powers over assessment, the right to create a central assessment committee as a standing committee of the LCC and power to 'by fiat alter the totals of any valuation list in respect of any hereditaments which they shall decide to have been wrongly assessed'.[14] In February 1893 these centralizing provisions appeared in a second draft Bill by Cripps.[15]

To the secondary authorities the Council's actions over assessments were unsettling. Probably few of them sympathized greatly with Marylebone and St George's; those who had endeavoured to apply the 1869

---

[6] LCC Local Government and Taxation Com., Presented Papers, 30 Sept. 1892. For earlier Progressive criticism of Edlin's immodest appeal for a salary increase see W. Saunders, *History of the First London County Council* (1892), 371–2.

[7] Report by Blaxland, LCC Local Government and Taxation Com., Presented Papers, 23 June 1893.

[8] Blaxland to Marylebone Assessment Committee (4 Dec. 1893), ibid., 8 Dec. 1893.

[9] Blaxland memorandum LCC Local Government and Taxation Com., Presented Papers, 29 June 1894.

[10] For the judgment see ibid., 26 Sept. 1894.

[11] LCC Local Government and Taxation Com. Minutes, 1 Feb. 1895.

[12] Ibid., 15 July 1892. See also LCC Minutes, 28 June 1892.

[13] LCC Local Government and Taxation Com., Presented Papers, 4 Nov. 1892.

[14] Ibid., 20 Dec. 1892.

[15] Ibid., 1 Feb. 1893.

Act accurately knew that they were paying for their probity.[16] Never-theless, the LCC's inquisitorial methods and its conspicuously low opinion of the local committees probably caused concern; rumours of an imminent centralizing Bill certainly did. When the Council convened its second assessment conference in March 1893, the atmosphere was far more hostile than in 1890. Knowledge of the existence, but not the terms, of the Council's Bill accentuated the latent suspicion so characteristic of the two-tier relationship in these years; Costelloe, the chairman, later recalled that at the first session some delegates had 'menaced us with demonstrations a little like those . . . in the French Parliamentary Assem-bly'.[17] The atmosphere deteriorated further when the inveterate *pro-vocateur* J. F. Kelly of Clerkenwell, informed the sixth session that he had acquired, 'through a dark channel, but a perfectly honest one', a copy of the Bill.[18] The proposal came as 'a mine . . . sprung upon the Con-ference' not so much because its provisions were unexpected as because the Council's reticence seemed to confirm the suspicion of delegates that they had been assembled merely to rubber-stamp its policy. The situation was retrieved only by some submissive diplomacy on the part of Costelloe, for which he was criticized in the Council,[19] by the admission of local nominees to two-thirds of the places on the proposed central assessment committee, and by the dropping of the fiat clause. The Bill which emerged from the Conference, later to founder in Parliament, was therefore far more localist than that originally drafted. That it could satisfy both McKinnon Wood and the representatives of the Kensington Vestry[20] is a lesson in the power of compromise.

Compromise had been made necessary over assessments, over districts, over public health, and even over housing, by the force of the Vestries' reaction to any executive interference with their powers or areas. Both Ritchie and the LCC had underestimated the second-tier solidarity gen-erated during the 1880s by rising first-tier rates and the threat of reform. The battles of these years had shown that Vestry opinion could not be lightly overriden, and that would remain true as the problem evolved during the 1890s.

---

[16] See, for example, the letters from Kensington, Islington and Battersea Vestries in LCC Local Government and Taxation Com., Presented Papers, 12, 28 Nov. 1890.

[17] LCC Local Government and Taxation Com., Presented Papers, 10 Mar. 1899.

[18] Transcript of sixth session of assessment conference in LCC Local Government and Taxation Com., Presented Papers, 8 May 1893.

[19] *London*, 30 Nov. 1893.

[20] LCC Local Government and Taxation Com., Presented Papers, 22 June 1894; Ken-sington Vestry Minutes, 9 May 1894.

But while unanimity was assured in opposition to generalized threats to second-tier independence, events were already beginning to emphasize the divisions within the system that generally characterize the 'metropolitan problem'. The unabated rise of first-tier expenditure was making more strident the perennial complaints of wealthier areas as they saw parochial control over local taxation diminish. The most significant feature of the assessments issue was not that LCC heavy-handedness turned it into another general battle over second-tier autonomy, but that it had begun as an attempt by some of the wealthier parishes to deflect the first-tier burden on to other areas. Once the West End might have expected to be able to put itself at the head of a general second-tier campaign for first-tier economy, as it had done to some extent in 1888, but times had changed. The recent emergence of social politics had emphasized the gulf between rich and poor London, while at the same time raising hopes that municipal action could alleviate social distress. The LCC had identified itself with a social municipalism that clearly entailed the redistribution of metropolitan wealth through first-tier spending. Its policies were admired, and were beginning to be imitated, in those poorer parts of London which stood to benefit from them. They were resented in the West End.[21] The essence of second-tier division was contained in an exchange at a Vestry conference on housing convened by the LCC after the passing of the 1890 Act, when an attempt by a Kensington delegate to localize some of the cost of housing schemes was resisted by a Limehouse representative, arguing that the proposal 'was inimical to the East End and misleading; the improvements required in the East End must, he contended, be paid for by the Council'.[22]

If rising rates and social politics helped underline the divergence of interests within the second tier, the belated but pointed party politicization of London government in the late 1880s helped clarify the battle lines. Liberal Progressives had become firmly identified with municipal enterprise, with redistribution, and with metropolitan integration. Conservative municipal policy was more ambiguous, but hostility to the Radical LCC was pushing the party into a minimalist stance, and into the arms of the West End. Party labels helped intensify division.

All these developments were making the London problem harder to solve. Between 1888 and 1892 Ritchie had come commendably close to

---

[21] For Kensington's acerbic reaction to the Boundary Street scheme see Kensington Vestry, *Annual Report* (1890–1), 65–6.

[22] LCC Housing Department Records, 'Minutes of a Conference between the Housing of the Working Classes Committee and Delegates of the Vestries and District Boards', 4.

a single-handed settlement of the problem, with the first tier reformed, a two-tier concordat reached on housing and sanitary powers, and a district councils Bill in draft. His efforts had foundered then on the Vestries' protectiveness of their own independence; within a few years it would become clear that a would-be reformer would have not only to satisfy the legitimate aspirations of both tiers but also to arbitrate within the second tier between rich and poor, West and East. A settlement would become still more elusive.

6

The Cost of Progress, 1889–1895

Campaigning for the Moderates before the 1895 Council election, Sir John Lubbock, who should have known better, claimed that the Progressives had turned the final MBW rate of 10d. in the pound into an effective rate of 18·1d. in the new estimates.[1] To reach this conclusion it was necessary to conceal the fact that the Council had inherited the justices' duties as well as the Board's, to turn the Council's Exchequer contribution into a rate without treating the Board's coal dues similarly, and to treat the sums raised statutorily by the Council for poor-rate equalization as part of its own expenditure. At the same time, the Progressives produced an election leaflet detailing all these disabilities without mentioning the assistance received from the Exchequer. 'It is pitiable', recorded Beatrice Webb, 'to think of the degradations brought about by the competitive lying of an election.'[2]

Any valid comparison of the Council's rate and those of its predecessors required so many qualifications as to render it unsuitable for electioneering, as the structure of metropolitan finance had been completely overhauled by the 1888 Act. In London, as elsewhere, the Act replaced existing Treasury subventions in aid of poor and county rates by regularized Exchequer Contributions derived from the receipts from probate, beer and spirit, and licence duties. As recipient of the full Exchequer Contribution the LCC was bound to reimburse the poor-law authorities for the loss of the former grant-in-aid. It was also made responsible for the collection and distribution of a grant to the guardians of 4d. per head per day for indoor paupers, and it was empowered to pay half the salary of the Medical Officer of any Vestry which sought such assistance.

By the early 1890s grants-in-aid which had totalled around £2·85 million in 1887/8 had been replaced by Exchequer contributions aver-

---

[1] *Local Government Journal*, 19 Jan. 1895.
[2] Beatrice Webb's Diary, xv. fo. 1374 (17 Feb. 1895).

aging £6·18 million p.a. for the whole of England and Wales.[3] In London the position was less healthy. A total grant of £628,000 in 1887/8 had given way to an average Exchequer Contribution of £1,160,000 p.a. for the early 1890s, which meant a fall in London's share of central payments from 23·01 per cent in the period 1885–8 to 18·77 per cent in 1890–3.[4] Since the metropolis paid around 24 per cent of Imperial taxation,[5] and carried heavier social burdens than any other part of the country, it was arguable that the capital had been harshly treated. The change in the ratio was due to the new methods of apportionment adopted in 1888. The licence-duty receipts were to be shared out in proportion to the number of licences taken out in each county, a method which had the advantage of being self-regulating but which bore no necessary relation to the purposes of rate relief. London's share of licence-duty receipts for 1890–3 represented only 16 per cent of the whole.[6] The probate duty and beer- and spirit-duty grants were originally intended by Ritchie to be distributed in proportion to the extent of indoor pauperism, which would have brought relief 'to no part of the country more than to the poor districts of the Metropolis'.[7] The Liberal opposition, presented with few targets in what was an unexpectedly radical Bill, decided to attack this metropolitan bias, Harcourt even suggesting, with all the tact that made him so popular, that the distribution reflected the fact that Ritchie, Goschen, and W. H. Smith represented London seats.[8] The eventual arrangement was a distribution in the same proportions as the grants-in-aid in their final year. The discontinued grants had to some extent reflected London's special needs, directly through the size of the pauper-lunatic grant, and indirectly through the massive grant for the metropolitan police, but it was obviously a less direct reflection of spending needs than a grant based on indoor pauperism. On top of this, the year 1887/8 had seen London's share of grants-in-aid—at 21·9 per cent—at a lower level than in any of the four preceding years; a quinquennial average would have increased London's share of the probate-duty grants by about £30,000.[9] The effect of the adoption of these methods was that central rate relief was calculated without reference to the assessments on which

[3] See G. L. Gomme's report, 'London and the Imperial Exchequer' in *London Statistics*, IV (1893–4), 565–87, esp. 568, 570.
[4] Calculated from ibid. 568, 570.
[5] *London Statistics*, II (1891–2), xi and III (1892–3), xxvi.
[6] Gomme, 'London and the Imperial Exchequer', 568.
[7] *Hansard*, 3rd ser., CCCXXIII, 1674 (19 Mar. 1888).
[8] Ibid., CCCXXVIII, 612 (6 July 1888).
[9] Gomme, 'London and the Imperial Exchequer', 570.

the rates themselves were levied. James Stuart pointed out in the debate on the Bill that the anticipated levels of relief from licence- and probate-duty receipts amounted to $4d$. in the pound of rateable value outside London and only $1·75d$. within the capital.[10]

Nevertheless, whatever the relative shares, the amount of central support for metropolitan rates did rise by around 85 per cent as a result of the 1888 Act. The effect of this was muted, however, by the coincidental cessation of the coal and wine duties during 1888/9. The Progressives were widely blamed for their approval of the coal dues' abolition, which added around $2d$. to the county rate, but the dues were doomed anyway. Both national parties and the Treasury were hostile to them as an indirect tax upon a necessity, and both the Gladstone and the Salisbury governments had refused MBW and Corporation appeals for renewal. Had a Conservative LCC talked the government into retention of the coal dues, Liberal pressure upon the metropolitan share of Exchequer Contributions would surely have been stepped up, and it is hard to see how both dues and contributions could have remained unimpaired. Nevertheless, the passing of the dues significantly offset the new rate relief, and was a factor unique to London. The average annual Exchequer Contribution over the period of the first two Councils was the equivalent of a rate of $3·7d$. in the pound. Of this, $1·19d$. went to replace the former grants-in-aid, leaving a surplus of $2·51d$. The coal dues had, in their last year, produced $1·83d$., so that the net gain was no more than $0·68d$. in the pound.[11] When this consideration is added to those already mentioned, the limited effect of Exchequer support becomes clear. Expressed as a percentage of rates levied in London—the best way of assessing the ratio of aid to need—the Exchequer Contribution in 1889/90, the first year without the coal dues, comes to only $12·51$ per cent against a national average of $19·19$ per cent. Only 3 of the 114 counties and county boroughs receiving Exchequer support could show a smaller share.[12]

These explanations are a precondition of any assessment of the Progressives' impact upon the rates. In order to make a valid comparison

[10] *Hansard*, 3rd ser., CCCXXIX, 573 (26 July, 1888).
[11] For these figures see Gomme's draft memorandum on London rates in LCC Local Government and Taxation Com. Presented Papers, 1 Feb. 1895.
[12] See Gomme's table in 'London and the Imperial Exchequer', 586–7. As with many of Gomme's exercises, one must be wary. Although the table was drawn up in 1894, it refers only to 1889/90, before the payments in respect of police superannuation (which, like most police grants, disproportionately favoured London) began. As a measure of the inadequacy of licence and probate duty contributions, however, the exercise is valid. The Council did not, of course, benefit from police superannuation payments.

between the Council's rate and those of its predecessors, it is first necessary to remove from consideration the payment made statutorily by the
Council to advance rate equalization, the indoor pauper grant. Equalization levies did not represent new taxation upon the county as a whole,
merely a redistribution of resources within it. Since the necessary sums
were raised on the county rate but applied in relief of local rates, the
Council incurred the odium of the levy without compensating acknowledgement of the benefits conferred. The payments should have been
confined to a separate account, and the Council made sure that this was
done with the Vestry rate equalization of 1894.[13]

When the Council's rate is reduced to the same basis as the rates of
its predecessors it emerges that even by the end of the second Council's
term the total of rates and rate support was less than a penny in the
pound higher than in the last year of the old regime. The main artificial
aid enabling the Council to achieve this had been the quinquennial
valuation of 1891, which, by increasing the county's assessment by around
4 per cent, made possible the convenient reduction in the poundage rate
in the year before the second election. Against that should be set the cost
of new duties imposed upon the LCC since 1889, accounting for 0·97*d.*
of the rate levied in 1894/5.[14] Overall the Council's impact upon the rates
had been marginal. 'Surely', wrote Sidney Webb, 'never was revolution
so cheap'.[15]

There was nevertheless reason to doubt whether the revolution had
actually arrived. Certainly there was heavy expenditure still to come. A
report drawn up by Costelloe in July 1892[16] showed that works already
authorized would cost an estimated £2·44 million, the most costly items
being the Blackwall Tunnel and the Boundary Street housing scheme in
Bethnal Green. An expenditure of £2·25 million to improve the main
drainage network was becoming increasingly urgent. The Council would
eventually have to clarify its position on street improvements. The Strand
Improvement alone would cost £2·25 million, and other schemes

---

[13] See Costelloe's 'Memorandum on the Effect of the Equalisation Bill', in Local Government and Taxation Com., Presented Papers, 5 July 1893, and J. Stuart to H. H. Fowler,
2 May 1893, in the Equalisation Bill Papers, PRO HLG/29/42/24.

[14] Local Government and Taxation Com., Presented Papers, 1 Feb. 1895 (Gomme
Memorandum).

[15] S. Webb, 'The Work of the London County Council', *Contemporary Review*, 67 (1895),
152.

[16] B. F. C. Costelloe, *Memorandum as to Legislative Proposals Concerning the Powers of the
Council* (15 July 1892), LCC *Official Publications*, III, No. 52. For the figures given here see
Appendix V, 24.

TABLE 6.1. First-tier Authorities' Rates (*d.* in £), 1886/7 to 1894/5

	1 Metropolitan Board of Works[a]	2 County Justices[b]	3 Coal or Wine Dues (Rate Equivalent)	4 London County Council[c]	5 LCC Equalization Payments	6 County Rate for LCC Purposes[d]	7 Exchequer Contributions (Rate Equivalent)	8 Total Rates + Rate Support
1886/7	7·13	1·95	2·61	—	—	—	—	11·69
1887/8	7·82	1·81	2·48	—	—	—	—	12·11
1888/9	8·86	1·54	2·18	—	—	—	—	12·58
1889/90	—	—	—	12·53	2·48	10·05	1·57	11·62
1890/1	—	—	—	13·25	2·47	10·78	2·91	13·69
1891/2	—	—	—	11·75	2·63	9·12	3·38	12·50
1892/3	—	—	—	12·50	2·55	9·95	2·66	12·61
1893/4	—	—	—	13·00	2·41	10·59	2·52	13·11
1894/5	—	—	—	14·00	2·54	11·46	2·02	13·48

a. Adjusted to correspond to financial years, to allow inclusion of the Board's last precept, Jan. to Mar. 1889.
b. Average weighted by 1891 population.
c. County Rate as levied.
d. Column 4 minus column 5.

Sources: Return in *London Statistics*, II (1891–2); Gomme's draft memorandum in LCC Local Government and Taxation Committee, Presented Papers, 1 Feb. 1895; Analysis of County Rate 1889–95 in *London Statistics*, VI, 412–13. Coal Dues figures from Local Taxation Returns 1888/9 in *PP 1890*, LXII.

projected in 1892 totalled £1·3 million; even if the Council secured the
'betterment' levy that it sought on properties enhanced in value by its
improvements, a 3 per cent levy on half the enhancement would not raise
£3·5 million.[17] Reversal of the first Council's decision to apply the
beer and spirit duties to rate relief rather than technical education was
anticipated, together with an estimated £230,000 'natural increase' in the
parks and housing budgets. Overall Costelloe envisaged an addition of
£9 million to the Council estimates, putting a further 4·1*d.* on the county
rate.[18]

Nor was this all. Costelloe's memorandum covered only expenditure
plans which had already been formulated, together with the 'natural
increase' of existing budgets. This would have implied that the projects
already under way represented the limit of Progressive ambitions, which
was not the case. Costelloe believed that £3 million would be needed
adequately to implement the Cross Act in London,[19] an estimate which,
since Boundary Street alone absorbed over £300,000, might appear conservative. Water purchase was one of the Progressives' most potent causes,
but the initial burden of compulsory purchase was even more daunting
than it had been in 1880, following the inflation of water profits by three
subsequent quinquennial valuations. Several Progressives must have been
inwardly relieved that the jaundiced Royal Commission of 1892–3 rejected
criticisms of the existing supply.[20]

The metropolitan rating system was already creaking. Total rates in
1894/5 varied between 4*s.* 6½*d.* and 7*s.* 7½*d.* in the pound,[21] levels even
higher on average than those which had been considered intolerable in
the 1860s. They were raised upon an assessment that was some 70 per
cent higher than then and a good deal more sensitive. Costelloe believed
London authorities to be 'literally at a deadlock'[22] so far as even the
most necessary improvements were concerned. For the Council, effective
retrenchment on its own account was extremely difficult. In the first
place, it was heir to the debt created by the expansionary improvement
projects of the MBW in the late 1870s and 1880s, debt which would
diminish only gradually. By May 1890 the Council's gross debt came to

[17] For an explanation of the Council's proposals see the House of Lords SC Town
Improvements (Betterment), *PP 1894*, XV, Q. 1244 (C. Harrison). Also Lord Hobhouse,
'The House of Lords and Betterment', *Contemporary Review*, 65 (1894), 438–52.
[18] Costelloe, *Memorandum on Legislative Proposals*, 24.
[19] SC Town Holdings, *PP 1890*, XVIII, Q. 5098 (Costelloe).
[20] RC Metropolis Water Supply, *PP 1893–4*, XL.
[21] *London Statistics*, V (1894–5), 216–19.
[22] SC Town Holdings, *PP 1890*, XVIII, Q. 4515 (Costelloe).

£29·65 million, of which only some £426,000 was stock raised by the Council and £645,000 was debt due to the Justices' creditors. The net debt, after allowance for reloans and surplus land holdings, was still £17·84 million.[23] Repayment and interest instalments accounted for virtually 8*d*. in the pound of the county rate for the Council's first two years, a level higher than the total MBW rate until 1888.[24] Some 66 per cent of the money raised by the Council for its own purposes in 1888/9 therefore went to debt repayment, and could not be renounced. The remainder of the budget was scarcely more tractable, as will be seen.

2. THE ORGANIZATION QUESTION AND THE ONE-PARTY
COUNCIL

The most significant feature of the county rate table (Table 6.1) is the steady upward trend from the LCC's first year, a trend which was broken by the quinquennial valuation of 1891 but which gathered pace again during the years of the second Council. It is explained by two connected circumstances, one organizational, the other ideological. The organizational factor was the decentralized nature of the Council's constitution. This was in itself an administrative asset, if not a necessity. The MBW had been able to handle much of its administration through its Works and General Purposes Committee, a committee of the whole Board, with much of its proceedings arranged, it was alleged, by a small 'inner ring' of members. Had the LCC depended upon its plenary sessions to get things done, London would have remained ungoverned. At the weekly public sittings, as Burns explained, 'the municipal Dr Jekyll has a tendency to pose as a political Mr Hyde',[25] with the result that the full Council became a lively, and sometimes uproarious, debating chamber. 'Anything more unlike the House of Lords it would be impossible to conceive', was Rosebery's first impression.[26] After only two months as an alderman, Frederic Harrison was 'sick of the L.C.C., who talked raging platitudes to their electors' at the early meetings.[27] Farrer spoke of having got

---

[23] SC Town Holdings, *PP 1890*, XVIII, Appendix 5, 353.

[24] See the analysis of the County Rate 1889–95 and estimates for 1895/6 in *London Statistics*, VI, 412–13.

[25] J. Burns, 'The London County Council. I. Towards a Commune', *Nineteenth Century*, 31 (1892), 499.

[26] Quoted in *London*, 22 Mar. 1894.

[27] Harrison to J. Morley, 13 Apr. 1889, Frederic Harrison Papers 1/68.

through more business in three hours at the Board of Trade than could be done in three weeks at the LCC.[28]

Nevertheless, things did get done. The municipal Dr Jekyll in fact lived and worked in committee. The Council's eighteen or so standing committees enjoyed considerable practical autonomy from the start. 'Whole sections of administration', wrote Sidney Webb at the end of his first three years on the Council, 'are delegated en bloc to particular Committees, and are heard of in Council only by quarterly or annual reports'.[29] Committee independence extended to the nomination of committee chairmen and vice-chairmen, and it was committee work which reared most of the relative 'unknowns' who became influential in Council politics—Costelloe, Dickinson, Charles Harrison, Hutton—as well as two men who were already familiar by the time of their election, but who none the less made their mark on the Council through their labours in committee—John Burns and Sidney Webb. For Beatrice Webb, writing of her husband's first year on the LCC, 'the weekly Council meetings are perhaps the least important part of the Council's proceedings.... The Council is a machine for evolving Committees, the Committee a machine for evolving one man.'[30]

Committee policy reports reached the Council as long and definitive proposals, so that the weekly agenda paper was 'literally as long as one volume of a thirty-one-and-sixpenny novel'.[31] Much would pass without comment. The Council as a whole could amend or veto any report, but it lacked the capacity to initiate policy or, more important, to set one proposal in the context of general policy. The implications of this for the Council's budget are obvious. They had been anticipated, in fact, by the 1888 Act, which had stipulated that all proposals involving more than £50 expenditure be submitted to the Finance Committee for approval.[32] Most Progressives on the first Council found this provision objectionable, partly because of the cumbrous procedure actually envisaged,[33] but mainly because of the composition of the Finance Committee itself. The first committee elections in 1889 had been the last to be invested with any

---

[28] RC Amalgamation, *PP 1894*, XVII, Q. 14166.

[29] Webb, 'The Work of the LCC', 133.

[30] Beatrice Webb's Diary, xiv(ii), fo. 1293 (30 July 1893).

[31] Webb, 'The Work of the LCC', 131.

[32] 51 & 52 Vict., c. 41, s. 80(3). Cf. W. H. Dickinson before the Amalgamation Commission: 'The less we say about section 80 the better. I do not think that it was intended to mean what it says', *PP 1894*, XVII, Q. 1039.

[33] See A. G. Gardiner, *John Benn and the Progressive Movement* (1925), 148–9, who gives the impression that the procedure was observed.

degree of impartiality, and Moderates with specific talents had been drafted on to the relevant committees with comparatively little regard for party. As always, several Moderates were able financiers, and the first Finance Committee included seven Moderates among its fifteen members. The chairman, Lord Lingen, was a nominal Progressive but avowedly unpartisan and, more to the point, a committed retrencher, with a sensitive awareness of his Committee's function under the 1888 Act.

Literal observation of the Act would have brought a series of battles between the Finance and the spending committees, which would probably have culminated in a purge of the former by the Progressive majority. In fact the spending committees circumvented the requirements of the Act by submitting all proposals directly to the Council, which would pass them, if it did so, subject to the submission of an estimate by the Finance Committee.[34] This cast upon the committee the onus of rejecting schemes which already had the Council's approval, rather than adapting projects before they reached the Council. Lingen railed against such an arrangement, asking on one occasion whether his committee was to become 'a mere register of the decrees of the Council',[35] and a level of tension built up between Lingen, supported by Lubbock, Farrer, Rosebery and most of the Moderates, and the Progressive radicals.

This culminated, towards the end of the first Council, in the public dispute between Lingen and Charles Harrison, effective leader of the radicals, over the comparatively trivial question of the method of loan repayment. Neither the annuity system nor the instalment system of repayment was fiscal heresy.[36] The Local Government Board favoured annuities when giving loan sanction to guardians; the Treasury had favoured instalments for the Metropolitan Board. Lingen, after twenty years at the Treasury, supported instalments. Possibly only twenty years

[34] Memorandum by Special Organization Com. on Finance in LCC General Purposes Com., Presented Papers, 9 May 1892.

[35] *Metropolitan*, 15 Nov. 1890. The occasion was the presentation of the Boundary Street estimates.

[36] Under the instalment system, equal amounts of principal were paid off each year, and interest payments fell in step with the principal. Under the annuity system the entire loan, with interest, was paid off at the end of its term by means of a sinking fund fed by equal annual payments sufficiently large to enable the fund to accumulate at interest to meet the burden of repayment. The annuity system was cheaper in the early years of repayment, as the generation of interest by the sinking fund kept the annuity payments low, but was more burdensome in the later years and overall because interest was paid on the entire loan throughout. For a blow by blow example see Charles Harrison's memorandum of 30 Oct. 1890, in LCC *Official Publications*, 1, No. 13.

at the Treasury could have convinced anybody that the difference between annuity and instalment was a resigning matter, but there were questions of principle involved. Harrison objected to the existing loan system for capital improvements *in toto*, so long as occupiers paid the rates, feeling that while it was possible for a ninety-nine-year leaseholder to pay off most or all of a sixty-year loan within his term, Council improvement projects merely enhanced the value of a freeholder's property at the expense of the occupier.[37] Adoption of the annuity system, which fell less heavily in the earlier years of repayment, would at least reduce the impact upon the occupier, possibly until such time as landowners could be made to contribute to the rates. Harrison's opponents glossed this to imply that his 'only rule of finance', to quote the Liberal Unionist Progressive W. W. Bruce, 'was to put off payments from the present day and defer them to a future day ... a well-known and simple rule, which was in active operation in several South American republics'.[38] Lingen and his supporters believed that the greatest part of the burden of repayment should be carried by the generation which opted to contract the loan, and that in any case the Council should not tamper with accepted financial practice for political reasons.[39] Lingen resented the Council's interference with technical decisions made by his committee. The passing of a series of reloans on the annuity principle in December 1891 led to Lingen's resignation, shortly followed by the resignation of the vice-chairman Benjamin Cohen and three other finance committee Moderates.[40]

The loans question represented the first serious defeat for the junta which had been raised to power in 1889—Rosebery, Lubbock, Farrer, and Lingen—at the hands of the Progressive rank and file. If Rosebery had really believed, as Farrer said,[41] that the battle would diminish Harrison's influence, he had misjudged both the mood of the Progressive party and Harrison's importance within it. The affair raised serious doubts as to whether the Progressive party was amenable to any overall control. Lingen had martyred himself for the sake of a somewhat exalted view of the role of his committee, which he believed to have been 'meant by the Local Government Act of 1888 to be the government; appointed

---

[37] See e.g. SC Town Holdings, *PP 1890*, XVIII, Q. 3463 (Harrison); LCC *Official Publications*, I, No. 13 (Harrison Memorandum), 6.

[38] *London*, 15 Feb. 1894.

[39] See the correspondence in *The Times*, 23, 25 Jan. 1892. Also Farrer to Lubbock, 22 Dec. 1891, Avebury Papers, Add. MS 49657, fo. 171.

[40] LCC Minutes, 15 Dec. 1891, 19 Jan., 2 Feb. 1892.

[41] Farrer to Lubbock, 2 Feb. 1892, Avebury Papers, Add. MS 49658, fo. 39. Farrer was 'not sure of this'.

indeed, and removable by the Council (Parliament) but when appointed, and while appointed meant to exercise very real power (regulation and control of finance)'.[42] This was a generous interpretation of the statute, but the deposition of the Finance Committee did draw attention to the absence of any effective central controlling body within the Council. 'The whole case illustrates the need of something like a ministry, which could resign if beaten on a point of vital policy', wrote Farrer to Lubbock in January 1892. 'The Council must learn that if they choose leaders and mean to keep them they must not kick them.'[43] Lubbock himself contributed an article to the *Fortnightly Review* in February, stressing the lack of any executive in the Council and suggesting the chaos that would result if parliamentary government operated in a similar way.[44] Rosebery, in a letter declining nomination for St George's-in-the-East in 1892, indicated that the organization question would be the first great problem facing the second Council.[45]

There were strong administrative arguments for the creation of an executive on the Council, but they ran counter to many Progressive instincts. What Burns stigmatized as 'centralised, secret and internal control' was likened to the closet administration of the MBW and contrasted with 'the public, popular, open policy of letting committees who really know most about the work decide the lines on which that work should be conducted'.[46] The committee work of the rank and file Progressives was impressive. Their exertion was generally unpublicized, and they did not wish to see its results suppressed by executive fiat. For the labour men in particular, persistent committee work was the means of winning improvements in the wages, hours, and conditions of the Council employees;[47] the Council's 'moral minimum' of 24s. per week had been attained in practice by 1892 without ever being ratified by the full Council.[48] On top of this, most Progressives felt irritated enough by existing external constraints upon the Council, which an increasingly

[42] Lingen to Rosebery, 28 Dec. 1891, RP MS 10090, fo. 258.

[43] Farrer to Lubbock, 30 Jan. 1892, Avebury Papers, Add. MS 49658, fo. 36.

[44] Sir John Lubbock, 'A Few Words on the Government of London', *Fortnightly Review*, 57 (1892), 159–72. For the genesis of this article, which Lubbock believed to have been written 'not from a polemical point of view', see Lubbock to Farrer, 26 Dec. 1891, Sir Thomas Farrer Papers, 2572/93/4.

[45] *The Times*, 6 Feb. 1892.

[46] J. Burns, 'Let London Live', *Nineteenth Century*, 31 (1892), 684–5.

[47] Burns joined the Main Drainage Committee in 1889 precisely because it was the largest employer: J. Burns, 'Towards a Commune', 503.

[48] As Farrer complained: RC Labour, *PP 1893–4*, xxxix, Pt. I, Q. 3780 (Webb), Q. 7711 (Farrer).

hostile Unionist government did nothing to relax, and by Ritchie's attempts to bring LCC spending under tighter Local Government Board control in the summer of 1891,[49] to see no virtue in voluntary submission to internal curbs.

In any case, the Progressive party was simply not amenable to the sort of hierarchical guidance that the proposal envisaged. The party's strengths lay in the caucus at Spring Gardens, at which the rank and file prevailed by weight of numbers, and in the revitalized Liberal Associations in the constituencies. The national Liberal party apparently provided little more than moral support for the London Progressives, and the Progressive organization at Spring Gardens was unable to provide financial support for the local associations at election time.[50] The Liberal Associations were much less ready than their Conservative counterparts to call upon the central or metropolitan party organizations for candidates, and although candidates were generally expected to defray much of the cost of their campaigns, they were also expected to subscribe to the Progressive programme to the satisfaction of their constituency associations.[51] Under these circumstances, the Progressive hierarchy had no stronger sanction than 'moral suasion' available should it find itself at odds with the party as a whole, and the loans question, among other battles on the first Council, had shown how ineffective that was.

After the loans battle, Farrer had consoled himself with the thought that the next Council 'will not be so C. Harrisonian as the present'.[52] In fact the landslide of March 1892 created an enlarged Progressive party more radical and partisan than its predecessor. One of its first acts was to demonstrate that it would not have a chairman imposed upon it, let alone an executive. The Liberal Party hierarchy had been grooming Lord Carrington for the chair since his return from the governorship of New South Wales in the summer of 1891; in September Francis Schnadhorst and James Stuart had urged him to contest Hoxton 'with a view to becoming chairman'.[53] An embarrassing brush with the 'Shoreditch 200 Liberal "desperadoes" ' had aborted the Hoxton project,[54] but Carrington was eventually adopted and elected by West St Pancras. On meeting the

---

[49] By the amendment of Standing Order 194. See PRO/T1/8576 C/9115.

[50] Cf. J. W. Benn to J. R. Seager, 24 June 1891, Progressive Party Minutes, and report on interview with LLRU executive, Minutes, 14 July 1891.

[51] Among the reasons for Carrington's rejection by Hoxton in 1891 was that he was 'not disposed to go far enough as to betterment': Carrington Diaries, 18 Nov. 1891.

[52] Farrer to Lubbock, 7 Feb. 1892, Avebury Papers, Add. MS 49658, fo. 49.

[53] Carrington Diaries, 25 Sept. 1891.

[54] Ibid., 16 Nov. 1891.

Progressive caucus after the March elections, however, he was rejected both for the chairmanship—to which Rosebery returned as a temporary 'unity' candidate—and for the vice-chairmanship—to which John Hutton was elected unanimously. 'Carrington (wily dog) after his experiences of toadies in the Colonies professed his inability to fill the office'—recorded Burns, ' "wanted to learn", "willing to be a private", his humility will yet win him the chair'.[55] It did not. When Rosebery stepped down in July the Progressive slate for the leadership—Hutton as chairman, Charles Harrison as vice-chairman, and W. H. Dickinson as deputy-chairman—comprised good party men and good committee men. Harrison's nomination was particularly distasteful to the Moderates. Benjamin Cohen asked whether he had 'the qualification of absence of party "spirit" ' and expressed regret that 'the arrangement under which communications had been passed between the various sections of the Board [sic] with the view to secure nominations which would be acceptable to all had not been followed in the case of the present and recent vacancies'.[56] Selection of committees on the new Council had been equally partisan. Whereas in 1889 there had been five Moderate committee chairmen, in 1892 there were only two. On the second Council, therefore, an enlarged and more radical Progressive majority acted without the constraint of the previous centrist leadership and without most of the Moderate committeemen.

These circumstances might have strengthened the case for the executive proposal, but they hardly strengthened its chances of success, and it met with a frosty reception when it came before the new Council. A Special Committee on Organization was appointed in March 1892, and at its first meeting Rosebery raised the question of a 'Central Committee of Policy'.[57] It was opposed by, among others, Burns, who 'succeeded in preventing a vote, yea I believe killed it'.[58] The Special Committee appointed three sub-committees, including one concerned with financial management. The executive was again discussed at the second meeting of the organization Committee and again left unresolved. A fourth sub-committee was appointed to consider the role of the General Purposes Committee, which Lubbock had seen as an embryonic executive.[59] After the meeting Burns spoke with Rosebery for an hour on the subject, coming away with the impression that 'I at last convinced him he was

---

[55] Burns Journal, 9 Mar. 1892, Add. MS 43612.
[56] *Local Government Journal*, 23 July 1892.
[57] LCC Minutes, 22 Mar. 1892; LCC General Purposes Com. Minutes, 23 Mar. 1892.
[58] Burns Journal, 23 Mar. 1892, Add. MS 43612.
[59] LCC General Purposes Com. Minutes, 23, 28 Mar. 1892.

wrong'.[60] Whether or not this was true, the question was not raised again in this form. Instead it was left to the various sub-committees to return their reports. The sub-committee on the General Purposes Committee rejected the idea of an executive, recommending only that the Committee 'be assigned the duty of keeping in the mind of members a comprehensive view of the action of the Council, and its relation to any particular proposition laid before the Council', without expressing an opinion on the wisdom of the proposition itself.[61] On the finance sub-committee, however, Lubbock, with the assistance of the Moderate Beachcroft and the defection of one of the three Progressives, pushed through a recommendation· to institute strict observance of the system of financial scrutiny laid down in the 1888 Act.[62] The Organization Committee blocked this by sending it to the various committees for comment; only five of the fourteen committees which replied approved the proposal, and it dropped.[63] The Council was therefore left with no executive, merely an upgraded General Purposes Committee serving as 'half revising Cabinet, half "maid of all work" to the others',[64] with no independence in matters of policy.

TABLE 6.2.   LCC Estimated Rate for Council Services, 1889/90 to 1894/5 (*d.* in £)

	1889/90	1890/1	1891/2	% increase 1889–92	1892/3	1893/4	1894/5	% increase 1889–95
Main Drainage	1·098	1·228	1·274	16·13	1·349	1·637	1·302	18·58
Parks	·404	·445	·483	19·55	·588	·621	·711	75·99
Fire Brigade	·644	·651	·668	3·73	·673	·759	·867	34·63
Traffic Routes	·225	·235	·256	13·78	·274	·355	·308	36·89
Building Act	·011	·014	·010	−9·09	·024	·023	·016	45·45
Industrial Schools	·130	·098	·112	−13·85	·122	·127	·137	5·38
Technical Education	—	—	—	—	·003	·033	·295	—
Judicial	·444	·467	·481	8·33	·455	·508	·470	5·86
Lunacy	·267	·392	·619	131·84	·536	·480	·528	97·75
Other Services	·101	·189	·164	62·38	·238	·219	·241	138·61
Establishment	·804	·815	·806	0·25	·925	·993	1·160	44·28
TOTAL	4·128	4·534	4·873	18·05	5·187	5·755	6·035	46·20

Source: County Rate analysis 1889–95 in *London Statistics*, VI, 412–13.

The result was not only that it was very difficult to co-ordinate Council policy, but also that it was very difficult to bridle the enthusiasm of the

[60] Burns Journal, 28 Mar. 1892, Add. MS 43612.
[61] General Purposes Com. Presented Papers, 9 May 1892.
[62] Ibid., Memorandum from Special Organization Committee on Finance.
[63] General Purposes Com. Minutes, 4 Apr. 1892, Presented Papers, 9 May 1892.
[64] Webb, *Work of LCC*, 141.

spending committees. Table 6.2 demonstrates the consequences. An increase of less than 12 per cent in the county rate over the period of the first two Councils masked a rise of more than 46 per cent in the non-debt rate. If the 0·97d. attributed to services introduced since 1889 in the 1894/5 estimates is entirely disregarded, there remains an underlying increase of 22·7 per cent in the rate levied for council services over only six years, and this despite an increase of more than 7 per cent in the assessment of the administrative county. That such an increase could occur even before many of the most cherished Progressive projects had borne fruit should have disturbed the party. LCC spending was not out of control—councillors were conscious of the electoral dangers of rising rates—but the forces encouraging expansion simply outweighed those inhibiting it. The economies of scale inherent in a large authority can be more than offset by the kind of organizational wastage afflicting large commercial concerns;[65] something of this sort affected the early LCC.

Most Progressives were reluctant to accept a stark choice between progress and economy. Their rhetoric had assumed the existence of untapped sources of revenue which could afford rate relief without inhibiting the Progressive programme, but by the end of the second Council's term the Progressives had made no advance on water purchase, the absorption of the City, or the taxation of land values. Limited tramway purchase had provided London's only remunerative debt. Yet the Council had inherited a first-tier rate level already considered oppressive, and had been unable to prevent its upward drift. As if to emphasize the point, the estimates for 1895/6, announced only four days before the 1895 Council election—an obvious opportunity for expedient retrenchment—envisaged another penny on the county rate.[66]

The Progressives' position was worsened by the acceleration of second-tier rates in the early 1890s. When total rates were considered high, each of the major spending authorities in the London system—Vestries, Guardians, County Council, or School Board—operated on the margin of ratepayers' tolerance, inhibited in fresh expenditure by the levies of the other bodies, yet unable to reduce those levies. Although it was suggested earlier that the ratepaying public is more likely to blame the rating than the precepting authority for rising rates in a two-tier system, the enormous publicity and controversy surrounding the LCC made it

---

[65] J. Dearlove, *The Reorganisation of British Local Government* (Cambridge, 1979), 6–7.
[66] The Chairman of the Finance Committee, Evan Spicer, was 'an alderman and an honest man'; Beatrice Webb's Diary, xv. 1373–4 (17 Feb. 1895).

more prominent than the second-tier bodies in the 1890s. McKinnon Wood attributed just two opinions to the London ratepayer: 'first, that the rates, somehow, always tend to increase, and secondly that the whole of that increase is due to the action of the London County Council'.[67] This was special pleading, and cannot be proved, but there is little doubt that the Progressives were vulnerable as long as they piled an increasing county rate upon second-tier rates that were rising still faster. Whilst they undoubtedly approved of the revival of the second tier in the 1890s, they must have been conscious of the threat that it posed to their own position.

3. THE REVIVAL OF VESTRYDOM

For Robert Donald the 'leading note' struck by the LCC was to be found not so much in its own work as in the 'energising influences which the Council has started'.[68] With many of the cherished projects of the LCC Progressives stifled by the want of legal power, it is arguable that Progressivism found a better outlet in the second tier than the first. It is also true that in some areas the rejuvenation of Vestrydom had begun before 1889, and it is probably more accurate to speak of the first- and second-tier revivals sharing common ancestry in the emergence of social politics and the overhaul of London Liberalism in the later 1880s. In the space of less than a decade the Vestries underwent a municipal evolution that had occupied up to forty years in the provinces. The ascendancy of the shopocracy, with its dated tone of 'economist' Radicalism, faded in the late 1880s. The static nature of Vestry politics since the 1860s had meant that the Vestries, like the MBW, had aged with the 1855 system, and the late 1880s and early 1890s saw death or retirement remove many of the men who had dominated parish life for up to thirty years—Robert Gladding of Whitechapel, G. P. Meaden of Wandsworth, Edward Dresser Rogers of Camberwell, John Runtz of Hackney, Robert Furniss of St Pancras. At the same time the post-Redistribution Liberal constituency organizations began to turn their attention to Vestry elections. The late 1880s saw the transformation of Vestry politics from the old system of ostensibly apolitical ratepayers' associations to one of party political

---

[67] *London*, 22 Mar. 1894. Cf. C. Harrison's draft manifesto for 1895, Benn Papers, vi. 5.
[68] R. Donald, 'How We Are Governed: London's Parliament at Work', *Windsor Magazine*, i (March 1896), 278.

contests. An editorial in the *Westminster Times* on the 1887 Vestry elections within its circulation area[69] provides a microcosmic analysis of this evolution: in St Martin's, politically quiescent like most central parishes, the election had 'already taken place very quietly'. In St Margaret and St John the single active Ratepayers' Association had drawn up its slate and no contest was anticipated. In St George, Hanover Square the two ratepayers' associations had failed to agree on a joint list and would fight as rivals, but without political affiliation. In Chelsea, where Dilke had canvassed for the nomination of his supporters by the Parochial Protection Society, party lists were being run.

The running was usually made by the 'Liberal and Radical' constituency associations, advocating the brand of social politics that had gained ground in the early and mid-1880s, and would soon be voiced on the LCC. The emergent Vestry Progressive parties comprised many of the radicals who had supported municipal reform on the Vestries earlier in the decade, together with middle-class sympathizers with the social programme, and the few working men who managed to satisfy the Vestry qualification. Their programmes of municipal enterprise were frequently unpalatable to the older retrenchment-minded Liberals. Some, like William Robson of Clerkenwell, who had remained loyal to Liberalism after Home Rule and had been president of the Central Finsbury Liberal Association in 1887, crossed the floor during the 1890s. Others, like Mark Judge of Paddington, survived as militant independents, but many representatives of the older Vestrydom simply accepted their alienation from the new Radicalism.[70]

The injection of politics was a major element in the revival of the long-static Vestry system. It brought dramatically increased turnouts at elections[71] and raised the 'turnover' of Vestry membership.[72] By increas-

[69] *Westminster Times*, 14 May 1887.
[70] For example, J. A. Lyon of Camberwell, who 'had always thought that I was a Liberal amongst Liberals, but the new class of Liberals, or Progressists, won't have me, and I can't go over to the Tories' (*London*, 17 June 1897), and W. S. Upton, a veteran of the Tower Hamlets Liberal Association opposed by the Mile End Progressives in 1894, who considered himself 'a Radical as it was understood in the Chartist days, not the mixture of Socialist-Republican of the present, with which he had no sympathy'. (Obituary in the *Shoreditch Guardian*, 8 June 1895.)
[71] For example in Camberwell, where no more than 2 of the 6 wards had been polled in any year before 1882, all 6 were polled for the first time in 1888, and never fewer than 4 thereafter: Camberwell Vestry, *Annual Report* (1899–1900), 291–2.
[72] For example in Shoreditch the rate of change of Vestrymen 1886–96 was double that of the previous ten years: F. Sheppard, 'St Leonard, Shoreditch', in D. Owen, *The Government of Victorian London* (Cambridge, Mass., and London, 1982), 342.

ing the accountability of Vestrymen it must have contributed to the surge of second-tier activity in the 1890s. But this increasing activity was evident even in the central and West End parishes where the challenge of Progressivism was weakest. The Vestry revival was not confined to the East and inner South, but was a general phenomenon, reflecting the local authorities' reaction to the image of negligence propagated in the 1880s, and their anxiety for the second tier's future.

The growth of first-tier rates during the 1880s, and in particular that of the two authorities precepting upon the Vestries—the MBW and the School Board—had had the effect of depressing Vestry expenditure, or at least of restraining its growth. The Vestries' share of all metropolitan local taxation fell from 30 per cent in 1878/9 to a low of 22 per cent in the MBW's last year, 1888/9.[73] 'The continual increase of these central precepts has the effect of starving local work', complained H. M. Robinson, the Progressive Vestry Clerk of Shoreditch.[74] In the early 1890s the emergence of local Progressivism and the more general diffusion of municipal enterprise in the second tier encouraged the Vestries to abandon their attempts to absorb first-tier expansion. Between 1888/9 and 1893/4 the rates levied by Vestries and District Boards for their own purposes rose by nearly 40 per cent, despite a 31 per cent increase in all first-tier levies.[75]

These years saw an expansion of Vestry activity in almost every field, from the routine to the ostentatious. The housing crisis and its effect upon the Vestries' reputation had put a premium upon the most mundane duties of sanitary management, and pressure was maintained by the voluntary efforts of the Mansion House Council.[76] The number of sanitary inspectors in London was said to have risen from 53 to 208 between 1885 and 1894,[77] and sanitation assumed a new prominence in second-tier politics.[78] Overall, however, it was the expansion of capital projects that marked the Vestry revival. The LCC sanctioned loans totalling £317,000 for the provision of parks and open spaces by the Vestries during the

---

[73] See Appendix 3.

[74] Shoreditch Vestry, *Annual Report* (1892–3), Clerk's Report, 4.

[75] See Appendix 3.

[76] Several parishes were subjected to Home Office inspections following the representations of the Mansion House Council. See the reports in *PP 1886*, LVI (Clerkenwell, Mile End); *PP 1888*, LXXXI (Bethnal Green); *PP 1889*, LXV (Rotherhithe); and *PP 1890–1*, LXVIII (Shoreditch).

[77] By Asquith, deriving his figures from Webb, at the Queen's Hall. *Daily Chronicle*, 8 Dec. 1894.

[78] For a lively account of Progressive sanitation in Newington see J. W. Horsley, *'I Remember': Memories of a 'Sky Pilot' in the Prison and the Slum* (1911), 240.

1890s, and no less than £1·8 million for paving works;[79] the Fulham Progressives considered it an electioneering point in 1893 that seven miles of new streets had been laid out since 1886.[80] The rash of Queen Anne municipal buildings still prominent in London provides the Vestries' most conspicuous memorial. Between 1885 and 1900 seventeen new town halls or Vestry halls were planned or built.[81] In the ten years from 1886 eighteen baths and washhouses were opened, and thirty-four parishes adopted the Public Libraries Acts, where only two had done so before.[82] More selectively, St Pancras, Hampstead, and a handful of other authorities undertook municipal electric lighting, an adoptive Vestry function under Acts of 1882 and 1888.[83] Camberwell Vestry opened a school of art and supported a technical college.[84] Shoreditch opened its Municipal Technical Schools in May 1893 and carried through the most imaginative second-tier housing project at Moira Place, while embarking on the Pitfield Street library, town hall, and dust-destructor scheme, completed in 1899.[85]

In working-class areas Vestry Progressivism, like LCC Progressivism, embraced an active labour policy. Its preconditions were the trend towards direct labour over the previous three decades and 'the growing demand that public bodies should be model employers'.[86] Booth cited a 123 per cent increase in the number of municipal employees in London between 1861 and 1891, with a 40 per cent increase during the 1880s alone, making local authority work the eighth fastest growing London employment sector.[87] By 1890 John Cole, secretary of what was then the London Vestry Employees' Union, could claim that the Vestry direct labour force outnumbered contract labour by three to two.[88] The Progressive Battersea Vestry dispensed with the contractor completely in 1895.[89] In the late 1880s and early 1890s this long-term trend towards direct

---

[79] *London Statistics*, x (1899–1900), 763.

[80] 'How Fulham is Governed', *London*, 30 Mar. 1893.

[81] From the table compiled by C. Cunningham, *Victorian and Edwardian Town Halls* (London, Boston, and Henley, 1981), Appendix 2, 252 ff.

[82] *London Statistics*, x (1899–1900), 228–67 and 304. The baths total includes rebuildings.

[83] *London*, 2 Nov. 1893, 15 Mar. 1894, and 4 Apr. 1895.

[84] Ibid., 16 Apr. 1896, 6 Jan. 1898.

[85] Ibid., 2 Mar., 4 May 1893. For Moira Place see ibid., 26 Mar. 1896 and 14 Oct. 1897; for Shoreditch see also *Municipal Journal*, 1 June 1900.

[86] A. L. Baxter, 'Civil and Municipal Service', in C. Booth, *Life and Labour of the People of London* (1902), 2nd ser. iv, 27.

[87] Booth, *Life and Labour*, 2nd ser. v, 60.

[88] *Metropolitan*, 29 Nov. 1890.

[89] For the Battersea experiment, culminating in the opening of the municipal workshops in 1898, see *London*, 6 Jan. 1898.

employment coincided with more limited but intense public anxiety over sweating to produce a widespread improvement in municipal wages. The pressure for wage increases was political rather than economic. Booth's collaborator A. L. Baxter had no doubt that 'even where the wages are very low the supply of labourers is always largely in excess of the demand', or that every Vestry could pay its sweepers as little as 18s. per week and still secure an adequate supply of men.[90] The comparative resilience of municipal labour during the recession years of 1892–5, when 'new unionism' generally faltered, supports his view, as does the virtual absence of strikes for higher pay.[91] Table 6.3 shows the Board of Trade figures for individual wage increases from 1893 to the end of the decade; if the returns stretched back to the late 1880s they would be more striking still, for the indications are that the greatest advances were made in the wake of the gas and dock strikes of 1888–9. Table 6.4, constructed from Baxter's breakdown of his own 1895 survey and of a return compiled by Battersea Vestry in 1891, nevertheless shows a significant improvement in those four years.

The other element of labour policy was unemployment relief. A succession of Local Government Board circulars to Vestries from 1886, urging the expedition of labour-intensive projects to alleviate distress, encouraged the belief that the local authorities could significantly reduce unemployment. Such exhortations were unhelpful: 'we had their circular, but they did not give us the legal power to carry it out', as the Shoreditch Vestry Clerk complained,[92] but while the West End authorities could afford to ignore what the Kensington Vestry Clerk stigmatized as the LGB's 'pass it on policy',[93] working-class parishes were subjected to pressure from below as well as from above. In Shoreditch itself in 1893 'the unemployed came in a threatening manner until the Vestry agreed to put on so many men to do the dusting and scavenging twice as often as before ... One thousand of these men on several occasions marched down from Tower Hill and endeavoured to block the entrance to the Town Hall'.[94] Most Vestries in working-class areas took action of this

[90] Baxter, 'Civil and Municipal Service', 27, 30.
[91] John Cole told the LVEU annual meeting in 1890 that the union operated not through strikes but through the polls (*Metropolitan*, 29 Nov. 1890). Cole's successor J. W. Fitch claimed in 1897 that the union had never needed to strike (*London*, 4 Mar. 1897).
[92] RC Amalgamation, *PP 1894*, XVII, Q. 11846 (Robinson).
[93] Letter from W. C. Leete to *Local Government Journal*, 18 Nov. 1893.
[94] RC Amalgamation, *PP 1894*, XVII, Q. 11845 (Robinson). For similar pressure in Newington see Newington Vestry, *Annual Report* (1892–3), 79, and in St George the Martyr see *London*, 7 Feb. 1895.

TABLE 6.3.　Strength of National Municipal Labour Union and Number of London Municipal Employees Affected by Increases in Wages during the 1890s

Year	Members	NMLU[a] Annual Income	Expenditure per member	Increases in wages[b]
1891	3377	£ 661	8s. 1½d.	—
1892	5793	1771	5 1½	—
1893	5674	2205	8 2	775
1894	4530	1852	7 10	986
1895	4500	1729	7 7¾	1034
1896	4505	1663	7 4¾	1763
1897	4766	1612	7 2	1175
1898	4732	1662	7 3	627
1899	3918	—	—	2354

a. Despite its title the NMLU recruited almost exclusively from London; see C. Booth, *Life and Labour*, 2nd ser., iv. 42. In 1891 the union appears as the National Labour Union of Municipal and Vestry Employees; the name changed to the National Municipal and Incorporated Vestry Employees Labour Union in 1892, and to the National Municipal Labour Union in 1898.

b. Board of Trade Labour Department, Reports on Wages and Hours of Labour in *PP 1894*, LXXXI (II); *PP 1896*, LXXX (I); *PP 1897*, LXXXIII; *PP 1898*, LXXXVIII; *PP 1899*, XCI; *PP 1900*, LXXXI.

Source: Board of Trade Chief Labour Correspondent, Statistical Tables in *PP 1893–4*, CII; *PP 1894*, XCIV; *PP 1895*, CVII; *PP 1896*, XCIII; *PP 1897*, XCIX; *PP 1898*, CIII; *PP 1899*, XCII; *PP 1900*, LXXXIII. Membership figures for year end.

sort, whether willingly or not, but the feeling that 'where a Royal Commission on this subject has failed to provide any specific remedy, it would appear doubtful if local authorities ... will excel [their] efforts'[95] engendered an understandable defeatism. Want of power or funds inhibited such ambitious projects as John Cole's £10,000 of parochial reflation in Camberwell[96] and H. M. Robinson's light railways and municipal farms for Shoreditch.[97] The Vestries' horizons were usually limited to short-term and casual employment—street sweeping or snow clearing.[98]

[95] Fulham Vestry, *Annual Report* (1894–5), 227.
[96] *Local Government Journal*, 25 Nov. 1893.
[97] *London*, 21 Dec. 1893.
[98] A summary of Vestry relief work in the winter of 1892–3 is given in *London Statistics*, IV (1893–4), xxiv.

TABLE 6.4.	Vestry Wage Rates: Comparison of Booth/Baxter Return for 1895 and Battersea Vestry Return for 1891

| | Battersea Sample 1891 | | | | Booth/Baxter Sample 1895 | | | |
| | All occupations | | Sweepers | | All occupations | | Sweepers | |
Weekly Wages	No.	%	No.	%	No.	%	No.	%
Below 20s.	732	20	258	$29\frac{1}{2}$	189	5	150	13
20–25s.	2129	58	584	$66\frac{1}{2}$	1156	$29\frac{1}{2}$	424	36
25–30s.	513	$14\frac{1}{2}$	37	4	1830	$46\frac{1}{2}$	597	51
30–35s.	147	4	—		508	13	—	
35–40s.	55	$1\frac{1}{2}$	—		117	3	—	
40–45s.	22	$\frac{1}{2}$	—		87	$2\frac{1}{2}$	—	
Above 45s.	37	1	—		27	$\frac{1}{2}$	—	
SAMPLE TOTALS	3635	(100)	879	(100)	3914	(100)	1171	(100)

Source: Booth, *Life and Labour*, 2nd ser. v. 44.

This expansion of second-tier activity was general, and not confined to Vestries under Progressive control. Obviously the Progressives of any Vestry were more likely to identify themselves with municipal action, and the Moderates with municipal retrenchment. Progressives may have been more committed to sanitary reform—the Fulham Medical Officer who admitted privately that 'the Progressives are his best friends'[99] was probably not alone—and they were almost always more committed to fair wages and unemployment policies, but these were marginal distinctions within a general pattern of increasing activity. Jesse Argyle's comment on Hampstead, that 'the Vestry, tho' largely composed of men who wd. probably call themselves Moderates, is really very Progressive in its general policy',[1] could have been applied to several Moderate parishes. The enhanced public demand for municipal enterprise, the Vestries' own anxiety to refurbish the second-tier image and the competitive atmosphere created by party politics combined to drive minimalist retrenchment out of fashion. Significantly, in a politically marginal parish, Clerkenwell, though the Progressives suffered electorally for the cost of their policies, the incoming Moderates did not reverse them: 'all the reforms instituted have been maintained'.[2] Similarly in Mile End, where the Moderates

[99] Jackson, Booth MS, B 260, 101.
[1] Ibid., B 214, 119.
[2] Revd J. E. Wakerley, ibid., B 237, 79–81.

regained control after a period of Steadmanite Progressivism, 'the distinct Progressive tone . . . is maintained'.[3]

A sense of the passing of the old order was shown by some of the Vestrymen and officials interviewed for the Booth survey. Paddington no longer saw '25% of a Vestry elected by 9 people, and the beadle sent out as a scout to fetch up 8 or 9 people to vote'.[4] In St Luke it was no longer the case that 'the med. officer only came once a fortnight, & . . . one man combined the offices of [sanitary] inspector & street keeper'.[5] St Pancras no longer employed 'men without knowledge as sanitary inspectors, such as army pensioners, etc.'[6] Clerkenwell, conscious of 'past notoriety', 'used to be a guzzling body, but [has] now gone to other extreme'.[7] The working-class Vestrymen admitted by the abolition of the qualification in 1894 secured attention disproportionate to their numbers.[8] They aroused much naked snobbery, but the valid point was made by one Hackney Vestryman that their admission had destroyed the cloying social homogeneity of some of the old authorities: 'Formerly the members were all of one type & thought much alike on most questions. Now they represent all classes, so there is more difference of opinion & matters in the Vestry are fully debated which formerly would have gone through without comment.'[9]

Incompetent and recalcitrant officials survived,[10] but most of them belonged to the older generation. Most prominent in the Booth interviews was the new breed of energetic Vestry official, self-confident and given to executive brusqueness: Foot, the chief sanitary inspector of Bethnal Green, who was 'zealous to a fault, perhaps, for the public health', Sykes, the St Pancras Medical Officer, who advocated 'a little tyranny for the people's good'.[11] Argyle wrote of H. M. Robinson, Shoreditch Vestry Clerk, that 'the work is with him no mere official duty—he believes in it, almost lives in it, its friends are his friends, its

[3] Jutsum, ibid., B 381, 193.

[4] Dethridge, ibid., B 255, 9.

[5] Yarrow, ibid., B 235, 167.

[6] Menzies, ibid., B 214, 11.

[7] Glaister, ibid., B 238, 31.

[8] See e.g. Wetenhall, ibid., B 214, 173; Preston, B 238, 53; Robinson, B 235, 63; Harcourt, B 292, 107–9; Clarke, B 189, 101.

[9] Hosgood, ibid., B 189, 57.

[10] For example Shaw, Rotherhithe MOH, 'evidently past his work now', ibid., B 383, 39; Edmunds, St James, 'rather an old dodderer', B 245, 77; for Greenwich DB officials—'aged and past their work'—see Hall, B 384, 117. For recalcitrance, Jutsum, Mile End, B 381, 195.

[11] Ibid., B 381, 3; B 214, 41.

enemies are almost his personal foes'.[12] It was an ironic measure of the greater confidence of the Vestry officer that some of Booth's respondents believed the local authorities to be run by their permanent officials.[13] This was an exaggeration. The most effective officials were those actively encouraged by their Vestries. The municipal revival in Shoreditch in the 1890s occurred because the retirement of the Clerk, Medical Officer, and Surveyor in quick succession ('thus getting rid of the weight of old-fashioned officialism') coincided with the emergence of Vestry Progressivism.[14] Elsewhere an active Medical Officer might run up against 'the ways of the men who have kept whelk stalls, etc',[15] and diplomacy was more effective than authoritarianism. In Clerkenwell the Medical Officer acknowledged that 'a few property owners on Vestry . . . can retard the work of sanitation', but they could 'not prevent anything being ultimately carried out'.[16] Dr Waldo of St George-the-Martyr, perennially at war with his Vestry, was regarded as unnecessarily fractious.[17] The general impression is one of co-operation, in a climate which favoured municipal action.

The Booth material hints at the change in public mood. Most interesting is the evidence of the willingness of tenants to complain of insanitary property, particularly if protected by a guarantee of anonymity.[18] The sanitary debate had previously assumed a sullen indifference to improvement on the part of the slum tenant, and the 1884–5 Royal Commission had solemnly turned over the question of whether pig made sty or sty made pig.[19] The expansion of Vestry sanitary powers in 1891 and the greater publicity given to those powers had generated a consumer demand for action. There are even signs that landlords were more willing to co-operate with the sanitary authorities,[20] perhaps because lodging-house registration, however cumbersome as a means of imposing sanitary standards, was believed to affect house values.[21]

---

[12] Ibid., B 235, 59.

[13] For example Aves, ibid., B 227, 211; Duthy, B 269, 91.

[14] Ibid., B 235, 61.

[15] Yarrow, St Luke's, ibid., B 235, 167.

[16] Glaister, ibid., B 238, 31.

[17] Andrews and Allen, Strand, ibid., B 245, 125.

[18] Harris, MOH Islington, ibid., B 202, 73; Wetenhall, B 214, 175 (who believed that tenants would complain to escape paying rent arrears); Revd H. E. Stone, B 220, 19.

[19] RC Housing of the Working Classes, *PP 1884–5*, xxx, Report, 14, 15; see also the evidence of J. Bates, QQ. 4163 ff.

[20] 'Get on much better than used to do with landlords; authority recognised & owners give in more readily': Rygate, MOH St George's E, Booth MS, B 381, 69.

[21] Taylor, MOH Mile End, ibid., B 381, 209.

The questionnaire drawn up by Booth for his religious influences investigation in the late 1890s, and sent to clergymen, nonconformist ministers, and other local dignitaries, asked about the standard of local government in the respondent's area. Not all interviewees expressed any opinion, and the repetition of such phrases as 'active and efficient' in the interview transcripts suggests that Booth's secretaries often glossed what may only have been vague expressions of approval. Obviously the replies came from an exceptionally articulate, well-educated and perhaps charitable section of the community. Ministers of religion were more concerned with standards of sanitary provision in poor areas and strikingly less concerned with the level of rates than one would imagine ordinary householders to have been. Nevertheless, the survey does provide a unique contemporary expression of opinion on local government, solicited rather than offered, and taken from people who did not necessarily have axes to grind. Expressions of bland approval predominate, although where dissatisfaction was voiced, it was usually voiced sharply.[22] An almost instinctive concern over councillor calibre persisted in the face of abundant and acknowledged evidence of Vestry enterprise,[23] although Battersea Vestry incurred the unusual charge of not having enough tradesmen on it.[24] Occasional unspecific allegations of corruption[25] suggest that some of the mud thrown in the 1880s had stuck. But the strongest impression left by the interviews was that 'local govt. was never more hopeful than now';[26] an awareness of recent and substantial improvement was expressed in parishes across London.[27] At the end of the Vestries' lives they commanded more respect than for most of their span, and more than their

[22] 'As to the work of the vestries ... it is "beastly" ': Revd A. Girdlestone, Clapham Park, ibid., B 300, 13. 'A bear garden when they meet': Henderson, Battersea, B 301, 63. 'Local government was very bad—the publicans' influence ruled': Revd H. E. Arnold, St Pancras, B 215, 31.

[23] For example Revd W. H. Allen, Fulham Road, 'Vestry "is to say the least vulgar" ': ibid., B 265, 205. See also G. Miller, Westminster, B 254, 43; H. Lewis, Bermondsey, B 275, 69; W. Reed, Wandsworth, B 299, 157; R. J. Somers, Camberwell, B 283, 103.

[24] Revd G. Harcourt, ibid., B 292, 107–9.

[25] 'There was much corruption and log rolling': Revd W. J. Mills, Newington, ibid., B 277, 27. 'There is a great deal of jobbery': F. C. Bainbridge, Lambeth, B 269, 17. See also I. Pugh, St Luke's B 234, 13; J. Adams, A. R. Shrewsbury, Hammersmith, B 268, 31, 63; H. Curtis, Wandsworth, B 300, 27.

[26] Revd W. Stevenson, ibid., B 201, 24.

[27] For example Revd W. Abbott, Paddington, ibid., B 250, 129–31; W. H. Bleaden, Marylebone, B 248, 141; H. Thomas, Holborn, B 241, 21; H. W. Goodhart, S. Buss, Shoreditch, B 231, 99, B 232, 47; B. Sackett, St George's E, B 224, 33; H. H. Selby Hale, Rotherhithe, B 279, 109; R. A. Hulls, St George Martyr, B 278, 137; R. B. Harrison, Newington, B 276, 79; W. R. Finlay, Camberwell, B 281, 65; C. R. Lilly, Lambeth, B 272, 43.

memory would command after the publication of the polemics of Jephson and Robson.

This was only achieved at a price. The burst of capital projects raised Vestry debt to £5·26 million by 1900, 16 per cent of rateable value against 7·1 per cent in 1886.[28] Current expenditure rose by 32·5 per cent between 1883/4 and 1893/4.[29] The new labour policy put a substantial and consistent pressure upon Vestry budgets.[30] Table 6.5 shows the effect of these increases on the eve of rate equalization. The 32·5 per cent increase in current expenditure was accommodated overall by an 18 per cent increase in the rate and a 17 per cent increase in assessments. Neither figure represents a drastic increase over the best part of the decade, but when each is broken down by Vestry income groups, disparities appear. Whereas the twelve richest authorities could sustain a 37 per cent increase in expenditure by means of 13 per cent increases in rates and rateable value, the poorer parishes, with higher poundage rates to begin with and a greater susceptibility to default, required a 23 per cent rate increase and a 28 per cent assessment increase to raise expenditure by 36 per cent. With Progressive sentiment and the pressure from Vestry labour and from the unemployed strongest in the poorer areas, but with the local rate-level already onerous and regressive in its incidence, these authorities faced apparently intractable problems. In 1892 the working-class parish of St George-in-the-East, with total rates already at 5s. 6d. in the pound, warned the LGB that its make-work suggestions, if systematically applied, 'would only end, either in a successful revolt of the ratepayers or in a financial collapse'.[31] By 1893/4 forty-eight of the eighty-one rating units outside the City paid total rates of 6s. or over, eight of them paying more than 7s. in the pound.[32] Each of the nine components of the Whitechapel District Board was rated at 6s. or more. Poplar DB averaged 7s. 7½d. with Bow parish rated at 7s. 11d. Levels such as these had no precedent since the crisis years of the 1860s. They made the pressure for rate equalization irresistible.

[28] Figures from parliamentary local taxation returns.
[29] See Table 6.5.
[30] For example in Fulham the wages bill rose from £6,565 in 1886/7 to £13,784 in 1894/5 (Fulham Vestry, *Annual Report* (1894–5), 226). In Bethnal Green the Surveyor's labour account rose from £4,252 in 1887/8 to £10,689 in 1894/5 (Bethnal Green Vestry, *Annual Report* (1887–8), 8 and (1894–5), 5–7). In Hackney the wages bill rose from £10,786 in 1890/1 to £16,927 in 1893/4: Booth MS, B 189, 97–9 (Lovegrove).
[31] *Local Government Journal*, 26 Nov. 1892.
[32] Return of Rates Raised, 1893–4, in *London Statistics*, IV (1893–4), 346–9.

TABLE 6.5. Effect of the Expansion of Vestry Services, 1883/4 to 1893/4

Vestry/DB Groups[a]	Aggregate Current Expenditure (£)[b]		Average Vestry Rate (£)[c]		Aggregate Rateable Value (£)		% Increases		
	1883/4	1893/4	1883/4	1893/4	1883/4	1893/4	Expenditure	Rate	R.v.
R.v./head over £10.28 (12 authorities)	521,288	716,596	0·060	0·068	9,399,010	10,673,798	37·47	13·33	13·56
R.v./head £6.72–£9.79 (6 authorities)	361,267	516,195	0·082	0·093	4,083,502	5,077,940	42·88	13·41	24·35
R.v./head £5.00–£5.56 (13 authorities)	676,379	819,876	0·079	0·091	7,797,461	9,214,529	21·22	15·19	18·17
R.v./head £3.30–£4.89 (9 authorities)	349,071	475,467	0·089	0·110	3,777,722	4,384,208	36·21	23·60	27·97
TOTAL	1,908,005	2,528,134	0·078	0·092	25,057,695	29,350,475	32·50	17·95	17·13

a. Grouped by rateable value per head in 1891.

b. The two parishes (Hammersmith and Battersea) which seceded from their respective District Boards between 1884 and 1893, have been treated as if separate throughout, and their expenditure figures for 1883/4 estimated on the basis of their rateable value as a proportion of those of their District Boards.

c. Averages weighted by population in 1881 and 1891. All first-tier precepts deducted.

Sources: Returns of Metropolitan Rates in *PP 1884/5*, LXVII and *London Statistics*, IV (1893/4), 345–8. The comparison of individual years is necessary because no complete rate series survives for 1891/2 or 1892/3, while those for subsequent years are affected by equalization. Expenditure figures for 1883/4 from *PP 1884–5*, LXVI, 479–87 and for 1893/4 from LCC *Statistical Abstract for London* (1899), 47. Assessment figures for 1883 from the table in RC Local Taxation, Appendix XXVII, *PP 1898*, XLII, 660, and for 1893/4 from *Statistical Abstract*, (1899), 46.

4. EQUALIZATION

It was remarkable that the Vestry system could have survived until 1894 without any rate equalization mechanism or Exchequer support for Vestry expenditure. This had been possible because the first tier had accounted for a good deal of the expansion of local government activity down to the late 1880s, and supported it through a common rate. The explosion of Vestry expenditure in the early 1890s, however, drew attention once again to the disparity of local rates. Equalization had always been a preoccupation of the LCC Progressives, who had set up a sub-committee on the subject in the Council's first months. In 1892 it became a legislative possibility following the election of a Liberal government and a larger metropolitan Liberal contingent, including several Progressive Councillors. The first London Equalization of Rates Bill was introduced by H. H. Fowler, President of the Local Government Board, in 1893. Like other sops to Liberal sectionalism it fell victim to the second Home Rule Bill, but the force of the metropolitan reaction to its abandonment ensured reintroduction by Fowler's successor, Shaw-Lefevre, in 1894. In that year it passed.[33]

The Act provided for a levy of 6*d.* in the pound on the rateable value of the entire administrative county, including the City, to form an equalization fund which would then be redivided among the parishes in proportion to population. The result was that areas with a rateable value per head higher than the London average emerged as net contributors while those below the average were recipients. The size of an area's contribution or grant would reflect its divergence from the mean rateable value per head. If the principle of equalization was accepted—and R. V. Barrow's original Commons resolution of February 1893 had passed without a division[34]—the scheme now put forward was hard to oppose either on administrative or political grounds. Its mechanical operation removed the dangers of discretion; neither the LCC nor the Local Government Board could be called upon to scrutinize second-tier expenditure, determine 'desirable' level of local spending, or penalize extravagance.

Objections of varying degrees of validity were nevertheless raised against the Bill.[35] The strongest, that population was counted decennially

[33] As 57 & 58 Vict., c. 53.

[34] *Hansard*, 4th ser., IX, 335–61 (24 Feb. 1893).

[35] The most articulate criticisms of equalization, both from contributing parishes, are by C. H. Campbell, Kensington Vestryman and LCC Moderate: *Memorandum on London*

while rateable value was assessed each year, was met by providing for a separate London census in 1896 and for the Registrar General to make annual estimates of population thereafter. This change allowed examination of the underlying complaint that population was not a valid determinant of the size of grant in the first place. Such claims prompted impatient denials from the Bill's supporters—'that the needs of a place are roughly proportionate to its resident population does not seem to admit of any reasonable doubt',[36] asserted MacKinnon Wood. The victims of a population-based system were in fact few. The riverside parishes of the St Saviour's and St Olave's District Boards were made net contributors by their highly rated warehouse property although they contained some of the deepest poverty in London; the contributions paid by central and West End parishes did not reflect wear and tear on their streets—and consequently upon their local rates—resulting from their location. Such hard cases showed that rateable value per head was not above criticism as an indicator of the relationship of needs to resources in any area, but they could not prove that any better measure was available. Any more detailed assessment of parochial needs would have entailed discretionary powers still more distasteful to the Bill's Conservative opponents. Such powers would have threatened something of the arbitrariness and opacity which has marked twentieth-century control of local finance; the Local Government Board did not seek them, and indeed considered 'any minute control by a Central Authority' to be 'at variance with the principles of modern legislation'.[37]

G. C. T. Bartley professed to believe that the population basis for payments would encourage overcrowding.[38] Several critics pointed out that London's rating disparities were enhanced by the prevalence of compounding in poor areas, and that a high rate systematically discounted was not a high rate at all.[39] This was true to a point, but was not a valid criticism of an Act which distributed its rewards according to rateable value per head rather than the rate actually levied; the variation within

---

Rates, copy in LCC Clerk's Dept., CL/FIN/1/4; and 'Report by H. Wilkins (St James Vestry) on London (Equalization of Rates) Bill', copy in Lord Randolph Churchill Papers, RCHL 1/31/4498, and reprinted in St James' Vestry, *Annual Report* (1893–4), 103–11.

[36] Memorandum by T. MacKinnon Wood in London (Equalization of Rates) Bill Papers, PRO HLG/29/42/37.

[37] Memorandum in PRO HLG/29/42/43.

[38] *Hansard*, 4th ser., XXVII, 850 (24 July 1894).

[39] 'It is absurd to call a rate 7/- in the pound when the real rate paid by so many is 7/- minus 30 per cent, and to contrast such a rate with a lower rate in a Parish where compounding is not permitted on anything like the same scale': Campbell Memorandum, 5.

the rateable value per head series was real enough. Rather inconsistently, many of the same critics also pointed to cases where the Act penalized parishes with rates already above average or benefited parishes with low rates. Islington, two-thirds of the way down the rateable value per head league in 1891 but with rates below the metropolitan average, had its thrift rewarded by constant sniping from the supporters of retrenchment. St Luke's, its rates inflated by the debt incurred for the Whitecross Street improvement, emerged as a net contributor with above average rates. In fact, as Shaw-Lefevre put it, 'if we were to wait for a scheme which would remove all anomalies we might wait for the Greek Kalends'.[40]

The Bill was projected to leave around 60 per cent of the parishes affected with local rates of between 2s. 2d. and 2s. 7d. in the pound, as Table 6.6 indicates.

TABLE 6.6.   Anticipated Effect of the Equalisation Act, 1894

Local (General and Lighting) Rate in £	Before Act	After Act
	(no. of parishes)	(no. of parishes)
< 2s. 2d.	21	15
2s. 2d.–2s. 7d.	19	46
2s. 7d.–2s. 9d.	14	10
2s. 9d.–3s.	19	5
> 3s.	5	2

Source: Figures from PRO HLG/29/42/8.

Liberal and Progressive criticism of the Bill generally asserted that it had not gone far enough. Costelloe's original memorandum on equalization had suggested a 1s. rather than a 6d. levy,[41] and Fowler claimed to have thought hard before settling on the lower figure.[42] His caution ensured, in Dilke's words, that 'of the rich parishes that will pay not one will by its payment be raised above the average rate of London, while of the poor parishes that will receive hardly one will be reduced below that rate'.[43] In the poorest parishes the Act would be seen as inadequate by the end of the decade.[44]

---

[40] *Hansard*, 4th ser., XXVII, 824 (24 July 1894).

[41] See the commentary in PRO HLG/29/42/8.

[42] *Hansard*, 4th ser., XXVIII, 84 (3 Aug. 1894).

[43] Ibid., XXVII, 940 (25 July 1894).

[44] An attempt was made to increase the levy to 1s. when the London Government Bill passed through Committee; see ibid., LXIX, 428 (24 Mar. 1899) and LXXI, 807 (16 May 1899).

This moderation may have inhibited political criticism, but the greatest obstacle faced by the Bill's opponents was simply that many more people stood to gain than to lose by it. Its mechanism was such that areas with a higher than average rateable value per head became net contributors and those below the average net beneficiaries. Such had been the upward thrust upon rateable value per head in the City and the West End, where the process of commercialization had both raised assessment and hastened depopulation, that the handful of wealthiest areas forced up the arithmetical mean, leaving most of the rest of London below it. The imbalance between the thirty-five net contributors and the forty-eight net beneficiaries did not appear great, but the former included all the minuscule Schedule C authorities and the small parishes clustered in the central area. The population basis for the distribution of the equalization fund meant that more than 77 per cent of the 1891 population lived in areas which gained by the Act.[45] The victims were confined almost exclusively to the central business district and the West End, where Chelsea alone was a very marginal beneficiary. Most of the largest grants went to the East End, but all the outer suburbs except Hampstead were net recipients.

This made the Bill hard to attack. Attacks were only likely, of course, from the London Unionist Members, and only those representing central or West End seats had any direct interest in opposition. Some of the rest prefaced their speeches with magnanimous declarations that they were about to criticize a measure which would greatly benefit their constituents, but they did not carry their altruism to the length of voting against the Bill. Shaw-Lefevre's conviction that 'most of the Tory members for London dare not vote against it'[46] proved justified as the negative amendment to the second reading was not pressed to a division. Goschen, whose constituency of St George, Hanover Square suffered substantially from equalization, found himself 'practically deserted by half of the Metropolitan Members'[47] in his opposition.

Goschen's frustration epitomizes the reaction of the contributors. The City and the West End parishes had long been aware that their high assessments made them potentially the milch cows of a more integrated metropolitan system. Since the early 1880s they had felt increasingly helpless in the face of the growth of the first-tier precepts, over which

[45] For contributors and recipients see Table 6.7.
[46] G. J. Shaw-Lefevre to Sir W. Harcourt, 10 May 1894, MS Harcourt, Dep. 91/95.
[47] G. J. Goschen to Lord George Hamilton, 17 Jan. 1895, with Hamilton to A. J. Balfour, 24 Jan. 1895, Add. MS 49778, fos. 25, 21.

TABLE 6.7. Equalisation Act, 1894: Net Contributions and Receipts, 1895–1900

(Average Annual Rate Equivalent, *d.* in £)

Net Contributors		Net Recipients	
Staple Inn (Schedule C)	5.99	Plumstead	8.18
Lincoln's Inn (Schedule C)	5.95	Bethnal Green	7.71
Savoy (Strand DB)	5.74	Mile End Old Town	7.49
Inner Temple (Schedule C)	5.72	Bromley (Poplar DB)	6.49
Rolls (Strand *DB*)	5.72	Bow (Poplar DB)	5.97
Middle Temple (Schedule C)	5.66	Newington	5.71
City	5.65	St George-in-the-East	5.40
Charterhouse (Schedule C)	5.46	Mile End New Town (Whitechapel DB)	5.15
Furnival's Inn (Schedule C)	5.41	Camberwell	4.70
Gray's Inn (Schedule C)	5.26	St George-the-Martyr	4.34
St Olave and St Thomas (St Olave DB)	5.13	Limehouse (Limehouse DB)	4.16
St Paul, Covent Garden (Strand DB)	5.11	Poplar (Poplar DB)	3.85
St Martin-in-the-Fields	4.92	Hackney	3.77
St Mary-le-Strand (Strand DB)	4.76	St Paul, Deptford (Greenwich DB)	3.72
St James, Westminster	4.59	Old Artillery Ground (Whitechapel DB)	3.66
St Sepulchre (Holborn DB)	4.52	Fulham	3.66
St Clement Danes (Strand DB)	4.34	Bermondsey	3.65
St George, Hanover Square	4.06	Christchurch (Whitechapel DB)	3.57
Saffron Hill (Holborn DB)	3.97	Ratcliff (Limehouse DB)	3.51
St Saviour's (St Saviour's DB)	3.46	Greenwich (Greenwich DB)	3.45
Glasshouse Yard (Holborn DB)	3.39	Battersea	3.31
St Margaret and St John	3.06	Islington	3.13
St Anne, Soho (Strand DB)	2.38	Rotherhithe	2.93
Kensington	2.06	Shadwell (Limehouse DB)	2.67
St Peter, Westminster (Schedule C)	1.91	Hammersmith	2.60
St Giles and St George	1.77	Lambeth	2.54
St Marylebone	1.72	Shoreditch	2.48
Paddington	1.50	Whitechapel (Whitechapel DB)	2.25
Hampstead	1.30	St Nicholas, Deptford (Greenwich DB)	2.15
Christchurch (St Saviour's DB)	1.12	Tooting (Wandsworth DB)	2.10
St Andrew and St George (Holborn DB)	1.10	Clerkenwell	1.98
Horselydown (St Olave's DB)	0.60	Woolwich	1.81
St Luke	0.36	Stoke Newington	1.72
		Wandsworth (Wandsworth DB)	1.69
		Norton Folgate (Whitechapel DB)	1.66
		Lewisham (Lewisham DB)	1.58
		Clapham (Wandsworth DB)	1.53
		Penge (Lewisham DB)	1.37
		Streatham (Wandsworth DB)	1.29
		Putney (Wandsworth DB)	1.09
		Charlton (Lee DB)	1.08
		St Pancras	1.08
		Aldgate (Whitechapel DB)	0.85
		Lee (Lee DB)	0.70
		Eltham (Lee DB)	0.64
		Wapping (Limehouse DB)	0.64
		Kidbrooke (Lee DB)	0.48
		Chelsea	0.01

Source: Calculated from the table in *London Statistics*, x (1899–1900), xciii.

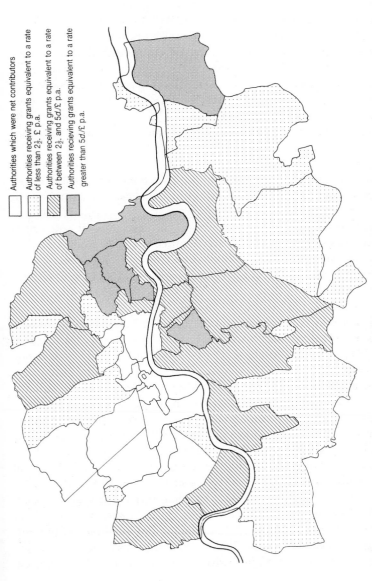

Authorities which were net contributors

Authorities receiving grants equivalent to a rate
of less than 2½. £ p.a.

Authorities receiving grants equivalent to a rate
of between 2½. and 5d./£ p.a.

Authorities recieving grants equivalent to a rate
greater than 5d./£ p.a.

Equalisation of Rates Act, 1894: Average Annual Contributions and Receipts, 1895/6 to 1899/1900

they had no direct control. The attempts to peg assessments were attributable to this, as was the virulence of the West End reaction to the sins of the MBW. The toppling of the Metropolitan Board had only led to its replacement by a body which was politically unsympathetic to the wealthier areas, and which, with its social projects, its direct labour operations, and its trade union wages, spent much of its precept income upon objects to which these Conservative areas were deeply hostile. First-tier rates had not fallen with the coming of the LCC, and by 1893/4 their growth was accelerating under the most radical Council of the whole Progressive era.

In the thirty years since 1863 the proportion of metropolitan taxation accounted for by common charges had risen from 27 per cent to 62 per cent.[48] Equalization, when fully effective, would consummate this trend, driving the figure up to almost 70 per cent. It was a pointed statutory assertion of the principle of metropolitan integration. Whereas first-tier levies supported common services from which the wealthy parishes derived some benefit, equalization payments represented a clear loss for contributing areas. Kensington would provide nearly £18,000, St George, Hanover Square £31,000, and the City as much as £96,000 simply to aid the rates of other parishes.[49] The principle of equalization had been promoted by the government and accepted by Parliament, but many in the West End continued to see it, in Lubbock's words, as a departure from 'the old principle of the Liberal Party . . . that taxation and representation should go together'.[50] For the West End and the City, self-government meant self-taxation before all else. The impression left by the period of Vestry expansion was that the poorer parishes, having indulged themselves beyond their means in a spree of municipal enterprise, were leaving the West End and the City to pick up the bill. The wealthy areas, having failed to halt the expansion of the first tier, now faced a demand to subsidize that of the second tier. Equalization followed five years of parochial suspicion of the centralizing motives of the LCC, and coincided with the deliberations of the Royal Commission on the amalgamation of City and County, widely misinterpreted as a Progressive step towards the single municipality. The Equalization Bill was believed, probably rightly, to be 'far more the Bill of Messrs Costelloe, Stuart, Pickersgill, C. Harrison, and other Progressives of the Council, aided by certain MPs

[48] See Appendix 3.
[49] Figs. from *PP 1894*, LXXIV (II), 543–8.
[50] *Hansard*, 4th ser., XXVII, 838 (24 July 1894).

of London, than of the Government of the day'.[51] It provided material endorsement of the West End parishes' distrust of the Council and significantly influenced their later moves towards municipal secession.

[51] Campbell Memorandum, 4.

7

Amalgamation and Devolution

While the equalization debate was being played out, the attention of most Progressives was fixed elsewhere, upon the deliberations of the Royal Commission on the Amalgamation of the City and County of London. For the Corporation more was at stake in 1893–4 even than the £94,000 that it was set to lose to the equalization fund. Amalgamation threatened the City's jealously cherished autonomy and the exclusive possession of its private wealth. It would mean not only the loss of all that the Corporation had sought to preserve since the 1830s, but submission in the process to an enemy whose radicalism was bitterly unpalatable to the overwhelming majority of Corporators. The threat of amalgamation with the LCC would bring the Corporation back on to the London political stage for the first time since 1884.

Progressive eagerness to deal with the City was almost universal. The overlap between the LCC Progressive party and the Firthite London Municipal Reform League has been exaggerated, but it was still significant, and antipathy towards the Corporation was the element of the League's programme common to the greatest proportion of its membership. All but three of the seventy Progressives who replied to the *Pall Mall Gazette* questionnaire in 1889 favoured making the City a district under the Council.[1] When Rosebery sought to promote a broad Progressive platform for the 1892 election, distinct from the 'advanced' programmes of the Metropolitan Radical Federation and the LLRU, he made Corporation reform its most urgent item.[2]

To Progressives the Corporation was the most offensive of the vested interests feeding upon the London community. Its independent wealth appeared to offer a form of rate relief more tangible and accessible than public-utility profits or ground rents. To those schooled in the Firthite tradition, the Corporation had been the obstacle depriving London until 1889 of the municipal rights enjoyed by other cities. Even after the

---

[1] *Pall Mall Gazette* 'Extra' on the London County Council (1889), 87–8.
[2] Letter to the electors of St George-in-the-East, *The Times*, 6 Feb. 1892.

Council's creation the failure of a number of the first Council's legislative projects[3] heightened Progressive frustration at the fact that theirs was a county rather than a municipal authority, and one which remained hampered by constraints designed for the MBW. The return of a Liberal majority in the general election of 1892 made absorption of the City plausible once more, and this was reflected in the legislative memorandum with which Costelloe greeted the incoming ministers. With an uncharacteristic economy of purpose he deferred dock municipalization and Guild reform, and delegated land-value taxation to the Chancellor of the Exchequer. He concentrated upon the argument that 'the people of Greater London are still deprived of any real municipal life' for want of 'the powers long since conferred upon all the great municipalities of the Kingdom' and those 'which have remained from ancient times in the hands of the Corporation of London itself'. Since the second category included the first and more, Costelloe concluded that the amalgamation of City and County 'seems to afford the key to the whole position'.[4]

Liberal gains in 1892 had given the parliamentary party a larger London contingent and increased the number of LCC spokesmen in the House. One of the new recruits, John Williams Benn, tabled a Commons question in February 1893 concerning the amalgamation of City and County. The President of the Local Government Board, H. H. Fowler, in a reply drafted by Rosebery,[5] proposed a Royal Commission 'to consider the proper conditions under which the amalgamation of the City and the county of London can be effected, and to make specific and practical proposals for that purpose'.[6] The appointment of the Royal Commission was an indication, as Fowler's reply virtually acknowledged, that the government, facing another Home Rule struggle, and with Welsh disestablishment, death duties, employers' liability, and local option to contemplate, wished to make a conciliatory gesture to the London Liberals without adding to the legislative burden. Part of the gesture was to phrase the Commission's reference in such terms as would preclude consideration of the *desirability* of amalgamation. It is hard to accept that the practical details of amalgamation warranted a Royal Commission by themselves; in the event the Commission would devote much of its time to second-tier reform.

---

[3] Listed as Appendix I in B. F. C. Costelloe, *Memorandum as to Legislative Proposals Concerning the Powers of the Council* (1892), LCC *Official Publications*, III, No. 52.
[4] Costelloe, *Memorandum on Legislative Proposals*, 1, 7.
[5] See H. H. Fowler to Rosebery, 10 Feb. 1893, RP MS 10091, 19.
[6] *Hansard*, 4th ser., IX, 35 (21 Feb. 1893).

It was chaired by Leonard Courtney, a Liberal Unionist MP and brother-in-law to the Webbs, with a marginal but consistent interest in London affairs. Provincial municipalities were represented by R. D. Holt, who had been the first Lord Mayor of Liverpool,[7] and E. O. Smith, Town Clerk of Birmingham. The LCC and the Corporation were both offered representation. The Council, with some misgivings on the Progressive left[8] accepted the government's suggestion of Sir Thomas, now Lord, Farrer. The Corporation, in the shape of its Special Committee, curiously showed no qualms about participating, and unanimously nominated the City Solicitor, H. H. Crawford, to represent it.[9] It can only have assumed that the Commissioners would not interpret their brief literally and would allow discussion of the *principle* of amalgamation. The brisk treatment of Corporation witnesses in the early sessions was enough to convince the Special Committee that the Commission was hostile, and in November 1893 it recommended that Common Council seek a pledge from the Commissioners to hear evidence upon 'the desirability as well as the convenient practicability' of amalgamation.[10] The balance of opinion of the Corporation's senior officers favoured a refusal to tender further evidence, but there remained an anxiety not to leave the Commission to its own devices, and there was general consent that Crawford should continue to serve.[11] An indication from H. H. Fowler early in December that the Corporation would not be 'prejudiced in any future parliamentary action' by its witnesses' continued appearance, was taken as adequate by a Special Committee still anxious not to boycott the Commission.[12]

Farrer was probably justified in his belief that the Corporation eventually withdrew 'because the Commission asked them for a balance sheet'.[13] The crisis was precipitated by the Council's Statistical Officer, G. L. Gomme, an earnest Progressive, who produced for the Commission the first thorough analysis of the Corporation's opaque published accounts.[14] Finance was, in the early 1890s, a growing worry for the Corporation. In May 1887 the then City Chamberlain, Benjamin Scott, had written to

[7] For Holt see P. J. Waller, *Democracy and Sectarianism: A Political and Social History of Liverpool, 1868–1939* (Liverpool, 1981), 494–5.
[8] *London*, 9 Mar. 1893.
[9] *Local Government Journal*, 4 Mar. 1893.
[10] Corporation of London, Special Com. Minutes, 13 Nov. 1893.
[11] MS Memorandum of Officers' Conference, 21 Nov. 1893, in Special Com. Minute Papers, Nov. 1893.
[12] Special Com. Minutes, 4 Dec. 1893.
[13] *London*, 23 May 1895.
[14] RC Amalgamation, *PP 1894*, XVIII, Appendix XI, 417–518.

the Lord Mayor indicating his concern at the impending extinction of the Corporation's Reserve Fund.[15] This fund had been set up in the 1860s to offset the reversion of the City's leasehold interest in the Finsbury Estate, and had stood at over £500,000 in 1872. It had been drawn upon in each year since then, indicating that the Corporation had failed to stay within even its own massive resources for fifteen consecutive years, until it stood at only £35,000 by the end of 1885.[16] The importance of this was underlined by the non-renewal of the coal dues, which ended, so far as the Corporation was concerned, in July 1888. Coal dues receipts had been devoted to improvements since the Act of 1861, so their expiry did not directly reduce the Corporation's general income, but they stood as security for nearly £900,000 of debt in 1888 for which the City estates were contingent security.[17] Scott estimated that interest payments of £21,000 p.a. would fall upon the City lands as a result of the cessation of the dues, together with repayments of principal.[18] By 1889 the Reserve Fund needed to be augmented by the sale of Corporation property, and in the early 1890s the sale of property became regularized as a means of offsetting continuing deficits.[19] At the same time market profits were applied, after the payment of interest on the market debt, to the general requirements of the Corporation, leaving no provision for repayment of market debt principal between 1889 and 1893.[20] The Corporation remained solvent in the early 1890s only by selling off assets and deferring the repayment of debt.

The Corporation found difficulty in controlling expenditure for much the same reason as the Council did—the centrifugal nature of its policy-making machinery—and Scott's suggestions for reform in 1887 included one proposal which echoed the spending provision in the Local Government Act—that all proposed expenditure over 100 guineas should be

[15] B. Scott to Lord Mayor, 2 May 1887, entered in the Corporation's Special Com. (Finance) Minutes, 13 Dec. 1887.

[16] See ibid. for the size of each year's deficit. For details of the larger payments from the reserve fund see Special Com. (Finance) Minute Papers, 24 Feb. 1888.

[17] Ibid., 5 Mar. 1888.

[18] Ibid., 25 May 1888.

[19] RC Amalgamation, *PP 1894*, XVIII, Appendix XI, 426. Between 1850 and 1888 the Corporation's sales of property had been more than balanced by reinvestment, so that some £75,000 was added to the City's capital estate. From 1889 to 1893 only £18,000 of the £102,000 realized by property transactions was reinvested, the remainder being carried to the City cash. See G. L. Gomme's second analysis of Corporation accounts in *London Statistics*, v (1894–5), 307–8.

[20] Gomme analysis, *PP 1894*, XVIII, Appendix XI, 439. See also second analysis, *London Statistics*, v, 306.

submitted to the Coal, Corn, and Finance Committee before being sent to Common Council.[21] In the Corporation's case, however, the difficulty was heightened by the near impossibility of any but the most assiduous Common Councilman forming any overall impression of Corporation finance. Scott considered finance to be 'a subject which, for divers reasons, it is undesirable to discuss in the public meetings of the Council',[22] and the accounts which he produced were both massive and unorthodox. Common Council therefore lacked the clear estimates and accounts which helped plot—even if they did not check—the expansion of the LCC budget. It also lacked, since the Corporation was not a rating authority except in respect of the City police, both the ability to stem short-term deficits by increasing the rates, and the political corrective to extravagance that could be applied by a ratepaying electorate. Common Council was certainly made aware in the late 1880s that Corporation revenues were not to be regarded as unlimited. A Special Committee on Finance was set up in 1887, which made some rather cautious recommendations of retrenchment in December 1888.[23] The decision to limit wine consumption at the Lord Mayor's banquet in 1889 must have convinced even the most insensitive Corporator that times were hard.[24] Nevertheless, little had been done to remedy matters by the time Gomme's analysis revealed the growing deficits, the depletion of the reserve fund, the sales of assets, and the deferment of market debt.

The Corporation's position was not as desperate as Scott suggested, and it did not justify occasional Progressive professions that taking on the City would be an act of fiscal sacrifice on their part. In the first place some 28 per cent of Corporation expenditure in the late 1880s had been, in Scott's view at least, voluntary and dispensable.[25] Secondly, the City's rental income continued to rise, and in 1893 stood some 31 per cent higher than ten years before.[26] The City was not to be amalgamated and it has never gone bankrupt. Nevertheless, the Gomme memorandum had drawn attention to some features of the unreformed municipality which had been familiar enough sixty years earlier but which appeared

[21] Scott to Lord Mayor, 2, 23 May 1887, in Special Com. (Finance) Minutes, 13 Dec. 1887. This object was attained by the amendment of the 47th Standing Order to the form suggested in ibid., 5 June 1888.

[22] Scott to Lord Mayor, 2 May 1887, in Special Com. (Finance) Minutes, 13 Dec. 1887.

[23] Special Com. (Finance) Minutes, 4 Dec. 1888.

[24] *Metropolitan*, 23 Nov. 1889.

[25] Scott to Lord Mayor, 23 May 1887, Special Com. (Finance) Minutes, 13 Dec. 1887; ibid., Minute Papers, 5 Mar. 1888.

[26] See the rent table in Gomme's second analysis, *London Statistics*, V, 354–5.

uncomfortably anachronistic in the 1890s—alienation of property, insufficient debt provision, inadequate accounting. W. H. Pannell, a chartered accountant and member of the Special Committee, acknowledged privately that Gomme's analysis was 'damaging to the Corporation's case' and that he could not 'disprove the accuracy of it in any material degree'.[27] Scott, having originally told the Special Committee that he could answer Gomme,[28] eventually 'sent a retired official to represent him' before the Commission, to the annoyance of at least one of the Commissioners.[29] The revelation of the Corporation's financial incontinence provided a powerful indictment of City management, and made it far less attractive for the Corporation to press for consideration of the desirability of amalgamation. During December, therefore, the Special Committee raised its price again, calling upon the Commissioners to hear evidence on the position and functions of the secondary authorities.[30] This was arguably implicit in their reference, and would be the subject of their later sessions, but the Commissioners were now impatient of Corporation filibustering, and declined.[31] In response the Special Committee decided not to tender any more evidence, and in February 1894 Crawford resigned from the Commission.[32]

In the early months of 1894, then, the Corporation was in a distinctly vulnerable position. As it awaited the Commission's inevitable endorsement of amalgamation it had no chance of affecting their deliberations and no reservoir of public sympathy to draw upon. The option of manufacturing support, as in 1884, had been discredited by the Malversation Committee, and requests for employment from the veterans of that campaign, who resurfaced at the first hint of the City's distress, were ignored.[33] Although the Special Committee had reaffirmed its faith in separate municipalities as soon as amalgamation was mooted, the recent

---

[27] W. H. Pannell to Sir John Monckton, 18 Dec. 1893, in Special Com. Minute Papers, July–September [sic] 1893.

[28] Ibid.

[29] E.O. Smith, interviewed in *London*, 9 May 1895.

[30] RC Amalgamation, *PP 1894*, XVII, Q. 6546.

[31] Ibid., Q. 6547.

[32] Special Com. Minutes, 16 Feb. 1894; RC Amalgamation, *PP 1894*, XVII, Q. 8354.

[33] M. J. Cunningham spontaneously created a Metropolitan Municipalities Federation, advocating 'the principle of "Federation"' in Mar. 1894; see Cunningham to Monckton, 2 May 1894, Special Com. Minute Papers, July–October [sic] 1894. See also Cunningham to Monckton, 10 Apr., 20 July 1894, C. W. Stokes to Monckton, 11 Sept., 4 Oct. 1894, J. H. Johnson to Monckton, 13, 16 Jan. 1895, Cunningham to Faudel Phillips, 23 Oct. 1895, all in Special Com. Minute Papers. The Special Com. Minutes show that all these approaches were ignored.

overhaul of the first tier made the policy less plausible; the Common Serjeant believed that 'to attempt at the present day to wipe out a popularly elected body like the County Council is ... an idle dream'. He advocated adopting the stance of 'beati possidentes', trusting to the legislative build-up and the delicate balance of parties to prevent the enactment of any Amalgamation Bill, and waiting for reprieve from a Unionist government.[34] With the incumbent Liberal ministry less than eighteen months old, this policy induced restlessness in Common Council, where a senior Councilman complained in February 1894 that the Special Committee 'seemed to have fallen into a stupor or sleep'.[35] The pace was quickened by a young Common Councilman, T. H. Brooke Hitching, who promulgated a naïve separate municipalities scheme of his own, by which fourteen distinct authorities would control their own fire brigades, parks, poor law, and education.[36]

The Special Committee's dilemma was solved for it by the Kensington Vestry. Kensington's overwhelmingly Moderate Vestry had been a critic of Progressive policies virtually since the Council's inception. It had responded particularly tetchily to equalization, which cost the parish some £18,000 p.a., circulating a critical pamphlet by the Moderate Councillor and Kensington Vestryman C. H. Campbell, and organizing public protest meetings.[37] Like many West End parishes, it took the appointment of the Amalgamation Commission to be a step towards the single municipality, and when the Commission refused to hear evidence on the desirability as well as the practicality of amalgamation, it moved in sympathy with the Corporation. In December 1893 R. A. Robinson, future Moderate chairman of the LCC, moved that 'in any scheme for the better government of the metropolis, the powers, duties and responsibilities of local authorities should be enlarged rather than curtailed, and that this can best be attained by the establishment and incorporation of a number of municipalities vested with full municipal life and privileges'. The motion was passed unanimously, after an adjournment, in January.[38] It concluded with a rider that it be forwarded to the Corporation 'with an intimation that in the event of a satisfactory

---

[34] Memorandum by F. Fulton, 4 Dec. 1893, Special Com. Minute Papers, Dec. 1893.

[35] *Local Government Journal*, 3 Feb. 1894.

[36] For Brooke Hitching's scheme see the pamphlet *Home Rule for London* in Special Com. Minute Papers, Nov./Dec. 1894, also the interview in *Local Government Journal*, 31 Mar. 1894.

[37] C. H. Campbell, *Memorandum on London Rates*, LCC Clerk's Dept., CL/FIN/1/4; *Local Government Journal*, 24 June 1893; see also 11 July, 4 Oct., 19 Nov. 1894, 25 Jan. 1895.

[38] Kensington Vestry Minutes, 20 Dec. 1893, 17 Jan. 1894.

scheme being formulated on the above basis, it will receive the favourable consideration of this Vestry'.

The Kensington move was important in that it provided the first instance of Vestrydom seeking alliance with the City on the London government question. Over the previous forty years, although the Corporation and the Vestries appeared to display a common localism, their practical aims differed radically. The City sought administrative decentralization in order to render the central body less potent and to reduce the anomaly of its own independence. Such devolution was plausible, if at all, only with a less fragmented second tier. 'Tenification' would entail the wholesale agglomeration of existing secondary bodies, and was an implicit slur upon the Vestries. In general the Vestries were not greatly interested in administrative devolution. They had grown used to the existence of a first tier which relieved them of burdens that would have overwhelmed them, and which provided rate support and cheap loans for their capital projects. They sought greater security from the 'empire-building' of the MBW and the LCC and protection from the sort of subjection threatened in 1884, but they did not wish to dismember the central body. Above all, the amalgamation of existing secondary bodies, necessary to administrative decentralization, was anathema to them.[39] If Chelsea and Kensington could not tolerate even the hint of amalgamation in 1890, the wholesale grouping implicit in 'tenification' was impossible. Accordingly, the Corporation had made little effort over the years to court the Vestries, and in 1884, when they faced an obvious common threat, it had devoted most of its energy to the propagation of the phoney charter movements. Developments since then, however, had brought the outlook of the West End Vestries closer to that of the City. The increase in first-tier rates had emphasized the cost to these areas of metropolitan integration. The politicization of local government and the capture of the LCC by Radicalism had given an added edge to the Conservative West End's resentment of the first tier. The Council's stress upon social politics had led to its spending less of its income in the West End than had the MBW, and equalization had drawn a material distinction between the one-third of authorities—mostly in the West End—who contributed, and the two-thirds who benefited. In the West End, therefore, a specific hostility to Progressive policies was heaped upon the general resentment of LCC 'imperialism', and when the Council picked its fight with the City, Kensington responded sympathetically.

[39] Chelsea Vestry resoundingly condemned the Brooke Hitching proposals in February: *London*, 8 Feb. 1894.

On receiving the Kensington resolution, the Special Committee invited a delegation from the Vestry to a conference. It took place in March, and can be considered the inception of the parochial incorporation movement.[40] Having established that the Vestry was 'absolutely hostile' to the LCC's amalgamation scheme, and that it considered 'attempts to absorb property of Corp^n a robbery', means were examined of strengthening the second tier. It was taken as axiomatic that local municipalities should be established, more powerful than the Vestries, and that a central authority should exist for 'central matters'. The Vestry Clerk, W. C. Leete, suggested optimistically that the time had almost arrived for a return to an indirectly elected central body. On the vital question of areas, opinion tended towards municipalizing the twenty-eight post-Redistribution parliamentary boroughs, a half-way house between 'tenification' and municipalizing the Vestries. Leete observed that 'Parly Boroughs would dispel opposition of large Boroughs such as Islington, Lambeth, Camberwell'; he could have added that such a solution would avoid forcing Kensington and Chelsea into diffident wedlock. The retreat from 'tenification' was obviously necessary, but it was made without any consideration of the relationship between the size of the second-tier authorities and the extent of possible devolution. This would become a characteristic of West End attitudes during the lifetime of the incorporation movement. Kensington considered itself the '5th City of England', and had no fear of devolution. It placed more stress upon what it saw as its own right to municipal independence than upon any general scheme for the whole metropolis.

By symbolic accident, the Royal Commission received a request to hear evidence from the Kensington Vestry on the day that the City's withdrawal was confirmed.[41] From March to June it took second-tier evidence of the sort that it had told the Corporation was beyond its brief. Leete and a leading Vestryman, T. W. Wheeler, put the Kensington case before the Commissioners. They met an unenthusiastic response, and did not influence the eventual report, but this mattered little, since during the spring and summer of 1894 the case for separate municipalities was adopted with a new enthusiasm elsewhere. Devolution became the leading theme of London Municipal Conservatism.

---

[40] For this paragraph see the rough notes of the meeting in Special Com. Minute Papers Mar./Apr. 1894.
[41] RC Amalgamation, *PP 1894*, XVII, proceedings of 15 Mar. 1894.

2. THE SEARCH FOR A MODERATE POLICY

The emergence of devolution as a fashionable cause in the City and the West End resolved the search for a distinctive Conservative municipal policy that had been begun in 1889. It became received Conservative opinion that the years of Moderate opposition derived from their quixotic refusal to fight the 1889 elections on party lines, which had left them vulnerable to the politically mobilized forces of Radicalism.[42] This was untrue; the political nature of the 1889 contests was recognized at the time, and several Conservative associations can be shown to have adopted candidates.[43] It is true, however, that the Conservatives lacked the sort of central direction of the local campaigns provided for the Progressives by the London Liberal and Radical Union, and that largely as a consequence of this there was no distinctively Conservative municipal programme in 1889. The Bristol University collection of election addresses reveals the extent to which the social politics of the 1880s permeated the 1889 campaign. Virtually every address outlined a form of 'active' programme, with housing, sanitation, and public-utility purchase the leading elements. Even at the end of a decade which had seen London local taxation rise by 37 per cent,[44] bringing the violent hostility shown towards the first-tier bodies in the late 1880s, demands for pure retrenchment were confined to a few of the several eccentric independents. Conservatives who had attributed the rising MBW precept to peculation trusted to direct election to curb the rates. Many must have assumed that with the party controlling five-sixths of London's parliamentary representation, the Council would display a Conservative complexion.

Defeat in 1889 was crucial, as it enabled the Progressives to appropriate the most attractive municipal policies for their own programme, where they became tainted by association with those elements of Radicalism which Conservatives found most unpalatable. Thus water purchase, which for all its procedural difficulties was almost universally desired and which had been attempted by a Conservative government in 1880, and housing reform, once a preoccupation of Salisbury's and an area in which

---

[42] See e.g. T. G. Fardell, 'The London County Council, I: The Impeachment', *New Review*, 6 (1892), 257.

[43] The Hackney Central Conservative Association adopted candidates for the first elections (Minutes, 16 Nov. 1888), and the Strand Association attempted, apparently unsuccessfully, to bind candidates to Association policy (Minutes, 9 Dec. 1888). The Bristol University collection of election addresses shows that several candidates on both sides admitted to party sponsorship in 1889.

[44] See Appendix 3.

three of the most important pieces of legislation had been passed under Conservative ministries, became linked with the taxation of ground rents, temperance, the most lurid side of London's missionary Nonconformity, and the suspicion of deference to organized labour. Conservatism was not incompatible with municipal enterprise, as the contemporary work of Conservative councils in Liverpool, Sheffield, and elsewhere, and the 'Tory municipalism' of figures like A. K. Rollit demonstrated. In principle the Moderates had still the option of a 'commonsense' municipalism—Progressivism stripped of its 'fads' to leave something like Chamberlain's municipal capitalism, emphasizing the absorption of structural monopolies and the application of their profits to aid the rates. In practice, however, as the Progressives came to inherit the antipathy towards first-tier rates that had helped cripple the MBW the appeal of a purely negative opposition became more seductive. On the first Council a perceptible rift developed between those Moderate municipalists like R. M. Beachcroft and G. B. Longstaff, who worked with Progressives on the Housing and Building Act Committees, and the 'worst Tories' who sought 'to make the Council a bear-garden and a failure'.[45] This division was advertised by the celebrated vote of June 1891 when a cluster of right-wing Moderates left the Council chamber simply to render inquorate a special meeting on tramway purchase, thus frustrating the wishes of a clear majority on the Council and several of their own party.[46] Faced with the choice between sniping at its opponents' alleged extravagance and devising a positive Moderate municipalism which it was in no position to implement, the party drifted into the 'mere negative propaganda'[47] that so discredited it in 1892.

The 1892 Council election was a fiasco for the Moderates. Initial preparations, revolving around the attempt of R. W. E. Middleton, Conservative national agent, to build a campaign around the figure of Earl Cadogan, standing in the City in order to become chairman of a Moderate second Council, foundered on Salisbury's opposition. Salisbury retained the misgivings he had felt about the size and scope of the Council in 1888. After the first elections he had been unperturbed by the Progressive majority, confident that with the chance to 'play the drunken helot', the

---

[45] Sir Thomas Farrer to T. C. Farrer, 25 July 1890, T. C. Farrer Papers, 1888–90, 2572/1/17.
[46] *Metropolitan*, 13 June 1891; W. Saunders, *History of the First London County Council* (1892), 473–5. Under the 1870 Act tramway purchase required the support of a simple majority, with two-thirds of the Council voting. The first Moderate whip found his party 'a difficult crew to manage': W. H. James to Norfolk, 8 Jan. 1893, Norfolk Papers.
[47] J. Chamberlain to L. Holland, 12 July 1894, Chamberlain Papers, JC 5/43/1.

Council would find the rope to hang itself.[48] In 1892 he still did 'not believe it *can* succeed in its present state', and warned Cadogan that the anticipated political benefits of Moderate gains would be outweighed by 'the more permanent evils which the association of one of our number with the career of the County Council might involve'.[49] Cadogan did not stand, and the City candidature, together with the leadership of the second Council Moderates, passed to the fifteenth Duke of Norfolk. If the Moderates *had* to be led by a peer and a London ground landlord standing for the City, they could have done with Cadogan's talent. Norfolk's electioneering overtures to the 'respectable tradesmen' of Shoreditch proved embarrassing; on the Council he would speak only twice in four years.[50]

In the absence of any direction from Central Office, the Moderate campaign became dangerously associated with the activities of the London Ratepayers' Defence League. This body, an offshoot of the fiercely right wing Liberty and Property Defence League, was founded by the tenth Earl of Wemyss during the autumn of 1891 and launched at a public meeting at the Guildhall in November. It sought to fight what Wemyss stigmatized as 'the progressists of the London County Socialistic Council'[51] and to avert the 'danger of having a State and municipal bureaucracy established in our midst on the ruins of individual liberty'.[52] Believing, wrongly, that the LCC had been 'intended to keep our streets clean and our water-closets in sanitary working order' but had been carried by 'vaulting ambition' into the sphere of municipal enterprise,[53] Wemyss advocated an unashamedly negative programme,[54] hostile to virtually every aspect of Progressive municipalism. He attacked public utility purchase,[55] taxation of land values, municipal housing, and even the

---

[48] Quoted R. Taylor, *Lord Salisbury* (1975), 126.

[49] Salisbury to Cadogan, 13 Jan. 1892, Cadogan Papers, CAD/514. See also Middleton to McDonnell, 15 Dec. 1891 and 8 Jan. 1892, HHP.

[50] J. Stuart, 'The London Progressives', *Contemporary Review*, 61 (1892), 530; *Local Government Journal*, 18 Jan. 1896.

[51] London Ratepayers' Defence League, 'Report of Inaugural Meeting . . .' (1891), quoted in K. Young, *Local Politics and the Rise of Party* (Leicester, 1975), 51.

[52] Wemyss to Sir H. James, 31 Jan. 1892, Wemyss Papers, RH 4/40/12.

[53] Earl of Wemyss, *Memories, 1818–1912* (privately printed, Edinburgh, 1912), on microfilm in WP, RH 4/40/19, 139.

[54] 'For remember that it was a negative policy, in the main, that was given to men by the greatest of law givers', Wemyss, *Modern Municipalism: An Address to the Paddington Ratepayers' Defence Association* (1893), 10. For the 8th Commandment as a text upon the taxation of ground rents see Wemyss to H. Wilkins, 19 Mar. 1892, WP, RH 4/40/12.

[55] Wemyss, *Modern Municipalism*, 7–8.

Public Health Act,[56] and contemplated a statutory ceiling for poundage rates.[57]

The support of Wemyss and his League was a substantial liability to the Moderates. With a General Council including twenty peers even in August 1891,[58] and with the support of the open-handed Duke of Westminster, the image of the League as protector of privilege could not easily be countered, but for all its titled supporters the League was perpetually short of funds[59] and lacked the organizational power to offset the odium that it inspired. It was emphatically not a front to unite Conservatives and Liberal Unionists,[60] however necessary such an organization might have been. In February 1892 Devonshire declined to attend a League meeting, for fear of embarrassing Sir Henry James in his opposition to the 'Gladstonian London Council'.[61] and it is probable that Wemyss's stridency alienated both Liberal Unionists and liberal Conservatives. The leaders of the Council Moderates avoided any public association with Wemyss's League,[62] but their own drift into reaction during the first Council prevented their presenting a sufficiently positive programme to divert attention from it. A Moderate working party charged with organizing the 1892 campaign was chaired by the Liberal Unionist Sir Henry James, who 'asked for a Programme and could get none'; the party 'drifted in default of a Programme into a purely negative position'[63] little different from that of Wemyss. They opposed municipal trading generally, held that water purchase should wait upon the impending Royal Commission Report, urged that revision of the incidence of taxation be left to Parliament, accepted tramway purchase, working-class housing, and direct labour operations only if advantageous to the ratepayers, and called for Council wages to be regulated 'by the custom of the trade for the time being'. Police transfer and the absorption of the City and the Livery Companies were opposed outright; second-tier reform should wait for Parliament.[64]

With this manifesto the Moderates won only 34 of the 118 seats in the

---

[56] Wemyss to H. Spencer, 16 Feb. 1892, WP, RH 4/40/12.

[57] Wemyss, *Modern Municipalism*, 5; see also Wemyss to Cranborne, 11 Dec. 1892, WP, RH 4/40/12.

[58] According to an LRDL prospectus enclosed with W. B. Broderick to Norfolk, 5 Aug. 1891, Norfolk Papers.

[59] It was £90 in debt by late 1892: Wemyss to Cranborne, 11 Dec. 1892, WP, RH 4/40/12.

[60] As Young claims in *Local Politics*, 51.

[61] Devonshire to Wemyss, 22 Feb. 1892, WP, RH 4/40/12.

[62] See Wemyss to H. Spencer, 16 Feb. 1892, WP, RH 4/40/12.

[63] James to L. Holland, 8 Nov. 1893, copy in Joseph Chamberlain Papers, JC 5/43/4.

[64] For the programme see *Metropolitan*, 20 Feb. 1892.

1892 LCC election. Four months later the Conservatives would win 34 seats out of 59 in the general election, despite a Liberal swing. The Progressive dominance of the Council in this period depended upon a Moderate performance in municipal elections significantly poorer than that of their Conservative equivalents in parliamentary contests. There was no obvious structural explanation. The two franchises differed slightly before 1900, with the parliamentary lodger voters excluded from the municipal roll, and peers and women occupiers on the Council register denied the parliamentary vote, but if anything these differences should have helped the Moderates.[65] The Moderates frequently claimed that Conservatives were less likely to vote in local elections than Liberals. This cannot be disproved, but it is noteworthy that only 3 of the 22 seats which retained one or two Progressives to the Council but elected a Conservative to Parliament had a below-average turnout in the 1892 LCC election.[66] It probably is true that the Moderates were robbed of the benefits of superior resources by the tight provisions of the Corrupt Practices (Municipalities) Act,[67] but it would be tendentious to argue that Conservative parliamentary dominance in London was based on 'Tory gold'.

The explanation for the divergent results of the two 1892 elections, and for the broader paradox of Progressive control of the Council at a time of Unionist dominance of London parliamentary elections, is more political than psephological. The Moderates had committed themselves to a retrenchment-oriented campaign critical of every Progressive initiative; in a sense thay gave vent to the West End reaction to rising first-tier rates that had been so curiously muted in 1889. West End hostility to the process of metropolitan integration which the Council partly represented was a potent force, but the West End was not the whole of London, and its antipathy towards the Council was not felt so intensely elsewhere. In

[65] Lodgers were generally taken to be Liberal in London, women voters to be Conservative—Costelloe heard from agents of both parties that the women's vote 'was cast against progress by a majority of about ten to one' in 1892 (interview in *Women's Signal*, 7 Feb. 1895). Successive occupation votes could be claimed for moves anywhere within the county in LCC elections, whereas they were confined to moves within the parliamentary borough in general elections, but this benefit seems to have been rarely claimed: for the difficulties involved see Seager's letter in *South London Press*, 17 Aug. 1889.

[66] Election figures from *Pall Mall Gazette* 'Extra' (1892), 39–45.

[67] The Act treated London constituencies as wards of a parliamentary borough. Sidney Webb complained of having to fight Deptford, population 100,000, on a budget of £100: N. MacKenzie (ed.), *The Letters of Sidney and Beatrice Webb* (London and Cambridge, 1978), i. 373. Carrington and Collins won St Pancras W. on a joint expenditure of £155 in 1895 and £161 in 1898: Carrington Diaries, 2 Mar. 1895 and 13 Mar. 1898. Dickinson was elected for Wandsworth, a Conservative parliamentary seat with a 16,000 electorate, for £155 in 1892: M. Pugh, *Electoral Reform in War and Peace, 1906–18* (1978), 190.

the West End the combination of very high assessments and very low second-tier poundage rates had enhanced the pain of the Council's levies, and had apparently blinded Wemyss and his confrères to the fact that the aggregate rate raised by the LCC actually dropped both in 1890/1 and in 1891/2.[68] Their root-and-branch opposition to Progressivism led them to forget that the liberal Conservatism of the suburbs was more receptive to the philanthropic side of the Council's social programme, and that rated householders had some sympathy for the taxation of land values and for water purchase. In consequence the Progressives won seats in 1892 in predominantly middle-class suburbs which consistently returned Conservatives to Parliament: Clapham, Brixton, Norwood, and Lewisham returned two Progressives, North Hackney and Wandsworth one, although each was regarded as a safe Conservative seat in Parliament. The difference between West End and suburban Conservatism was more significant in municipal than in national elections because the West End felt itself victimized by the local taxation system. Equalization and the eventual failure of the incorporation movement would drive the point home.

Moderate alienation of the Conservative vote was still more pronounced in working-class seats. In the five general elections between 1885 and 1900 the Conservatives won 61 of the 120 contests in Henry Pelling's Category C—'predominantly working class'—seats,[69] but in 1892 they won only 2 Council seats out of 48, and their best performance throughout the Progressive era was to secure 8 seats in 1895. In municipal politics the initiative in working-class areas lay with the Liberals. Those elements of populist Unionism which helped the party in parliamentary contests— jingoism, anti-alienism, the residual protectionism of the riverside districts, and hostility to Home Rule—were irrelevant to municipal contests. Where Progressives offered working-class housing, parks, and fair wages, the Moderates displayed equivocation or hostility towards municipal enterprise. The psephological consequences of this political difference were disproportionate. The 1885 redistribution in London had been based upon population rather than registered electorate. With a smaller electorate in poor districts, votes in working-class seats were worth more than elsewhere, as Table 7.1 illustrates.

The Conservative *London Argus* complained after the 1898 election that 21,000 votes in four Tower Hamlets divisions returned 8 Progressives

[68] See Appendix 3.
[69] For Pelling's London categories see H. Pelling, *Social Geography of British Elections, 1885–1910* (1967), ch. 2.

TABLE 7.1. Municipal Electorate by Pelling's Categories, 1892

	LCC Seats	Registered electorate per seat
Category A (Predominantly Middle Class)	40	11,049
Category B (Mixed Class)	30	9,504
Category C (Predominantly Working Class)	48	7,863

while 20,000 votes in Wandsworth returned only 2 Moderates,[70] and it is true that the Moderates suffered from the caprice of electoral arithmetic in the Council contests. in 1892 they secured 43·19 per cent of the vote even with 5 of their safest seats uncontested, but won only 19 per cent of the seats.[71] Three years later they would win 30,000 more votes than the Progressives, but an equal number of seats. Their failure to look beyond the West End proved disproportionately costly.

In April 1893 Colonel Rotton won a by-election at Clapham for the Moderates on a platform that can best be described as limited Progressivism, promising to 'accept accomplished facts'.[72] Two months later the anti-Progressive *Local Government Journal* admitted that Conservatism 'does not exist in municipal politics in London because it has no raison d'être'.[73] C. A. Whitmore, Conservative MP for Chelsea, produced a plea in the *National Review* for April 1893 for a more positive Conservative approach to the exercise by the Council of powers within its scope, and for consideration of new powers, such as gas and water control, on their merits.[74] Ironically, however, the minimalist Moderate policy of 1892 threatened to feed upon its own failure, as defeat in all but the safest Conservative strongholds had virtually confined the

[70] *London Argus*, 12 Mar. 1898.
[71] Calculation based upon aggregate vote totals, adjusted to allow for seats in which one party put up only one candidate. In these seats (4 Moderate, 3 Progressive) the 'surplus' successful candidate has been taken as the man second in the poll; he has been treated as unopposed and his vote discounted. The two seats (St Pancras N. and E.) in which both parties put up only one candidate, and a contest was necessitated only by independents, have been treated as uncontested, and all votes cast discounted. The Moderate poll would have been higher had not 5 of their strongholds been completely uncontested.
[72] *London*, 6 Apr. 1893. He promised to support the Council's wages policy, water purchase, cheap trains, and improvements in parks and housing, and acknowledged that ground rent taxation needed settlement.
[73] *Local Government Journal*, 3 June 1893.
[74] C. A. Whitmore, 'Conservatives and the London County Council', *National Review*, 21 (1893), 175–86.

party on the Council to the West End. The impetus for the founding of first the London League and then the London Municipal Society came from Conservatives outside the Council.

The London League was formed in May 1893 with a meeting at the house of Ernest Beckett. Its originators included William Hillier, fourth Earl of Onslow, who was to be the most important Conservative municipal figure in London for the remainder of the decade, Lionel Holland, younger son of Viscount Knutsford and, as prospective parliamentary candidate for Bow and Bromley, necessarily an 'advanced' Conservative, and A. A. Baumann, Member for Peckham, and one of the most strident opponents of the LCC on the Conservative back-benches. Ten meetings of the London Programme Committee under Baumann's chairmanship resulted in the formulation of a programme which demonstrated amply the difficulty of elaborating a constructive Moderate policy.[75] With the exception of a rather subjective labour clause[76] and an unspecific commitment to parks and street improvements, there was nothing directly bearing on the LCC. The Council was not mentioned in the programme. A proposal for Local Government Board regulation of gas and water companies was advanced to keep the public utility question off the rates. Suggestions for the treatment of sick paupers, and an unduly elaborate programme of burial reforms had limited appeal; other proposals—for control of alien immigration, better market accommodation, shorter shop hours, rights of compensation for tenants effecting sanitary improvements, and the outlawing of house-farmers—would require changes in the law. The negative programme of 1892 had only been replaced by an evasive one, which Holland considered 'indefinite and half-hearted'. It had soon become clear that 'a final programme could not be completed without such difference of opinion as might endanger the unity of the body'.[77] The main obstacle was apparently Baumann, who had spent the early 1890s determinedly sabotaging LCC Money and General Powers Bills, had been prominent in the opposition to the Public Health Act, and did not wish to see the 'progressive views' which Holland considered 'vital to the success of our party'[78] introduced by the Moderates. Holland and the advanced wing of the party attempted to persuade Lord Randolph

---

[75] London Programme Com., printed programme in Lord Randolph Churchill Papers, RCHL 1/30/4367.

[76] All local authority contracts to pay 'the wages generally recognised as fair in the trade affected', ibid.

[77] Holland to Churchill, 26 Oct. 1893, RCHL 1/30/4366.

[78] Ibid.

Churchill publicly to endorse the forward programme in the hope of forcing Baumann and his followers to reach an accommodation. Churchill's response is unclear, but, in the face of continued hostility on the part of the Conservative leadership,[79] the League could produce only the anodyne manifesto published in December 1893.[80] This contained no more specific policy commitment than the pledge in Article V 'to formulate and support a London policy which will, without discouraging the granting of larger powers to local authorities, tend to the prompt exercise of the powers already possessed'. The actual formulation of such a policy remained, at the end of 1893, no nearer than before.

This was the position when the deliberations of the Amalgamation Commission and the forced withdrawal of the Corporation suddenly made a Conservative revival more urgent. The probability is that the threat to the City, Conservative trophy since 1874, jogged the party leadership out of its detachment. Certainly the spring and early summer of 1894 brought a flurry of pronouncements from front-bench figures, pointing towards separate municipalities. At the end of April 1894 Balfour, replying to the Metropolitan Division of NUCCA called for 'a division of the vast metropolitan area into municipalities, who [*sic*] should deal with all those subjects which are not, from the nature of the case, necessarily under the control of a central body.[81] In mid-May Ritchie, writing to *The Times* on unification and centralization, released the red herring that the Conservatives had always intended to create strong local bodies in 1888 but had been cheated by pressure on parliamentary time.[82] Most significantly Salisbury himself spoke on unification to the Grocers' Company at the end of May, urging that 'if the City of London has populations near to it which desire municipal institutions ... let other sister municipalities be set up by its side'.[83] In June he endorsed Brooke Hitching's advocacy of separate municipalities.[84]

It is possible that the leadership also smiled upon the creation of the London Municipal Society in May. The LMS shared common ancestry with the London League but, being relatively free of back-bench obstructionists of Baumann's stamp, it was able to commit itself to an 'advanced' programme with less friction. Onslow and Holland were joined by liberal

[79] See Young, *Local Politics*, 53.
[80] Copies in Hatfield House Papers (Middleton to Salisbury, 18 Dec. 1893) and Norfolk Papers (Onslow to Norfolk, 4 Dec. 1893).
[81] *Local Government Journal*, 5 May 1894.
[82] *The Times*, 18 May 1894.
[83] *Local Government Journal*, 2 June 1894.
[84] Ibid., 16 June 1894.

Conservatives like H. P. Harris, Moderate whip on the second Council, and C. A. Whitmore, supposedly the author of the LMS constitution,[85] and by some influential Liberal Unionists, including Lubbock, H. B. Farquhar, and R. M. Beachcroft. Their adhesion created 'the uneasy feeling about that this new Municipal Society is in some sense a Liberal Unionist lodge'[86] a feeling which probably alienated NUCCA and some constituency parties,[87] and which was heightened by the shift in sponsorship from Churchill to Chamberlain. During 1894–5, and indeed during the whole period of opposition from 1892, Chamberlain was engaged in the attempt to give Unionism a more overt commitment to a 'forward' policy.[88] His interest lay in encouraging urban against rural Unionism; what he had once hoped to effect through a new redistribution benefiting London and the larger towns[89] he may now have sought through urban municipalism. Certainly he made a cogent attempt to articulate a Unionist municipal philosophy in an article appearing in the *New Review* in June 1894;[90] the arguments used were largely derived from London local politics and the only authority specifically mentioned was the LCC. Chamberlain was occasionally credited with the inspiration of the initial LMS manifesto of May 1894. Its programmatic nature,[91] its 'advanced' tone, and the inclusion of an irrelevant commitment to old age pensions[92] suggest his influence; the call for slum clearance and street improvement to be 'systematically carried out on a general plan in all parts of London'[93] was to be echoed in Chamberlain's Limehouse speech of January 1895, and is itself reminiscent of the Birmingham Improvement Act. Nevertheless, other aspects of the programme derived from the London League,[94] and others still from the battles within the

[85] *Local Government Journal*, 21 July 1894.

[86] Norfolk to Salisbury, 21 Oct. 1894, HHP.

[87] For the issue of parallel programmes by NUCCA and the LMS see Young, *Local Politics*, 66–7. The Strand Conservative Association declined to form an LMS branch because 'they are now and have been for some years past carrying out the objects of your society', Minutes, 22 Oct. 1894.

[88] See R. Jay, *Joseph Chamberlain: A Political Study* (Oxford, 1981), ch. 7.

[89] J. Chamberlain, Occasional Diary, 12 June 1891, Joseph Chamberlain Papers, JC 8/1/5.

[90] J. Chamberlain, 'Municipal Government: Past, Present and Future', *New Review*, 10 (1894), 649–61.

[91] London Municipal Society, 'Draft of Objects ...' in Norfolk Papers, dated in pencil 26 May 1894.

[92] Ibid., II, 5.

[93] Ibid., III, 2.

[94] For example local taxation of personalty and alien immigration control. The commitment to leasehold enfranchisement for working-class occupiers was Onslow's suggestion: see Balfour to Onslow, 4 July 1894, copy, Balfour Papers, Add. MS 49879, fo. 16.

LCC,[95] with which Chamberlain was not familiar. Given the leanings of its hierarchy, the LMS was bound to adopt a forward policy of some sort.

The danger of Chamberlain's efforts reviving the tension between the 'forward' and the 'negative' Moderates was, however, dispelled by the emergence of decentralization as a platform with broad appeal. To those Vestries suspicious of LCC 'imperialism', to the victims of rate equalization, to the Corporation (which contributed £2,000 to the LMS between July 1894 and February 1895),[96] and to the Unionist politicians who dabbled in London questions, it had obvious attractions. Generally, it offered the Moderates a positive means of challenging the Progressives without having to outbid them in expensive social reforms. In May 1894, then, it became the leading item in the first draft LMS programme, which promised 'the establishment of municipal corporations to be entrusted with large powers' so that 'the vast and widespread population of the Metropolis will be enabled to enjoy full advantages of self-government; proper dignity and importance will be imparted to the local authorities; the heavy and growing responsibilities of the central body will be lightened; and undue centralization will be avoided'.[97] Four months later the cause received unexpected encouragement from the Amalgamation Commission.

3. THE AMALGAMATION REPORT

The Amalgamation Commission reported in September 1894. It recommended the unification of City and County,[98] with conviction, although not without an oblique criticism of the terms of reference. The terms of amalgamation echoed much, although not all, of the scheme prepared by the Council's exclusively Progressive and distinctly Radical Special Committee on London Government. Corporation and Council would be merged to form a new Corporation founded upon the Municipal Corporations Act.[99] The City estates and markets, with their associated liabilities, would pass to the new Corporation, as would the Guildhall, its library, and its school of music. The new Corporation would elect the

[95] For example LCC budgetary control and greater emphasis upon street improvements to provide employment.

[96] Special Com. Minutes, 11 July 1894, 25 Jan., 8 Feb. 1895.

[97] LMS, 'Draft of Objects', 1.

[98] RC Amalgamation, Report, in *PP 1894*, XVII.

[99] Although with some features of the 1888 Act incorporated, including the contentious s. 80 on budgetary control, presumably at Farrer's insistence.

Lord Mayor from the entire citizen body, severing the mayoralty from the Livery Companies. Common Council's administrative duties would pass to the new Corporation, along with such of the City Commissioners of Sewers' functions as were performed by the LCC outside the City. The City Commissioners' second-tier functions would pass to the new local authority for what the Royal Commission called the 'Old City'.

Most of this was predictable, although it was still received with unbridled enthusiasm by Progressives, and Farrer told Courtney that he could find himself 'the First Lord Mayor of United London'.[1] What was not expected was that the Commissioners, like their predecessors in 1853–4, would dabble gratuitously in second-tier reform. In reality, as Farrer later argued,[2] 'the logic of facts' dictated that if the Commissioners were to make recommendations for the allocation of residual second-tier powers in the City area, they would have to consider both general second-tier powers and the two-tier balance. Their specific conclusions were adventurous, however. They recommended local municipal councils, with mayors but not aldermen, and specified nineteen Vestry and District Board areas which appeared fit for immediate transformation. The new councils would inherit Vestry and all other second-tier powers, excepting the poor-law, and, more provocatively, it was urged that 'no duties shall be thrown upon the central body that can be equally well performed by the local authorities'.[3] The author of these suggestions was almost certainly Farrer. In 1889 he had acted to push the Council's sub-committee on London government towards a more positive commitment to decentralization than had been contained in Hughes's original scheme, and had moved successfully that the sub-committee 'proceed on the principle of decentralisation, by making the District Councils as important as possible, and vesting in them all such executive functions as are not essentially and necessarily the business of a central authority'.[4] On second-tier reform, as on LCC budgetary control, Farrer used his membership of the Royal Commission to put over opinions on a matter not central to it.[5]

These recommendations had no connection with the emergence of Conservative decentralization proposals during the spring and summer of 1894. They represented opinions formulated by Farrer five years

---

[1] Farrer to Courtney, 3 Oct. 1894, Courtney Papers vi. 6.

[2] Quoted in *London*, 7 Nov. 1895. ·

[3] RC Amalgamation, *PP 1894*, XVII, Report, 17, 28, 30.

[4] LCC Sub-Com. on Completion of London Government, Minutes, 14 Nov. 1889.

[5] The second-tier recommendations were therefore made because of Farrer's presence rather than despite it, as Young claims in *Local Politics*, 55.

earlier, at a time when limited devolution had not been seen as controversial. The Commissioners were not calling for a separate-municipalities solution, and they had treated the Kensington secessionists with an impatience otherwise reserved for the spokesmen of the City. Farrer supported decentralization as a measure of administrative rationalization, not as a means of saving the 'stupid old City'.[6] Nevertheless, proposals for local mayors and the devolution of LCC powers, at a time when decentralization had become official Moderate policy, touched the Progressives on a raw nerve.

During the early 1890s Progressive attitudes towards the second-tier question derived from several conflicting preoccupations. Respect for local municipal enterprise was tempered by some suspicion of parochial competence and by a faith in metropolitan unity and integration. The urgency of the problem seemed, however, to have diminished when the London Liberals succeeded in smuggling the metropolis into the 1894 Local Government Act. This 'revolution in a clause'[7] secured many of the most desirable reforms that London Liberals would have sought in a District Councils Bill—expansion of the Vestry franchise by the amalgamation of the parliamentary and county registers, admission of women to Vestries, removal of the prohibitive qualification for Vestry membership—without tampering with the two-tier balance.[8] The Act also empowered Vestries to petition the Local Government Board for the transfer of baths and library commissioners' and burial boards' powers within their areas; such 'horizontal' transfers helped build up the secondary bodies without despoiling the Council. The survival of the District Board system was an anomaly, of course, but otherwise most Progressives probably felt that after the 1894 Act 'the transition from Vestries to future District Councils will be little else than a matter of form',[9] and that the second-tier problem was settled. They would therefore have welcomed a decisive rebuttal by the Amalgamation Commissioners of 'tenification' and of the incorporation proposals being voiced by the Kensington witnesses. That the Commission opted instead for an endorsement of the principle of devolution at a time when decentralization was being adopted by the Progressives' opponents was, in the indiscreet words of the *Daily Chronicle*, 'an awkward incident'.[10] The Commissioners' second-tier

---

[6] Farrer to Benn, 17 Jan. 1895, Benn Papers, vi, quoted in Young, *Local Politics*, 67.
[7] London Reform Union, *First Annual Report for 1892–3* (1894).
[8] 56 & 57 Vict. c. 73, s. 31.
[9] *London*, 11 Jan. 1894.
[10] *Daily Chronicle*, 28 Nov. 1894.

proposals contained nothing intrinsically unacceptable to Progressives—
the LCC Special Committee incorporated them in its draft Bill based on
the report and considered their implementation 'of the highest importance'[11]—but the timing and tone of the recommendations was still an
embarrassment.

For the Moderates, though, they were tactically invaluable, enabling
the party to beg the awkward question of the lengths to which it would
go to defend the City. Norfolk, Moderate leader on the second Council,
admitted privately that amalgamation posed difficulties for several in the
party who did not wish for too close an identification with the 'simply
"non possumus" attitude' anticipated from the City.[12] The strategy
eventually adopted was embodied in Lubbock's amendment to the Progressive motion approving the report in November 1894, to the effect
that the Commissioners' second-tier proposals should be implemented
before those for amalgamation.[13] As the 1894 Vestry elections and the
1895 Council elections approached, this hardened into a commitment to
second-tier municipalities.

4. THE MEANING OF DEVOLUTION

The gains made by the Moderates in the 1894 Vestry elections and their
attainment of parity with the Progressives in the 1895 Council elections
appeared to vindicate the new policy. In fact the swing against the
Progressives probably owed little to the public response to the Amalgamation Report, let alone popular sympathy for the Corporation. As
Courtney, 'with his superior air', told Beatrice Webb, 'this election won't
be fought on anything so remote as Unification ... If you win you will
win on your administration, if you lose you will lose on the increase or
supposed increase in the rates'.[14] The increase was not imaginary. The
county rate yield had risen by 28 per cent over the period of the second
Council, with a further 10 per cent increase already projected.[15] Rising
rates probably brought back into line those Conservative suburbs which
had previously returned Progressives. In North Hackney, which had
returned one Progressive in 1889 and 1892, the Stoke Newington Rate-

[11] 'London Government Bill' and 'Notes on the Clauses', in LCC Clerk's Dept. CL/LOC/1/2.
[12] Norfolk to Salisbury, 1 Nov. 1894, HHP.
[13] LCC Minutes, 24 Nov. 1894.
[14] Beatrice Webb's Diary, xv. fo. 1372 (15 Feb. 1895).
[15] See Appendix 3.

payers' Association had showed itself sympathetic to the Progressives' 'rate support' proposals[16] and, resisting Wemyss's flattery in 1891,[17] supported Progressives in each of the first two elections.[18] It did not live to fight the third, but in the Vestry elections of December 1894 its ticket was identical to the Conservative list.[19] North Hackney, Brixton, Lewisham, Norwood, Wandsworth, and Clapham returned two Moderates in 1895, and only one of the Progressives' twelve Category A seats of 1892 survived.

The Moderates could probably, then, have prospered just as well on 'mere negative propaganda' as on a devolution platform. Nevertheless, negative propaganda was divisive in a way that decentralization appeared not to be and devolution had gathered a momentum that justified its adoption. Defining it was more difficult, and not altogether necessary for the purposes of the election. But it was a policy which meant different things to different groups, and the diverse components were not always compatible, as the next four years would show.

The philosophy of what became the incorporation movement could embrace anything from full-blooded 'tenification' involving a structural shift from a predominantly centralized to an almost entirely decentralized system, obliterating the LCC in the process, to a mere tidying up of the two-tier margin and the honorific enhancement of second-tier dignity. The majority of the Vestries were unambitious in their demands. They sought a constitutional reform that would remove the bad odour of 'Vestrydom' and curb the encroachment of the LCC upon second-tier powers. They sought devolution of those Council powers which they considered intrinsically local, Building Act powers being most frequently mentioned. Whilst all secondary authorities found growing first-tier rates an incubus, however, and were eager to limit LCC 'extravagance' where it was demonstrated, the two-thirds of sanitary authorities below the average rateable value per head were aware that wholesale devolution was

[16] A joint sub-committee of the Stoke Newington and W. Hackney Associations in December 1888 agreed that candidates should be questioned on poor-rate equalization, taxation of ground rents, and gas and water control (SNRA Minutes, 31 Dec. 1888), and the SNRA advanced the same questions in 1892 (ibid., 8 Feb. 1892).

[17] Ibid., 14 Dec. 1891. Wemyss's attempt to make the LRDL a federation of ratepayers' organizations had little success. Only seven parishes and one City ward sent delegates to the meeting of March 1892 (W. B. Brodrick to Wemyss, 31 Mar. 1892, WP, RH 4/40/12). After the 1892 election the Fulham RA contemplated secession 'in consequence of the delegates of the Association not having been consulted on anything' (*West London Observer*, 19 Mar. 1892).

[18] SNRA Minutes, 7 Jan. 1889, 8 Feb. 1892.

[19] Ibid., 10 Dec. 1894.

likely to be burdensome to them, and saw the advantage of calling upon
the rateable wealth of all London to defray the cost of marginal functions.
They had before them the example of West Ham, a living instance of a
'separate municipality', which the City had helped secure incorporation
in 1886.[20] The difficulty of supporting a fire brigade, a school board, and
other municipal accoutrements amongst a predominantly working-class
population had sent the rates up to 7s. 4d. in the pound.[21] At a time when
the Moderates of Kensington were contemplating secession from the
county of London, the Progressives of West Ham sought admission to it,
by which they would benefit in 'very much the same way that a poor man
would benefit by marrying a rich woman',[22] especially after the passing
of the Equalization Act. Extensive devolution of LCC functions was
potentially oppressive for most Vestries. If it could be sustained only by
wholesale amalgamations of secondary areas it was still less attractive, as
the Chelsea furore in 1890 had shown. The Vestry revival had generated
a good deal of localized civic pride, and while localism obviously fuelled
much Moderate rhetoric against the allegedly centralizing LCC Progressives, it was just as potent a weapon against 'tenification'. Administrative devolution was incompatible with parochialism.

This was not obvious to the West End Vestries. They were not
interested in a purely honorific second-tier reform: 'a mere change of
name' would not satisfy the Kensington Vestry.[23] They wished to remedy
a situation in which, for example, only 19 per cent of rates raised in St
James' in 1893/4 was applied to local purposes.[24] They had much less to
lose by an estrangement from the LCC, to which they attributed an anti-
West End bias and which they blamed for equalization. They were as
anxious to preserve parochial identities as any secondary authorities—
Kensington had been no more eager to join Chelsea in 1890 than Chelsea
had Kensington—and their support for extensive devolution could not
lead them to 'tenification'. Usually they squared the circle by declining
to look at the second-tier question as a general problem. Their rhetorical
approach was to ask why, say, Kensington, with a population large enough
to make it a county borough had it been outside London, and a rateable

[20] SC Malversation, *PP 1887*, X, QQ. 1519–22 (G. P. Goldney). In 1894 T. H. Brooke
Hitching still considered West Ham 'the proud pioneer of the coming federation of London
corporations': *London*, 21 June 1894.
[21] Ibid., 14 June 1894.
[22] Ibid., 31 Oct. 1895. For the absorption movement in West Ham see *Stratford Express*,
3, 10 Mar., 16, 23 June 1895.
[23] RC Amalgamation, *PP 1894*, XVII, Q. 10,629 (Leete).
[24] *London Statistics*, IV (1893–4), 348–9.

value exceeded only by Liverpool and Manchester of the provincial municipalities, should be denied full municipal institutions, and to claim the right 'to be placed in as advantageous a position as the various County Boroughs throughout the Country'.[25] When pressed to name powers amenable to *general* devolution, however, the proposals of the Kensington men were less rousing: building inspection, sky-sign regulation, technical instruction, infant life protection, shop hours regulation, slaughterhouse and dairy inspection, and the naming and numbering of streets.[26] Sidney Webb calculated that all the transfer proposals specified by Conservative witnesses before the Commission accounted for only £12,000 of the Council's £2 million budget.[27] The West End authorities wished rather to 'contract out' of the metropolitan system themselves than to reshape it generally, because the latter option would raise again all the questions to which metropolitan integration had originally been the answer.

The City's main concern was self-preservation, as always. In its perception of the means to this end, though, policy was changing. On the face of it the Corporation's policy was still traditional 'tenification', and there was an argument for saying that while amalgamation remained a threat 'tenification' would be indispensable, since the only way to justify the City's position would be by creating similarly independent local municipalities. 'Tenification' alienated the parishes, however, and was practically implausible. With the initiative taken by Kensington earlier in the year, the Corporation had for the first time been encouraged to identify the common ground that it shared with the West End local authorities, and to refine the clumsiness of 'tenification'. In October 1894 a group of Corporation officers drew up a new scheme for second-tier reform at the instigation of the Special Committee, and it was resolved to approach 'Lord Salisbury, Mr Balfour, Mr Chamberlain and others'.[28] The importance of the scheme[29] lay in the fact that it abandoned previous attempts to cast other secondary authorities in the City's mould. Confident, presumably, that the immediate danger of legislation on the Amalgamation Report could be resisted, the officers recommended that

[25] Statement of Supplemental Evidence by T. W. Wheeler and W. C. Leete, LCC Clerk's Dept. CL/LOC/1/3.
[26] Ibid.
[27] *London*, 7 Nov. 1895.
[28] Special Com. Minutes, 11 Oct. 1894.
[29] The elements of the officers' scheme adopted by the committee are given in Special Com. Minutes, 19 Nov. 1894. The most important transfers were Technical Instruction Act powers, powers under Part III of the 1890 Housing Act, some Building Act regulatory powers, and powers over offensive businesses, slaughterhouses, and dairies.

future threats be forestalled by an extension of the City's boundaries, to offset the liability of its dwindling population. The second-tier question could then be considered without reference to the City, and the officers proposed separate municipalities of indeterminate number and areas. They would receive a considerable number of powers transferred from the LCC, few of which, however, were particularly important or expensive. Without, for instance, police powers, powers relating to large-scale clearances under Part I of the 1890 Housing Act, open spaces powers, or powers under the Tramways Act, the new boroughs would be markedly weaker than the Corporation. Nor were the transfers specified likely to make much difference to the ratio of first- to second-tier rates in the West End. The officers acknowledged the need for a Central Council, which would inherit all other LCC functions, together with a general default over the secondary bodies and the right to audit their accounts. They sought to curb it not by stripping it of power, but by a partial return to indirect election, by which aldermen would not be co-opted, as on the LCC, but would be returned by the secondary bodies. The only hope for the committed decentralizers lay in the provision by which the Central Council could in the future choose to devolve existing or fresh statutory powers to the new municipalities, an open-ended provision that would become familiar during the next few years. Without extensive devolution either of functions or of finance, there was less need to toy with the contentious question of second-tier amalgamations and, with a tact not characteristic of previous City schemes, the Special Committee resolved 'that it is undesirable to particularly indicate at present the extent of a new area of the City or what should be the precise areas of the other municipalities'.[30] The new scheme was not published and had no overt influence upon events, but it is significant as an indication of the evolution and refinement of the thinking of a Special Committee which, nine years earlier, had sought to confine the central body to main drainage, water, and light.

No such subtlety infused the pronouncements of the Unionist politicians who involved themselves in the question. Salisbury and Chamberlain aimed at the political emasculation of Progressivism, and saw the emasculation of the Council as a means to that end. Both were therefore unrepentant tenifiers. Salisbury, no longer assured that the LCC would destroy itself, attacked it in the conventional terms of the Conservative right. Rallying the Moderate troops at the Queen's Hall in November

[30] Special Com. Minutes, 24 Nov. 1894.

1894 he spoke of the Council as 'a place where Collectivist and Socialist experiments are tried ... where the new revolutionary spirit finds its instruments and collects its arms'.[31] He hinted at the establishment of municipalities of up to a quarter of a million people, confining the central body to main drainage, management of the Thames, and water supply[32]— in short to 'all those things which depend on the natural law that water will go down and not up'. Chamberlain's position was more delicate. He would have betrayed his pedigree by departing from the belief that 'municipal government is the most potent agent of social reform'[33] and could not afford a purely nihilistic attitude towards the Council, but he had supported 'tenification' since his Liberal days and found no difficulty in dressing it in Radical clothes now. He treated the Amalgamation Report as if it were an attempt to revive the Harcourt Bill. At Stepney in February 1895 he charged the Commissioners and the Progressives with seeking to create a 'vast overreaching centralized despotism', and proposed instead to create new municipalities roughly equal in size to his Birmingham.[34]

Although Salisbury was concerned for the City, and Chamberlain sought to 'appeal to the Home Rule feeling which undoubtedly exists in the separate districts now administered by Vestries and Local [*sic*] Boards',[35] neither had any real understanding of London government. Metropolitan Unionists, often closer to the local bodies, were more cautious. The Metropolitan Division of NUCCA spoke in its 1895 programme merely of 'separate municipalities' in 'well defined areas'[36] which could mean anything and posed no explicit threat to the LCC. The LMS was more cautious still, advocating the preservation of existing districts and the devolution of those powers 'which ought to be administered locally'.[37] Elucidating this programme, H. P. Harris and R. M. Beachcroft, though drawing a rather careless analogy with provincial county boroughs, acknowledged that 'the district communities of London cannot, from the circumstances of their geographical position, be as completely self-governed as the large provincial towns'. Their specific transfer

---

[31] The best reports are in *The Times* and *Daily Chronicle*, 8 Nov. 1894.

[32] A pregnant aside which apparently passed unnoticed.

[33] Speech at Stepney, reported in *The Times*, 7 February 1895.

[34] Ibid.

[35] Memorandum on the Amalgamation Report, enclosed with Chamberlain to Norfolk, 22 Oct. 1894, Norfolk Papers.

[36] For the NUCCA programme see *Tory*, Feb. 1895.

[37] For the LMS programme see R. M. Beachcroft and H. P. Harris, 'The Work and Policy of the London County Council', *National Review*, 24 (1895), 828–46.

proposals merely echoed the limited suggestions made before the
Amalgamation Commission.[38]

In other words, the Moderate proposals could imply anything from a
slight adjustment of the two-tier balance to a comprehensive decentralization of London government. They could satisfy all their backers
only as long as they were not more explicitly defined. The policy was
most valuable as a means of fighting fire with fire in the face of the
amalgamation threat. With Rosebery, still an elected member of Council,
having become prime minister in March 1894, the will to legislate on the
Royal Commission report existed. Discussions on the shape of a unification Bill were held in the closing months of 1894, attended by Rosebery, Asquith, Shaw-Lefevre, Charles Harrison, Sir Henry Jenkyns, and
others.[39] Although no draft Bill survives, it is clear that proposals of some
detail were mooted both for unification and for second-tier reform.[40]
Lefevre gave the subject priority amongst his department's suggestions
for the Queen's Speech, and legislation was accordingly promised for the
1895 session.[41] The legislative timetable was the main obstacle. The
curious idea of trusting the measure to introduction in the Lords was
dropped, and in the Commons any Bill would have had to queue behind
Welsh Disestablishment and Local Option. The City Remembrancer was
justifiably confident that 'the present prospects of the Session hardly
suggest a probability of such a Bill being seriously pressed forward'.[42] In
June the government fell. The incoming Unionist ministry buried the
Amalgamation Report, ending the immediate threat to the City, but if
that threat were not to revive in the future, the opportunity to enact a
plausible second-tier reform had to be taken. The internal contradictions
of the Moderate devolution proposals would then become critical.
Attempts to resolve them were to occupy the next four years.

[38] *National Review*, 24 (1895), 837–8.
[39] G. J. Shaw-Lefevre to Rosebery, 7, 30 November 1894, RP, MS 10099, fo. 77, 320; C.
Harrison to Rosebery, 16 Dec. 1894, MS 10100, 124; Lefevre to Rosebery, 23 Jan. 1895, MS
10101, 170.
[40] See the memorandum 'London Unification: Points for Discussion', RP, MS 10100, fo.
239, n.d. but probably originally with MS 10099, 320 of 30 Nov. 1894.
[41] RP, MS 10147, fo. 38; *Hansard*, 4th ser. xxx, 3–4 (5 Feb. 1895).
[42] Report on Legislative Proposals in Special Com. Minute Papers, Feb. 1895.

8

The Slow Death of the Incorporation Movement

While the LCC Moderates campaigned for decentralization, a cluster of spontaneous movements for parochial incorporation emerged. Kensington again led the way, resolving on 30 January 1895 to seek 'to possess a Charter of Incorporation, and to be vested with that fuller Municipal life which the granting of the same would bring about'.[1] In February St Pancras passed a similar resolution, and Marylebone and Paddington sent the subject to committees (both would adopt their favourable reports in the summer).[2] In March Westminster Vestry resolved, on Onslow's motion, in favour of incorporation in principle, and in April Chelsea decided to seek incorporation should any other parish achieve it.[3] On 1 July an informal meeting of the embryonic incorporation movement agreed to summon a formal conference of 'concurring' Vestries.[4] The Westminster Vestry Clerk, J. E. Smith, produced a draft Bill for the incorporation of his parish, adaptable for each of the nineteen authorities the Amalgamation Commission had considered ripe for elevation.[5] These were probably the authorities to receive a circular from Onslow, coyly marked 'confidential', inviting them to apply for charters.[6] The letter bore fruit in Hammersmith, Hampstead, Lambeth, and St James, so that ten Schedule A parishes, together with St Paul, Deptford of the Greenwich District Board, gathered in January 1896 to ask Salisbury and Henry Chaplin, President of the Local Government Board, for legislation to create second-tier municipalities in London.[7]

---

[1] Kensington Vestry Minutes, 30 Jan. 1895.

[2] St Pancras Vestry Minutes, 13 Feb. 1895; Marylebone Vestry Minutes, 7 Feb., 14 Mar., 2 May 1895; Paddington Vestry Minutes, 19 Feb., 21 May, 18 June 1895.

[3] Westminster Vestry Minutes, 27 Mar. 1895; Chelsea Vestry Minutes, 30 Apr. 1895.

[4] See Chelsea Vestry Minutes, 9 July 1895.

[5] 'Draft Outline of a Bill for the Incorporation of the United Parishes of St Margaret and St John, Westminster as a Municipal Borough', 1895, in Box 1 of the material relating to Westminster Incorporation, 1895–9, in Westminster Archives. See also Westminster Vestry Minutes, 23 Oct 1895.

[6] *London*, 25 July 1895.

[7] Westminster Vestry Minutes, 13 Nov. 1895, 22 Jan. 1896.

Although the hidden hand of the Corporation assisted many of the parochial movements[8], pressure for incorporation in the 1890s was spontaneous and did not represent a revival of the phoney charter movements of 1884. The parishes involved were all under Moderate control, a measure of the extent to which the second-tier question had become politicized since the 1895 Council elections. Some sought incorporation to prevent what they saw as the danger of being reduced to LCC cyphers—'County Council number thirty', as one Paddington Vestryman feared.[9] The West End parishes which led the movement still resented equalization and may have hoped to escape it,[10] but Hammersmith, Lambeth, St Pancras, and St Paul, Deptford were beneficiaries of the 1894 Act, and Chelsea lay on the margin. In Hammersmith the proponents of incorporation assumed that success would mean the loss of their equalization grant.[11] The parish lay some way down the rateable value per head table, and secession made little administrative sense, but the Vestry had embarked upon an adventurous programme of municipal expansion during the 1890s and found the Council's precepts an incubus on top of rising second-tier rates—to the Moderate Vestryman Thomas Chamberlen 'the County Council had been taking £20,000 a year out of Hammersmith, and if it had not done that they could have had half a dozen parks with the money'.[12] This attitude was far more deeply rooted in the West End, where high assessments and low second-tier rates emphasized the first-tier burden: T. W. Wheeler told a Kensington incorporation meeting that £450,000 of the £590,000 raised in rates in the parish went to other bodies.[13] The hope of throwing off the first tier entirely depended upon complete secession from the metropolitan system. In the early stages of the movement the proponents of incorporation argued as if this was feasible: incorporation advocates in Marylebone and Hampstead prefaced their motions with surveys of the powers generally

---

[8] T. D. Sewell, joint secretary to the Westminster incorporation movement, was a Corporation employee. H. H. Crawford, City Solicitor, and Sir John Monckton, Town Clerk to the Corporation, were present at the second inhabitants' com. meeting. (Minutes, 16 Oct. 1896, Westminster Incorporation material.) Crawford also assisted the movements in Marylebone and Camberwell (Sewell to J. E. Smith, 3 Mar. 1897, Box 1, Westminster Incorporation material). The Camberwell movement was initiated by a Common Councilman, Matthew Wallace, and that in Marylebone by T. H. Brooke Hitching. The abortive movement in Fulham was led by F. A. Jewson, a Corporation employee.

[9] *Paddington Times*, 22 Feb. 1895.

[10] Although the City's semi-independence had not exempted it from the Act.

[11] *West London Observer*, 19 Feb. 1897.

[12] Ibid., 20 April 1895.

[13] *West London Observer*, 15 Jan. 1897.

available to provincial municipalities, including the right to a separate commission of the peace, and the establishment of police courts and Quarter Sessions.[14] There was no prospect of such powers being generally devolved across London; the effect of the spontaneous generation of the incorporation movement in a cluster of separate parishes was to create a particularistic attitude which aimed more at contracting out of the metropolitan system than at a general devolution scheme. This posed obvious problems for the LCC Moderates, whose perspective was metropolitan rather than parochial. A series of secessions of Conservative areas from the administrative county might benefit the parishes concerned, but it would weaken the Moderate position on the Council and thus strengthen Progressivism elsewhere. It became still more necessary for the Moderates to construct a general devolution scheme.

2. THE TRANSFER CONFERENCE OF 1896

The return of the two parties in equal numbers in 1895 made the task of managing the third Council, to James Stuart, 'one of the most interesting pieces of work I have had to assist in directing'.[15] In fact the surviving Progressive aldermen and the greater Moderate propensity to absenteeism ensured continued Progressive control, but the Moderates were able to secure a larger share of Council posts and a better deal on the committees. On the third Council they would make significant changes in budgetary control and tramway policy, among other things. On the London government question, little changed while the Rosebery government survived and the amalgamation of City and county remained a possibility. The Progressives carried a motion in May 1895 prodding the government to act on the Amalgamation Commission's report, while the Moderates reiterated their unspecific call for the enhancement of the local bodies.[16] The Unionist victory in the July general election changed the position. It provided yet another providential deliverance for the City and increased the likelihood of second-tier legislation. This necessitated a more constructive definition of Moderate policy on the subject, which was affected by another consequence of the election. Both C. T. Ritchie, the creator of the Council and Moderate leader since his election as an alderman in

---

[14] *Marylebone Mercury*, 16 Mar. 1895; *St John's Wood, Kilburn and Hampstead Advertiser*, 25 July 1895.
[15] J. Stuart, *Reminiscences* (privately printed, 1911), 237.
[16] LCC Minutes, 14, 21 May 1895; *London*, 16, 23 May 1895.

March, and Cadogan, elected Councillor for Chelsea, were drafted into important ministerial posts. With the approach of the new Council session in September the Moderates elected Onslow, whose duties as Under-Secretary at the India Office did 'not involve very great labour in quiet times like this',[17] as their leader.

Onslow provided his party with a purposeful leadership previously lacking. He saw his 'principal object in politics' as being to 'undermine and destroy' the power of Progressivism on the Council,[18] and from the time of his election to the Westminster Vestry in 1894 to his resignation as LCC Moderate leader in 1899, sought to achieve that object through second-tier reform. His precise reform aims were generally concealed by the tactical reticence characteristic of the whole decentralization movement, but from the evidence available he appears as a militant tenifier, favouring large authorities,[19] decentralization which would extend even to water control,[20] and the reduction of the LCC to a supervisory authority.[21] As a Westminster Vestryman he was one of the leaders of the parochial incorporation movement, but as a Moderate Councillor he was aware of the need to build a general second-tier scheme. He sought to harness local particularism and general decentralization by building upon the conventional Moderate support for the devolution proposals of the Royal Commission. In November 1895 he moved in the Council that a conference be convened between the LCC and the secondary authorities to consider the question of transfer of powers.[22]

Although Progressives called for all sections of the Amalgamation Report to be honoured, they could hardly resist Onslow's proposal, which was referred to the Local Government Committee for implementation. In due course each Vestry—Schedule A or B—and each District Board was invited to send three representatives to Spring Gardens. The Council supplied twenty-four members—half nominated by each party—in an advisory role, entitled to speak but not to vote.[23] Sir Arthur Arnold, Chairman of the Council, chaired the conference. The entire statutory powers of the Council were tabulated, and delegates invited to propose

[17] Salisbury to Onslow, 20 Sept. 1895, OP, 173/7/29.
[18] Typescript notes of speech to a Moderate Party meeting, n.d. but Mar. 1897, OP, 173/7/35.
[19] Interview in *Westminster*, 1 Dec. 1896.
[20] He believed water control could be handled by groups of second-tier municipalities: Onslow to Salisbury, 14 Feb. 1897, HHP.
[21] *Local Government Journal*, 25 Apr. 1896; *Westminster*, 1 December 1896.
[22] LCC Minutes, 5 Nov. 1895; *London*, 7 Nov. 1895.
[23] LCC Minutes, 17 Dec. 1895.

powers suitable for either full transfer or the exercise of concurrent powers by the secondary bodies.

The incorporation movement parishes, though instinctively sympathetic to devolution, had their doubts about the conference's value. They looked to their prospective charters to effect the transfers appropriate to their areas and had not considered the question in its metropolitan context. With the separate representation of the Schedule B parishes—only one of which belonged to the movement—the incorporators would be heavily outnumbered at the conference, and felt some diffidence about pressing the case in so broad a forum. Kensington Vestry's Government of London Committee, conscious of 'the desirability of concerted action being taken' by the movement, convened a meeting of its members before the conference.[24] It was decided to participate but, apparently, to qualify participation by a prefatory explanation, moved by Paddington and Marylebone at the opening session, that decisions reached by the conference should not prejudice their applications for incorporation.[25] This somewhat superfluous safeguard permitted the incorporating parishes to play a very limited role in the proceedings of the conference.

If the conference seemed to offer only limited benefits to the incorporation movement, it provided an important opportunity for those secondary authorities which sought only to clarify the two-tier margin and erect a barrier to LCC interference. The need to spell out the parochial attitude to second-tier reform had been clear since the threat to Chelsea in 1890; St James' Vestry had approved a second-tier scheme in 1891 and Camberwell in 1892.[26] The announcement of the transfer conference in 1896 prompted the clerks of two south-eastern authorities to draw up their own plans for marginal transfers. In Lee, George Whale believed that 'whilst the Local Authorities have been for upwards of forty years left with almost the same powers as in 1855, the powers of the Central Authority have been much increased, and many mere local details inconsistently thrust upon it'; reporting to the District Board in January 1896 he identified twenty-four of these local details in the Council's circular and listed them for transfer.[27] In Plumstead, Edwin Hughes, the

[24] Kensington Vestry Minutes, 15 Jan. 1896.

[25] LCC, *Proceedings of a Conference ... on the Question of Transfer of Powers* (1896), 7–8.

[26] St James' Vestry, Special Com. Minutes, 2 Nov. 1891, Vestry Minutes, 12 Nov. 1891; Camberwell Vestry Minutes, 25 May 1892.

[27] Lee DB Minutes, 16 Feb. 1898, 22 Jan. 1896.

Moderate Councillor and Tory MP who served as clerk to the Vestry, picked out as many as forty-one of the Council's listed powers for transfer or concurrent exercise.[28] In neither case was any of the LCC's major branches of expenditure threatened; the items covered related chiefly to those areas of Building Act operation and the various inspection and regulation powers where the two-tier division was irrational. The aim of Whale and Hughes was to tidy up a system that had evolved haphazardly. The aim of their employers was to 'secure complete independence and responsibility to every member of the [two-tier] system'[29] and to dispel the spectre of 'that municipal monstrosity, one authority only to govern all London'.[30] Decentralization could secure both aims, but was not sought as a means of crippling the LCC or of reversing metropolitan integration.

Neither Lee nor Plumstead wished to take on large-scale transfers at their own expense, and Whale announced his intention of moving for an extension of 'the principle of a common fund' to cover new transfers and existing powers concerning highways and public health.[31] If this was important to Lee it was still more important to the East End parishes where the financial weakness of the 1855 system was now most obvious. It was already clear that equalization had only partially offset the steady increase in expenditure during the 1890s. In 1895/6 the poundage rates within the Tower Hamlets varied from 6s. 5d. in St George's to an unprecedented 8s. 2d. in the Bow and Bromley parishes of the Poplar District Board, while St James' Westminster still paid only 4s. 9d. in the pound.[32] In October 1895 Bromley Vestry convened a conference of East End authorities which called for an extension of the 1894 equalization scheme, further poor-rate equalization, and greater metropolitan support for local expenditure.[33] With the existing situation unsatisfactory to them, the prospect of a transfer conference apparently intended to make the metropolitan system still more unbalanced deeply concerned the East End authorities.

There was, therefore, no more a uniform second-tier attitude to transfer than there was a uniform LCC attitude when the conference opened at the end of January 1896. The first session was crowded, with each of the

---

[28] Plumstead Vestry Minutes, 29 Jan. 1896.
[29] Ibid.
[30] Lee DB Minutes, 22 Jan. 1896.
[31] Ibid., 5 Feb. 1896.
[32] *London Statistics*, VI (1895–6), 474–7.
[33] Bromley Vestry Minutes, 16 Oct. 1895; *East London Observer*, 7 Dec. 1895.

invited authorities represented, in recognition, perhaps, of the fact that this was the first occasion in the entire London government debate when second-tier opinion had been seriously canvassed. The first day's events could hardly have pleased Onslow. After the opening pleasantries H. M. Robinson, Clerk to the Progressive Shoreditch Vestry, which had endorsed the Bromley conference resolutions in January 1896,[34] moved that the conference call for an increase in the equalization levy proportionate to the cost of any powers recommended for transfer. He added that, if his motion failed, Shoreditch would view transfer in a different light.[35] Onslow defused this unwelcome reminder of the financial aspect of decentralization by securing its postponement until the final session, so that individual transfers could be assessed 'on principle only, reserving for subsequent consideration the manner in which such transfer might have financial consideration',[36] but so early an airing of the question must have affected subsequent debates. Two rather shabby votes on the first day emphasized that finance was never far from delegates' thoughts, as first the non-riparian majority of parishes resolved to take the maintenance of the Thames Embankment roadways off the county rate, and secondly the majority of parishes not receiving main-road grants from the Council resolved to deprive the nine authorities which did.[37]

The Chelsea representatives, with the prospect of an embankment roadway to support, left the first session of the conference 'not very strongly impressed with its utility thus far'[38], and the Poplar and Limehouse delegates contemplated a protest about their prospective joint loss of £3,000 in main-road grants.[39] The five subsequent sessions, however, proved less acrimonious and more business-like. Their result was substantial approval of the programmes of marginal transfer drawn up by Whale and, in particular, Edwin Hughes, who effectively managed the conference.[40] The most significant among them related to the operation of the Building Act, long a parochial grievance, and the consequent transfer of control over 'an officer called "District Surveyor", who, like Rider Haggard's "She", must be obeyed'[41]. A series of Public Control

[34] Shoreditch Vestry Minutes, 21 Jan. 1896.
[35] LCC, *Transfer Conference Proceedings*, 6.
[36] Ibid., 17.
[37] Ibid. 13–17.
[38] Chelsea Vestry Minutes, 4 Feb. 1896.
[39] *East End News*, 8 Feb. 1896.
[40] For the conference resolutions see Table 8.1.
[41] 'Local (Hammersmith) Government As It Is and As It Might Be, II', *West London Observer*, 28 Nov. 1891.

Department powers of inspection and regulation were recommended for transfer, together with a collection of individual powers relating to the stopping-up of streets, removal of obstructions, common lodging house inspection, electric lighting inspection, and Shop Hours Act enforcement. Twenty-five transfers were recommended in all, with a further five powers proposed for concurrent exercise by the two tiers. Twenty transfer proposals were negatived by the conference and fifteen, requiring amendment of the law, referred to the Council's Local Government Committee.

The significance of the conference lay in the limited nature of its recommendations, 'more numerous than important', in Salisbury's dismissive phrase.[42] In all they accounted for an annual expenditure of just under £25,000—about a sixth of a penny on the county rate.[43] None of the Council's major spending powers was affected. LCC Progressives concluded that the conference 'has made it clear, once and for all, that there is no power or function of any magnitude or importance which could be transferred from the central to the local authorities',[44] although the discovery did not make them any more open-handed over the transfers that were proposed. Even the London Municipal Society concluded, 'as a result of the conferences held between the LCC and the local bodies, that there are very few powers who can advantageously be transferred from the former to the latter'.[45] The parishes seeking incorporation were obviously unhappy. The Westminster representatives attributed what they saw as the conference's failure to the 'very contracted views' of many of the delegates, who 'steadily opposed any transfer of powers to local authorities which, however much such transfer might add to their importance and dignity, might be expected to involve the local area ... in any additional expenses'.[46] The Kensington delegates concluded that their movement 'is not likely to be materially assisted by the holding of the Conference or the result arrived at'. They blamed Sir Arthur Arnold for too precise an interpretation of his chairman's brief, so that transfers were considered item by item and 'no debate took place on the general policy'.[47] In fact the incorporation movement had been weakened more

[42] Quoted *London*, 12 May 1898.
[43] See Haward's Table in LCC Local Government and Taxation Com. Presented Papers, 27 Nov. 1896.
[44] Sidney Webb, quoted in *London*, 23 Dec. 1897.
[45] J. G. Hay Halkett, LMS Secretary, interviewed by Jesse Argyle, May 1897, Booth MS, B 181, 5.
[46] Westminster Vestry Minutes, 24 June 1896.
[47] Kensington Vestry Minutes, 4 Nov. 1896. Dr Young claims that the conference was 'dominated' by the richer Vestries and the LCC Moderates: K. Young and P. Garside, *Metropolitan London* (1982), 78.

by its own refusal to descend to particulars than by Arnold's failure to rise above them. Although T. W. Wheeler, one of the Kensington leaders, apparently believed that the central body could be confined to 'questions relating to the fire brigade, the main drainage, theatres and bridges',[48] there was no attempt to put such a minimalist philosophy, or indeed any co-ordinated incorporation movement policy, before the conference. Only three of the twenty-five transfer proposals that were adopted came from the movement, along with fourteen of those referred to the Local Government Committee, none of any great importance. The incorporators appeared inhibited by their minority position, and by their view of the conference as a distraction, at a time when they sought their own emancipation through individual charters.

In view of this, the calling of the transfer conference appears a tactical mistake on Onslow's part. At a time when the incorporation movement was gathering steam, the conference provided an unsolicited demonstration of the commitment of the majority of parishes to metropolitan integration. But Onslow's problems were more than tactical. The conference had driven home the lesson of the 1892 LCC election and of the Equalization Act, that the municipal interests of the West End were not necessarily mirrored in the suburbs, even Conservative suburbs. That the Progressive East End and inner South would resist devolution was predictable, but that the delegate from the impeccably Moderate Lewisham District Board should announce that 'for the mere honour of having these things under our own control we should not be willing to undertake extra expense' was significant.[49] Lewisham was a recipient under the Equalization Act and, like many suburban parishes in the process of 'filling up', it had embarked upon considerable local expenditure. Its rates stood as high as 7s. in the pound in 1895/6.[50] The readiness of Hammersmith to risk bartering the benefits of integration for those of autonomy was not widely shared.

Onslow had probably calculated upon an uncritical acquisitiveness on the part of the secondary authorities overcoming such anxiety. For most of the 1890s the local bodies had voiced strong criticism of LCC encroachment upon second-tier prerogatives. In moving for the conference Onslow had cited the memorial signed by twenty-seven authorities after the Chelsea amalgamation threat, containing an unspecific plea for broader

---

[48] *West London Observer*, 15 Jan. 1897.
[49] LCC, *Transfer Conference Proceedings*, 30.
[50] *London Statistics*, VI, 474.

TABLE 8.1. Major Proposals of the Transfer Conference, 1896

	Proposals of Conference	Views of LCC	1899 Bill	1899 Act
Building Act	1. Removal of posts and bars	Accepted transfer	Proposed transfer*	Transferred*
	2. Sanction of new streets	Accepted subject to LCC approval	—	—
	3. Appointment of District Surveyors	Opposed transfer	—	—
	4. Approval of building plans, etc.	Opposed except *re* wooden structures	Wooden structures only	Transferred *re* wooden structures
	5. Sanction of working class dwellings	Opposed transfer	—	—
	6. Action *re* dangerous structures	Referred back	—	—
	7. Consent to balconies, etc.	Opposed transfer	—	—
	8. Removal of sky signs	Transferred with default power	Transferred with default power	Transferred with default power
	9. Storage of timber	Concurrent powers	Concurrent powers	Concurrent powers
	10. Demolition of illegal buildings	Concurrent powers	Concurrent powers	Concurrent powers
Highways	11. Maintenance of embankment roadways	Accepted transfer	Transferred on LCC request	Transferred on LCC request
	12. Lighting, etc., of embankments	Accepted transfer	Transferred on LCC request	Transferred on LCC request
	13. Main road maintenance	Accepted transfer	Proposed transfer	Transferred
	14. Testing and inspection of electricity supply	Opposed transfer	—	—

		No objection	Power to promote and oppose Bills	Power to promote and oppose Bills
Improvements	15. Concurrent power for improvements			
Local Govt.	16. By-laws for 'good rule and government'	Opposed transfer	—	—
Parks	17. Powers under Disused Burial Grounds Act, 1884	No action	—	—
Public Control	18. Appointment of Shop Hours Act inspectors	Opposed transfer	—	—
	19. Power to declare offensive businesses	Opposed transfer	—	—
	20. Sanction of new offensive businesses	Opposed transfer	—	—
	21. Licensing of slaughterhouses, etc.	Opposed transfer	—	—
	22. Inspection of slaughterhouses, registration of dairies	Accepted with LCC default power	Proposed transfer with LCC default power	Transferred with LCC default power
	23. Registration and inspection of common lodging houses	Opposed transfer at present	Proposed transfer with default power	—

* Under s. 6 of the original Bill, Building Act powers were to be reviewed by the Privy Council.
Sources: Table in LCC Clerk's Dept. Records, CL/LOC/1/3 and 62 & 63 Vict., c. 14.

powers.[51] But local rates had risen steeply since 1890, making the majority of secondary authorities more conscious of the advantages of metropolitan rate support through the Council, and of equalization, and less anxious to take on gratuitous fresh burdens. The conference had proved what should have been obvious—that extensive devolution was impossible with more than forty second-tier authorities. But if this pointed back to 'tenification' it raised still deeper problems. The localist crusade that had gathered pace since 1893 had depended in part upon the parochial pride generated by the Vestry revival, and upon the second-tier reaction to the alleged centralizing tendencies of the LCC. The Chelsea episode had shown that parochial localism made second-tier amalgamations more difficult. Since the mid-1880s, in fact, the trend had been towards still further fragmentation of the second tier, with the secession of various Schedule B parishes from their District Boards. The year 1886 had brought independence to Fulham and Hammersmith, previously yoked unhappily in the Fulham DB,[52] and in the following year Battersea, more radical and more working-class than the other components of the Wandsworth District, was raised to Schedule A.[53] In 1894 Plumstead had detached itself from its own District Board, after an acrimonious tussle with the other component parishes, which were then reconstituted as the Lee DB.[54] In the same year the Hackney District Board, which had 'never worked harmoniously'[55] was dissolved, and its two components, Hackney and Stoke Newington, transferred to Schedule A.[56] The incongruous adhesion of St Paul, Deptford to the incorporation movement was part of the parish's attempt to leave the Greenwich District, with which it had been 'leading a cat and dog life for the last thirty or forty years'.[57] These manœuvres were chiefly prompted by impatience at the restrictive nature of the district board system, but the parochialism they generated augured badly for the prospect of second-tier amalgamations.[58]

Some of the adherents of the incorporation movement had in fact

[51] *London*, 7 Nov. 1895.
[52] Fulham and Hammersmith were separated by 48 & 49 Vict. c. 33, s. 3.
[53] Battersea was emancipated by 50 & 51 Vict. c. 17, which also raised the two parishes of the Westminster DB (St Margaret and St John) to Schedule A status as a joint Vestry.
[54] For the details see F. E. Mayes, 'Local Government in Woolwich', in Woolwich and District Antiquarian Society, *Annual Reports*, 21 (1954–7) 27–59.
[55] *London Argus*, 21 May 1898.
[56] Plumstead and Hackney DBs were both dissolved by 56 & 57 Vict. c. 55.
[57] Interview with T. A. Simpson, Greenwich Vestry Clerk, in *London*, 3 Mar. 1899.
[58] Especially when secession was motivated by a reluctance to support the other DB parishes financially. Limehouse Vestry considered secession for this reason in 1894: see *East London Observer*, 7 July 1894.

joined to protect themselves against the possibility of amalgamation. Hampstead had been moved by a rumoured proposal 'to tack Hampstead on to another parish or divide it between two or three parishes'[59] and the seconder of the incorporation motion in Paddington had cited the threat of amalgamation with Marylebone or Kensington.[60] Chelsea's urge for self-preservation had shown itself in 1890, and a committee of the St James' Vestry, set up in the wake of the Chelsea episode, had expressed its 'deliberate and mature opinion that the autonomy of the parish should not be interfered with'.[61] Whether these expressions represented true localism or merely the job-protective instincts of Vestrymen is impossible to say, and not immediately relevant; the decentralization movement had been built upon second-tier enthusiasm and could not afford to ignore Vestry opinion. The incompatibility of parochial particularism and administrative devolution was becoming clear, and made still harder Onslow's task of harnessing the localist zeal of the incorporation movement to the cause of general decentralization. For the moment, however, the failure, in his eyes, of the transfer conference threw him back upon the enthusiasm of the incorporators.

3. PIECEMEAL INCORPORATION

The incorporation movement had advanced as the transfer conference sat. In March 1896 Paddington Vestry received a reply from the Privy Council Office to a petition of 1895 calling for the strengthening of second-tier powers. The reply, which displayed the curious passivity that would typify the governmental response to the incorporation movement over the next eighteen months, was probably intended also as an oblique answer to the Westminster memorialists. Written under Devonshire's imprint by Sir Charles Lennox Peel, Clerk of the Council, it admitted that there was no prospect of early legislation, but stressed that

although the existing law relating to the government of London may affect the question, there is no specific provision in the Municipal Corporations Act, 1882, which excludes districts in London, and it would therefore appear to be competent

[59] *Hampstead and Highgate Express*, 20 July 1895.
[60] *Paddington Times*, 22 Feb. 1895.
[61] St James, Piccadilly, Vestry, Special Com. Minutes, 2 Nov. 1891. St Martin-in-the-Fields later joined the movement on the 'express understanding' that it would not be merged into any conglomerate larger than the Strand parliamentary borough (J. E. Smith, notes to 'Proposed Municipalities for London', Box 1, Westminster Incorporation material). The understanding was not honoured.

for the Inhabitant Householders of any such District to petition Her Majesty in Council for the grant of a Municipal Charter.[62]

This Delphic challenge was taken up not by Paddington but by Onslow's own Vestry, Westminster, which in 1896 resolved to set in motion the machinery stipulated by the 1882 Act in order to incorporate the joint parish of St Margaret and St John. Between September 1896 and January 1897 an inhabitants' committee met and an executive committee was formed, a craft petition was approved and a successful public meeting held, and the 'somewhat tedious task' of canvassing for signatories to the petition undertaken. Respect for the requirement of the law meant that the Westminster petition was characterized by a meticulous integrity lacking in the City-sponsored petitions of 1884, and the achievement of persuading 62 per cent of eligible signatories to subscribe was impressive.[63] In January 1897 the Privy Council Office received a petition with nearly five thousand signatures.[64] In the meantime the same procedure was set in motion in Kensington.[65]

Nobody believed that Parliament had intended the 1882 Act to apply to London, but although the Act was considered one of the best drafted on the statute book,[66] it made no specific exclusion of the metropolis. Counsel consulted by the LCC advised that the Queen could grant a charter under s. 210 of the Act, and that a scheme under s. 213 could probably transfer powers from the existing local authorities to the new borough.[67] Westminster's advice, however, was that it would be 'extremely difficult if not impossible' to make the alterations implicit in transfer without an amending Act,[68] and Paddington's reason for not acting upon the Privy Council Office's hint was the improbability of a charter being granted except as part of a general scheme.[69] Nevertheless, J. E. Smith, Westminster Vestry Clerk, and co-ordinator of the

---

[62] The memorial and the reply are reprinted in the Paddington Vestry, *Annual Report* (1895–6), 27–30.

[63] These events are summarized in the report of the Executive Committee to the General Committee of the Westminster Incorporation movement; General Com. Minutes, 26 Feb. 1897, Westminster Incorporation material.

[64] The petition is in PRO PC1/1018.

[65] Kensington Vestry, *Annual Report* (1896–7), 64–71.

[66] By M. D. Chalmers, the Parliamentary Draftsman, quoted in W. B. Odger, *Local Government* (1901), 79, n. 1. (I am grateful to Philip Waller for this reference.)

[67] Opinion of A. Macmorran in LCC Local Government and Taxation Com. Presented Papers, 29 Jan. 1897.

[68] J. E. Smith to W. C. Leete, 28 Oct. 1896, Westminster Incorporation material, Letter-book, 8.

[69] Paddington Vestry Minutes, 3 Nov. 1896.

Westminster movement, believed recent provincial charters to indicate 'an unrestrained power to vary and adapt existing Acts to the new requirements'.[70] The hope was that enough doubt existed to justify a test case.

If the incorporators hoped also to jolt the government into legislative action they were to be disappointed. Salisbury, writing 'as a citizen of Westminster and as a member of the Cabinet', alerted Devonshire to the Westminster petition in November 1896. He supported it 'very heartily' and urged the Lord President not to 'refuse it hastily' but gave no indication that its object would be better met by legislation.[71] The problem posed by the Westminster petition therefore came back to the Privy Council Office to settle. Counter-petitions came from the LCC and what J.E. Smith was pleased to call 'certain vestries of secondary importance'.[72] These were headed by Islington, in fact the most populous parish in London and a Progressive trophy from the 1894 Vestry elections.[73] Islington representatives had been among the most vocal opponents of the incorporators at the transfer conference, and in February 1897 the Vestry resolved to petition against the granting of a charter without consideration of the reform of London government as a whole.[74] The LCC made the same point, opposing any transfer of powers contingent upon a charter 'without simultaneous consideration of the whole subject of powers and areas in London'.[75] This objection was the more potent now that the transfer conference had demonstrated the gulf between the aspirations of the incorporation movement and those of the other secondary authorities. Piecemeal incorporation threatened to make London's patchwork system still more complex if it entailed the multiplication of special county rate arrangements of the kind already necessitated by the City's exemptions, with different levels in each area if the extent of transfer varied.[76]

The legal doubt as to the applicability of the 1882 Act led the Privy Council Office to consult the Law Officers before embarking upon the mandatory public enquiry. The Attorney General and Solicitor General

[70] Smith to Leete, 28 Oct. 1896, loc. cit.
[71] Salisbury to Devonshire, 30 Nov. 1896, Devonshire Papers.
[72] Westminster Vestry, *Annual Report* (1896–7), 5.
[73] For the other petitioners see the epitome in Box 1, Westminster Incorporation material.
[74] Islington Vestry Minutes, 19, 26 Feb. 1897.
[75] LCC Minutes, 16 Feb. 1897.
[76] As W.W. Bruce pointed out in the Council debate: *London*, 18 Feb. 1897.

reported in March 1897, endorsing the view already expressed by some LCC lawyer Moderates[77] that the Act was inapplicable.

> It would not be in accordance with the [1855] Statute that Charters of Incorporation should be granted to these local bodies in London. The Legislature has prescribed that they are to be Vestries and District Boards, and we do not think that any change can properly be made by Charter either in form or in substance.[78]

The Law Officers went on to spell out the obvious implication that if the government wanted change it would have to legislate for it. After a four-month gap, during which the second charter petition, from Kensington, was received,[79] Balfour communicated the Law Officers' opinion to the Commons in July.[80] The public burial of the two charter petitions virtually obliged the government to consider legislation, and the London Government Act of 1899 was really conceived at this point. Before considering its gestation, however, a distraction staged by the Corporation needs attention.

4. SOUTHWARK AND THE CITY

The Corporation's Special Committee had resolved at the time of the Amalgamation Report that the City could best be defended by expanding its jurisdiction. Although no evidence appears to prove that the Corporation initiated the attempts of the northern Southwark parishes to secure inclusion in the City, the fact that the measure advanced *pari passu* with the other change approved in 1894—the absorption of the City Commission of Sewers by the Corporation proper[81]—makes Special Committee instigation probable.

The Corporation had acquired jurisdiction within the six Southwark parishes defined as the ward of Bridge Without in 1550,[82] although over the centuries it had 'gradually withdrawn from the government of the Ward, maintaining that the Corporation came to Southwark mainly to

[77] Notably H. B. Poland in the Council (Quoted in *London*, 18 Feb. 1897), an expression which Onslow privately admitted 'takes the fight out of one' (Onslow to Smith, 19 Feb. 1897, Box 1, Westminster Incorporation material).
[78] Report of R. E. Webster and R. B. Finlay, 16 Mar. 1897, PRO PC8/479/78562.
[79] PRO PC1/996. Sir Arthur Arnold was a signatory.
[80] *Hansard*, 4 ser., LI, 176–7 (15 July 1897).
[81] Approved by the Special Com. on 24 Nov. 1894 and achieved by 60 & 61 Vict. c. cxxxiii.
[82] D. J. Johnson, *Southwark and the City* (Oxford, 1969), 113. See 367–81 for an account of the amalgamation movement.

judge thieves and not to govern citizens'.[83] It none the less retained various rights within 'the Borough', appointing the High Bailiff and the parliamentary Returning Officer. Bridge Without elected no Common Councilmen, and became an aldermanic Chiltern Hundreds, receiving the member of the Court most eligible to retire from active service. The inhabitants had petitioned the Corporation for unqualified inclusion in 1788, 1814, 1835, and 1892 without success,[84] but the fresh initiative taken by H. J. Coles, a member of the largely decorative Corporation of Wardens in St Saviour's, Southwark, and a Moderate on the St Olave's District Board, in October 1894 coincided with the City officers' recommendation to the Special Committee that the Corporation's area be extended. Following Coles's report to the Wardens, the St Saviour's Vestry approved a report advocating amalgamation in January 1895, and convened a conference of the Vestries and District Boards in the Bridge Without area.[85] This sat three times between March and June.[86] By December 1895 the five parishes comprising the St Saviour's and St Olave's District Boards had resolved to seek inclusion, leaving only Progressive St George-the-Martyr outside.[87]

The benefits to the Southwark parishes were obvious. They were minuscule authorities which owed their retention of a separate identity to the parochialism of the 1855 Act, and they were unlikely to survive a second-tier reform unscathed. If amalgamation was inevitable, the City offered a tempting dowry, with its estate revenues and high assessments to aid the Southwark rates.[88] The City's self-indulgent administration and its uneconomic localization of some first-tier functions made Southwark's prospective gains smaller than might have been anticipated, but Coles none the less estimated that had the amalgamation been in force during

---

[83] Report of the Bell Warden to the Wardens of St Saviour's, 22 Oct. 1894, in Southwark Archives, material relating to Bridge Ward Without, 352.031.

[84] Johnson, *Southwark and the City*, 354 ff.; see also the Report of the Bell Warden, loc. cit.

[85] St Saviour's Vestry Minutes, 2 Jan. 1895.

[86] *South London Press*, 16 Mar., 27 Apr., 1 June 1895.

[87] St Thomas, Southwark, Vestry Minutes, 9 Apr. 1895; St Olave's Vestry Minutes, 3 May 1895; St John, Horselydown, Vestry Minutes, 15 May 1895; Christchurch, Southwark, Vestry Minutes, 16 Dec. 1895.

[88] 'Changes of necessity will soon take place in the Government of Greater London. Christchurch will probably be absorbed into some municipality ... If Christchurch be not attached to the City, it will most probably be joined to the old Borough of Southwark, including Bermondsey and Rotherhithe, which would mean an increase of from 6d to 9d in our rating ...': Christchurch Vestry Minutes, 16 Dec. 1895.

1895/6 the Southwark poundage rates would have fallen from between 6s. 5½d. and 7s. 2d. to 6s. 0½d.[89]

Southwark's gains would have to be recovered elsewhere. The LCC stood to lose £5,500 from the Southwark parishes in respect of services transferred to the City Commissioners or the Corporation, offset by an unspecifiable saving in the cost of executing those powers in Southwark, and a slight reduction in the county debt charge.[90] The other parishes in the two poor-law unions concerned[91] would suffer heavily from the loss of the highly assessed warehouse property in the riverside parishes; Bermondsey and Rotherhithe faced an extra 4d. in the pound on the poor rate, Newington and St George-the-Martyr an extra 3d.[92] The City would suffer from the admission of a dependent poor population of the kind that it was popularly believed to have spent forty years banishing from its own area. It was nevertheless glad of an opportunity to augment its dwindling resident population. A 40 per cent decline in population between 1881 and 1896 threatened to undermine its case for municipal independence, previously rather dubiously supported by the optimistically precise 'day census' estimates of its working population.

Despite some opposition from City ratepayers,[93] the Special Committee welcomed the Southwark petitioners, and its report in favour of the amalgamation was adopted 'amidst general and hearty applause' by Common Council in April 1896.[94] In June the Corporation's legal officers recommended the promotion of a private Bill, although, with a reticence characteristic of the City's manœuvres in the 1890s, they urged that the Corporation should support rather than actively sponsor the measure.[95] At the December wardmotes the Southwark Bill was the subject of some rousing hyperbole from leading corporators. W. H. Pannell, of the Special Committee told Bassishaw Ward that it would 'settle the question of London government for some time to come', a rather Guildhall-centred interpretation. The Lord Mayor, George Faudel-Phillips, an avowed 'tenifier', who privately looked upon Southwark as 'the first leaf of the

---

[89] Memorandum on Southwark rates in Southwark Archives, 352.031.

[90] LCC, *Report by the Statistical Officer . . . on the City of London* (*Inclusion of Southwark*) *Bill* (1897).

[91] Bermondsey and Rotherhithe in the St Olave's Union, Newington and St George-the-Martyr in the St Saviour's Union.

[92] LCC, *Report by the Statistical Officer*, 18–19.

[93] Johnson, *Southwark and the City*, 373.

[94] *Report of the Delegates of Southwark Parishes on the City of London* (*Inclusion of Southwark*) *Bill*, Special Com. Minute Papers, Mar./Apr. 1898.

[95] Opinion of the Law Officers, 24 June 1896, Special Com. Minute Papers, June–Dec. 1896.

artichoke',[96] told Farringdon Within that it would make the City 'safe for all time', and Portsoken that 'even if it did cost the ratepayers a little, it would be nothing compared to what they would have to pay if the unification of London took place'.[97]

The City of London (Inclusion of Southwark) Bill was introduced in January 1897. It proposed to give the Southwark parishes an extremely modest quota of sixteen Common Councilmen against the 206 representing the City's smaller population, and to transfer those county powers exercised by the LCC in Southwark but not in the City to the City Commissioners of Sewers, leaving the Council with those powers which it exercised in the City under the 1855 Act and its amending Acts. There was no mention of LCC powers within the City deriving from other legislation, and no provision for the discharge of county or police debt, elementary omissions suggesting that the City's law officers had indeed stood aside from the drafting. Nor was there any provision for compensating the remaining parishes of the St Olave's and St Saviour's Unions for loss of poor-rate, in consequence of which Bermondsey, fearing that the proposal would 'materially add to the burden of our already highly rated parish', sent a committee to confer with Rotherhithe, while St George-the-Martyr convened a special Vestry meeting to oppose the Bill.[98] Their concern was understandable but unnecessary. Even had it been better drafted, the Bill proposed too extensive a disturbance of the London government system to be smuggled through by private Act. The government left it to its parliamentary fate, and it fell on second reading in March 1897.[99]

5. TOWARDS LEGISLATION

The idea that the City and Southwark Bill represented the first step towards solving the London problem was plausible only to those who viewed the issue from the Guildhall. The Government still had to face the problems posed by the Westminster and Kensington petitions and

---

[96] G. Faudel-Phillips to Salisbury, 20 Apr. 1896, HHP. Faudel-Phillips, whom *London* (8 Oct. 1896) considered 'the most dangerous man who has ever been elected to the Mansion House', sought 'twelve municipalities with control of water' (Faudel-Phillips to Salisbury, 20 Apr. 1896), and with the City as their 'foster-mother' (*London*, 4 Mar. 1897).

[97] Reports of wardmotes in *Local Government Journal*, 26 Dec. 1896.

[98] Bermondsey Vestry Minutes, 25 Jan. 1897; Rotherhithe Vestry Minutes, 19 Jan. 1897; St George-the-Martyr Vestry Minutes, 15 Jan. 1897.

[99] *Hansard*, 4th ser., XLVII, 1077–1103 (22 Mar. 1897).

the Law Officers' pronouncement. Early in June 1897 the Cabinet discussed 'plans for increasing the number of municipalities in London'
with a view to legislating in 1898.[1] In August Devonshire told Sir Charles
Lennox Peel of the Privy Council Office, weighing up the Kensington
application, that the government wished to 'enable the Privy Council to
deal with that and similar petitions'.[2] At this stage it took the narrowest
possible reading of the Law Officers' opinion: if the existing law did not
allow the granting of charters within the metropolis, it should be changed
to make London charters legal. There was no reference to the transfer of
powers implicit in any such grant, or to its effect upon the rest of the
London system.

The fact that the problem remained with the Privy Council suggests
that the government still aimed at piecemeal incorporation rather than a
general scheme. The Privy Council Office was accustomed to assessing
individual applications for charters under a procedure comprehensively
defined by statute; it was not used to drafting general legislation. Faced
with the need for a general Bill to allow individual applications, it
recruited Sir Henry Jenkyns, Parliamentary Counsel to the Treasury,
and Courtenay Ilbert, his Principal Assistant, as drafting advisers.[3] Both
men conveyed rather overdue doubts as to the consequences of piecemeal
devolution through incorporation. Jenkyns, who was in any case critical
of the Privy Council Office's habitual failure to assess charter applications
in the context of 'local government in general', warned that piecemeal
transfers would 'throw local government in London into the melting
pot'.[4] Ilbert, in a clarificatory memorandum of November 1897, assumed
that 'no one would seriously suggest' the municipal secession of individual
areas,[5] an incautious overestimation of the government's rationality on
the issue for which he was rebuked by Halsbury.[6] Later that month the
point was repeated by Sir Hugh Owen, Permanent Secretary to the Local
Government Board, who spelled out the administrative inconvenience
that would result from the proliferation of exemptions from the county
rate and other anomalies already occasioned by the semi-independence

---

[1] Salisbury to Victoria, 3 June 1897, PRO CAB 41/24/15.
[2] Memorandum, Devonshire to Peel, 9 Aug. 1897, PRO PC 8/483/79006.
[3] See J. H. Harrison to the Secretary to the Treasury (draft), 11 Aug. 1897, in
PRO PC 8/483/79006.
[4] H. Jenkyns to C. L. Peel, 28 Sept. 1897, PRO PC 8/479/78562.
[5] Memorandum on London Local Government, 2 Nov. 1897, PRO HLG 29/63/2.
[6] See Devonshire to Salisbury, 17 Nov. 1897, HHP, and Devonshire to James, 14 Nov.
1897, James Papers, M 45/927.

of the City.[7] All three officials assumed that, whether or not a change of *status* could be conferred upon individual authorities, any transfer of *powers* would need to be general. The problem was that general transfer would not satisfy the incorporators unless it went beyond the transfer conference proposals,[8] and although most second-tier authorities valued the change of status that would dispel the slur of Vestrydom, there was force in Devonshire's observation that 'Londoners must be a very strange people if they can be enthusiastic over the gold chains and furred robe'.[9]

Early in November the Westminster Conference—as the incorporation seekers now styled themselves—took stock after the failure of the two petitions. Onslow, speaking with authority, assured the incorporators of the government's goodwill, and suggested another deputation to seek the removal of 'the disability under which the Queen in Council at present labours'.[10] During the closing months of 1897 the incorporation movement developed a broader base as a new circular invitation brought replies from eleven authorities not previously attached to the movement. Onslow's selection was now more judicious; in 1895 he had apparently contacted the parishes singled out by the Royal Commission, a sample including such Progressive strongholds as Shoreditch, Bethnal Green, Newington, and Poplar, while excluding Vestries like Camberwell, Plumstead, and Rotherhithe which now joined the movement. The recruitment of Bermondsey, Mile End and, most conspicuously, Islington, the leading opponent of Westminster incorporation, had been made possible by Moderate gains in the elections of 1896 and 1897. The West End parish of St George, Hanover Square was a natural incorporator only previously inhibited by the suspicion of expansionary designs on the part of the Westminster Vestry, but the conversion of the 'shopocratic' Vestries of Clerkenwell and Fulham, the large and socially mixed parishes of Lambeth, Islington, and Camberwell, and above all the poor parishes of Mile End, Bermondsey, Rotherhithe, and Plumstead, was important. By the time that T. W. Wheeler introduced the next Westminster Conference deputation to Salisbury in February 1898, he could claim that thirteen of the twenty-three authorities represented were net beneficiaries of the Equalization Act—a proportion which almost matched that of London as a whole.[11]

[7] Memorandum of 27 Nov. 1897, PRO HLG 29/63/4.

[8] Devonshire to Salisbury, 17 Nov. 1897, HHP.

[9] Devonshire to Onslow, 4 Feb. 1898, OP 173/7/72.

[10] MS notes of address to Westminster Conference, Box 1, Westminster Incorporation material.

[11] *Proposed Municipalities for London: Report of Proceedings of a Deputation to the Prime Minister and the Lord President of the Privy Council* (1898), 4.

The broadening of the movement was a measure of the success of the tactic adopted by Onslow after the transfer conference of playing down the importance of administrative devolution. The counsel retained by the Westminster incorporation movement for the anticipated public inquiry had been instructed 'not to press that part of the Petition having reference to the transfer of powers',[12] and in April Onslow had gone as far as to say that Westminster 'was not now pressing for any transfer of powers, their main object and desire being primarily to obtain an alteration in the title of "Vestry"'.[13] With this proviso it became possible for the movement to appeal to all the parishes in Moderate hands since the elections of 1896.[14] John Loftus, the 'pillar of East End Conservatism'[15] who represented Mile End in the deputation to Salisbury in February 1898, explained that his Vestry had joined the movement only when convinced that the West End was not seeking to shed its metropolitan obligations, and stressed the need to protect equalization.[16] Camberwell Vestry instructed its delegate to do nothing to imperil the parish's equalization grant.[17]

If the civic pride of Vestrydom was to be given its head, Onslow could not afford to inhibit it by pressing for more extensive devolution than most secondary authorities could accept. His policy at this stage would appear to have been to divorce the question of transfer from that of the elevation of Vestry status and to harness second-tier enthusiasm in pursuit of the honorific improvement. The transfer conference resolutions could be included in any second-tier reform, but beyond them there was no need to expand the vague assertion that experience of the new authorities 'would soon demonstrate the desirability of a still further devolution of powers from the Council to such Municipalities'.[18]

Onslow's playing down of the transfer question in his dealings with the Vestries was facilitated by a growing conviction, as the Council elections of March 1898 approached, that a Moderate Council could provide the devolutionary impetus that the second tier as a whole had not produced. Writing to Salisbury in November 1897 he had argued

---

[12] Westminster Incorporation material, Inhabitants' Com. Minutes (Executive Com.), 26 Feb. 1897.

[13] Reply to Islington Vestry, quoted in *London*, 15 Apr. 1897.

[14] All 23 parishes were Moderate-controlled: *London*, 3 Feb. 1898.

[15] *London Argus*, 25 Sept. 1897.

[16] *Proposed Municipalities for London*, 7.

[17] D. C. Preston, quoted ibid., 7.

[18] Manuscript petition from Westminster Conference deputation to Salisbury, Box 1, Westminster Incorporation material.

that if 'the Vestries are clothed by Parliament with the dignity of municipalities and authorised to exercise such powers as the Council may transfer
to them, a Unionist majority on the Council might so strengthen the
Local and weaken the Central authority that even with a sympathetic
majority in the House of Commons the Council would in the future be
powerless to do much mischief'.[19] At first sight the devolutionary crusade
seemed to have overreached its premisses. The attempts to disestablish
the Council made sense only if its Progressive majority was unassailable;
if it was necessary to capture the Council to implement them, the energy
spent might have been better devoted to the creation of a durable Moderate ascendancy on the LCC. Nevertheless, what worried Onslow was the
inbuilt redistributionary potential of a first-tier body, and the existence on
the Council of 'a party aiming to obtain supreme control within it in
order to make all sorts of attacks on property'.[20] By these criteria structural
reform was essential. It could not, of course, be achieved by winning a
Council election. It would depend upon legislation, but the election of a
Moderate Council would smooth the passage of the necessary Act and
ensure that full use was made of whatever devolutionary mechanism it
created.

6. SUICIDE AND THE 1898 ELECTION

With the retirement of the 1892 aldermen who had preserved Progressive
control on the third Council, even limited gains in 1898 would guarantee
Moderate control. Onslow expected 'to win several seats and unless the
wave of reaction is too strong to hold those we at present have'.[21] The
1898 election saw the most intensive Moderate campaign before their
victory in 1907, with several leading Unionist statesmen speaking for the
party, with the 'organised co-operation' of London's Conservative agents
'put in force to an extent it never was before',[22] and with a corps of a
thousand women canvassers, led by the Marchioness of Tweedsdale,
Countess Cadogan, and Lady Onslow, sent to scour London for the
deference vote.[23] Ironically, most of this effort had to be devoted to
counteracting the effects of a Conservative *faux pas* committed at the

[19] Onslow to Salisbury, 11 Nov. 1897, HHP.
[20] Quoted in the *Local Government Journal*, 22 Jan. 1898.
[21] Onslow to Salisbury, 11 Nov. 1897, HHP.
[22] *Primrose League Gazette*, 1 Feb. 1898.
[23] *Local Government Journal*, 15 Jan. 1898.

start of the campaign, when Salisbury 'performed that well-known acrobatic feat of opening his mouth and putting his foot into it'.[24]

Five days before Salisbury was due to address an NUCCA conference at the Albert Hall in November 1897, Onslow had written requesting him to make reference to London local politics, in the hope of securing Council candidates from an audience including a substantial section of metropolitan Conservatism. Salisbury eventually devoted about a third of his speech to London affairs, and raised the Moderate standard for the 1898 campaign.[25] Forced to speak at short notice, however, he was unable to do more than fall back upon conventional abuse of the Progressives, and his own deep-seated view that the Council was unworkable. Arguing that London's 'so-called municipality' was 'something like ten or twelve times larger than any other municipality in the country', Salisbury, ignoring the existence of the second tier, inferred that it had ten or twelve times as much work to do. Its problems, therefore, stemmed from Parliament's failure to 'look upon London as what it is—not as one great municipality but as an aggregate of municipalities'. Only moderately-sized municipalities could secure the best men; large bodies were overloaded, and required full-time councillors. The LCC, which Salisbury had already dismissed as a 'little Parliament', was therefore in the hands of men who were 'running a danger of becoming professional politicians'. London threatened to go the way of those favourite Conservative examples of municipal megalomania, Paris and New York, unless the Council responded to the danger 'in a wise, a patriotic, and enlightened spirit'. In a phrase that would echo throughout the campaign, he acknowledged that this might appear 'a suicidal course to recommend to it'. Whether or not in elucidation of this opaque threat, he went on to suggest that the requirements of London government would best be met by giving 'a large portion of the duties which are now performed by the County Council to other smaller municipalities', and professed 'very little doubt' that legislation would be introduced in 1898.

Although Lord James considered Salisbury's later speeches 'lamentable both in matter and delivery',[26] the remarks on London suggest not so much senility as the sort of impromptu indiscretion to which Salisbury was prone throughout his career. They probably stemmed from Onslow's explanation of tactics in the letter of 11 November, when he had suggested Moderate-inspired devolution to limit the harmful power of future Coun-

[24] *Local Government Journal*, 20 Nov. 1897.
[25] For the speech see *The Times*, 17 Nov. 1897.
[26] Lord James, typescript Diary, 1886–1909, 106, James Papers, M45/1864.

cils,[27] but it is most unlikely that Onslow had intended this line of thought to be made public. It was supremely tactless for Salisbury to celebrate the imminent dismemberment of the Council while soliciting candidates for it, to urge men to come forward while denying that 'if you elected the best county council in the world ... you would have solved the problem of London municipal government'.[28] The reference to the Council's suicide was sufficiently cryptic to allow Onslow's retreat into semantics—'by suicide, I do not think Lord Salisbury actually meant "*felo de se*" ',[29]—and denials by several government speakers of any intention to 'smash' the Council,[30] but by any reading of the speech, Salisbury had maintained that the LCC was structurally unfit to govern London, and advocated extensive devolution of its powers. 'Sulla locutus est', as Harry Lawson put it.[31] Salisbury was in office and had promised legislation; his threats had more significance in 1897 than when he had supported 'tenification' in 1894.

On the Progressive side, Carrington foresaw that the speech would 'be of immense service to use in the election in March.[32] Mackinnon Wood ignored Rosebery's pusillanimous warning that the issue lacked staying power[33] and produced within a fortnight a manifesto which declared the Council's future to be the 'one fundamental issue' of the campaign.[34] Progressive opposition was promised to any attempts to divide London into 'cities of the rich and parishes of the poor'—a phrase more redolent of piecemeal incorporation than of Salisbury's 'tenification', but still a powerful election cry. The Moderate leadership responded with uncomfortable evasiveness. Although the LMS had pressed for—and duly received—a promise of London legislation in the Queen's Speech,[35] it is unlikely that the Moderate leadership wished to make second-tier reform the central issue of the campaign before legislative proposals were formulated. Onslow stressed to the *Daily News* that the Moderates had

[27] Onslow to Salisbury, 11 Nov. 1897, HHP.
[28] *The Times*, 17 Nov. 1897.
[29] Interview in *Daily News*, 14 Jan. 1898.
[30] For example Ritchie at Croydon, Chamberlain at Birmingham (*Local Government Journal*, 27 Nov. 1897), and T. W. Russell, Parliamentary Secretary to the Local Government Board (ibid., 8 Jan. 1898).
[31] H. L. W. Lawson, 'The County Council Election', *Fortnightly Review*, 69 (1898), 197.
[32] 'He advised the Tories to capture all the seats and then to commit suicide. What a noble, patriotic municipal programme.' Carrington Diary, 17 Nov. 1897, Bodleian MS Film 1102.
[33] Rosebery to T. Mackinnon Wood (copy), 28 Nov. 1897, RP, MS 10131, fo. 158.
[34] Reprinted in *London*, 2 Dec. 1897.
[35] LMS, Executive Com. Minutes, 13 Oct. 1897.

'no hard and fast proposals' for municipalities, that they would wait to see the promised Bill and, incautiously, that 'we look to this election to show what the people of London themselves desire in the matter'.[36] Privately he asked Devonshire not to publish the Bill before the elections or to give details of its likely shape.[37]

Devonshire was probably right to question this tactic, as 'the Progressives will get their knife quite as effectually into a policy which you cannot or will not disclose as into one the principles of which are laid down'.[38] Salisbury's language had been menacing enough to justify an attack upon crude 'tenification', and that was what emerged, despite ministerial disclaimers and an open letter from the Prime Minister denying any wish to restore the MBW.[39] Cornwall and Freak spoke of 'a crisis in the history of London', Wallace Bruce of Salisbury's desire 'to reduce the Council to a Drainage Board', Monkswell and Shaw-Lefevre of 'a mischievous and impracticable scheme for creating separate municipalities in London'. Jackson and Peppercorn feared 'a consequent enormous increase in the rates' in Greenwich, and, like many candidates, inferred a threat to equalization.[40] The target of 'the proposed Moderate plan, which is devised to enable the richer districts to escape from an equitable share of those burdens which necessarily fall upon poorer London'[41] was kept constantly before the electorate. Lord Dunraven, the erstwhile Tory Democrat elected for Wandsworth in 1895, privately pressed Salisbury to promise not to disturb equalization.[42] Several Moderate candidates in recipient parishes pledged themselves spontaneously.[43]

Progressives realized that the protection of parochialism offered the best defence against 'tenification'. Several candidates stressed their commitment to 'the transformation of the existing Vestries into dignified and powerful Councils'.[44] Sidney Webb disavowed the proposals for thirty

[36] *Daily News*, 14 Jan. 1898.
[37] See Devonshire to Onslow, 4 Feb. 1898, OP 173/7/72.
[38] Ibid.
[39] *Local Government Journal*, 4 Dec. 1897.
[40] 1898 Election addresses for Bethnal Green NE, Bow and Bromley, Haggerston, Greenwich (Bristol University collection).
[41] Benn and Organ, 1898 election address, Lambeth, Kennington (Bristol University collection).
[42] Dunraven to Salisbury, 7 Dec. 1897, HHP.
[43] Braby and Finch (Bethnal Green SW), Beachcroft and Rutland (Central Finsbury), Clough and Thynne (Islington N.), and other Moderates wanted the scheme's extension (Bristol University collection).
[44] Webb and Phillimore (Deptford). Cf. Costelloe (Bethnal Green SW), Bruce (Bow and Bromley), Baker (E. Finsbury), etc. Mackinnon Wood and Stuart (Hackney Central) cited the local provisions of the Amalgamation Report (Bristol University collection).

district councils in his 'London Programme' and asserted that 'the practical difficulties of merging areas that have been independent for over 40 years' were insuperable.[45] Dissident Moderates also threw their weight behind localism. The anonymous 'well-known Moderate leader' who was 'astonished at a policy which is repugnant to nine out of ten among London Conservatives'[46] may have inspired the proposals for 'a scheme of "fortyfication"' published by the *Pall Mall Gazette* 'on the highest authority' in December 1897.[47] Edwin Hughes, expiating his mistake of 1890, could not 'believe that by consent less than 37 areas will meet the case' and devised another second-tier scheme of his own.[48]

The most trenchant Conservative criticism of 'tenification' came from C. A. Whitmore, MP for Chelsea and a Moderate alderman since 1895, who had 'differed sharply'[49] from Onslow on several policy issues, including London government. In a speech of December 1897 he made a barbed assertion of the impossibility of wholesale transfer to 'those who know anything about the local government of London',[50] and in the following month, with what must have been a veiled reference to Onslow, he attacked those Moderate policy-makers who had convinced themselves that 'these District Councils, or municipalities, might be few, exercising their powers over large areas'. He denied that the extent of transfer depended upon the size of the secondary areas, or that larger areas would attract better men. As a veteran of Chelsea's fight for independence in 1890, he stressed that 'the unit of local administration must be a district in which some local patriotism lives, and in which some habit of combination for local purposes exists'. Invoking Salisbury's phraseology, he argued that 'to create artificially a few huge municipal districts in London would be a real example of gratuitous megalomania'.[51] Whitmore spoke for the significant, and probably preponderant, element within London Conservatism unwilling to sacrifice parochial identity for the sake of devolution. Onslow considered large areas necessary for significant decentralization, but was aware that second-tier amalgamations would be even more sensitive than the transfer question, and had avoided being specific. Salisbury, with his tactless reference to ten or twelve municipalities, had negated Onslow's discretion and worried many localist Conservatives.

[45] Interview in *London*, 23 Dec. 1897.
[46] *Local Government Journal*, 20 Nov. 1897.
[47] *Pall Mall Gazette*, 6 Dec. 1897.
[48] *London Argus*, 27 Nov. 1897.
[49] C. A. Whitmore to Onslow, 12 Mar. 1897, OP, 173/7/62.
[50] *London Argus*, 11 Dec. 1897.
[51] C. A. Whitmore, 'Not Tenification', *St James' Gazette*, 28 Jan. 1898.

In the election the Moderates were driven back almost to their 1889 position, winning only forty-eight seats. Their aggregate poll fell by less than 5 per cent, but that of their opponents rose by 19 per cent,[52] suggesting that the alleged threat to the Council brought out some of the Progressive abstainers of 1895. The 1898 election, like that of 1892, proved that 'the London County Council is a much more popular institution than West End opinion has supposed'.[53] Progressive swings in the suburbs were not sufficient to reclaim many of the Moderate gains there in 1895, but the threat to the Council 'sapped the Moderate voting strength in every working-class division'.[54] In the East, where two-thirds of the Tower Hamlets population—in Limehouse, Poplar, and Whitechapel—lived under the dead hand of the District Board system, the Council was the most conspicuous agent of municipal improvement.[55] It had provided Boundary Street and the Blackwall Tunnel, and gained credit for pursuing water purchase in an area hit by 'water famines' in successive summers in the mid-1890s. When the Westminster conference deputation called upon Salisbury, the *East London Observer* had noted that 'the whole of East London, which is equal to two Birminghams, was represented by the Mile End Vestry'.[56]

The East's reaction to 'tenification' fed upon more than a decade's experience of its assigned role as the centre of 'Darkest London', subject to a regular influx of social observers and journalistic voyeurs. With Toynbee Hall and the People's Palace appearing in Baedeker,[57] the East wearied of 'wealthy and idle men and women ... picking their way down the alleys of Bethnal Green and into the courts near Aldgate'[58] and reiterating 'its meanness and its monotony'.[59] An East London Defence Alliance had been formed as early as October 1886 to protect the area from philanthropists and journalists;[60] in May of the same year a correspondent of the *East London Observer* had urged the 'descriptive ones' to direct their investigations elsewhere.[61] Five years later that paper's

[52] For the 1898 polls see *London*, 10 Mar. 1898.
[53] C. A. Whitmore, 'Our Defeat and Some Morals', *National Review*, 31 (1898), 263.
[54] Ibid.
[55] 'There is very little of what can be called Local Government in East London. The Boards are not in touch with the people.': Canon Barnett, 'Toynbee Hall and Local Government', MS notes, n.d. in Barnett Papers, GLRO, F/BAR/553.
[56] *East London Observer*, 5 Feb. 1898.
[57] R. A. Woods, 'The Social Awakening in London', *Scribner's Magazine*, 11 (1892), 402.
[58] *Link*, 20 Oct. 1688.
[59] W. Besant, *East London* (1901), 14–15.
[60] *Metropolitan*, 30 Oct. 1886.
[61] 'Is East London as Black as It's Painted?', *East London Observer*, 8 May 1886.

proprietor had founded his East End Defence League.[62] To most of the East End the incorporation movement embodied the exclusive and patronizing attitude of the West; insistence upon the duties of integration was a self-defensive response.

The Progressives made a clean sweep of the seven Tower Hamlets seats, both Bethnal Green seats, both Shoreditch seats, and South and Central Hackney. They were similarly successful in working-class constituencies south of the river, claiming the three Southwark seats, both Newington seats, Lambeth North, and Battersea. As always, Moderate failure in working-class areas left them vulnerable to the inbuilt bias of the London constituency system. 49·44 per cent of the poll gave them only 40 per cent of the seats, and restored the Progressives to a comfortable majority.

The results left Onslow 'a crushed heap'.[63] Convinced that the ' "Have nots" of the East End ... have the larger ratepayers and property owners at their mercy', he feared for 'landowners, shareholders *et hoc genus omne*'.[64] On the London government question, the defeat meant that devolution would still have to be wrung from a reluctant Council. It did not make legislation less likely—and in practice it probably made very little difference to its form—but Onslow had come to favour enabling devolutionary legislation which would then be enthusiastically implemented by a Moderate Council. Not only was a Progressive LCC guaranteed until the likely end of the 1895 Parliament, but the case for devolution had been presented in the worst possible way by Salisbury, and consequently attacked from almost all sides. The incorporation movement never quite regained the momentum that had been generated in the last months of 1897.

7. THE BILL AND ACT OF 1899

The greatest irony of the Salisbury speech is that, despite the promise of early legislation, the government had not decided upon any specific second-tier policy by November 1897, and certainly not the policy so injudiciously outlined by the prime minister. The majority of the Cabinet

[62] J. J. Bennett, 'East End Newspaper Opinion and Jewish Immigration, 1885–1905', M.Phil. thesis (Sheffield University, 1979), 128. For the defence of East London in the *East London Observer* see 128–9.

[63] Onslow to Lady Gwendolen Onslow, 19 March 1898, quoted in the typescript 'Family History' by the Fifth Earl (*c.* 1924), v. 1153, OP, 173/1.

[64] Onslow to Cadogan, 11 Mar. 1898, Cadogan Papers, CAD/1321.

probably still favoured the easy option of a short enabling Bill to permit the creation of metropolitan municipalities by the Privy Council, in the hope that the problem could then solve itself. Within ten days of Salisbury's speech, Ritchie and Chamberlain had each spoken of the need to empower the Privy Council to satisfy London petitions.[65] Ridley was still advocating this policy in February 1898 and Halsbury in April.[66] It ignored the departmental objections to piecemeal incorporation and the question of general transfer.

Consideration of the question in Cabinet in December and January at least clarified the choice between general transfer, bringing administrative uniformity but only limited devolution, and piecemeal incorporation, allowing extensive transfers to individual petitioning areas but creating administrative chaos. The first option was pressed by Lord James, who argued that the question of the granting of charters should be considered as separate from that of the transfer of powers, and that any transfers should be general, and not dependent upon a demand for incorporation. Realizing that voluntary general transfer was likely to be limited, James suggested vaguely that 'some additions' be made to the resolutions of the transfer conference to provide 'a fairly sufficient number of duties for a municipal body to deal with'.[67] This was answered early in January by Salisbury, in a memorandum presenting the case not for the 'tenification' that he had thrown to the London electorate in November, but for piecemeal incorporation. He sketched the heads of a Bill to allow the granting of charters to Vestries seeking them, by which each new municipality would inherit all existing Vestry functions, and could apply for the transfer of any LCC powers that it sought by Provisional Order of the Privy Council.[68]

This system would leave the uniformity of the two-tier structure entirely dependent upon the attitude of the Privy Council Office. The officers charged with drawing up whatever legislation was settled upon were unequivocally hostile to any but a general transfer of powers. Urged by Ilbert to 'fortify my position'[69] by demonstrating the administrative confusion involved, Owen agreed that 'the public would never be able to understand why they had to go to the County Council in the case of one

[65] *Local Government Journal*, 27 Nov. 1897.

[66] For Ridley at Battersea see *Morning Post*, 18 Feb. 1898. For Halsbury's view see Devonshire to Halsbury, 6 Apr. 1898, Add. MS 56371.

[67] Memorandum on the London Government Bill, 16 Dec. 1897, PRO CAB 37/45/55.

[68] The memorandum appears not to have survived either in the PRO or at Hatfield. It is summarized in PRO HLG 29/63/12.

[69] Ilbert to Owen, 22 Jan. 1898, PRO HLG 29/63/16.

street and to the local authority in the case of another street close by'.[70] An order to turn the Salisbury proposals into a presentable Bill would require a daunting degree of legislative dexterity.

In Cabinet Chamberlain assured Salisbury that 'I entirely agree with you as to London Municipal Government & greatly prefer your plan to Lord James'.[71] Ritchie and Chaplin professed to agree with Salisbury that individual parishes could be incorporated, but both argued that transfer should none the less be general—to new boroughs and old Vestries alike—which left them in practice much closer to James's position.[72] Ritchie in fact believed that the government would 'be hopelessly beaten' if it attempted piecemeal transfer, and viewed the change from Vestry to municipality as 'mainly a change of name'.[73] Devonshire, as Lord President, was still assumed to be responsible for the measure. Although he had 'no love for the County Council',[74] he had long been suspicious of the incorporators,[75] and while he acknowledged that 'Ilbert is no doubt too fond of incursions into politics',[76] he agreed with him that it was 'quite out of the question' to detach individual parishes from the London system.[77] Accordingly, although his office prepared, on Balfour's suggestion, a draft along the lines of the Salisbury memorandum,[78] his mind remained open.

'As we stand now', he wrote to Onslow on 4 February, 'municipalization may mean anything or nothing'.[79] Addressing Onslow's Westminster conference deputation the previous day, he had put forward three options for the forthcoming Bill—the creation of municipalities without any transfer of power, general devolution to all secondary authorities, and a third option involving the separation of powers into two schedules—the first listing those for general transfer, the second those which would go to municipalities only.[80] Only this third option was likely to interest his audience. It probably represented the departmental

---

[70] Owen to Ilbert, 24 Jan. 1898, PRO HLG 29/63/17.

[71] Chamberlain to Salisbury, 14 Jan. 1898, HHP.

[72] For Ritchie's memorandum of 15 Jan. 1898 see PRO CAB 37/46/5. For Chaplin's of 20 Jan. 1898 see CAB 37/46/7.

[73] PRO CAB 37/46/5.

[74] Devonshire to Salisbury, 17 Nov. 1897, HHP.

[75] See Devonshire to James, 9 Dec. 1897, James Papers, M45/930.

[76] Devonshire to Salisbury, 17 Nov. 1897, HHP.

[77] Devonshire to James, 14 Nov. 1897, James Papers, M45/927.

[78] See Devonshire to Salisbury, 15 Jan. 1898, HHP. This draft appears not to have survived.

[79] Devonshire to Onslow, 4 Feb. 1898, OP, 173/7/72.

[80] *Proposed Municipalities for London*, 9.

refinement of Salisbury's proposals, ensuring the standardization of such transfers as did take place and avoiding what the bureaucrats found the most worrying implication of piecemeal incorporation—that the extent of transfer could vary between incorporated areas. The price to be paid was the creation of two classes of secondary authorities—municipalities and Vestries—with different sets of powers.

Devonshire had ended with an appeal to the incorporators to produce proposals of their own. In response they met in March. Their immediate demands were modest: the implementation of the transfer conference resolutions, replacement of LCC by Local Government Board loan sanction, the 'horizontal transfer' of adoptive Act powers and the title of municipal corporation for the new bodies. 'It was not thought desirable' to raise the question of areas.[81] In due course, though, the Westminster Conference's executive committee of fourteen Vestrymen and Vestry clerks, led by Onslow and T. W. Wheeler, produced a draft Bill which they unveiled in August.[82] It proposed that the twenty-three parishes and districts then comprising the movement should be granted charters, except for St James, St Martin's, and the Strand, which would be grouped. Any other Schedule A Vestry or District Board could apply for a charter. The new bodies would have mayors who would become ex-officio aldermen of the LCC. This innovation, suggested by Cadogan,[83] was the closest feasible approach to the politically impossible return to an indirectly elected central body, which had become more attractive to Conservatives in view of the radicalism of the LCC. It amounted to another attempt to circumvent the electorate's refusal to return a Moderate Council, as most of the incorporating parishes were Moderate strongholds.

Specific transfers were again limited to the conference resolutions, but it was stressed that these were 'by no means complete or exhaustive'.[84] Acting on Devonshire's hint that municipalities could enjoy more extensive powers than other secondary bodies, the Westminster men devised an elaborate mechanism to allow them to wring these powers from the LCC. On the application of a majority of the new municipalities the Council could, if it saw fit, transfer specified powers to all of them, retaining those powers in areas still under Vestries. If the Council did

---

[81] The meeting's decisions are summarized in Bermondsey Vestry, *Annual Report* (1897–8), 30. See also Chelsea Vestry Minutes, 15 Mar. 1898.

[82] PRO PC 8/509/81344.

[83] See Onslow to Cadogan, 24 Dec. 1897, Cadogan Papers, CAD/1274.

[84] PRO PC 8/509/81344 (Memorandum).

not see fit, the petitioning municipalities could appeal to the Local Government Board. No specific provision was made to offset the cost of transfer, other than to deduct the cost of transferred services from the LCC precept, but, presumably in response to the reaction to Salisbury's speech, it was stressed that the Equalization Act was not affected.[85] It remained, of course, an adoptive—and therefore piecemeal—measure. Its authors claimed that 'the spirit of emulation and desire for autonomy will speedily bring the whole of London into line',[86] and may have believed as much, but Devonshire's indication that municipalities could be given a separate status from other authorities appeared to have made the problem of uniformity less pressing.

Publication of the Westminster Bill prompted Islington Vestry, back under Progressive control, to convene a Vestry conference to criticize its provisions.[87] The call was answered by most of the Progressive Vestries, and by some of the constituents of the Westminster Conference, to Onslow's disgust. Sixty-four delegates braved November fog and rain to attend the conference and reaffirm the opposition of the second-tier authorities outside the movement to any but general transfers.[88] Without any expression of opinion upon the extent of such transfer or upon second-tier areas, the conference's value was limited, but its resolutions were conveyed to the Privy Council Office, and would have reinforced the bureaucratic opposition to partial transfer.

The Queen's Speech of 1899 once again promised a London Bill.[89] The measure was by now well advanced, although it is not until the 'notes on clauses' of 17 January and the draft of 24 January that its evolution can begin to be traced.[90] The diary of Courtenay Ilbert, the draftsman, shows that he took advice chiefly from figures outside the Onslow circle— H. P. Harris, a leading Moderate Councillor, but one who wished to 'preserve existing areas as far as possible' and opposed the Westminster proposals,[91] C. W. Tagg, the 'clever, pushing'[92] Vestry Clerk of Camberwell, who was a member of the Westminster Conference committee

---

[85] Ibid., s. 20.
[86] Ibid., Memorandum.
[87] Islington Vestry Minutes, 5 Aug. 1898.
[88] *London and the Municipal Journal*, 1 Dec. 1898.
[89] *Hansard*, 4 ser., LXVI, 4 (7 Feb. 1899).
[90] PRO HLG 29/63/37 and 44.
[91] Speech to the Paddington Parliament, in *Paddington Times*, 18 Nov. 1898. Harris expressed his disagreement with the piecemeal incorporation proposals of the Westminster Bill, by which 'the districts which most needed reform would not get it'.
[92] Onslow to Cadogan, 24 Dec. 1897, Cadogan Papers, CAD/1274.

but also a Progressive,[93] and C. J. Stewart, the Clerk of the LCC.[94] Ilbert reported to a Cabinet committee comprising Balfour, now charged with the Bill instead of Devonshire, probably to allow its introduction in the Commons, Devonshire himself, Ritchie, Chaplin, Akers-Douglas, and Hamilton.[95] Without Salisbury, Chamberlain, and Onslow (who was not in the Cabinet) the hawkish side of the decentralization movement was not represented. During 1899 Ilbert recorded only one meeting with Onslow,[96] who depended upon his contact with Balfour and Hamilton to make his views known.

Under these circumstances the original Westminster Conference Bill became rather blunted.[97] The first and most important change was the decision, apparently from the start, that the constitutional second-tier reform should apply across the whole of London, with the obvious exception of the City. Since the transfer conference, Onslow and the incorporators had sought to devise means by which parishes anxious to secure greater devolution than the conference had offered could attain a status and powers superior to those of other areas. The Westminster Conference proposals had been based upon Devonshire's suggestions in this direction. The source and timing of the abandonment of this proposal are unclear, but it presumably derived from the intense opposition of Ilbert and the other officials to the creation of different classes of authorities within the second tier. Its effect was compounded by the adoption of a set of specific transfers even more limited than those of the transfer conference. The original conference resolutions had been referred by the LCC to a sub-committee of the Local Government and Taxation Committee,[98] chaired by Onslow but with a Progressive majority which ensured that he 'by no means had it all my own way'.[99] It had sounded all the committees affected by the proposals and consulted their permanent officials, a procedure guaranteed to stimulate all the Council's possessive instincts. As a result only twenty of the thirty-three conference proposals were approved, with two transfers subjected to an LCC default power

[93] See *London*, 16 Feb 1893. In 1887 he had been political secretary of the Peckham Liberal Club: see *South London Press*, 5 Feb. 1887.
[94] For these meetings see the Ilbert Diary, 7, 9, 10, 16, 17, 19, 23, 24 Jan., 14, 15 Feb., and 3 Mar. 1899.
[95] Ibid., 9 Feb. 1899.
[96] Ibid., 25 Jan. 1899.
[97] The surviving drafts are compiled in PRO HLG 29/63. The Bill as introduced is in *PP 1899*, VI, Bill 93.
[98] LCC Local Government and Taxation Com. Minutes, 15 May 1896.
[99] Onslow to Cadogan, 31 Dec. 1897, Cadogan Papers, CAD/1279/1.

and four qualified in other ways.[1] With two more transfers referred back by the full Council, barely half the conference proposals remained intact.[2] Ilbert adopted only this limited selection of specific transfers, and reduced it further by delegating all Building Act transfer for the separate consideration of the Privy Council.[3]

These setbacks for the incorporators were qualified by some successes. The least important concerned the title of the new authorities. Ilbert objected to the use of the term 'borough' for authorities that could not enjoy the complete independence of provincial municipalities. Invoking Lord Bowen's denunciation of 'the evil practice of defining a cow so as to include a horse', he warned that casual definition could bring the new councils inadvertently under the Municipal Corporations Act and effect 'an unexpected and unintended transfer of powers'.[4] Echoing the Amalgamation Commission, he used the term 'municipal councils' throughout the early drafts, but the Cabinet committee, anxious to preserve the political symbolism of the 'borough' title in what was becoming a rather stunted Bill, insisted against Ilbert's 'strong protest' that the new authorities be styled 'metropolitan boroughs'.[5] To enhance the resemblance to real municipalities, the new authorities received not only mayors but aldermen, although the Cadogan proposal for local mayors to be ex-officio LCC aldermen was dropped.[6]

To offset the limited extent of specific transfer, a version of the Westminster Conference's future transfer mechanism was built into the Bill. By what became known as the 'suicide clause'[7] it was proposed that in the event of the LCC and one borough agreeing to the transfer of a particular Council power, the Local Government Board could ratify that transfer by Provisional Order. The LGB could then extend the transfer to any other borough seeking it, and when it had passed to the majority of boroughs it could be compulsorily imposed upon the rest on the application of the LCC.

It is unlikely that Ilbert felt much enthusiasm for this arrangement, by which, at a given moment, some former LCC powers might be exercised by all the boroughs, some by a majority of them (if the LCC

---

[1] See the report and table in LCC Local Government and Taxation Com., Presented Papers, 21 July 1897.

[2] LCC Minutes, 21 June, 4 Oct. 1898.

[3] *PP 1899*, VI, Bill 93, ss. 5, 6 and Second Schedule.

[4] Notes on Clauses, 16 Mar., 17 Jan. 1899, PRO HLG 29/63/78 and 37.

[5] Ilbert Diary, 13 Feb. 1899.

[6] It had been dropped by mid-February: see PRO HLG 29/63/54.

[7] Sydney Buxton in *Hansard*, 4th ser., LXXI, 166 (9 May 1899).

had not applied for general transfer), some by a minority, and some by a single borough. It was, however, a significantly muted version of the Westminster proposals. In the first place the LCC had acquired a final veto that the Westminster men had denied them, and the fate of the transfer conference recommendations suggested that the Council would not be open-handed. In any case, transfer now depended upon powers being sought not by the majority of the incorporating parishes, but by the majority of all metropolitan boroughs. With existing equalization levels and a fragmented second tier there was no guarantee that the boroughs would be more ambitious than their predecessors at the transfer conference.

Onslow therefore sought to restructure the second tier to make it more receptive to devolution. First he approached the question of funding transfer—a question which he and his movement had begged during and since the transfer conference. The Westminster Conference proposals had made no financial provision for transfer, but they had assumed devolution only to 'consenting' authorities. With reform extended to the whole second tier, and with the 1898 election having demonstrated the widespread fear of higher rates through devolution, Onslow realized that transfer would be precluded without some financial guarantee to the weaker authorities, and engaged J. E. Smith to construct a scheme extending equalization to offset transfer costs. The consequent production of a scheme for equalizing the cost of main road maintenance in November 1898[8] brought the supreme irony of a movement which had derived much of its initial impetus from the reaction to equalization being forced to advocate its extension. Making a virtue of necessity, Onslow convinced himself, and sought to convince Balfour, that 'by the adoption of another equalisation principle, relief can be given to the poorer parishes and those which might take most objection to being "grouped", at a cost to the richer parishes which they will hardly feel and which I venture to think they will not consider more than commensurate with the political advantages they will gain by the Bill'.[9] Equalization schemes could at least be subjected to statutory limits in a way that first-tier rates could not. Whether these processes were communicated to Ilbert is unclear. If they were he resisted the call to add yet another form of rate equalization

[8] J. E. Smith to Onslow, 9 Nov. 1898 ('Municipalities—Extension of Equalization'), Box 1, Westminster Incorporation material.
[9] Onslow to Balfour, 21 Nov. 1898, in 'Family History', v. 1154, OP, 173/1.

to the complex structure of metropolitan finance, as the Bill envisaged only straightforward grants from the county rate.[10]

The need for such support would depend upon the independent strength of the secondary authorities, which raised the always sensitive question of amalgamations. Like most sensitive questions, it was evaded by the Bill. Sixteen of the more robust existing authorities were scheduled to become Metropolitan Boroughs, but the fate of most of the remaining twenty-seven was left to a corps of Boundary Commissioners, guided only by the stipulation of a 100,000 to 400,000 population range and a £500,000 minimum rateable value.[11] One important amalgamation was, however, scheduled. This was 'Greater Westminster', reviving the former parliamentary borough as a second-tier unit, joining Westminster Vestry with St George, Hanover Square, St James, St Martin's, and the Strand District Board. This conglomerate was accurately seen as 'a concession to Lord Onslow and his Incorporation Committee, given as a kind of reward for the assiduity with which they have pushed the municipalities question in London politics'.[12] Other rewards would depend upon the Boundary Commissioners. Onslow hoped that they would create 'municipalities at least as populous, as large, as valuable and as self-contained as Lambeth',[13] and from early February set out to 'prepare public opinion in the Districts affected'.[14]

The Bill, therefore, entered Parliament with neither the extent of transfer nor the size of the secondary areas settled. It ran only to twenty-eight clauses, of which nineteen required subsequent action by extra-parliamentary bodies—Boundary Commissioners, the Privy Council, the Local Government Board, and others.[15] Although the Westminster men had actually lost important ground during the drafting, continued ambiguity over transfers and areas left room for opposition attacks. The

[10] Transfers by the 'suicide clause' could be supported from the county rate to an extent specified by the LGB under s. 8 of the Bill.

[11] The population and rateable value minima apparently derived from the Moderate Councillor G. B. Longstaff. See his article 'The Work of a London Boundary Commission', *London Argus*, 22 Jan. 1898, and Owen's adoption of the proposal in his Memorandum of 20 Apr. 1898 (PRO HLG 29/63/19).

[12] *Local Government Journal*, 4 Mar. 1899.

[13] Memorandum enclosed with Onslow to Balfour, 3 Feb. 1899, Sandars Papers, Bodleian MS Eng. Hist., c. 730, 64. Onslow was to address a Lambeth audience. Lambeth had the second largest population, by the 1896 census, and the fourth largest assessment, by the 1898 valuation, of the London sanitary authorities. See the return in *PP 1899*, LXXXIV, 570–3.

[14] Onslow to Balfour, 3 Feb. 1899, Sandars Papers, Bodleian MS Eng. Hist. c. 730, 62.

[15] As was stressed by W. F. Dewey in his report for Islington Vestry (Minutes, 17 Mar. 1899).

'suicide clause' allowed the LCC Progressives to predict a future Moderate Council scattering London's municipal patrimony to the second tier. Burns warned a Battersea audience that the Bill 'aimed at mutilating, maiming and degrading the London County Council',[16] and Dickinson issued an extravagantly apocalyptical warning of the weakness of a fragmented metropolis during an epidemic or water shortage, or 'in case of war, when London might be within a fortnight of starvation'.[17] They vented their fantasies at the end of March, when the Bill was condemned *seriatim* in the Council's first nocturnal session,[18] despite unprecedented privation[19] and the efforts of the press corps to curtail the debate.[20]

Vestries in the unscheduled parishes noted that the Boundary Commissioners' instructions would in theory allow them to reduce the twenty-seven authorities concerned to as few as five.[21] This was unlikely, but the example of Greater Westminster, rolling five authorities into one, was disturbing.[22] Virtually every unscheduled parish or district either petitioned for inclusion or, if its case appeared hopeless, investigated union with a neighbouring authority to prevent more comprehensive amalgamation. Clerkenwell and St Luke's, Holborn and St Giles, and Limehouse and Mile End contemplated such alliances, while Whitechapel and St George's actually petitioned Balfour to be joined.[23] The shadow fell most obviously over the East End, where only Poplar was listed, where the local authorities were financially weak, and where one of the local Unionist Members, Lionel Holland, had tabled a series of 'tenifying' amendments.[24] The greatest outcry, though, came not from the East but from Greater Westminster, where the extent of amalgamation was known. A Strand Borough Joint Committee was formed by St James, St Martin's, and the Strand to oppose the conglomerate, and a public meeting was held in April, chaired by that hardened sponsor of lost causes, the Earl

---

[16] *South Western Star*, 21 Apr. 1899.

[17] *Municipal Journal and London*, 31 Mar. 1899.

[18] LCC Minutes, 28 Mar. 1899. The debate ended at 2.15 a.m.

[19] Carrington was reduced to ordering wine from the National Liberal Club (*Local Government Journal*, 1 Apr. 1899).

[20] By withdrawing to the retiring room, 'fondly believing that if they were absent from their accustomed places the debate must conclude' (*Municipal Journal and London*, 7 Apr. 1899).

[21] LCC, *Report by the Statistical Officer on the London Government Bill* (1899).

[22] See St Luke's Vestry Minutes (Special Com. on London Government Bill), 13 Apr. 1899.

[23] Clerkenwell Vestry Minutes, 13, 20 Apr. 1899; St Giles DB Minutes, 6 Mar. 1899; Holborn DB Minutes, 20 Mar. 1899; *London*, 28 Apr. 9 June 1899.

[24] For Holland's views see the amendments in PRO HLG 29/59, and his speeches in *Hansard*, 4th ser., LXXI, 984–6 and 987–8 (18 May 1899).

of Wemyss.[25] In Westminster as elsewhere the perpetuation of parish boundaries by the 1855 Act had bolstered parochial consciousness against the erosion of localism threatened by London's growth. Uncritical deference to those boundaries would have prevented any rationalization of the second tier, but the 1890s had shown that local identity could not be obliterated lightly. Chelsea, having defended its autonomy so vigorously in 1890, was scheduled without query from the first surviving draft, although containing less than the minimum population required for boroughs in unscheduled areas.

In the Commons the task of introducing the Bill fell to Balfour, although 'ministers on his right and left, particularly Mr Ritchie, together with the law officers, had to prompt him all the time he was on his feet'.[26] He met little opposition from the Liberal front bench, where Campbell-Bannerman greeted the Bill with an unguarded admission that it could have been worse, and Herbert Gladstone had to be briefed by Burns on its inadequacies.[27] Liberal energies were then spent on a futile amendment to include the City. The lengthy committee stage, however, was more informed, dominated by the London Liberals and moderate London Unionists like Whitmore and Hughes. What had entered as a curiously unspecific Bill emerged with far fewer gaps, and whatever benefits Onslow and the incorporators had sought from legislative imprecision were lost. Balfour was responsive to informed amendments, especially when backed by significant Conservative support. In committee the proportion of aldermen on the new councils was reduced from one-third to one-sixth, as on the LCC, loan sanction was restored to the LCC, with an appeal to the Local Government Board, and the clause transferring LCC lodging-house regulation powers to the boroughs was removed altogether, as was that empowering the Privy Council to assess the two-tier allocation of Building Act powers. The 'suicide clause' was significantly altered. Where the Bill had provided for a three-stage transfer mechanism, first to individual councils, then to other consenting councils, and finally to unwilling councils, the Act stipulated that transfer could only be made to all councils simultaneously, on the application of a majority of them *and* the LCC.[28] The tortuous attempts to devise a machinery by which a

[25] St James Vestry Minutes, 2 Mar. 1899; St Martin-in-the-Fields Vestry Minutes, 13 Feb. 1899; Strand DB Minutes, 1 Mar. 1899; St George, Hanover Square Vestry Minutes, 9 Mar. 1899.
[26] *Municipal Journal and London*, 3 Mar. 1899.
[27] *Hansard*, 4th ser., LXVIII, 1575–98 (21 Mar. 1899); Burns Journal, 13 Mar. 1899, Add. MS 46317.
[28] For the Bill as amended, see *PP 1899*, VI, Bill 217.

minority of ambitious authorities could force the pace of transfer had eventually failed, and piecemeal incorporation finally expired.

The question of areas remained. The omission of two-thirds of London from the first schedule had caused anxiety, which Balfour eventually quelled by filling in the areas of the new boroughs himself. Hackney, Bethnal Green, and Shoreditch were added to the schedule intact and the separatism of St Paul, Deptford, and Stoke Newington was respected,[29] although Plumstead and Woolwich were joined despite the opposition of both authorities.[30] Seven more new boroughs were created by amalgamation, although more than two existing sanitary authorities were merged only in the two poorest areas—inner Southwark, where the St Saviour's and St Olave's districts were added to Newington and St George-the-Martyr, and the East End, where the Whitechapel and Limehouse districts were joined to St George's and Mile End to form the Metropolitan Borough of Stepney.

When the Bill emerged from the Commons, then, it proved to have avoided radical change either in the two-tier distribution or in the secondary areas. Specific transfers were limited to those transfer conference resolutions which the LCC accepted, and Building Act transfer was dropped. The 'suicide clause' now depended upon the initiative being taken by the majority of local bodies, which made it practically unworkable.[31] Although the number of second-tier authorities had been reduced by a third, the amalgamations effected had united parishes of similar social and economic composition—Rotherhithe and Bermondsey, Holborn and St Giles, Clerkenwell and St Lukes, Lewisham and Lee parish, Greenwich, Charlton and Kidbrooke, Plumstead and Woolwich, and the new Westminster, Southwark, and Stepney amalgamations.[32] No attempt had been made to link poor areas with rich ones, as Lionel Holland advocated,[33] to facilitate extensive devolution. With twenty-eight Metropolitan Boroughs the second tier remained localist, and 'tenification' was dead.

---

[29] Although the extra-metropolitan district of South Hornsey was added to Stoke Newington, an addition already approved by the Vestry as a means of avoiding reunion with Hackney (Stoke Newington Vestry Minutes, 7 Feb. 1899).

[30] Plumstead Vestry Minutes, 13 Mar. 1899; Woolwich Local Board Minutes, 14 Feb., 13 May 1899.

[31] According to Young and Garside only one minor transfer was made (in 1933), under the provisions of the 1899 Act and s. 64 of the 1929 Local Government Act: Young and Garside, *Metropolitan London*, 300–1, n. 12.

[32] For the 28 eventual secondary areas see London Government Act, 62 and 63 Vict. c. 14, First Schedule.

[33] Speech at Bromley, *East London Observer*, 4 Mar. 1899.

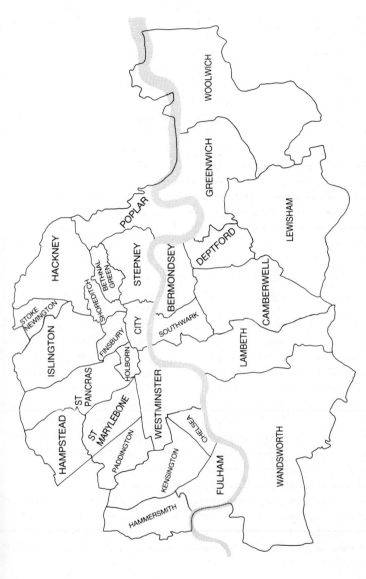

Local Authority Areas under the London Government Act, 1899

'How greatly the Govt. of London Bill has grown in Arthur's hands!' commented Chamberlain to Salisbury in January 1899. 'It may be all right, but I do not think it is what you intended.'[34] Even in October 1898 Onslow had feared that the government's prime concern was 'how easily they may be able to get the Bill through the House of Commons'.[35] By the summer of 1899 he was convinced that somebody was ' "getting at" the London members' and worried that 'County Council (Moderate as well as Progressive) influences will prove too strong for the Government'.[36] The eventual Act fell far short of Onslow's aspirations, and would not provide the institutional brake on Progressivism that he sought. Resignation from the Moderate leadership in 1899 ended 'by no means the smoothest passage in his career'.[37]

Onslow had sought to change the balance of power within the London two-tier system, replacing what had evolved into a predominantly centralized structure by a predominantly decentralized one. This required both devolution of powers and the creation of secondary authorities large enough to handle the powers devolved. He had first anticipated that a general parochial appetite for powers would create a demand for devolution, but the transfer conference had disproved this. The conference had shown the structural obstacles to devolution, and the pursuit of charters by individual West End parishes, even had they been legal, would not have solved the general problem. Onslow's response had been to broaden the appeal of incorporation by deferring the question of transfer, while looking to a future Moderate Council to force the pace of devolution from above. Defeat in the 1898 elections precluded this and led him to seek a separate status for the incorporating parishes, with an extended degree of transfer determined by the ambitions of the majority. This option was ruled out in the drafting stage, probably through the antipathy of the officials involved, and Onslow was forced once again to pursue a general scheme. He conceded the extension of equalization to facilitate transfer, and hoped to mitigate its effect by an extensive reconstruction of second-tier areas. This was blocked by a Parliament and a minister more responsive than Onslow to parish localism. In the meantime the future transfer mechanism had been neutered first by Ilbert and then by Parliament. The end product was an Act providing for a

---

[34] Chamberlain to Salisbury, 26 Jan. 1899, HHP.
[35] Onslow to J. E. Smith, 9 Oct. 1898, Box 1, Westminster Incorporation material.
[36] Onslow to J. E. Smith, 'Friday', n.d. but probably May 1899, ibid.
[37] 'Family History', v. 1132, OP, 173/1.

marginal readjustment of powers, a sensitive reorganization of areas which kept the second tier localized, and an honorific enhancement of local dignity. As such it could almost have been devised to implement the local provisions of the Amalgamation Report of 1894, which fell far short of Onslow's ambitions.

The years since 1895 had seen the steady rejection of the alternatives to the existing system of a strong first tier, a localized second tier, a high proportion of first-tier expenditure and second-tier rate equalization. Wholesale transfer had failed because the second tier as a whole did not want it. Individual parochial secession and the later proposals to differentiate between Vestry and municipal powers had foundered chiefly upon bureaucratic objections to the extensive administrative confusion they would have caused. Second-tier amalgamations ran counter to a prevalent localism that transcended political divisions. Reduction of rate equalization would have alienated all the 1894 Act's beneficiaries, and was never proposed; Onslow finished by advocating further equalization. What remained was little more than a measure to tidy up the existing system—as the tenifier Lionel Holland told the Commons with dismissive irony, 'a mere vestry reform bill'.[38]

[38] *Hansard*, 4th ser., LXXI, 988 (18 May 1899).

9

Conclusion: The Process of Reform

It is a humbling fact that, at the close of a century which will ever
be remembered as the century of great cities, it is at all necessary
to consider the elementary principles of municipal reform.

John Williams Benn at Stepney, October 1894[1]

It remains extraordinary that the local government of the world's largest
city should have reached the pitch of disorganization that the London
system had reached by the 1880s before an executive and a legislature
based in that city would grasp the nettle of reform. London displayed to
a marked degree the disincentive to action characteristic of most local
government reform problems—the combination of limited public concern
with considerable resistance from the interests affected. It is broadly true
that most of those sufficiently familiar with the system to hold opinions
on the reform question were already part of it, as county councillors,
Vestrymen, or officials. Given the weakness of ratepayers' associations
and other outlets for the local government 'consumer', it took the party
politicization of London government to advance reform. Municipal
reform became an emblem of London Radicalism in the 1880s, and the
London Municipal Reform League was successful in working upon
a Liberal government to introduce legislation, but the comprehensive
alienation of existing authorities by the 1884 Bill ensured maximum
resistance from within the system, and demonstrated the difficulty of
operating through an external pressure group. Party involvement in first-
and second-tier elections from the late 1880s, however, served to give
political colour to the divisions inherent in metropolitan development,
between rich and poor parishes, West End and East End. It ensured that
subsequent reform proposals, whether Liberal or Conservative, would
have their supporters within the system. It also provided an organizational
link between partisans within the local bodies, the London MPs on each
side, and the national party leaders.

What it did not do was produce a politically partisan solution. Herbert
Morrison and W. A. Robson argued that the Conservatives tried to curb

[1] Quoted in *London*, 1 Nov. 1894.

the LCC by structural reform in 1899,[2] but it remains the case that a system largely cast by Conservative legislation nevertheless operated in a redistributionary way and was dominated by a first-tier body then in Radical hands. Arguably in 1888 the government had no reason to anticipate a protracted Radical ascendancy on the LCC. In 1899, however, it was moved to legislate by continual prompting from Onslow, the London Municipal Society, and the West End, but yet produced an Act that failed to 'smash' the LCC and did little to reduce the 70 per cent or so of metropolitan taxation that was already centralized.

This was because the London problem contained too many variables to be open to crudely partisan solutions or, to be more precise, because the crudely partisan solution proposed by one section of metropolitan Conservatism in the West End was not acceptable even to Conservatives elsewhere. It is true that party politics helped define the evolving distinction between those areas which gained from metropolitan integration and those which suffered by it. It is also true that broader political principles helped determine party stances on the reform question: Radicals' advocacy of redistribution and hostility to privilege led them to support municipal enterprise and rate equalization and to attack the City and the West End, while Conservatives' hostility to 'confiscation' and municipal collectivism made them protective of the City and suspicious of the LCC. But these political impulses were subject to qualification by other circumstances. Dr Young equates Conservatism with decentralization, local autonomy, and the Vestries, and Radicalism with centralization, integration, and the LCC, but to do this he is forced to claim that the Conservatives invented the LCC only to appease Goschen, that the Vestries supported their own abolition in 1886, and that the 1896 transfer conference was a triumph for the West End.[3] There is little room in this analysis for the rate equalization of 1894, a Liberal measure which strengthened the second tier. The conclusion must be that although political motivation provided the impulse to reform, it could not by itself determine the shape of reform. It was one force among many.

The others cut across party lines. The most potent of them was the interdependence of the various component areas of the metropolis.

[2] H. Morrison, *How Greater London is Governed* (1935), 100–1; W. A. Robson, *The Government and Misgovernment of London* (1939), 93–4. See also the dispute between Robson and Keith-Lucas in *Public Administration*, 50 (1972), 95, 213.
[3] K. Young, 'The Politics of London Government, 1880–1899', *Public Administration*, 51 (1973), 96 n. 4; K. Young, *Local Politics and the Rise of Party* (Leicester, 1975), 37–8; K. Young and P. Garside, *Metropolitan London: Politics and Urban Change, 1837–1981* (1982), 57–8, 77–80.

Metropolitan growth brought the differentiation of commercial, industrial, and residential quarters, and the social segregation of rich and poor
areas. The concentration of wealth in the central business district and the
West End left those areas to carry much of the burden of an increasingly
integrated metropolitan system, as the 1894 rate equalization emphasized.
This meant that the West End reaction to the growing cost of integration,
though voiced in mid-century terms of autonomy, could easily be por-
trayed by its opponents as a sectional and selfish movement. 'Metropology' provides many examples of successful selfishness, of course, but
the West End started from a disadvantageous position owing to London's
particular social configuration. Modern 'metropology' typically has
exclusive outlying suburbs naming their price for inclusion in the metropolitan system, and this was true of some of the earlier instances of
boundary extension,[4] but the most select residential area of Victorian
London lay not on the fringes but in the centre, physically locked
into the metropolis. Extrication demanded the strained constitutional
expedients sought first by the City and then by Onslow and the West
End. By the 1890s the City had settled for an undeclared compromise by
which it accepted heavy equalization payments and a high level of fiscal
integration in return for the preservation of its constitutional autonomy.
With less autonomy to defend, the West End continued to seek the
reduction of its fiscal burdens through constitutional change, but by
the time the drawbacks of metropolitan integration had become clear to
the West End, its advantages had become clear to most of the rest of
London.

This was most tellingly true of the suburbs. These areas were predominantly Conservative in national politics, but most of them had still
to develop the social homogeneity they would acquire in the twentieth
century (when 'the suburban housing tracts of the twenties and thirties
... carried the physical separation of the classes to new extremes')[5] and
the 'fierce suburban separatism'[6] that went with it. They had more in

---

[4] 'A long chapter of compromises and concessions' preceded the enticement of the
suburbs into Greater New York in 1898: B. S. Coler, quoted in V. Jones, *Metropolitan
Government*, (Chicago, 1942), 317. Similarly for Greater Birmingham in 1911: A. Briggs,
History of Birmingham (Oxford, 1952), ii. 151–5. Broughton and Pendleton were 'seduced
into incorporation' in Salford in 1853 by over-representation: J. Garrard, *Leadership and
Power in Victorian Industrial Towns, 1830–80* (Manchester, 1983), 39.
[5] J. Cox, *The English Churches in a Secular Society: Lambeth, 1870–1930* (Oxford, 1982),
31.
[6] K. Young and J. Kramer, *Strategy and Conflict in Metropolitan Housing: Suburbia
versus the GLC, 1965–1975* (1978), 12.

common with American suburbs of the same period, which combined localism with an eagerness to benefit from superior central city services.[7] London's suburban authorities valued their equalization grants and LCC support for capital projects; they were not prepared to forgo either for the sake of the West End, despite their political affinity. The same applied *a fortiori* to Conservative-controlled working-class parishes, so that while Onslow eventually managed to assemble most Moderate Vestries beneath the incorporation banner, he could do so only by playing down the devolution of expensive first-tier powers and denying any threat to equalization. Under these circumstances political affinity provided little more than a token allegiance, unable to override material interests that conflicted with it. Onslow's belated espousal of equalization in 1898–9 indicates his acceptance that integration might be the price to pay for the political advantages of dismembering the LCC, but it must be doubtful whether any reform involving the extension of equalization would have had much appeal for the West End.

The second obstacle to a purely political solution was the developing *esprit de corps* of the second tier. Second-tier solidarity had been fashioned in the Chadwick era, and hardened during the 1880s with resistance to the 1884 Bill and with the attack upon the MBW. As the reform question became polarized in the 1890s the divisions between second-tier bodies came to appear more important than their common interests, but there remained a shared determination to resist interference with existing local powers and areas. The two-tier battles of 1889–91 demonstrated this second-tier resilience and marked the beginning of the process of separate development of the two tiers which has continued since. The links established before the 1890s—drainage sanction and loan sanction by the LCC, default powers over housing, and above all the first tier's reloans and contributions to local capital projects—all survived, but there was little prospect of further 'vertical integration'. The 'suicide clause' of the 1899 Act, providing for transfer of powers between the tiers, was voluntaristic and in practice inoperative. The election of the first tier by the second had died with the MBW, and Balfour rejected Onslow's suggestion that local mayors be made ex-officio county aldermen. There was never any chance of the boroughs having county councillors thrust upon them. Onslow had assumed that parochial self-esteem could be harnessed in the cause of devolution, but this had proved misguided. What the majority of the second tier had wanted was an honorific

[7] J. C. Teaford, *City and Suburb* (Baltimore and London, 1979), 63.

enhancement of their status, to dispel the stigma of Vestrydom, and a marginal adjustment of the two-tier balance, to reduce the scope for LCC interference. These the 1899 Act provided.

Second-tier resilience was integral also to the third major obstacle to 'tenification'—the survival of parochialism. The development of the system since 1855 had shown that a second tier based on the fragmented and irregular parish network necessitated a strong first tier. The attack upon the LCC therefore demanded consolidation of the local bodies. After the Chelsea furore of 1890 this came to appear a greater threat to parochial autonomy than the extension of LCC surveillance. Onslow thus found that the cultivation of Vestry enthusiasm for local municipalities only made second-tier amalgamations less likely, and it was this that led him down the blind alley of piecemeal incorporation. To make matters worse, Fig. 9.1 suggests that classical 'tenification' using the pre-1885 parliamentary boroughs would have improved only marginally the inequality of resources within the second tier. The problem was that rich areas adjoined other rich areas, poor ones other poor ones. To counteract this with the systematic and artificial linkage of rich and poor districts would have taken some spatial ingenuity. It would also have entailed the kind of amalgamation least popular within the second tier. Noticeably, all the voluntary amalgamations mooted after the publication of the 1899 Bill involved parishes of similar social composition.[8] Parochialism was a strong enough obstacle as it was, without compounding it by arousing the mutual social suspicion of rich and poor districts.

Obviously much Vestry parochialism could be ascribed to the *amour propre* which afflicts most local authorities. This could not explain, however, the force of the public reaction to the proposed Chelsea–Kensington amalgamation in 1890, or the conviction of many London Conservatives who were not merely apologists for the Vestries that a vital local government system required the adoption of 'natural' secondary areas, and that the old parliamentary boroughs were not natural. The assumption that the parishes *were* natural had not been tested very deeply. It was suggested earlier that both middle-class and working-class communities were becoming more compact and introverted by the turn of the century, which would have argued against 'tenification' on the assumption that secondary areas should reflect existing communities. The

[8] When a committee of Clerkenwell Vestry suggested union not only with St Luke's but also with Holborn, part of the central business district, the proposal was rejected by the full Clerkenwell Vestry as well as by the Holborn District Board: Clerkenwell Vestry Minutes, 29 Mar., 13 Apr. 1899; Holborn DB Minutes, 13 Mar. 1899.

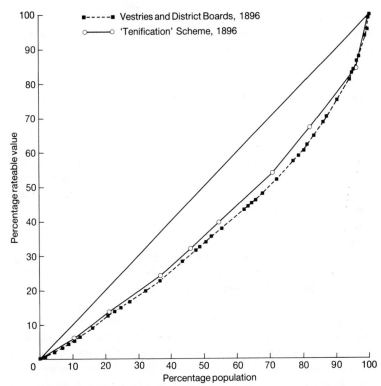

Key: Vestries and District Boards, 1896
'Tenification' Scheme, 1896

FIG. 9.1   Resource Distribution of London Local Authorities, 1896
Note: Evenness of spread of rateable value per head among secondary authorities
is measured by proximity to the 45° line. The projected 'tenification' scheme is
based upon grouping the parishes by the pre-1885 parliamentary boroughs, with
Lewisham and Lee added to Greenwich and with a new borough formed of
Wandsworth and Battersea. For the Lorenz curve method see Barlow, *Spatial
Dimensions of Urban Government*, 73–5.

parish network was more 'local', in that sense, but its components varied
immensely in size. Outer parishes like Islington, Lambeth, and St Pancras
were larger than most municipal units in Britain, and perhaps unwieldy
to manage.[9] They were too large to have represented unitary communities

---

[9] The clerk to the Lambeth Guardians told Jesse Argyle in 1900 that 'the parish is too
large for thoroughly efficient administration, Norwood in particular being remote from the
centre of Government': Booth MS B 383, 63–5 (Thurnall).

by any of the conventional physical definitions pertaining to residential mobility, spatial segregation, or school, church, and workplace catchment areas, but nobody suggested breaking them up. The statute-based British reform process could not reflect community as sensitively as the more voluntaristic American system, whatever its other advantages, and Londoners were denied even the petition stage essential to grants of provincial charters under the Municipal Corporations Act. What passed for localism in the London government debate was in fact a psychological deference to existing local areas, centuries old. London's omission from the Municipal Corporations Act and Hall's retention of the parish unit in 1855 had saved London from boundary commissioners and the designation of new areas, and given parochialism a prescriptive force. The most eloquent defence of the parish as community probably came from the Liberal Dilke in his *Speaker* article, but that this essentially conservative attitude should appeal to many metropolitan Conservatives hardly needs explanation. It moved many of the men whom Balfour consulted in 1898–9, figures like H. P. Harris and C. A. Whitmore, who were influential in shaping the Bill, and was another force impeding the radical Conservative solution of Onslow and the West End.

Under all these circumstances the solution arrived at by 1899, combining a strong first tier and a high degree of financial integration with small local areas, and a clear definition of second-tier powers, probably pleased more interested parties than any other. The weaknesses that became apparent in the 65 years of the system's operation, however, were inherent in the structure adopted then. Despite mayoral chains and the jealous protection of second-tier autonomy, 'the metropolitan boroughs [were] very much the poor relations of the London County Council' down to 1965.[10] Whether or not borough status had solved the Vestries' alleged 'councillor calibre' problem, limited and unattractive duties soon created an 'officer calibre' problem[11] perhaps more harmful in the twentieth century. Still more seriously, the adoption of small areas brought the structural problem of single-party monopolies in many boroughs.[12] The Victorians, always reluctant to acknowledge the role of party politics in local government, had rather glossed over this danger, but with the social segregation attendant upon metropolitan development it was always likely that areas small enough to represent self-contained communities

[10] Sir Frank Marshall, *The Marshall Inquiry on Greater London* (1978), 9.
[11] RC Local Government in Greater London, 1957–60, Minutes of Evidence, Q. 13080 (Robson).
[12] Ibid., Q. 13070 (Self).

would be too socially homogeneous to sustain political pluralism. 'In the real world', as the Centre for Urban Studies told the Herbert Commission, 'the criteria of representative local democracy conflict'.[13]

Consolidation of the second tier was therefore always a likely outcome of the Herbert Commission's deliberations in the 1950s. In the event it was extensive, and brought many forced marriages in 1965 that would not have been undertaken in the 1890s. Chelsea and Kensington were at last merged and Greater Westminster made greater still by the addition of Marylebone and Paddington. St Pancras was joined to commercial Holborn and Bohemian Hampstead in the new Camden borough, while Battersea was pushed into the new Wandsworth although it 'had no more to do with its new partners of Putney or Tooting than with Hammersmith or Dulwich'.[14] Second-tier witnesses before the Herbert Commission resisted amalgamations as tenaciously as any Vestryman in the 1890s, but the inclination of the wider public to defend existing authorities was much weaker. Chelsea and Kensington were merged with little more than conventional expressions of regret; in Camden 'the nostalgia for Hampstead, Holborn, and St Pancras Councils proved to be shortlived'.[15]

With the reappearance of Tower Hamlets, Hackney, Greenwich, Southwark, Lambeth and Westminster the new inner London boroughs savoured more than slightly of 'tenification'. There was inevitably a political motive to reform, but it was rather to end the thirty-year Labour monopoly of the first tier than to clip the first tier's wings. The LCC was not carved up but replaced by a much larger Greater London Council, and even if the union of inner and outer London represented 'an arranged marriage for which they are not well suited',[16] the most canvassed alternative in the 1950s had been to grant county borough status to a constellation of Middlesex suburbs—a step towards American fragmentation.[17]

Nevertheless, consolidation of the second tier removed one of the major impediments to abolition of the first. The extension of central government rate support during the twentieth century, reducing the importance of the first tier's redistributive role, has removed another. Their removal has emphasized that the strength of the first tier down to 1965 was due

---

[13] Ibid., Written Evidence, v. 651.

[14] B. Kosmin, 'Political Identity in Battersea' in S. Wallman *et al.*, *Living in South London: Perspectives on Battersea, 1871–1981* (1982), 42–3.

[15] E. Wistrich, *Local Government Reorganisation: The First Years of Camden* (1972), 285.

[16] R. Glass, 'The Mood of London' in D. Donnison and D. C. Eversley (eds.), *London: Urban Patterns, Problems and Policies* (1973), 426–7.

[17] G. Rhodes, *The Government of London: The Struggle for Reform* (1970), 17–18.

as much to the second tier's dependence upon it as to its own positive role. London's metropolitan authorities have never controlled police, water, electricity, or the docks. Central government relieved the LCC of its ambulances and trams, and the GLC of its reacquired transport powers. The sturdy independence of the second tier ensured that the idea, fashionable in the 1960s, of the GLC as a 'strategic' metropolitan authority never took root.[18]

Thus while the proposal to abolish the GLC advanced by the Conservatives in the 1983 general election and implemented in 1986, was politically motivated, the structural weakness of the first tier had by then made it administratively plausible. The more obvious populist justification that devolution would return power to the citizens was invoked only hesitantly, partly because very little devolution would actually take place, and partly because the enlarged second-tier authorities of 1965 were scarcely less remote and bureaucratic than the GLC. The Herbert Commission may have been influenced by the LSE group's characteristically unscientific assertion that the public would soon identify with whatever new boroughs were created,[19] but the group acknowledged by 1968 that there was little evidence of such identification.[20] Recent work in both Lambeth and Southwark suggests that residents professing any sense of locality at all were more likely to identify with parts of the borough than with the borough itself.[21] The 'managerialization' of modern urban government had made matters worse. In Lambeth, where no boundary change was involved,[22] the new borough 'was born, so to speak, looking a good deal more corporate than the old Metropolitan Borough council it replaced'.[23] In Hackney dissatisfaction with the new borough was expressed as nostalgia for its predecessors.[24] This was probably not

[18] For the difficulties of defining the 'strategic' authority see Marshall, *The Marshall Inquiry*, 105, and for a case study, K. Young and J. Kramer, *Strategy and Conflict*.
[19] RC Local Government in Greater London, 1957–60, Written Evidence, v. 460.
[20] RC Local Government in England, Research Study 2, *The Lessons of the London Government Reforms* (1968), 12.
[21] When asked to identify their neighbourhood only 4% of the Lambeth sample named the borough: 'People, Housing and District', IAS/LA/5 in Shankland Cox Partnership (in association with the Institute of Community Studies), *Inner Area Study: Lambeth* (1974–8), 51. For Southwark see P. Prescott-Clarke and B. Hedges, *Living in Southwark* (1976), 29.
[22] Lambeth is the only secondary area to have survived intact since 1855, excluding the City.
[23] C. Cockburn, *The Local State: The Management of Cities and People* (2nd edn.; 1978), 13.
[24] M. Young, H. Young, E. Shuttleworth, and W. Tucker, *Report from Hackney: A Study of an Inner City Area* (1980), 53.

so much a fault of the 1965 reorganization as the reflection of a problem inherent in modern metropolitan government. Mary Horton's research study for the Maud Committee in 1967 suggested an appreciably lower degree both of neighbourhood sense and of interest in local government in London than elsewhere.[25] Subsequent studies have also indicated the decline of community localism—with gentrification, immigration, the decay of kinship ties, and greater environmental dissatisfaction in the inner city[26]—and a corresponding disenchantment with local authorities.[27] Such spontaneous political activity as there is in London occurs well below the borough level, with tenants' and ratepayers' associations, neighbourhood councils, and the like.[28] A 1970 survey found that the need for such bodies was felt more strongly in urban than in rural areas and most strongly in London.[29]

The boroughs would therefore appear to have lost much of their representative capacity while acquiring a stronger administrative role. In the meantime, if the Livingstone years proved anything, they showed that the greater publicity inevitably accorded to a politicized first tier allows the metropolitan body to figure more prominently in the public mind than the second tier, whatever its structural weaknesses. Arguably the Victorian equation of the first tier with efficiency and the second with representation has been inverted. The tension between the administrative and the representative ideals of local government, inherent in every municipal system but particularly marked in the metropolis, thus resurfaces. With the capital now Balkanized against its wishes, few would claim that the London government problem has ever been solved.

---

[25] Ministry of Housing and Local Government, Com. on the Management of Local Government, iii, *The Local Government Elector* (1967). See Table 38, 29, for lower readership of local newspapers; Table 137, 100, for lower proportion of friends in council area; Table 139, 102 for degree of attachment to council area; also Tables 31 (24), 32 (25), 48 (36), 72 (52), and 99 (71).

[26] See e.g. M. Young *et al.*, *Report from Hackney*; R. Glass, 'The Mood of London', in Donnison and Eversley, *London Patterns, Problems and Policies*, 422; J. D. Eyles, *Environmental Satisfaction and London's Docklands: Problems and Policies in the Isle of Dogs* (Queen Mary College Dept. of Geography, Occasional Paper No. 5; 1976), 9 ff.: 'Study of Intending Migrants', IAS/LA/20 in Shankland Cox Partnership, *Lambeth*; Research Surveys of Great Britain Ltd., *The London Project Commentary* (1977), 30; E. Fernando and B. Hedges, *Moving out of Southwark* (1976), 15.

[27] M. Young *et al.*, *Report from Hackney*, 52 ff. Only 14% of their sample believed that they could influence the council: 'I honestly think if you go to a councillor you are wasting your time'; 'the biggest filing system in the borough is the waste paper bin'.

[28] D. Donnison, 'The Micropolitics of the City' in Donnison and Eversley, *London Patterns, Problems and Policies*, 383–404.

[29] J. Baker and M. Young, *The Hornsey Plan*, 2nd edn. (1973), 5.

Appendices

APPENDIX I   Local Authorities under the Metropolis Local Management Act, 1855

	Parishes, Districts, etc.	Rateable Value per Head		Representatives on	
		1856 £	1896 £	MBW 1855	District Board 1855
	City of London	9·44	144·09	3	—
Schedule A					
Vestries	Bermondsey	2.74	4·88	1	—
	Bethnal Green	1·16	3·49	1	—
	Camberwell	3·84	4·52	1[b]	—
	Chelsea	3·86	8·07	1	—
	Clerkenwell	3·32	5·95	1	—
	Hampstead	6·43	10·43	1	—
	Islington	4·58	5·26	2[a]	—
	Kensington	5·50	12·14	1[a]	—
	Lambeth	3·52	5·66	2[a]	—
	Mile End Old Town	2·66	3.60	1	—
	Newington	2·93	4·07	1	—
	Paddington	9·29	10·70	1[b]	—
	Rotherhithe	3·59	5·36	$\frac{1}{2}$[c]	—
	St George, Hanover Square	12·15	24·77	2	—
	St George-in-the-East	3·43	4·13	1	—
	St George-the-Martyr, Southwark	2·41	4·75	1	—
	St James, Piccadilly	11·30	34·76	1	—
	St Luke	3·02	8·36	1	—
	St Martin-in-the-Fields	10·15	43·52	1	—
	St Marylebone	6·34	11·35	2	—
	St Pancras	4·23	6·84	2[a]	—
	Shoreditch	2·30	5·65	2	—
Local Board	Woolwich	2·87	6·56	1	—
District	Fulham DB[e]	3·88		1	
Boards of	Fulham		4·93		15
Works (with	Hammersmith		5·63		24
Schedule B	Greenwich DB	3·57	5·15	1[b]	
Vestries)	Greenwich				30
	St Nicholas, Deptford				6
	St Paul, Deptford				21
	Hackney DB[g]	4·43		1[b]	
	Hackney		4·95		51
	Stoke Newington		6·23		6

Parishes, Districts, etc.	Rateable Value per Head		Representatives on	
	1856 £	1896 £	MBW 1855	District Board 1855
Holborn DB	3·84	13·02	I	
Glasshouse Yard				I
Saffron Hill				9
St Andrew and St George				33
St Sepulchre				6
Lewisham DB	8·51	6·63	½d	
Lewisham				24
Penge				3
Limehouse DB	3·06	5·20	I	
Limehouse				15
Ratcliff				12
Shadwell				6
Wapping				3
Plumstead DBg	5·34		½d	
Charlton				9
Eltham				6
Kidbrooke		7·33		I
Lee				9
Plumstead		3·38		12
Poplar DB	4·63	4·34	Ib	
Bow				9
Bromley				15
Poplar				24
St Giles DB	4·84	11·55	I	
St Giles-in-the-Fields				27
St George, Bloomsbury				21
St Olave DB	4·99	17·97	½c	
Horselydown				15
St Olave, Southwarkh				12
St Thomas, Southwarkh				I
St Saviour DB	4·51	13·74	I	
Christchurch, Southwark				15
St Saviour, Southwark				24
Strand DB	5·84	26·42	I	
Liberty of the Rolls				3
St Anne, Soho				18
St Clement Danes				15
St Mary-le-Strand				3
St Paul, Covent Garden				9
Precinct of the Savoy				I
Wandsworth DB	5·89		Ia	
Batterseaf		5·21		12
Clapham				18
Putney				6
Streatham		6·62		9
Tooting				3
Wandsworth				9

Parishes, Districts, etc.	Rateable Value per Head		Representatives on	
	1856 £	1896 £	MBW 1855	District Board 1855
Westminster DB[f]	3·91		1	
St Margaret		} 16·31		30
St John				27
Whitechapel DB	3·06	5·52		
Christchurch, Spitalfields				12
Holy Trinity, Minories[h]				1
Mile End New Town				6
Norton Folgate				3
Old Artillery Ground				1
Old Tower Without[h]				1
St Botolph Without, Aldgate[h]				6
St Katherine-by-the-Tower[h]				1
Whitechapel[h]				27
Extra-parochial Places (Schedule C) Charterhouse			—	—
Furnival's Inn			—	—
Gray's Inn			—	—
Inner Temple	42·81	84·79	—	—
Lincoln's Inn			—	—
Middle Temple			—	—
St Peter's Close			—	—
Staple Inn			—	—

a. By the Metropolis Management Amendment Act, 1885, 48 & 49 Vict., c. 33, s. 1, Islington, Kensington, Lambeth, St Pancras, and Wandsworth were each given three MBW representatives. Wandsworth was reduced to two representatives on the secession of Battersea from the DB in 1887 (50 & 51 Vict., c. 17, s. 6).

b. Camberwell, Paddington, Greenwich, Hackney, and Poplar were each given two MBW representatives by 48 & 49 Vict., c. 33, s. 1.

c. Rotherhithe and St Olave's shared one MBW representative.

d. Lewisham and Plumstead shared one MBW representative until given one each by 48 & 49 Vict., c. 33, s. 2.

e. Fulham DB was dissolved, and Fulham and Hammersmith Vestries raised to Schedule A, by 48 & 49 Vict., c. 33, s. 3.

f. By the Metropolis Management (Battersea and Westminster) Act, 1887 (50 & 51 Vict., c. 17), Battersea was raised to Schedule A and given one MBW representative and Westminster DB was dissolved, the component parishes being incorporated as a united Vestry in Schedule A.

g. By the Metropolis Management (Plumstead and Hackney) Act, 1893 (56 & 57 Vict., c. 55), Plumstead vestry was raised to Schedule A and the remaining components of the Plumstead DB reconstituted as the Lee DB, and Hackney and Stoke Newington were raised to Schedule A, dissolving the Hackney DB.

h. Under the powers of grouping small parishes granted to the LCC by the 1894 Local Government Act, St Olave and St Thomas, Southwark were united, Minories joined to Whitechapel, and St Katherine's and Old Tower Without joined to St Botolph Without, Aldgate in 1896. All the new groupings remained in Schedule B.

APPENDIX 2   The London Precept System

Source: Adapted from the table in *London Statistics* IX (1898–9), 435.

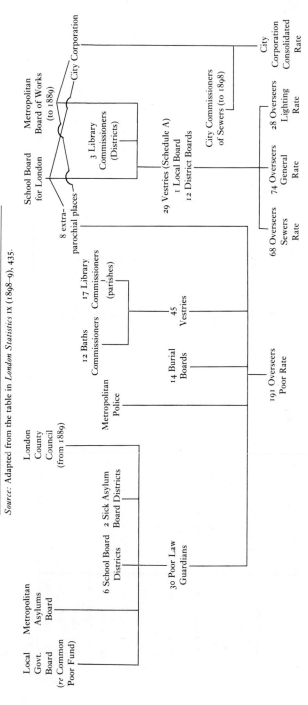

Numbers of authorities are those valid in 1899.

APPENDIX 3   Local Taxation in London, 1863/4 to 1899/1900

Rates Levied[a]	1863/4 £	%	1867/8 £	%	1873/4 £	%	1874/5 £	%	1875/6 £	%
First Tier										
County	178,681	6·34	196,726	6·65	208,890	5·19	256,639	6·04	204,490	4·73
MBW	289,633	10·28	417,106	14·09	218,780	5·44	345,817	8·14	443,908	10·27
Metropolitan Police	294,165	10·44	367,001	12·40	504,227	12·53	341,753	8·05	387,029	8·95
Corporation of London[b]	41,181	1·46	55,896	1·89	65,393	1·62	65,317	1·54	67,287	1·56
Metropolitan Asylums Board	—	—	8,777	0·30	121,376	3·02	143,394	3·38	191,960	4·44
London School Board	—	—	—	—	64,463	1·60	105,951	2·49	206,694	4·78
Total First Tier	803,660	28·53	1,045,506	35·32	1,183,129	29·40	1,258,871	29·64	1,501,368	34·73
Equalization										
Metropolitan Common Poor Fund	—	—	319,212	10·78	674,309	16·75	616,197	14·51	630,128	14·58
Indoor Pauper Grant	—	—	—	—	—	—	—	—	—	—
Equalization Rate	—	—	—	—	—	—	—	—	—	—
Total Equalization	—	—	319,212	10·78	674,309	16·75	616,197	14·51	630,128	14·58

Total First Tier and Equalization	803,660	28·53	1,364,718	46·10	1,857,438	46·15	1,875,068	44·15	2,131,496	49·31
Second Tier										
Poor Law	1,071,330	38·04	408,410	13·80	817,516	20·31	956,309	22·52	719,983	16·66
Burial Boards	*	*	21,100	0·71	11,181	0·28	8,778	0·21	9,803	0·23
Baths and Washhouses	*	*	10,589	0·36	*	*	*	*	*	*
Libraries	†	†	†	†	†	†	†	†	†	†
Vestries and District Boards^c	839,630	29·81	1,036,409	35·01	1,201,342	29·85	1,272,751	29·97	1,334,426	30·87
City Commissioners of Sewers	101,853	3·62	119,109	4·02	137,183	3·41	134,063	3·16	126,842	2·93
Total Second Tier	2,012,813	71·47	1,595,617	53·90	2,167,222	53·85	2,371,901	55·85	2,191,054	50·69
Grand Total	2,816,473	100·00	2,966,335	100·00	4,024,660	100·00	4,246,969	100·00	4,322,550	100·00

a Church rates excluded throughout.
b Including City Ward rate.
c Including Conservators of Commons.
* Included in poor-rate total.
† Included in Vestry rate total.

Appendix 3 (cont.):

Rates Levied[a]	1876/7		1877/8		1878/9		1879/80		1880/1	
	£	%	£	%	£	%	£	%	£	%
First Tier										
County	231,613	4·93	229,280	4·56	164,182	3·16	174,716	3·37	164,424	3·01
MBW	472,711	10·07	455,355	9·07	475,412	9·14	554,448	10·70	620,957	11·36
Metropolitan Police	420,904	8·97	426,540	8·49	435,435	8·37	438,728	8·47	443,626	8·12
Corporation of London[b]	72,109	1·54	64,155	1·28	66,629	1·28	67,154	1·30	81,653	1·49
Metropolitan Asylums Board	223,940	4·77	253,844	5·05	262,218	5·04	245,514	4·74	263,437	4·82
London School Board	331,275	7·06	452,610	9·01	506,351	9·74	541,717	10·46	585,567	10·71
Total First Tier	1,752,552	37·33	1,881,784	37·46	1,910,227	36·73	2,022,277	39·04	2,159,664	39·51
Equalization										
Metropolitan Common Poor Fund	640,403	13·64	663,267	13·20	676,046	13·00	722,384	13·95	765,676	14·01
Indoor Pauper Grant	—	—	—	—	—	—	—	—	—	—
Equalization Rate	—	—	—	—	—	—	—	—	—	—
Total Equalization	640,403	13·64	663,267	13·20	676,046	13·00	722,384	13·95	765,676	14·01

Total First Tier and Equalization										
	2,392,955	50·97	2,545,051	50·67	2,586,273	49·73	2,744,661	52·98	2,925,340	53·52
Second Tier										
Poor Law	767,178	16·34	823,303	16·39	887,303	17·06	770,318	14·87	778,084	14·24
Burial Boards	9,541	0·20	9,214	0·18	9,062	0·17	6,955	0·13	7,696	0·14
Baths and Washhouses	*	*	*	*	*	*	*	*	*	*
Libraries	†	†	†	†	†	†	†	†	†	†
Vestries and District Boards^c	1,411,699	30·07	1,443,629	28·74	1,568,376	30·16	1,517,477	29·29	1,580,561	28·92
City Commissioners of Sewers	113,480	2·42	201,678	4·02	149,690	2·88	140,686	2·72	173,780	3·18
Total Second Tier	2,301,898	49·03	2,477,824	49·33	2,614,431	50·27	2,435,436	47·02	2,540,121	46·48
Grand Total	4,694,853	100·00	5,022,875	100·00	5,200,704	100·00	5,180,097	100·00	5,465,461	100·00

a Church rates excluded throughout.
b Including City Ward rate.
c Including Conservators of Commons.
* Included in poor-rate total.
† Included in Vestry rate total.

Appendix 3 (cont.):

Rates Levied[a]	1881/2		1882/3		1883/4		1884/5		1885/6	
	£	%	£	%	£	%	£	%	£	%
First Tier										
County	187,377	3·25	171,630	2·87	185,537	2·95	192,727	2·93	178,434	2·60
MBW	639,582	11·09	706,885	11·81	716,186	11·37	759,714	11·56	837,575	12·22
Metropolitan Police	471,281	8·17	497,895	8·32	511,499	8·12	529,007	8·05	534,463	7·79
Corporation of London[b]	75,670	1·31	72,026	1·20	73,542	1·17	75,782	1·15	77,520	1·13
Metropolitan Asylums Board	466,596	8·09	457,078	7·64	453,730	7·21	610,006	9·28	427,140	6·23
London School Board	661,175	11·47	674,855	11·28	754,589	11·98	886,883	13·50	977,659	14·26
Total First Tier	2,501,681	43·39	2,580,369	43·12	2,695,083	42·80	3,054,119	46·47	3,032,791	44·23
Equalization										
Metropolitan Common Poor Fund	789,166	13·69	743,743	12·43	872,199	13·85	788,548	12·00	856,442	12·49
Indoor Pauper Grant	—	—	—	—	—	—	—	—	—	—
Equalization Rate	—	—	—	—	—	—	—	—	—	—
Total Equalization	789,166	13·69	743,743	12·43	872,199	13·85	788,548	12·00	856,442	12·49

	Amount	%	Amount	%	Amount	%	Amount	%	Amount	%
Total First Tier and Equalization	3,290,847	57·07	3,324,112	55·55	3,567,282	56·66	3,842,667	58·47	3,889,233	56·72
Second Tier										
Poor Law	711,858	12·35	905,343	15·13	905,172	14·38	872,858	13·28	1,089,498	15·89
Burial Boards	7,589	0·13	6,603	0·11	7,613	0·12	6,742	0·10	6,097	0·09
Baths and Washhouses	5,435	0·09	7,581	0·13	9,787	0·16	9,442	0·14	13,605	0·20
Libraries	1,209	0·02	1,352	0·02	1,725	0·03	2,216	0·03	2,070	0·03
Vestries and District Boards[c]	1,606,182	27·86	1,610,329	26·91	1,604,027	25·48	1,621,841	24·68	1,630,510	23·78
City Commissioners of Sewers	142,776	2·48	128,553	2·15	200,652	3·19	216,167	3·29	225,662	3·29
Total Second Tier	2,475,049	42·93	2,659,761	44·45	2,728,976	43·34	2,729,266	41·53	2,967,442	43·28
Grand Total	5,765,896	100·00	5,983,873	100·00	6,296,258	100·00	6,571,933	100·00	6,856,675	100·00

a Church rates excluded throughout.
b Including City Ward rate.
c Including Conservators of Commons.

Appendix 3 (cont.):

Rates Levied[a]	1886/7		1887/8		1888/9		1889/90		1890/1	
	£	%	£	%	£	%	£	%	£	%
First Tier										
County	177,956	2·57	167,924	2·41	184,902	2·60	1,611,449	21·32	1,311,559	16·55
MBW	895,553	2·92	960,653	13·77	1,074,062	15·13	—	—	—	—
Metropolitan Police	569,175	8·21	573,942	8·22	555,461	7·82	566,457	7·49	616,458	7·78
Corporation of London[b]	81,415	1·17	79,004	1·13	83,134	1·17	93,125	1·23	95,498	1·21
Metropolitan Asylums Board	229,999	3·32	329,571	4·72	334,737	4·71	356,095	4·71	371,058	4·68
London School Board	1,121,386	16·18	1,131,568	16·22	1,056,358	14·88	1,061,705	14·05	1,271,755	16·05
Total First Tier	3,075,484	44·38	3,242,662	46·47	3,288,654	46·32	3,688,831	48·80	3,666,328	46·27
Equalization										
Metropolitan Common Poor Fund	877,559	12·66	887,362	12·72	962,071	13·55	954,566	12·63	945,623	11·93
Indoor Pauper Grant	—	—	—	—	—	—	246,226	3·26	407,392	5·14
Equalization Rate	—	—	—	—	—	—	—	—	—	—
Total Equalization	877,559	12·66	887,362	12·72	962,071	13·55	1,200,792	15·89	1,353,015	17·07

Total First Tier and Equalization	3,953,043	57·04	4,130,024	59·19	4,250,725	59·87	4,889,623	64·69	5,019,343	63·34
Second Tier										
Poor Law	1,047,396	15·11	825,279	11·83	962,739	13·56	640,477	8·47	699,864	8·83
Burial Boards	5,828	0·08	6,084	0·09	6,038	0·09	5,353	0.07	5,218	0·06
Baths and Washhouses	16,415	0·24	18,110	0·26	16,607	0·23	22,742	0·30	30,936	0·39
Libraries	2,330	0·03	12,427	0·18	21,155	0·30	21,929	0·29	32,998	0·42
Vestries and District Boards[c]	1,688,705	24·37	1,706,241	24·45	1,570,694	22·12	1,760,360	23·29	1,811,606	22·86
City Commissioners of Sewers	216,112	3·12	279,930	4·01	271,967	3·83	217,926	2·88	324,258	4·09
Total Second Tier	2,976,786	42·96	2,848,071	40·81	2,849,200	40·13	2,668,787	35·31	2,904,880	36·66
Grand Total	6,929,829	100·00	6,978,095	100·00	7,099,925	100·00	7,558,410	100·00	7,924,223	100·00

a Church rates excluded throughout.
b Including City Ward rate.
c Including Conservators of Commons.

Appendix 3 (cont.):

Rates Levied[a]	1891/2 £	1891/2 %	1892/3 £	1892/3 %	1893/4 £	1893/4 %	1894/5 £	1894/5 %	1895/6 £	1895/6 %
First Tier										
County	1,255,466	15·10	1,365,743	16·05	1,450,357	16·12	1,607,783	17·23	1,768,348	18·21
MBW	—	—	—	—	—	—	—	—	—	—
Metropolitan Police	607,598	7·31	609,310	7·16	609,070	6·77	619,223	6·63	628,432	6·47
Corporation of London[b]	95,129	1·14	102,165	1·20	101,198	1·12	90,474	0·97	85,813	0·88
Metropolitan Asylums Board	382,265	4·60	623,865	7·33	681,622	7·57	546,333	5·85	605,836	6·24
London School Board	1,496,115	18·00	1,444,720	16·98	1,473,125	16·37	1,408,455	15·09	1,454,420	14·97
Total First Tier	3,836,573	46·15	4,145,803	48·73	4,315,372	47·96	4,272,268	45·78	4,542,849	46·77
Equalization										
Metropolitan Common Poor Fund	995,565	11·98	1,021,564	12·01	1,056,231	11·74	1,091,305	11·69	1,089,072	11·21
Indoor Pauper Grant	327,704	3·94	326,809	3·84	326,809	3·63	326,809	3·50	327,704	3·37
Equalization Rate	—	—	—	—	—	—	423,843	4·54	855,638	8·81
Total Equalization	1,323,269	15·92	1,348,373	15·85	1,383,040	15·37	1,841,957	19·74	2,272,414	23·39

Total First Tier and Equalization	5,159,842	62·07	5,494,176	64·58	5,698,412	63·33	6,114,225	65·51	6,815,263	70·16
Second Tier										
Poor Law	796,003	10·78	495,958	5·83	766,902	8·52	979,514	10·50	1,035,813	10·66
Burial Boards	8,647	0·10	9,604	0·11	9,862	0·11	10,767	0·12	14,519	0·15
Baths and Washhouses	33,793	0·41	45,164	0·53	57,204	0·64	61,419	0·66	77,264	0·80
Libraries	44,355	0·53	53,605	0·63	54,426	0·60	56,735	0·61	58,543	0·60
Vestries and District Boards^c	1,950,926	23·47	2,100,630	24·69	2,188,277	24·32	1,835,722	19·67	1,394,162	14·35
City Commissioners of Sewers	219,837	2·64	308,284	3·62	223,454	2·48	274,532	2·94	317,962	3·27
Total Second Tier	3,153,561	37·93	3,013,245	35·42	3,300,125	36·67	3,218,689	34·49	2,898,263	29·83
Grand Total	8,313,403	100·00	8,507,421	100·00	8,998,537	100·00	9,332,914	100·00	9,713,526	100·00

a Church rates excluded throughout.
b Including City Ward rate.
c Including Conservators of Commons.

Appendix 3 (cont.):

Rates Levied[a]	1896/7		1897/8		1898/9		1899/1900	
	£	%	£	%	£	%	£	%
First Tier								
County	1,877,160	18·25	1,735,458	16·37	1,759,232	16·94	1,715,784	15·38
MBW	—	—	—	—	—	—	—	—
Metropolitan Police	652,610	6·35	658,025	6·21	663,843	6·39	678,508	6·08
Corporation of London[b]	94,438	0·92	102,562	0·97	125,457	1·21	127,593	1·14
Metropolitan Asylums Board	679,841	6·61	754,879	7·12	774,246	7·45	817,174	7·33
London School Board	1,728,162	16·81	1,927,009	18·18	1,769,536	17·03	1,972,161	17·68
Total First Tier	5,032,211	48·94	5,177,933	48·84	5,092,314	49·02	5,311,220	47·61
Equalization								
Metropolitan Common Poor Fund	1,152,775	11·21	1,194,962	11·27	1,243,020	11·97	1,234,072	11·06
Indoor Pauper Grant	326,809	3·18	326,809	3·08	326,809	3·15	326,809	2·93
Equalization Rate	888,115	8·64	902,468	8·51	915,118	8·81	924,882	8·29
Total Equalization	2,367,699	23·02	2,424,239	22·87	2,484,947	23·92	2,485,763	22·28
Total First Tier and Equalization	7,399,910	71·96	7,602,172	71·71	7,577,261	72·94	7,796,983	69·90
Second Tier								
Poor Law	979,802	9·53	976,297	9·21	822,172	7·91	1,116,286	10·01
Burial Boards	16,353	0·16	19,460	0·18	15,504	0·15	12,468	0·11

Baths and Washhouses	66,075	0·64	84,121	0·79	85,856	0·83	107,354	0·96
Libraries	59,523	0·58	65,379	0·62	69,434	0·67	70,773	0·62
Vestries and District Boards c	1,478,599	14·38	1,571,661	14·83	1,541,682	14·84	1,693,261	15·15
City Commissioners of Sewers	283,142	2·75	282,167	2·66	276,098	2·66	360,674	3·23
Total Second Tier	2,883,494	28·04	2,999,085	28·29	2,810,746	27·06	3,357,816	30·10
Grand Total	10,283,404	100·00	10,601,257	100·00	10,388,007	100·00	11,154,799	100·00

a Church rates excluded throughout.
b Including City Ward rate.
c Including Conservators of Commons.

Source: This table is based upon the summary returns in *PP 1882*, LVII, 177 (for 1873–80), *PP 1893–4*, LXXVI, 27 (for 1881–1891), and *PP 1901*, LXIII, 1206–7 (for 1891–1900). Figures for 1863/4 are drawn from the First Report of SC Metropolitan Local Government, *PP 1866*, XIII. Appendix 6, 104–7 for aggregate Vestry and Poor Rate totals, Appendix 7, 108–9 for City and Metropolitan Police Rate totals, and Third Report, Appendix 7, 180–5 for county rate assessments. Poundage county rates for 1863/4 are calculated from poundage rates and assessments. Figures for the 1867/8 are taken from *PP 1865*, XLVII, 285; county levies are calculated from poundage rates and assessments. Figures for the 1867/8 are taken from Goschen's return in *PP 1870*, LV, 62–3; those for 1880/1 from that year's local Taxation Returns in *PP 1882*, LVII. Metropolitan Police levies in the Goschen return and in the return for 1873–80 were given as the rate raised in the entire Metropolitan Police area, which was substantially larger than the administrative metropolis; totals for the latter have been calculated by adding the levies from metropolitan parishes listed in the annual accounts of the Metropolitan Police in the Parliamentary Papers. All the summary returns failed to distinguish between the different types of poor rate levy; total contributions to the Common Poor Fund and the Asylums Board have been taken from the annual Local Taxation Returns. The overlap between the two, caused by the fact that the Asylums Board's maintenance rate could be charged by unions to the Common Poor Fund, has been calculated from the maintenance rates in the pound and the aggregate valuations given for 1867–1900 in the Metropolitan Asylums Board, *Annual Report* (1900), I. 56–7, and has been deducted from the MAB total. Indoor Pauper Grant totals have been taken from the annual Local Taxation Returns and deducted from the Vestry/DB totals. Figures given for the City Commissioners of Sewers after the Commissioners' abolition in 1897 are those for the second-tier rates—consolidated and sewer rates—determined by deducting the police, ward, and asylum rate totals (itemized in the equalization section of the Local Taxation Returns) from the Corporation total.

Metropolitan Borough	R.v./hd. (£) 1901	Component Metropolis Management Act Areas
Battersea	5·92	Battersea
Bermondsey	6·88	Bermondsey, Rotherhithe, St Olave's District
Bethnal Green	3·99	Bethnal Green
Camberwell	4·84	Camberwell
Chelsea	10·82	Chelsea
Deptford	5·43	St Paul, Deptford (Greenwich DB)
Finsbury	9·38	Clerkenwell, St Luke, Charterhouse (Schedule C), Glasshouse Yard, St Sepulchre (both Holborn District)
Fulham	5·38	Fulham
Greenwich	6·06	Charlton and Kidbrooke (both Lee District), St Nicholas Deptford, Greenwich (both Greenwich District)
Hackney	5·29	Hackney
Hammersmith	5·94	Hammersmith
Hampstead	11·46	Hampstead
Holborn	15·35	Furnival's Inn, Gray's Inn, Lincoln's Inn, Staple Inn (all Schedule C), Saffron Hill, SS Andrew and George (both Holborn District), St Giles District
Islington	5·69	Islington
Kensington	12·53	Kensington
Lambeth	6·15	Lambeth
Lee	6·60	Lee (Lee District), Lewisham (Lewisham District)
Paddington	10·04	Paddington
Poplar	4·63	Poplar District
St Marylebone	12·59	St Marylebone
St Pancras	7·64	St Pancras
Shoreditch	6·47	Shoreditch
Southwark	6·09	Newington, St George, Southwark, St Saviour's District
Stepney	4·70	Limehouse District, Mile End Old Town, St George-in-the-East, Whitechapel District
Stoke Newington	6·67	Stoke Newington
Wandsworth	6·58	Wandsworth District

Metropolitan Borough	R.v./hd. (£) 1901	Component Metropolis Management Act Areas
Westminster (City)	29·72	St George, Hanover Square, St James, St Martin-in-the-Fields, Strand District, Westminster
Woolwich	5·35	Eltham (Lee District), Plumstead, Woolwich

Bibliography

I. MANUSCRIPT AND UNPUBLISHED SOURCES

A. Private Papers, by location

Arundel Castle:
  Fifteenth Duke of Norfolk
Benn Brothers, Ltd, Tonbridge:
  John Williams Benn
Birmingham University Library:
  Joseph Chamberlain
Bishopsgate Institute:
  George Howell
Bodleian Library, Oxford:
  Third Earl Carrington
  Sir William Harcourt
  J. E. Thorold Rogers
  J. S. Sandars
British Library:
  First Baron Avebury
  A. J. Balfour
  John Burns
  Sir Charles Dilke
  W. E. Gladstone
  First Earl of Halsbury
British Library of Political and Economic Science:
  Charles Booth (notebooks compiled for the 'Life and Labour' volumes)
  Leonard Courtney
  F. W. Galton (MS Autobiography)
  Frederic Harrison
  Beatrice Webb's Diary
Chatsworth House:
  Eighth Duke of Devonshire
Churchill College, Cambridge:
  Lord Randolph Churchill
Greater London Record Office:
  Canon Barnett
  James Beal

Guildford Muniment Room:
 T. C. Farrer
 Sir T. H. Farrer[1]
 Fourth Earl of Onslow
Hatfield House:
 Third Marquess of Salisbury
Hereford and Worcester Record Office, Hereford:
 Lord James of Hereford
House of Lords Record Office:
 Fifth Earl Cadogan
 Sir Courtenay Ilbert
National Library of Scotland:
 Fifth Earl of Rosebery
Scottish Record Office:
 Tenth Earl of Wemyss

B. Central Government Records

Public Record Office, Chancery Lane:
 Privy Council Office (PC1, PC8)
Public Record Office, Kew:
 Cabinet Memoranda (CAB 37) and Prime Ministers' Letters to the Queen (CAB 41)
 Home Office (HO 45)
 Ministry of Housing and Local Government (HLG 29)
 Treasury (T1)

C. Local Government Records

(i) Minutes of First-tier Authorities
Corporation of London Record Office:
 Common Council, Minutes
 Corporation Special Committee, Minutes, Minute Papers
 Corporation Special (Finance) Committee, Minutes, Minute Papers
Greater London Record Office:
 London County Council, Minutes
 London County Council, Clerk's Department Records (CL/FIN/1 and CL/LOC/1)
 London County Council, General Purposes Committee, Minutes, Presented Papers

[1] Both the T. C. and T. H. Farrer papers are *en route* to Surrey County Record Office, Kingston.

London County Council, Housing Department Records (HSG/GEN/2/2)
London County Council Local Government and Taxation Committee
    Minutes, Presented Papers; Sub-Committee on Equalization of Assessments
    and Rates Minutes; Assessment and Valuation Sub-Committee Minutes;
    Sub-Committee on the Completion of London Government Minutes
London County Council, Special Committee on Amalgamation, Minutes
Metropolitan Board of Works, Minutes
Metropolitan Board of Works, Sub-Committee on Officers, Minutes
Metropolitan Board of Works, Sub-Committee on Surplus Lands, Minutes

(*ii*)   *Minutes of Second-tier Authorities*
Camden Archives, Swiss Cottage Library:
  Hampstead Vestry Minutes
  St Pancras Vestry Minutes
Chelsea Library (London Borough of Kensington and Chelsea):
  Chelsea Vestry Minutes
Finsbury Library (London Borough of Islington):
  Clerkenwell Vestry Minutes
  St Luke's Vestry Minutes
Greenwich Archives, Woodlands:
  Greenwich District Board Minutes
  Greenwich Vestry Minutes
  Plumstead District Board Minutes
  Plumstead Vestry Minutes
  Woolwich Local Board Minutes
Hackney Archives, Rose Lipman Library:
  Shoreditch Vestry Minutes
  Stoke Newington Vestry Minutes
Hammersmith Archives, Shepherd's Bush Library:
  Fulham District Board Minutes
Holborn Library (London Borough of Camden):
  Holborn District Board Minutes
  St Giles District Board Minutes
Islington Archives, Fieldway Crescent:
  Islington Vestry Minutes
Kensington and Chelsea Archives, Kensington Library:
  Kensington Vestry Minutes
Lambeth Archives: Minet Library:
  Lambeth Vestry Minutes
Lewisham Archives, Manor House Library:
  Lee District Board Minutes
  Lewisham District Board Minutes
Marylebone Library (City of Westminster):
  Marylebone Vestry Minutes

Paddington Vestry Minutes
Southwark Archives, John Harvard Library:
  Bermondsey Vestry Minutes
  Camberwell Vestry Minutes
  Christchurch Vestry Minutes
  Rotherhithe Vestry Minutes
  St George-the-Martyr Vestry Minutes
  St John, Horselydown, Vestry Minutes
  St Olave's Vestry Minutes
  St Saviour's Vestry Minutes
  St Thomas Vestry Minutes
Tower Hamlets Archives, Bancroft Road:
  Bromley Vestry Minutes
  Poplar District Board Minutes
  Whitechapel District Board Minutes
Wandsworth Archives, Battersea Library:
  Wandsworth Vestry Minutes
Westminster Archives, Buckingham Palace Road:
  St George, Hanover Square, Vestry Minutes
  St James, Piccadilly, Vestry Minutes
  St Martin-in-the-Fields Vestry Minutes
  Strand District Board Minutes
  Westminster Vestry Minutes

(iii)   Local Authority Reports (Greater London Record Office)
For publications of LCC see Section C.(i) of this bibliography
Metropolitan Board of Works:
  MBW 1000. Return of precepts upon and contributions to the Corporation of London, 1856–1880.
  MBW 2410. 'Return Showing the Amounts Expended and Liability Incurred by the Board in Each of the Several Localities of the Metropolis . . ., 1888'.
  MBW 236II. 'Translation of a letter from the Prefect of the Seine to the Chairman of the MBW . . .,' 1867.
  MBW 'Unnumbered Report' 0153. 'Statement Showing the Amount in the Pound of All Rates Raised in the Metropolis . . . 1876, 1878, 1880, and 1882'.
Vestries and District Boards, Annual Reports:
  Bermondsey Vestry, 1897–8
  Bethnal Green Vestry, 1887–8, 1894–5
  Camberwell Vestry, 1899–1900
  Chelsea Vestry, 1889–90, 1890–1
  Fulham Vestry, 1894–5
  Kensington Vestry, 1896–7

Newington Vestry, 1892–3
Paddington Vestry, 1888–9, 1895–6
St George, Hanover Square Vestry, 1885–6
St George-in-the-East Vestry, 1892–3
St James, Piccadilly Vestry, 1886–7, 1893–4

D. *Records of Political and Other Organizations*

Bethnal Green Ratepayers' Permanent Association, East Ward, Minutes, 1893–4 (Tower Hamlets Archives).

Chelsea Conservative and Constitutional Union, Hammersmith Branch, Minutes, 1869–73 (Hammersmith Archives).

De Beauvoir Town and Dalston Ratepayers' Association, Minutes, 1879–90 (Hackney Archives).

Hackney Central Division Conservative Association, Minutes, 1885–99 (Hackney Archives).

Kensington Ratepayers' Association, Annual Reports, 1888, 1889, 1892 (Kensington and Chelsea Archives).

London Liberal and Radical Union, Annual Reports, 1888–94 (British Library of Political and Economic Science).

London Municipal Reform League, Annual Reports, 1882–8 (British Library of Political and Economic Science).

London Municipal Society, Executive Committee Minutes, 1894–1900 (Corporation of London Record Office).

London Reform Union, Annual Reports, 1894–1900 (BLPES).

Marylebone Conservative Union, Ward 7 Branch, Report (Camden Archives, Heal Collection).

Metropolitan Asylums Board, Annual Report, 1900 (Greater London Record Office).

North Kensington Ratepayers' Association, Annual Reports, 1893, 1894, 1898, 1899 (Kensington and Chelsea Archives).

Plumstead Ratepayers' Association, Rules, 1887 (Greenwich Archives).

Progressive Party, London County Council, Minutes 1890–1900 (Greater London Record Office).

Stoke Newington Ratepayers' Association, Minutes, 1884–1894 (Hackney Archives).

Strand Conservative Association Minutes, 1888–1897 (Westminster Archives).

West Newington Liberal and Radical Association Annual Reports, 1886–1897 (Southwark Archives).

Westminster Conservative Association, Cash Book, 1869–1886, Index to Donors, 1866–1886 (Westminster Archives).

E. *Other Unpublished Material*

Bridge Ward Without, material in Southwark Archives, 352.031.

London County Council Election Addresses (National Liberal Club collection now in Bristol University Library).

London Government, papers of a conference of local authorities convened by Westminster District Board (Westminster Archives, E3391).

Middlesex Deeds Register (Greater London Record Office).

J. Toulmin Smith, collection of newspaper cuttings in Bodleian Library.

Westminster Incorporation movement, extensive collection of material in Westminster Archives.

II. PRINTED SOURCES

A. *Parliamentary*

(i) *Acts of Parliament*
Public General Acts

1 & 2 Wm. IV c. 60

15 & 16 Vict. c. 84 (Metropolis Water Act, 1852).

18 & 19 Vict. c. 120 (Metropolis Local Management Act, 1855).

23 & 24 Vict. c. 125 (Metropolis Gas Act, 1860).

24 & 25 Vict. c. 42 (London Coal and Wine Duties Continuance Act, 1861).

25 & 26 Vict. c. 93 (Thames Embankment Act, 1862).

32 & 33 Vict. c. 41 (Poor Rate Assessment and Collection Act, 1869).

32 & 33 Vict. c. 67 (Valuation (Metropolis) Act, 1869).

32 & 33 Vict. c. 102 (Metropolitan Board of Works (Loans) Act, 1869).

34 & 35 Vict. c. 47 (MBW (Loans) Act, 1871).

38 & 39 Vict. c. 36 (Artizans' and Labourers' Dwellings Improvement Act, 1875).

38 & 39 Vict. c. 65 (MBW (Loans) Act, 1875).

42 & 43 Vict. c. 64 (Artizans' and Labourers' Dwellings Act (1868) Amendment Act, 1879).

48 & 49 Vict. c. 33 (Metropolis Management Amendment Act, 1885).

50 & 51 Vict. c. 17 (Metropolis Management (Battersea and Westminster) Act, 1887).

51 & 52 Vict. c. 41 (Local Government Act, 1888).

53 & 54 Vict. c. 70 (Housing of the Working Classes Act, 1890).

54 & 55 Vict. c. 76 (Public Health (London) Act, 1891).

56 & 57 Vict. c. 55 (Metropolis Management (Plumstead and Hackney) Act, 1893).

56 & 57 Vict. c. 73 (Local Government Act, 1894).

57 & 58 Vict. c. 53 (London (Equalization of Rates) Act, 1894).

62 & 63 Vict. c. 14 (London Government Act, 1899).

Local Acts
31 & 32 Vict. c. cxxv (City of London Gas Act, 1868).
35 & 36 Vict. c. c (Port of London (Metage, etc.) Act, 1872).
60 & 61 Vict. c. cxxxiii (City of London Sewer Act, 1897).

(ii)   Debates
Hansard's Parliamentary Debates, Third and Fourth Series.

(iii)   Parliamentary Papers
Bills:
   Corporation of London Bill, *PP 1867–8*, I (Bill 106), *PP 1868–9*, II (Bill 40).
   Livery Companies Bill, *PP 1884–5*, III (Bill 210).
   Local Government (England and Wales) Bill, *PP 1888*, IV (Bill 182).
   London Government Bill, *PP 1884*, V (Bill 171).
   London Government Bill, *PP 1899*, VI (Bills 93 and 217).
   Metropolis Local Government Bill, *PP 1887*, IV (Bill 82), *PP 1888*, V (Bill 14).
   Metropolis Local Management Bill, *PP 1854–5*, IV (Bill 234).
   Metropolitan Corporation of London Bill, *PP 1870*, I (Bill 66).
   Metropolitan Municipalities Bill, *PP 1868–9*, IV (Bill 39).
   Municipal Boroughs (Metropolis) Bill, *PP 1870*, III (Bill 65), *PP 1875*, IV (Bill 61).
   Municipal Corporations (Metropolis) Bill, *PP 1867–8*, III (Bill 105).
   Public Health (London) Bill, *PP 1890–1*, VIII (Bill 231).

Select Committee Reports:
   London Corporation (Charges of Malversation) *PP 1887* (161) X.
   London Water Supply, *PP 1880* (329) X.
   Metropolis Local Taxation, First, Second, and Third Reports, *PP 1861* (211, 372, 476) VIII.
   Metropolitan Local Government and Taxation 1866, First and Second Reports, *PP 1866* (186, 452) XIII; 1867. First, Second, and Third Reports, *PP 1867* (135, 268, 301) XII.
   Town Holdings (volumes cited) *PP 1887* (260) XIII, *PP 1890* (341) XVIII.
   Town Improvements (Betterment) (House of Lords) *PP 1894* (292) XV.

Royal Commission Reports:
   Amalgamation of the City and County of London, *PP 1894* (c. 7493) XVII–XVIII.
   City of London Livery Companies, *PP 1884* (c. 4073) XXXIX.
   Corporation of London, *PP 1854* (1772) XXVI.
   Housing of the Working Classes, *PP 1884–5* (c. 4402) XXX.
   Labour, Fourth Report, *PP 1893–4* (c. 7063) XXXIX(1).
   Local Government in Greater London, *PP 1959–60* (Cmnd. 1164) XVIII.
   Local Taxation, *PP 1898* (c. 8765) XLII, *PP 1899* (c. 9150) XXXVI.

Metropolis Water Supply, *PP 1893–4* (c. 7172) XL.
Metropolitan Board of Works, Interim Report, *PP 1888* (c. 5560) LVI.
Municipal Corporations, Second Report, *PP 1837* (239) XXV.
Operation of Sanitary Laws in England and Wales, *PP 1871* (c. 281) XXXV.

Accounts and Papers:
 'Report of the Rt. Hon. G. J. Goschen M.P. . . . on the Progressive Increase
  of Local Taxation', *PP 1870* (470) LV.
 'Report on the Sanitary Condition of the Parish of Clerkenwell', *PP 1886*
  (c. 4717) LVI.
 'Return of the Number of Electors in Each Ward of the City of London . . .',
  PP 1882 (376) LII.
 'Return of the Result of Vestry Elections . . .', *PP 1886* (76–Sess. 1) LVII.
 'Return of Salaries, Fees or Other Emoluments, Received by the Officers of
  the Metropolitan Vestries and District Boards', *PP 1890–1* (14) LXIX.
 'Return Showing All Monies Owing at the Time of the Formation of the
  Metropolitan Board of Works . . .', *PP 1867–8* (360) LVIII.
 'Return Showing . . . the Amount of the Contribution of Each Parish to an
  Equalisation Fund of 6d. in the Pound on Rateable Value . . .', *PP 1894* (78)
  LXXIV(2).
 'Return Showing the Total Amount of Rates in the Pound Raised in the Years
  1889 to 1898', *PP 1899* (117) LXXXIV.
 Series Returns: 'Census Population Tables, 1851–1911'; 'Election Expenses,
  1865–1880'; 'Board of Trade Labour Department Returns, 1893–1900';
  'Local Taxation Returns, 1871–1900'.

Other:
 Committee of Inquiry on Local Government Finance (Layfield Committee),
  PP 1975–6 (Cmnd. 6453) XXI.

B.   Newspapers

(i)   National Daily Newspapers
Daily Chronicle
Daily News
Echo
Morning Post
Pall Mall Gazette
St James' Gazette
Star
The Times

(ii)   London Local Newspapers
Bayswater Chronicle
Chelsea News and Kensington Post
Citizen
City Press
East End News
East London Observer
Eastern Argus and Borough of Hackney Times
Hackney and Kingsland Gazette
[Borough of] Hackney Express and Shoreditch Observer
Hampstead and Highgate Express
Holborn Guardian
Islington Gazette
Kentish Mercury
Marylebone Independent
[Borough of] Marylebone Mercury
Paddington Times
St John's Wood, Kilburn and Hampstead Advertiser
Shoreditch Guardian
South London Chronicle
South London Press
South Western Star
Southwark Recorder
Stratford Express
West London Observer
West London Press and Chelsea News
Westminster
Westminster and Chelsea News
Westminster and Lambeth Gazette
Westminster Times

(iii)   Weekly and Specialist Newspapers
Democrat
Law Journal
Law Reports
Link
London (later London and the Municipal Journal; then Municipal Journal and
    London; finally Municipal Journal)
London Argus
Methodist Times
Metropolitan (later Local Government Journal)
Municipal Reform Gazette
Primrose League Gazette

Radical
Speaker
Tory
Women's Signal

C.   *Contemporary Publications* (pre-1914)

Place of publication London unless otherwise stated.

(i)   Books

Baines, F. E., *Records of the Manor, Parish and Borough of Hampstead* (1890).

Beal, J., *A Municipality for London* (c. 1862).

Besant, W., *East London* (1901).

Bevan, G. P., *The London Water Supply: Its Past, Present and Future* (1884).

Blanch, W. H., *Ye Parish of Camberwell: Its History and Antiquities* (1875).

Boase, F., *Modern English Biography* (1892–1921).

Booth, C. (ed.), *Life and Labour of the People of London* (17 vols.; 1902).

Buxton, C., *Self-Government in London: A Letter to the Rt. Hon. H. A. Bruce, M.P.* (1869).

Churchill, W. S., *Lord Randolph Churchill*, 2nd edn. (1907).

Clarke, Sir E., *The Story of My Life* (1918).

Dod's Handbook to the London County Council (1889).

Engels, F., *The Condition of the Working Class in England*, trans. W. O. Henderson and W. H. Chaloner, 2nd edn. (1971).

Firth, J. F. B., *London Government and How to Reform It* (1881).

—— *Municipal London* (1876).

—— *The Reform of London Government and of the City Guilds* (1888).

—— and Simpson, E. R., *London Government under the Local Government Act, 1888* (1888).

Gibb, T. E., *The Municipal Government of the Metropolis* (1886).

Hobhouse, L. T., and Hammond, J. L., *Lord Hobhouse: A Memoir* (1905).

Horsley, J. W., *'I Remember': Memories of a 'Sky Pilot' in the Prison and the Slum* (1911).

Jephson, H., *The Sanitary Evolution of London* (1907).

Judge, M. H., *The Working of the Metropolitan Board of Works* (1888).

Lloyd, J., *London Municipal Government: History of a Great Reform, 1880–1888* (1910).

London County Council, *London Statistics*, vols. I–XIII (1891–1903).

—— *Official Publications* vols. I–V.

—— *Proceedings of a Conference ... on the Question of Transfer of Powers* (1896).

—— *Report by the Statistical Officer ... on the City of London (Inclusion of Southwark) Bill* (1897).

—— *Report by the Statistical Officer on the London Government Bill* (1899).

—— *Statistical Abstract for London* (1899).

Masterman, C. F. G., 'Realities at Home', in Masterman, C. F. G. *et al.*, *The Heart of the Empire* (1901).
May's British Press Guide, 1884 (1884).
Mill, J. S., *Representative Government* (1861).
Newspaper Press Directory, 1884 (1884),
Odger, W. B., *Local Government* (1901).
Pall Mall Gazette 'Extra' on the London County Council (1889).
Phillips, W., *Sixty Years of Citizen Work and Play* (1910).
Proposed Municipalities for London: Report of Proceedings of a Deputation to the Prime Minister and the Lord President of the Privy Council (1898).
Robson, W., *Sir Charles Dilke and the Clerkenwell Vestry* (1884).
Saunders, W., *History of the First London County Council* (1892).
Scott, B., *A Statistical Vindication of the City of London* (1867).
Southwark, Lady, *Social and Political Reminiscences* (1913).
Stephen, L., *Life of Sir H. Fawcett* (1886).
Stuart, J., *Reminiscences* (privately printed, 1911).
Tanswell, J., *The History and Antiquities of Lambeth* (1858).
Torrens, W. M., *Twenty Years of Parliamentary Life* (1893).
Toulmin Smith, J., *The Metropolis and its Municipal Administration* (1852).
—— *The Metropolis Local Management Act* (1855).
Webb, S., *Socialism in England* (1890).
—— *The London Programme* (1891).
Wemyss, Earl of, *Memories, 1818–1912* (privately printed, Edinburgh, 1912; microfilm in Wemyss Papers).
—— *Modern Municipalism: An Address to the Paddington Ratepayers' Defence Association* (1893).

(ii) Periodical Articles
Baumann, A. A., 'The London Clauses of the Local Government Bill', *National Review*, 11 (1888), 539–52.
Beachcroft, R. M., and Harris, H. P., 'The Work and Policy of the London County Council', *National Review*, 24 (1895), 828–46.
Burns, J., 'Let London Live', *Nineteenth Century*, 31 (1892), 673–85.
—— 'The London County Council. I. Towards a Commune', *Nineteenth Century*, 31 (1892), 496–514.
Chamberlain, J., 'Municipal Government: Past, Present and Future', *New Review*, 10 (1894), 649–61.
Costelloe, B. F. C., 'London v. the Water Companies', *Contemporary Review*, 67 (1895), 801–16.
Donald, R., 'How We are Governed: London's Parliament at Work', *Windsor Magazine*, 1 (1896), 265–79.
Fardell, T. G., 'The London County Council, I: The Impeachment', *New Review*, Review, 6 (1892), 257.

Hobhouse, Lord, 'The House of Lords and Betterment', *Contemporary Review*, 65 (1894), 438–52.

—— 'The London County Council and Its Assailants', *Contemporary Review*, 61 (1892), 332–49.

Lawson, H. L. W., 'The County Council Election', *Fortnightly Review*, 69 (1898), 197–209.

Lubbock, Sir J., 'A Few Words on the Government of London', *Fortnightly Review*, 57 (1892), 159–72.

Rae, W. Fraser, 'Political Clubs and Party Organization', *Nineteenth Century*, 3 (1878), 908–32.

Salisbury, Lord, 'Artisans' and Labourers' Dwellings', *National Review*, 2 (1883), 301–16.

Stuart, J., 'The London Progressives', *Contemporary Review*, 61 (1892), 521–32.

Webb, S., 'The Work of the London County Council', *Contemporary Review*, 67 (1895), 130–52.

Wellsman, W., 'The Local Press of London', *Newspaper Press Directory* (1898), 12–14.

Whitmore, C. A., 'Conservatives and the London County Council', *National Review*, 21 (1893), 175–86.

—— 'Our Defeat and Some Morals', *National Review*, 31 (1898), 263–8.

Woods, R. A., 'The Social Awakening in London', *Scribner's Magazine*, 11 (1892), 401–24.

D. *Modern Publications* (post–1914)

Place of publication London unless otherwise stated.

(i) Books

Bahlman, D. W. R. (ed.), *The Diary of Sir Edward Walter Hamilton, 1880–1885* (2 vols.; Oxford, 1972).

Baker, J., and Young, M., *The Hornsey Plan*, 2nd edn. (1973).

Bakke, E. W., *The Unemployed Man* (1933).

Barker, M., *Gladstone and Radicalism* (Hassocks, 1975).

Barlow, I. M., *Spatial Dimensions of Urban Government* (Chichester, New York, Brisbane, and Toronto, 1981).

Bollens, J. C., and Schmandt, H. J., *The Metropolis: Its People, Politics and Economic Life* (New York, 1965); 4th edn. (1982).

Briggs, A., *History of Birmingham, II* (Oxford, 1952).

Centre for Urban Studies, *London: Aspects of Change* (1964).

Chilston, Viscount, *W. H. Smith* (London and Toronto, 1965).

Cockburn, C., *The Local State: The Management of Cities and People*, 2nd edn. (1978).

Committee for Economic Development, *Reshaping Government in Metropolitan Areas* (New York, 1970).

Committee of Inquiry on Local Government Finance (Layfield Committee), Appendix 10 (microfiche only), 16: *Report on a Survey of Public Attitudes to Local Government Finance* (1976).

Cox, J., *The English Churches in a Secular Society: Lambeth, 1870–1930* (Oxford, 1982).

Craig, F. W. S., *British Parliamentary Election Results, 1832–85* (1977).

—— *British Parliamentary Election Results, 1885–1918* (1974).

Crossick, G., *An Artisan Elite in Victorian Society: Kentish London, 1840–1880* (1978).

Cunningham, C., *Victorian and Edwardian Town Halls* (London, Boston, and Henley, 1981).

Daunton, M. J., *Coal Metropolis: Cardiff, 1870–1914* (Leicester, 1977).

—— *House and Home in the Victorian City* (1983).

Dearlove, J., *The Reorganisation of British Local Government* (Cambridge, 1979).

Dictionary of National Biography compact edn. (Oxford, 1975).

Donnison, D., 'The Micropolitics of the City', in Donnison, D., and Eversley, D. C. (eds.), *London Urban Patterns, Problems and Policies* (1973).

Doolittle, I. G., *The City of London and its Livery Companies* (1982).

Dyos, H. J., *Victorian Suburb: A Study of the Growth of Camberwell* (Leicester, 1961).

Eyles, J. D., *Environmental Satisfaction and London's Docklands: Problems and Policies in the Isle of Dogs* (Queen Mary College Dept. of Geography, Occasional Paper No. 5; 1976).

—— *The Inhabitants' Images of Highgate Village* (London School of Economics Graduate Geography Dept., Discussion Paper No. 15; 1968).

Fernando, E., and Hedges, B., *Moving Out of Southwark* (1976).

Finer, S. E., *The Life and Times of Sir Edwin Chadwick* (1952).

Fraser, D., *Urban Politics in Victorian England* (1976).

Gardiner, A. G., *John Benn and the Progressive Movement* (1925).

Garrard, J., *Leadership and Power in Victorian Industrial Towns, 1830–80* (Manchester, 1983).

Gattrell, V. A. C., 'Incorporation and the Pursuit of Liberal Hegemony in Manchester, 1790–1839' in Fraser, D. (ed.), *Municipal Reform and the Industrial City* (Leicester, 1982)

Gibbon, G., and Bell, R. W., *History of the London County Council, 1889–1939* (1939).

Glass, R., 'The Mood of London' in Donnison, D., and Eversley, D. C. (eds.), *London: Urban Patterns, Problems and Policies* (1973).

Gwynn, S., and Tuckwell, G. M., *The Life of the Rt. Hon. Sir Charles W. Dilke* (2 vols.; 1917).

Hamer, D. A. (ed.), *The Radical Programme*, by Joseph Chamberlain *et al.* (Hassocks, 1971).

Hanham, H. J., *Elections and Party Management* (1959).

Harris, J., *Unemployment and Politics* (Oxford, 1972).

Harrison, R., *Before the Socialists* (London and Toronto, 1965).

Harvey, D., *Social Justice and the City* (1973).

Haward, H. A., *The London County Council from Within* (1932).

Hennock, E. P., *Fit and Proper Persons* (1973).

Heren, L., *Growing up Poor in London* (1973).

Hirst, F. W., *The Early Life and Letters of John Morley* (1927).

Hobsbawm, E. J., 'The Nineteenth Century London Labour Market' in Centre for Urban Studies, *London, Aspects of Change* (1964).

Jay, R., *Joseph Chamberlain: A Political Study* (Oxford, 1981).

Johnson, D. J., *Southwark and the City* (Oxford, 1969).

Jones, V., *Metropolitan Government* (Chicago, 1942).

Joyce, P., *Work, Society and Politics* (Hassocks, 1980).

Kellett, J. R., *The Impact of Railways on Victorian Cities* (London and Henley, 1969).

Kosmin, B., 'Political Identity in Battersea' in Wallman, S., *et al.*, *Living in South London: Perspectives on Battersea, 1871–1981* (1982).

Lee, T., 'Cities in the Mind', in Herbert, D. T., and Johnston, R. J. (eds.), *Social Areas in Cities: Processes, Patterns and Problems*, 2nd edn. (Chichester, New York, Brisbane, and Toronto, 1978).

McBriar, A. M., *Fabian Socialism and English Politics 1884–1918* (Cambridge, 1962).

McCandless, C. A., *Urban Government and Politics* (New York, 1970).

MacKenzie, N. (ed.), *The Letters of Sidney and Beatrice Webb*, i (London and Cambridge, 1978).

MacKenzie, R. D., *The Metropolitan Community* (New York and London, 1933).

Marshall, Sir Frank, *The Marshall Inquiry on Greater London* (1978).

Matthew, H. C. G. (ed.), *The Gladstone Diaries*, vii and viii (Oxford, 1982).

Mineka, F. E., and Lindley, D. (eds.), *The Later Letters of John Stuart Mill* (vols. xiv–xvii of the Collected Works; Toronto, 1972).

Ministry of Housing and Local Government, Committee on the Management of Local Government, iii, *The Local Government Elector* (1967).

Morrison, H., *How Greater London is Governed* (1935).

Owen, D., *The Government of Victorian London* (Cambridge, Mass., and London, 1982).

Pelling, H., *Social Geography of British Elections, 1885–1910* (1967).

Prescott-Clarke, P., and Hedges, B., *Living in Southwark* (1976).

Pritchard, R. M., *Housing and the Spatial Structure of the City* (Cambridge, 1976).

Pugh, M., *Electoral Reform in War and Peace, 1906–18* (1978).

Ramm, A. (ed.), *The Political Correspondence of Mr Gladstone and Lord Granville* (Oxford, 1962).

Research Surveys of Great Britain Ltd., *The London Project Commentary* (1977).

Rhodes, G., *The Government of London: The Struggle for Reform* (1970).

Rhodes, G. (ed.), *The New Government of London* (1972).

Robb, J. H., *Working-Class Anti-Semite* (1954).

Robson, W. A., *The Government and Misgovernment of London* (1939).

Royal Commission on Local Government in England, *The Lessons of the London Government Reforms* (Research Study 2; 1968).

Royal Commission on Local Government in Greater London, 1957–60, *Minutes of Evidence*, Written Evidence (1960).

Shankland Cox Partnership (in association with the Institute of Community Studies), *Inner Area Study: Lambeth* (1974–8).

Sheppard, F., *Local Government in St. Marylebone, 1688–1835* (1958).

Smallwood, F., *Greater London: The Politics of Metropolitan Reform* (Indianapolis, New York, and Kansas City, 1965).

Smith, P., *Disraelian Conservatism and Social Reform* (1967).

Soutter, F. W., *Recollections of a Labour Pioneer* (1923).

Stedman Jones, G., *Outcast London* (Oxford, 1971).

Taylor, R., *Lord Salisbury* (1975).

Teaford, J. C., *City and Suburb* (Baltimore and London, 1979).

Thompson, F. M. L., *Hampstead: Building a Borough 1650–1964* (1974).

Thompson, P., *Socialists, Liberals and Labour: The Struggle for London, 1885–1914* (1967).

The Times, Tercentenary Handlist of English and Welsh Newspapers, Magazines and Reviews (1920).

Trainor, R., 'Peers on an Industrial Frontier: The Earls of Dartmouth and Dudley in the Black Country, c 1810–1914', in Cannadine, D. (ed.), *Patricians, Power and Politics in Nineteenth-century Towns* (Leicester, 1982).

Waller, P. J., *Democracy and Sectarianism: A Political and Social History of Liverpool, 1868–1939* (Liverpool, 1981).

—— *Town, City and Nation: England, 1850–1914* (Oxford, 1983).

Westergaard, J., and Glass, R., 'A Profile of Lansbury' in Centre for Urban Studies, *London: Aspects of Change* (1964).

Willmott, P., and Young, M., 'Social Class and Geography' in Donnison, D., and Eversley, D. C. (eds.), *London: Urban Patterns, Problems and Policies* (1973).

Wistrich, E., *Local Government Reorganisation: The First Years of Camden* (1972).

Wohl, A. S. (ed.), *The Bitter Cry of Outcast London*, by Mearns, A. (Leicester, 1970).

Wohl, A. S., *The Eternal Slum* (1977).

Young, K., *Local Politics and the Rise of Party* (Leicester, 1975).

—— '"Metropology Revisited": On the Political Integration of Metropolitan Areas', in Young, K. (ed.), *Essays on the Study of Urban Politics* (London and Basingstoke, 1975).

—— and Garside, P., *Metropolitan London: Politics and Urban Change, 1837–1981* (1982).

—— and Kramer, J., *Strategy and Conflict in Metropolitan Housing: Suburbia versus the GLC, 1965–1975* (1978).

Young, M., and Willmott, P., *Family and Kinship in East London* (1957).

——, Young, H., Shuttleworth, E., and Tucker, W., *Report from Hackney: A Study of an Inner City Area* (1980).

(ii)   Periodical Articles

Bedarida, F., 'Urban Growth and Social Structure in Nineteenth Century Poplar', *London Journal*, 1 (1975), 159–88.

Dennis, R., and Daniels, S., ' "Community" and the Social Geography of Victorian Cities', *Urban History Yearbook* (1981), 7–23.

Doolittle, I. G., 'The City's West End Estate: A "Remarkable Omission" ', *London Journal*, 7 (1981), 15–27.

Dunbabin, J. P. D., 'The Politics of the Establishment of County Councils', *Historical Journal*, 6/2 (1963), 231–3.

Dyos, H. J., 'The Slums of Victorian London', *Victorian Studies*, 11 (1967/8), 5–40.

Keith-Lucas, B., 'London Government', note in *Public Administration*, 50 (1972), 213.

Mayes, F. E., 'Local Government in Woolwich', Woolwich and District Antiquarian Society *Annual Reports*, 21 (1954–7), 27–59.

Newlyn, L., ' "In City Pent": Echo and Allusion in Wordsworth, Coleridge and Lamb, 1797–1801', *Review of English Studies*, 32 (1981), 408–28.

Pooley, C. G., 'Residential Mobility in the Victorian City', *Transactions of the Institute of British Geographers*, NS 4/2 (1979), 258–77.

Robson, W. A., 'London Government', note in *Public Administration*, 50 (1972), 95.

Wald, K. D., 'The Rise of Class-based Voting in London', *Comparative Politics*, 9 (1977), 219–29.

Ward, D., 'Victorian Cities: How Modern?', *Journal of Historical Geography*, 1/2 (1975), 135–51.

Young, K., 'The Conservative Strategy for London, 1855–1975', *London Journal*, 1 (1975), 56–81.

—— 'The Politics of London Government, 1880–1899', *Public Administration*, 51 (1973), 91–108.

E.   Theses

Baer, M. B., 'The Politics of London, 1852–1868; Parties, Voters and Representation', Ph.D.thesis (Iowa, 1976).

Bennett, J. J., 'East End Newspaper Opinion and Jewish Immigration, 1885–1905', M.Phil.thesis (Sheffield, 1979).

Butler, C., 'Some Aspects of the Work of Local Boards of Health, with Special

Reference to Woolwich Local Board of Health between 1848 and 1875', BA dissertation (South Bank Polytechnic).

Corbett, D. M., 'The Metropolitan Board of Works, 1855–1889', Ph.D.thesis (Illinois, 1943).

Davis, J. H., 'The Problem of London Local Government Reform, 1880–1900', D.Phil.thesis (Oxford, 1983).

Elliott, D. S., 'The Metropolitan Board of Works, 1855–1889', M.Phil.thesis (Nottingham, 1971).

Nicholson, F., 'The Politics of English Metropolitan Reform: The Background to the Establishment of the London County Council, 1876–1889', Ph.D.thesis (Toronto, 1972).

Wilkinson, A. M., 'The Beginnings of Disease Control in London: The Work of the Medical Officers in Three Parishes', D.Phil.thesis (Oxford, 1980).

Young, K. G., 'The London Municipal Society, 1894–1963', Ph.D.thesis (London, 1973).

F.   Other Unpublished Papers

Clifton, G., 'Corruption in Local Government and the Metropolitan Board of Works in the 1880s' (kindly lent by the author).

Smith, J. E., 'The Parliamentary Representation of Westminster from the Thirteenth Century to the Present Day' (1923; typescript in Westminster Archives).

Index

Northcote, Sir Stafford 84
Norwood 253 n.
Nottingham 39 n.

Onslow, Florence, Lady 227
Onslow, William Hillier, Fourth Earl 98,
  192, 193, 194 n., 205, 208, 211, 213,
  217, 218, 225, 226–33, 235, 236, 238,
  240, 241, 243, 246–7, 249, 250, 251,
  252, 254
Overseers of St Botolph, Aldgate v.
  Whitechapel District Board (1861)
  35 n.
Owen, Sir Hugh 224, 234–5

Paddington 5, 98, 112, 255
  Vestry 28, 163, 205, 206, 209, 217, 218
Pall Mall Gazette 176, 231
Pannell, W. H. 181, 222
Paris 228
parish government reform 133–4, 197
parks and open spaces 41, 158, 190
Peel, Sir Charles Lennox 217, 224
Pelling, Henry 190
Pendleton 250 n.
People's Palace, 232
Peppercorn, J. 230
Phillips, George 109
Phillips, William 71–2, 124–5
Pickersgill, E. H. 174
Plumstead 216, 244
  District Board 35 n., 80, 209–10, 216, 244
  Ratepayers' Association 26
  Vestry 216, 225
Poland, H. B. 220 n.
political organizations 23–5, 68–70, 71, 86,
  115–19, 120, 152, 156
  Central Liberal Association 116
  Conservative borough associations 24, 68
  Liberal borough associations 24, 25, 54–
  5, 60, 68, 69, 70, 90, 115, 157
  London Liberal and Radical Union 118,
  126–7, 185
  Metropolitan Radical Federation 176
  Radical borough associations 70, 90
  see also Conservative Party, Labour
  Party, Liberal Party, *and under*
  individual areas
Poor Law, poor rates 77, 142, 144, 155
Poplar 35, 232, 242
  District Board 166, 211, 225
Privy Council Office 217, 218–19, 224, 234,
  239, 243

Progressive Party, Progressivism 29, 73,
  118–28, 135–6, 141, 143, 146, 148–56,
  157, 158, 162–4, 166, 168, 170, 174,
  176, 186, 187–8, 190–1, 195, 196, 197,
  198, 207–8, 229, 232, 242, 246
  see also Liberal Party
public control, inspection 41, 129, 211–12
Putney 255

Quarter Sessions Boroughs 106–7

Radical Clubs 71, 86
Ratepayers' Associations 25–7, 28, 43 n., 85,
  157, 198–9, 248, 257
  see also under individual areas
rates, *see* local taxation
Reddish, John 30
Regent's Canal 6
Rendle, William 88
Ridley, Sir Matthew White 234
Ritchie, C. T. 84, 91, 102, 104, 105 n., 106–
  8, 126, 129, 131–4, 139–40, 142, 152,
  193, 207–8, 234, 235, 238, 243
Robinson, H. M. 158, 163, 211
Robinson, R. A. 182
Robson, W. A. 17, 108, 248–9
Robson, W. M. 90, 157
Rogers, E. D. 156
Rollitt, A. K. 186
Rosebery, Archibald Philip Primrose, Fifth
  Earl 5, 119, 147, 150–1, 153, 176, 177,
  204, 207, 229
Ross, John 90
Rotherhithe 6, 129, 221 n., 223, 244
Rotton, A. 191
Royal Commissions:
  Amalgamation of City and County
  (1893–4) 174, 176–84, 193, 195–8,
  201, 203, 204, 207, 208, 220, 225, 247
  City of London Livery Companies
  (1881–4) 74, 93
  Corporation of London (1853–4) 5, 13,
  60
  Housing of the Working Classes (1884–
  5) 91–2, 164
  Local Government in Greater London
  (1957–60) 4, 31, 50, 51, 255, 256
  Metropolis Water Supply (1892–4) 146,
  188
  Metropolitan Board of Works (1888) 30,
  103, 108–9
  Municipal Corporations (1835–7) 10, 54
  Operation of Sanitary Laws (1871) 46